UNDERSTANDING ■ OBJECTIVISM

UNDERSTANDING OBJECTIVISM

A GUIDE TO LEARNING AYN RAND'S PHILOSOPHY

LECTURES BY

LEONARD PEIKOFF

EDITED BY

MICHAEL S. BERLINER

NEW AMERICAN LIBRARY

NEW AMERICAN LIBRARY
Published by New American Library, a division of
Penguin Group (USA) Inc., 375 Hudson Street,
New York, New York 10014, USA
Penguin Group (Canada), 90 Eglinton Avenue East, Suite 700, Toronto,
Ontario M4P 2Y3, Canada (a division of Pearson Penguin Canada Inc.)
Penguin Books Ltd., 80 Strand, London WC2R 0RL, England
Penguin Ireland, 25 St. Stephen's Green, Dublin 2,
Ireland (a division of Penguin Books Ltd.)
Penguin Group (Australia), 250 Camberwell Road, Camberwell, Victoria 3124,
Australia (a division of Pearson Australia Group Pty. Ltd.)
Penguin Books India Pvt. Ltd., 11 Community Centre, Panchsheel Park,
New Delhi - 110 017, India
Penguin Group (NZ), 67 Apollo Drive, Rosedale, Auckland 0632,
New Zealand (a division of Pearson New Zealand Ltd.)
Penguin Books (South Africa) (Pty.) Ltd., 24 Sturdee Avenue,
Rosebank, Johannesburg 2196, South Africa

Penguin Books Ltd., Registered Offices:
80 Strand, London WC2R 0RL, England

First published by New American Library,
a division of Penguin Group (USA) Inc.

First Printing, March 2012
10 9 8 7 6 5 4 3 2 1

 REGISTERED TRADEMARK—MARCA REGISTRADA

LIBRARY OF CONGRESS CATALOGING-IN-PUBLICATION DATA:

Peikoff, Leonard.
Understanding objectivism: a guide to learning Ayn Rand's philosophy of objectivism/edited by
Michael S. Berliner.
p. cm.
ISBN 978-0-451-23629-6
1. Objectivism (Philosophy)   I. Berliner, Michael S.   II. Title.
B945.R234P45 2012
191—dc23   2011044769

Set in Baskerville MT Std
Designed by Ginger Legato

Printed in the United States of America

CONTENTS

PREFACE

■

Philosophy, and particularly Objectivism, is supposed to be an aid in life; and if it's chewed and concretized, that's how it functions. And that's the main reason I wanted to give this course on understanding Objectivism. Objectivism should help you to enjoy life. It should help to make you glad that you're alive.

—Leonard Peikoff, from "Understanding Objectivism," Lecture Eleven

On October 4, 1983, Leonard Peikoff presented the first lecture in his course "Understanding Objectivism." Dr. Peikoff's lectures continued for another ten weeks, live at the Hotel Roosevelt in New York City. Beginning in early 1984, the course was offered on tape to audiences in more than a hundred cities throughout the United States and Canada and in numerous other countries. "Understanding Objectivism" is still in use today, with a number of the lectures included in the curriculum of the Ayn Rand Institute's Objectivist Academic Center.

This course—and this book—should *not* be considered an introduction to Objectivism. As Dr. Peikoff stresses in the opening lecture, it "presupposes familiarity with Ayn Rand's works. . . . [I]f you don't know anything about Objectivism, this is the wrong lecture to be at."

The focus is on thinking methods: the right and wrong methods for trying to understand philosophy in general and for understanding and validating Objectivism in particular. But there is a "dividend," as Dr. Peikoff put it, which is to "get clear on some specific idea that we are applying the method to." The teaching of a method to understand

Objectivism necessitates the "chewing" of its essential ideas (for example, objectivity and life as the standard of value), and thus considerable time is spent on the content of Objectivism and Objectivism as a philosophical system.

Because the course was offered orally and much of it extemporaneously, a significant amount of editing was required to make it more amenable to the reading audience, but I tried to retain the less formal tone of the original oral discourse. I hasten to add, however, that I did not edit for philosophical content. I eliminated repetition, colloquial and conversational expressions, and even some material that was time-sensitive—that is, relevant to the live audience but not to readers—and I made some grammatical changes. I also eliminated (as repetitive or off topic) some questions and answers from the Q&A sessions following each lecture, and I moved some questions and answers to the lectures that contained those topics. All punctuation is mine, because I had access only to the tape recording, not to any original manuscripts. A word-for-word transcript of the tape recording of the course resides in the Ayn Rand Archives.

—Michael S. Berliner

FROM LEONARD PEIKOFF

People have often asked for a written version of my oral lecture courses, on the premise—with which I agree—that written lectures are much more accessible to the student. Writing, however, is in this context virtually a different language from speaking; a raw transcript of an extemporaneous speech, however excellent, is almost always filled with defects and confusions of one sort or another—and so is frequently boring as well. To turn a lecture course into an accurate, clear, and valuable book, a huge amount of time-consuming editing is required, a task that can be performed only by an individual with the necessary motivation, knowledge of the subject, and editorial skills. My own age and priorities make it impossible for me to undertake such a task.

I have therefore decided to authorize several individuals who possess the necessary qualifications to edit and bring out in book form certain of my courses, and to do so entirely without my participation. Although I have confidence in these editors to the extent that I know them, I have had no part in their work at any stage—no guiding discussions, no reading of transcripts, not even a glance at early drafts or final copy. Even a glance might reveal errors, and I could not then evade the need to read more, and so on, which is precisely what is out of the question.

In my opinion, the lecture course in this book is of real value to those interested in the subject. But when you read it, please bear two things in mind: Michael Berliner is an excellent, proven editor—and I have no idea of what he has done in this book.

P.S. If you happen to spot and wish to point out seeming errors in the text, please e-mail Dr. Berliner at the Ayn Rand Institute. If you like this book, I may add, do not give me too much of the credit. My course provided, let us say, the spirit, but Dr. Berliner gave it the flesh required to live.

UNDERSTANDING  OBJECTIVISM

■

The Role of Philosophy

If people who do not know what philosophy is and what it deals with attack it, that is not very significant. And there are, of course, a great many such people, people to whom philosophy stands only for a few disconnected bromides or sayings. They have no actual idea what the subject deals with, what the content of the topics are, or with its structure or organization.

If people *do* know something about what philosophy deals with, but equate philosophy with the worst, most irrational ideas—I mean people who equate it with self-sacrifice, or communism, or skepticism, or Linguistic Analysis—if those people attack it, it also doesn't mean very much.

But what about a different sort of person? I'm thinking of a person who knows, in some terms, what philosophy is. He knows its main branches, the issues it deals with, the overall structure of the subject, and, let us say, he has read Ayn Rand, and he is even sympathetic to her viewpoint—he's an advocate of egoism, and he's an atheist, and he's an advocate of capitalism, and so forth. What if people who fit *that* description attack philosophy? Yet every so often, I hear arguments against philosophy from such people. And, unless you lead a very insulated existence, you must all have heard them, too.

I want to begin this course on understanding Objectivism by giving you the three leading arguments (at least in my experience) against philosophy. Each of them claims that a happy man can't live according to a philosophy—not *any* philosophy, whether Objectivist or otherwise. They claim that every philosophy leads inevitably to serious problems for the person who holds it, problems that far outweigh whatever value the philosophy brings, so that philosophy is basically a source of harm, a grief to people. And the way to be happy, according to these arguments, is to kiss it good-bye and become a-philosophical, or anti-philosophical.

These arguments have been raised to me across the years by people from many different viewpoints, including former Objectivists. I say "former," because once they turn anti-philosophical, they usually abandon any philosophic affiliation. Some of these people I do not like or respect. But some I do. Some are honest, even if, in my judgment, they are badly mistaken; they sincerely believe these arguments, and sometimes they're very torn about them—they don't know what to answer, how to answer, or whether there *is* an answer.

I want to start by facing these issues head-on. These arguments are rarely formulated in detail, the way I will present them to you sympathetically. I disagree with them, of course, but the answers come much later in the course. The point now is this: Can you answer these arguments? Do you feel that there is something, anything at all, to them? Can I get to you for even a minute with regard to any one of them? Does any of them have a trace of momentary plausibility to you? For your own sake, I ask you to be fair; don't simply dismiss them out of hand because you know that I'm going to slaughter them in the fullness of time. If you actually confront them honestly, you will find that it is very helpful as a self-diagnosis, in regard to whether you understand Objectivism or not. (All my examples, by the way, are real—that is to say, they're taken from things actually said to me at least once.)

Number one: Philosophy stifles individuality or the self. Here is the argument: Philosophy, by definition, lays down a whole series of principles, telling people how to think, what to think, and what to value. It says, "Here is the truth on every important issue," including issues of value. It lays down rules on what you should believe, on every conceivable subject of significance: what you should think, do, feel. By definition, the argument continues, this leaves little or no room for individuality, for valuing or doing something that expresses your distinctive nature, your personal essence, your own self. The whole idea of philosophy, according to this argument—and this would be especially true of a philosophy that claims objectivity—the whole idea of a philosophy is to bring yourself under universal, impartial rules, rules that apply to *all* men at *all* times; the whole idea is to start to live in conformity with such rules, whether you like it or not. What does that mean? According to this argument, you have to repress your own personal self and start to behave like all the other advocates of that philosophy. You have to, in effect, become a robot or a follower, programmed to be just like all the other followers.

That is the abstract statement of this first argument. Now, let's take some examples. Lifestyles—take a young man, for instance, who discovers Objectivism, accepts it as true, loves *The Fountainhead*, but does not like skyscrapers. And there are such people. The sight of New York does not fill him with ecstasy—he may find it distasteful, noisy, dirty—he would much rather live on a ranch in California, or on an island in the Caribbean. The argument goes, if he gets into Objectivism, he's soon going to absorb the message "skyscrapers represent the heroic in man—greatness, achievement"—and his attitude, therefore, is anti-achievement, anti-man, and so on. He is indifferent to the good, and perhaps even an example of hatred of the good. And therefore he's wrong, he's low, he's bad. What's the result? If this boy tries sincerely to be a good Objectivist, he has to beat down this heretical feeling; he has to become a pro-skyscraper champion like everybody else, in the name of fidelity to his philosophy. But the price, therefore, is to cut himself off from his real feelings (in this case, the real lifestyle that he wants). He has to turn himself into what used to be called an other-directed, or an unreal, person, a mere follower.

Or take a case from art: Beethoven is the obvious example here. A person hears and is moved, deeply moved and stirred, by Beethoven's symphonies. Then he discovers esthetics; he discovers the Objectivist esthetics. He discovers that art is a sense of life issue, that it reveals your basic values, that your tastes reflect your metaphysical view of life. And then he hears that Ayn Rand personally disliked Beethoven, that she regarded his music as "malevolent universe"—that is, anti-values, anti-success, anti-man, the voice of doom. It would be the same pattern as with the skyscraper. Perhaps this person will consciously disavow Beethoven. Perhaps he'll just shy away from the issue and feel uncomfortable. But either way, his real personality, his tastes, his preferences are not being expressed. Instead, he's pushing the attitude that he has been taught is right.

I know a talented, creative artist, a Romantic artist, who believes that philosophy is incompatible with creativity. And his is a very sincere belief, because to be creative, this person feels, you have to be open to the new, to experiment. You have to give your subconscious absolute freedom in order to be able to come up with the groundbreaking, the untried, that which has so far never been conceived. But if you accept a philosophy, this artist feels, you get caged in with a whole set of esthetic rules telling you "art must be this, and it can't be that; this school is good, that one is based on determinism, and so on and so on." The result is that your subconscious is frozen in advance. If you take it seriously and really try to follow it, this person holds, you end up turning out inferior copies of whatever school or trend the philosophy happens to approve, instead of turning out your own individual works.

You can see how this sort of argument could be extended across the board. A person involved with Objectivism might repress his real career choice in order to obey the Objectivist idea of productivity. I'm sure you must have met a woman who wants children, who does not want a professional career in industry or the professions, like Dagny [Taggart, in *Atlas Shrugged*], and who feels she's inferior, she's guilty, she's violating the highest standards of Objectivist productivity thereby. A person might repress his real love or friend in the name of having the right kind, according to his philosophy, and so on and so on.

All of these people find themselves in the following position: If they pursue their own self, they feel guilty; if they repress it, they feel emptiness and frustration; so they're lost either way. So the conclusion they come to is that the problem, the culprit, is the attempt to impose a philosophy, any philosophy, on a person's individuality. By contrast, the man on the street seems to have a wonderful freedom, because he is in this position: It is not true that everything is significant for him. It's not true that all of life is a federal case. He doesn't need to be proving something every minute about what he likes and dislikes; he can be and do whatever he wants, and there's no censor, no rules, no guilt.

Ask yourself: How many people here desire something—it can be in the realm of vocation, career, sexual style, I don't care—something that you feel is perhaps not 100 percent Objectivism, as expressed in Ayn Rand's novels, and yet this is something that is important to you personally? If so, then ultimately you're going to have a problem. You will feel guilt, most likely, and then the pattern is that you will repress it, and then in time you will resent the necessity to repress what matters to you, and then in time it is good-bye. I've seen this happen many times.

This is an important issue, and it's part of the real need for this course on understanding Objectivism—to deal with and analyze this kind of problem with many actual, real-life examples, so that we can see what is and is not involved in living by a philosophy.

I want now to present a psychological variation of this same argument, and it goes as follows: If everybody were brought up as an Objectivist, and they were in an Objectivist world from the beginning, that would be fine, no problem. If they were taught only Objectivist ideas, their whole psychology would presumably be based on those ideas; everything about the person would be consistent, integrated—it would be terrific. But in actual fact, they say, life is not like that. People are brought up by irrational, or at least inadequate, parents, to say nothing of the environment—their neighbors, their teachers, politicians, and all the rest of it. The result is that by the time they discover Objectivism, they're filled with contrary ideas and with neuroses. Most often, they don't even *know* their subconscious ideas—they don't know how they got them, when they were drilled into them, or how to get rid of them. Then they hear Objectivism, and their mind approves, and they're left with a tremendous clash: the legacy of their upbringing versus a rational philosophy. And they're caught between the two, forever trying to fight their childhood conclusions, doomed to a life of inner conflict.

An example that I've heard a lot of times goes like this: Take a person brought up in a horrendously bad, irrational home, who never formed a strong career value or a strong career passion. His life was such a jungle growing up that it took his full strength just to survive it. But he preserved his mind, he heard Objectivism, he comes into it, he agrees, and he hears now "Career is a crucial top value." And he would like to have a career passion, but he cannot find one in him. He searches, and he can't find the kind of interests or values that he could start off with and build on. He's confronted with a blank. If he were a nonphilosophical person, he would still suffer scars from his upbringing; perhaps he never would be happy; but at least, the argument goes, he could at least struggle on, he could get something from other aspects of life. But if he's an Objectivist, he has the constant mandate hanging over him, the image of Roark. And therefore, by contrast, through constant self-criticism and self-condemnation, he's doomed to guilt for life.

Common to all the examples is the clash between an individual's feelings and philosophy. In the first cases, the person believed a feeling was him; in some sense, he was proud of it, it gave him pleasure; and then he felt philosophy is putting him down, squelching him as an individual. In this career case, he sincerely doesn't like the feeling—he wishes he had a career passion; he doesn't regard it as his essence that he's proud of—he wishes to high heaven he could get rid of it; but he can't, so he's condemned to a life of cursing himself. Again, what's common to them all is: "Myself—good or bad, like it or not, but me—versus philosophy."

In regard to the psychological variant, you might say, "There's an easy solution. If you have such deep problems, go find a psychotherapist." You might say, "True, it's often hard to find your own basic premises, uproot them, reintegrate them, and so on, but that's just what psychotherapy is for. So if you go and you work and you introspect and so on, in time you'll resolve the clash; all will be well."

I promise the answer you'll get is the answer I get—"What do you mean by 'in time'? How long?" Then the person says, "If psychology were so advanced, and psychotherapy so efficient that we could in a reasonable time identify and eradicate all of our bad premises, terrific. What's a reasonable time? Six months? Six years?" There are a lot of people who would go for six years. They think that would be a great investment. But, the argument says, in many cases, a person has problems of such a kind that with today's knowledge they're actually insoluble. He can go to a therapist—a good, rational, efficient therapist—he can sincerely try— but because of the primitive level of psychological knowledge in the world today, and the immense difficulties in changing a whole entrenched psychology, maybe *ten* years would not be enough, *twenty*, in order to change certain types of traits. So, the person concludes, "I'm condemned to fight *an entire life* of inner conflict if I continue to hold before myself a theoretical ideal of what I should be. But on the other hand, what if I say, 'I've got to be realistic—I can't change this attitude. I've tried, but it's immovable; that's how I'm going to be until I die,' so rather than perpetual conflict, I say, 'To hell with philosophy. I'm simply not built for it. I'm a certain way, call it sick or neurotic or warped, whatever you want, but I can't do anything about it, and I resign.'"

So, in one variant here, the person says, "This is me, and I want to be this way, and philosophy stamps me down," and the other says, "This is me, and I *don't* want to be this way, but I have no choice, I have to, and again, philosophy stamps me down." So in either case, there is constant inner conflict. And that is the argument of philosophy versus the individual, or philosophy versus the self.

Number two: Philosophy causes a life of outer conflict, or cultural alienation. It's philosophy versus the world. And here's the abstract argument:

Philosophy, by definition, lays down a set of rules and principles by which you should evaluate the things around you—other people, government practices, religions, everything. A person with a definite philosophy, therefore, is always judgmental; he's always saying, "This is right, true, good," or "That is wrong, false, bad." The world around you, however, rarely shares your philosophy. Sometimes a person may be in harmony with his environment, such as a very religious man at the height of the Middle Ages—so this argument wouldn't apply to him. But usually, the argument goes, the philosophically consistent person is at variance with the world. And this is *true*, because: He is consistent, the world is contradictory; he has a thought-out definite system, the world is eclectic; he has high standards, the world is pragmatic or expedient; he is independent, and most people, by definition, are conventional. So the philosophical person is in the position of constantly condemning what he sees around him, constantly running the world down as contrary to *his* standards, *his* principles, *his* values. Most cultures, after all, are a grab bag, a mixture of all kinds of elements, and most people are not very consistent, and the result is that there will be a tremendous amount to criticize from the point of view of *any* philosophy.

Now, the argument goes on, this is particularly true of Objectivism. Here is a revolutionary philosophy. It attacks wholesale the basic principles of the last twenty-five hundred years. It's confronting a society that reflects in countless ways, large and small, the exact opposite ideas. The result is that a sincere Objectivist has to live a life of cultural alienation. He has to feel constantly like an outsider, or a victim, or an outcast, facing a corrupt, hostile world. He's in effect a loner trapped among hordes of the irrational, the unjust. And on top of that, he can't simply remain silent, because he knows the principle that you mustn't sanction evil—you have to condemn it in order to be just—so his whole life becomes a protracted battle, a constant conflict with the people around him. His emotional feel of life, as a result, is loneliness, malevolence, trouble, pessimism. If he meets someone at a party, he can't, like an ordinary person, just chat over a drink, relax, and enjoy it. Whatever he talks about soon generates some sort of philosophic issue, because philosophy is everywhere. And the next thing you know, he's in a fight over religion, or politics, or something else. Even if he keeps quiet at the party, he's on edge, he's tense, he doesn't know what the next statement by some person or group is going to be, or what they're going to stay that he'll have to jump in and condemn in order to be true to his principles. So, leaving aside a few soul mates as isolated and in despair as he, his social life is continual anxiety, trouble, unpleasantness. If he goes to a movie—say he goes to see *E.T.*—he can't simply settle back and enjoy it like everybody else, because, since he's philosophical, he has to analyze it, he has to see it as a cultural symbol. And sure enough, in today's world, he's going to find all kinds of errors or evils in just about everything, which will end up putting the damper on, or entirely destroying, his enjoyment. *E.T.*, for instance, is definitely anti-adult; it's anti-science. Therefore, I've heard a number of people say it's an evil, irrational movie. (I can't resist saying that I love that movie. But more on that later.)

If an Objectivist goes to class at college, he supposedly either has to feel fear of what his professors are going to say, because he knows he's going to have to disagree and therefore be subject to the class's ridicule, or, at minimum, he's going to be filled with disgust, contempt, revulsion. Even if he goes to a party of Objectivists, he cannot have a good time, because he has to spend the evening on philosophy, on big issues. Everything has to be intellectual, and they end up discussing how awful the world is. And if somebody at the party just wants to relax, forget his troubles for the night, he stands a good chance of being accused of being evasive and anti-intellectual.

The conclusion of this argument is that it is simply not worth living if life is nothing but struggle, tension, condemnation, loneliness, and gloom. What's the solution? Get rid of the root of it all—this judgmental attitude, this constant concern with right or wrong, true or false—get rid of philosophy, and then simply enjoy yourself, like the man on the street (again, the symbol of a blissful existence). He just takes the world as it is. If he likes a movie, it would never occur to him to analyze it; if he meets someone at a party, he couldn't care less what that person thinks; he accepts the rule "never argue about religion or politics"; he's free, he's cheerful, he has no sense of being a cornered victim in a malevolent world. How does he do it? He's not enslaved by a philosophy.

Thus, according to the first argument, it's the self versus philosophy, or the inner world versus philosophy; and according to the second, it's the outer world versus philosophy. So it's a twofold torture chamber.

And that brings us to the last argument, which is the briefest, but it puts the capper on the first two. Why go through all this torture for nothing? Why for nothing? Because, argument number three claims, *philosophy is basically useless.*

The standard version of this you know: Who needs philosophy? It's all empty talk. But the version that I have in mind is more sophisticated: True, philosophy is important when you're young, or when you first discover it; it helps set your basic direction. You're swamped by so many possibilities and choices at that point, and you have no firm ideas as to what to choose or how. You're confronted with a mass of possible careers and religions and friends and lifestyles, you're just drowning in possibilities. You need a guide, so philosophy is really important or helpful at this stage; it kind of orients you to life.

But, the argument goes on, at a certain point your basic direction has been established. For example, if you come to Objectivism, you pretty soon give up religion, you resign from the Socialist Party, you reject a progressive education for your children, you pick out an appropriate career and a hardworking lifestyle, you choose certain appropriate friends, and so on. At this point, the argument asks, what more do you get out of philosophy? Of course, if you're a professional intellectual, then you might need philosophy, because you're actively dealing with its issues all the time. But what if you're not an intellectual? Suppose you're a full-time mother, or a businessman, or a lawyer, or a sculptor? All your basic decisions in life are made. So what do you do with philosophy then? What do you get from it? Your career is set, and most of your time is spent pursuing it. And philosophy is irrelevant to you there. You try cases or treat patients or sell bread, without need of any further philosophy. Your daily activities are set, your friends, your routines, your lifestyle—and you are overwhelmed with the demands and concretes of daily existence. Who has time for philosophy, and what for? The way I've sometimes heard this point is—What does being an Objectivist consist of? What do you do with Objectivism other than attend lectures by Peikoff?

I was discussing this argument recently with a friend, and he made the very perceptive comment that this argument is like deism in religion. In religion, there are three camps: the true believers, who hold that God is all-powerful and determines everything; the deists, who say no, God is necessary to start the universe off, but after that he retires from the scene and simply watches disinterestedly with no power to interfere; and then

the atheists, who say, "If we can get along without God for all those millennia, we can get along without Him at the very beginning, too." A very
valid development. A natural law without God altogether is the only consistent alternative. Deism was merely a stage in the atrophy of religion,
and the logical finale was atheism. So I think you see the parallel here.
The view that philosophy is necessary to start us off in a certain direction
but thereafter is useless in life is like the deism of this issue, and it leads in
logic to the same result—namely, that philosophy is dispensable even at
the beginning, because there is then some other way of reaching conclusions or making decisions in life, some nonphilosophical way. And if that
can work for the last forty or fifty years of your life, it can work for all of
your life in principle just as well.

So this argument, despite its appearance of making concessions to
philosophy, really amounts to an attack on the usefulness of philosophy
as such, at *any* point. It all comes down to the question, "If I intend to be
a decent, hardworking person, what on earth do I need philosophy for in
my daily life?"

That states the three arguments in essence. What is their common
denominator? The separation of philosophy from life, the dichotomy of
philosophy versus life. Philosophy is regarded as either useless in living,
removed from life, or a positive harm and hindrance to living, so that
there's life and there's philosophy, and you have to choose.

This viewpoint is extremely widespread today; it is not confined to
onetime Objectivists (although I focused on them for our purposes). The
whole culture is saturated with anti-philosophical ideas. We could divide
people into various categories on this basis, and you'd see how tremendously common the viewpoint is. In one category would be the explicit
skeptics about philosophy, those who openly scorn it as a waste of time,
hot air, no cash value—I mean the type of person for whom any term
descriptive of thought as such means removed from life. For instance,
they say, "It's abstract," and to them, "abstract" means nothing to do
with concrete reality; it's academic or scholastic, and to them, what goes
on in academies or schools, by definition, has nothing to do with reality;
it's "theoretical," and of course therefore has nothing to do with practice;

and so on. In another category would be those who profess certain philosophic ideas, and even respect them in a way, but who are careful to keep them as a side issue in their lives, without any central, ruling influence. This is what Ayn Rand called the "church on Sundays" attitude: One day a week, or a month, I pay homage to my ideas, but the rest of the time, in self-preservation, I forget about them and get on with the business of living. This is only a variant of the outright skeptic, because they both agree on the actual irrelevance of philosophy to life; the skeptic merely dispenses with the need of a weekly ritual. And last, just to complete this survey, there's another type of person—one who *does* take ideas seriously and really tries to live by them day and night. And where do the examples in *quantity* come from of this type? Only two sources that I know—religions and totalitarian movements. Nuns who retire from the world, renounce sex, take a vow of poverty, never speak, and so on; they live by what they preach all the time, or at least enough of it so that they're allowed the rest off. Or Nazis and Communists, who give up everything, body and soul, to the party. This third category embraces fanatics who sacrifice their lives *to* their philosophy. They, too, agree that it's your life or your philosophy, and then they merely give up their lives for philosophy. But the basic issue is still the same: life or philosophy. *Everybody* agrees—or almost everybody—that philosophy is removed from life. And the arguments I began with are only a kind of in-group version of this same basic attitude.

And yet Objectivists know—they *should* know—that something is wrong with all of this. Philosophy is not self-sacrifice. According to Objectivism, it's the means, the indispensable means, of achieving self-interest, prosperity, the enjoyment of life. So we know—or should—that philosophy is *not* detached from life, that it's not an impediment to living, but a vital necessity. So I'm turning now to the opposite viewpoint, the Objectivist viewpoint. I'm not yet answering the arguments I gave you; I'm merely reminding you of the exact opposite attitude to philosophy: that philosophy is the exact reverse of those three arguments. According to Objectivism, philosophy is essential to creating a self, to dealing with the world, to managing *at all* in daily life.

This course presupposes familiarity with Ayn Rand's works, with my lectures, and so on, so I'm going to be very brief on this part because I want to cover new material. This is in the nature of a reminder, and if you are here for the very first time, if you don't know anything about Objectivism, this is the wrong lecture to be at, because I'm taking for granted a context that will leave you utterly baffled. This is definitely aimed at an audience that already has an extensive knowledge of Objectivism. Therefore, to you, I'm merely reminding you what philosophy is. It's a science of fundamental ideas, the science that tells you the nature of the world, of man, of man's means of knowledge, and on that basis offers a code of values to guide his choices, actions, products, institutions. Do we need it? You've all read "Philosophy: Who Needs It" [the title essay in Ayn Rand's 1982 book]. You know that man needs philosophy by his essential nature. His mind needs the conclusions of philosophy to function at all. He has to know: what is reality, and can he count on it; what is knowledge, and how is it obtained; what is the good, and how should it be pursued? Does philosophy have any actual role in life? You must have read *The Ominous Parallels* [by Leonard Peikoff, 1982]. I claimed there, and I believe I proved, that philosophy is the factor ultimately moving everyone and everything, that it's inescapable even by people who denounce it, that it's responsible for the trends in economics, art, politics, literature, education, youth movements, movies, people's psychology, you name it.

What do you get out of holding a definite philosophy? When I was a college student, they used to say to freshmen—and they used to say this about philosophy in general to motivate; and it applies more to Objectivism inasmuch as it's a rational philosophy—they used to tell us that from philosophy you get a sense of certainty, as against agonizing doubt; you get a basic self-confidence, a sense of intellectual control, of control over your own mind and its method of thinking; you gain a fundamental understanding of the world, of why things are as they are, of what can be changed and what can't; and you get a sense of purpose, of priorities, of values, of what's important as against what's trivial, what counts in life, where you're going, what you need to know and do to be happy. That was the kind of speech that they used to give to freshmen in my day. And it's all true. Philosophy does all this and much more.

The man on the street whom the anti-philosophic arguments regard as blissfully free of philosophy (assuming he really is unphilosophical) is actually harmed by that fact, because however decent and nice he is, to him, the world is basically a mystery. He cannot fathom what is going on. And if he *is* decent, to that very extent, he can make no sense of the injustices he sees. He's not even sure that they *are* injustices, or what injustice *is*. He doesn't know, he has no answers, he doesn't even have any clear questions. He has no method to begin to untangle it all. So he just pulls his horns in and scrapes by. He may be productive, but he has no sense of control. He can't question or challenge in any serious way, and, quite without his knowledge or consent, he's being led systematically, step by step, to disaster.

So we can say this: On the one hand, philosophy is critically important; it—especially Objectivism—is a life-giving value; but on the other hand, there are all these arguments that philosophy is really a bane and not a blessing. So it's like A and non-A. What is the resolution?

I'm not going to answer in this lecture the three arguments that I started with. Each of them is complex, a mixture of several elements. Each of them has some valid points; they point to some real problems involved in living (albeit misapplied with the wrong conclusion). Each has many confusions that need painstaking straightening out. And they contain some very concrete errors about Objectivism. Objectivism does not, for instance, say that you have to like skyscrapers or that you have to come to lectures. But for detailed answers, you'll have to await the last half of this course. The argument about the uselessness of philosophy we're covering in lecture nine. Philosophy versus the self is ten and part of eleven, and philosophy versus the world is part of ten and eleven. So you've got a long time to wait. But this is a course, not a self-contained lecture, and so we have to lay a whole groundwork first.

What I want to do now is simply state, in general terms, the basic error common to all three of these arguments, the *basic* cause of people raising them, whatever else is involved. *More* than this is involved, but this is the basic cause.

The cause of the problems mentioned in all of these arguments is not philosophy, or Objectivism, but philosophy or Objectivism wrongly understood. And I don't mean here specific concrete errors; I mean wrongly understood in a fundamental, all-embracing way. Put another way—the cause is Objectivism improperly digested or assimilated. Or put still another way—the cause is Objectivism held as a series of abstractions not tied to reality. If a person did understand Objectivism—I'm using the word "understand" in a specific way: I mean grasping it in its actual relation to reality, not as floating generalities—I would say such a person, whatever problems he has, would not raise the arguments I mentioned. And I want now to develop this theme.

Nobody, certainly nobody sane and honest, could say, "Let's get rid of reality. It's too much trouble. It interferes with my self-expression, or it causes grief in dealing with other people, or it's useless in daily life." Reality, by definition, is all there is; it's what we live in and deal with every moment; and it's what we have to conform to if we are to survive and function at all, let alone prosper.

On the perceptual level, the level of sensory perception, there's no argument about this. If you started to walk into the path of a speeding truck, and someone screamed out to you, "Watch out for the truck!" no one apart from a deliberate suicide would dream of answering the following: "Don't try to impose rules on me, I want to express myself." Or, "I don't have views on trucks, because I don't want to argue all the time, and people have so many different ideas about trucks." Or, "I've already seen all the trucks I need to in my life when I was young; looking is a waste of time for me now, I'm too busy."

On the perceptual level, that is the analogue of the three arguments against philosophy. On that level, reality confronts us immediately, concretely, inescapably, and is not a matter of debate. The point is that this does not happen on the *conceptual* level—that is, the level of ideas, abstractions, thought. On that level, a gap is possible; an idea, sincerely held, mind you, but utterly unconnected to the world; and that is what makes possible a disdain for ideas. If ideas—and I mean here abstract philosophical ideas—were held by people with the same immediacy, the same reality, the same relation to actual perceptual concretes as the way we see trucks, none of the anti-philosophical line could arise, because it would be immediately obvious that it was an anti-reality line. If a person saw his philosophy in every concrete, and I mean see it, *really* see it, the way he now sees trucks, then no problems of the kind mentioned could arise. The person might still have problems with himself or with people, but he wouldn't have problems with philosophy; he wouldn't think the solution was to abandon philosophy.

The issue, therefore, is that many people, including a lot of honest, well-meaning, perfectly sincere people, do not see their philosophy that way. Let me put the exact same point in a different terminology, because it will illuminate another aspect. The essence of being in favor of reason is *proving* your ideas, *validating*, as against going by faith or blindly following authority. What does proving an idea consist of? Proof is *not* some formalized, ritualized deduction that would satisfy a pack of desiccated scholars somewhere. It is *not* some tricky, convoluted rigmarole designed to outwit dishonest adversaries. Proof is a very simple thing, and it is utterly nonsocial. It is the method of seeing firsthand that your ideas come from reality, that they actually reflect or correspond to facts of reality. That's all. Proof is really nothing but taking an abstract idea and endowing it with the vividness, the immediacy, the compelling quality of the percept of the truck that we talked about. So if you really proved an idea, it should stand in your mind like that truck, as a fact that is there, real, perceivable, unanswerable, absolute.

Of course, this is easy to say but hard to do. The question is: How do you achieve this state? How do you get your ideas, particularly philosophic ideas, into this kind of relation to reality? How do you take broad abstractions and make them, in your mind, seem like obvious transcripts of reality, so immediate that to you they are like percepts with all that clarity and compelling power? That is the question. And that is what I mean when I say that we have to learn to understand philosophic ideas and specifically Objectivism—I mean, grasp their relation to reality.

In a way, this problem exists for *all* abstractions, in any area or subject matter, whether philosophy or not. You know from the Objectivist epistemology that abstractions are symbols, shorthand symbols for integrations of concretes to enable us to deal with countless instances by a single word, held in a single frame of consciousness. And as such, abstractions by their nature are a step removed from reality. You know that there is a whole series of levels that get farther and farther removed: There are actual trucks that you can point to; then there is the concept "truck," which is a unit in your mind for which you have to think, "What does it stand for?" to connect it to reality; and then there's "vehicle," which is still broader, and includes trucks and cars and boats and so on, and is another step removed, and so on. And you know that there are all sorts of devices and methods inherent in concepts and necessary to keep them connected to reality, such as giving examples, offering definitions, and a lot more.

So the problem of understanding abstractions, keeping them tied to reality, exists for *all* abstractions. But the point I want to make now is that it is hardest and worst in regard to philosophy, because philosophy deals with the broadest abstractions. It's the most universal. You can look at it this way: Philosophy is at once the easiest and the hardest subject there is. It's the hardest and easiest subject there is for the same reason: It's the most universal. Therefore, in one way, it's the easiest—you don't need any specialized knowledge, it deals only with issues available at all times in all places to all professions; to engage in philosophy, you don't need to know science, engineering, medicine, no specialized knowledge; you just have to look at the world and grasp what's available in every age to every man; and in that way, it's the easiest. But in another sense, it's the hardest, because it is tremendously abstract. Here, your symbols, your words, are covering not just trucks, but existence, the totality; not just a toothache, but consciousness; not just going to a movie, but freedom or happiness. These types of concepts—"existence," "consciousness," "freedom," and so on—have so many concretes of such a bewildering variety, in so many different contexts and applications, and yet in philosophy, somehow, we have to hold this wealth of concretes together, disregard all these concrete differences, and move in a continual realm of tremendous abstraction. And most people simply cannot do it. They can grasp the ideas, but only by cutting loose from reality, only by forgetting about trucks, toothaches, movies, and so on, and functioning in a world made only of words, of abstractions. They don't know how to keep this level of abstraction connected to daily life, to actual reality—the reality they live in, work with, perceive. So for them, whatever their intentions, philosophy ends up like church on Sunday: It's something disassociated from life. It's a special occasional ritual; they may be sincere, but they can't keep it real. That's what it comes down to.

Here is the deeper reason—an epistemological reason—why philosophy is so widely scorned. It's not only because of the wrong ideas of philosophy that people have. It's the very nature of abstractions, of the difficulty that abstractions present to us, and that difficulty comes out worst in regard to philosophy.

To carry this a step further, if philosophy is the easiest yet the hardest subject, the same goes in spades for Objectivism. I could make a case that it's the easiest of all philosophies to assimilate and the hardest. Why the easiest? Because it's true. It's actually based on reality. That makes it much easier to grasp than fantasies about a supernatural dimension and the beauty of self-immolation for the collective unconscious. On the other hand, precisely because it does throw out fantasies, it's of no use at all if it's held in a cut-off-from-reality fashion. A false philosophy, to an extent, must be divorced from reality. And to that extent, it is not so difficult to hold. You don't have to work to see its relation to reality; it *has* no relation to reality; it's like a fairy tale, and you can usually follow it without much work or difficulty, no matter how weird it gets. There's no problem struggling to tie it in to reality, because the whole system says, in effect, "This is above reality; this is another dimension; you shouldn't think; just have faith, believe," and so on. But in Objectivism, by contrast, the whole thing about it—in every principle and detail—the whole thing is the tie to reality, to the concretes around us. Precisely because it is true, there is a tremendous amount of work involved in holding it, in keeping it connected to reality. And this is a giant task that is not imposed by a false philosophy. If you forget reality while reading Kant, that's not a problem; it can be very helpful. But if you forget reality in regard to Objectivism, it becomes ludicrous, and the whole thing is pointless.

However, it is not obvious how to keep a philosophy tied to reality. In fact, it's a very difficult and very rare feat. Good intentions and sincerity are not enough for this. You need a definite method of dealing with ideas, a method that is not self-evident. And I want to elaborate on that point.

I have watched Objectivists for many years—starting, I may say, with myself and my own struggles—try to assimilate the ideas of Objectivism. I've watched them try to grasp the proof, the tie to reality, in that truck-like fashion. I've seen well-meaning, educated students—intelligent, motivated, hardworking—I've seen them read all the materials, take courses in Objectivism, and yet they cannot really do it; they cannot digest the material. They can't do it with their eye steadily on reality. However much they try and wrestle with the material, it does not jell in their minds into a lucid, unanswerable perception of reality. They end up seeing it, in effect, as though through a glass darkly, or in a kind of fog.

I hasten to add that I myself went through a long period in this state, and by a long period I mean at least fifteen years, and that was my full-time field. At first I thought that everyone else understood but me, and that the problem was my own deficiencies. But eventually I saw the same problem and pattern repeated on person after person, and I came to conclude that a special method is necessary to grasp philosophy and keep it reality-oriented, a method with many aspects and specific steps calculated to add up in keeping ideas real. And I worked off and on for a number of years to define this method. Most recently we held a seminar with several very advanced Objectivists exploring our mutual mental processes—the method we used, the problems in understanding the ideas, what was really clear to them, what was not, how to make it better. And that is actually how this course arose, and what it's really all about. It's in effect tips from a veteran on how to really understand Objectivism. But what you have to see clearly at the outset is *why* a special method is necessary.

Many people have the idea that they can read a book on philosophy or Objectivism—now, we mean here that they're reading it in focus, they're sincere, they follow carefully—and they think that if they do that, and then at the end say, "This makes sense, I agree," that that constitutes understanding. It does not. Reading is not enough. The same is true of lectures. You can listen to someone else, the most wonderful lecturer in history, and you can be focused, sincere, honest, but that does not yield understanding in the sense we're talking about. I'm not downplaying reading or listening; that's obviously important, it's vital, it's the first step in learning a new philosophy. But the point is, it's only the first step. There's a whole process that has to come after that if you are to reach the stage of seeing, knowing, really grasping. There's a whole series of intervening steps required to bridge the gap. And I gave myself the assignment to try to identify the major steps that had to intervene. I do not have the last word on this question, but I think I have *some* word.

The question I set was this: Assuming that a person listens to a philosophy lecture or reads a book completely attentively, what else then has to go on in his mind in order for the ideas to emerge at the end as real knowledge that he possesses? My answer is essentially offered in this course. Without these steps, I believe, the best book or lecture simply fades away in your mind, and it has to by the very nature of thought, because the essence of these intermediate steps is how to make the material an actual part of your thinking, of your perception of reality. If you don't know the steps, if you don't perform them, then the material never becomes a part of you. It becomes merely the memory of somebody else's words. And however eloquent they are, that is necessarily a peripheral issue in your life; it has to fade away in time; it has to remain a side issue, because it has no real functioning reality in your mind. So reading and listening are not enough.

Something else is not enough. People often confuse *summarizing* an idea with *understanding* it. It is not enough to be able to give a summary, even a good, accurate summary. A summary does not signify understanding, in the sense that we're using it—that is, that's reality-based, like the perception of the truck. It is possible (and common) to give a very clear, accurate summary of an idea that is nevertheless floating and detached from reality.

Take the virtue of honesty, a topic we're going to be covering later in the course. In the seminar that I mentioned, a very intelligent woman whom I like and greatly admire gave a good example of this point. She volunteered to present her understanding of the virtue of honesty, of why you should be honest in life. She proceeded to give the following kind of statement: "If life is the standard of value, then the top virtue has to be rationality, exercising your mind. Rationality means grasping the facts of reality that you deal with. Honesty has to be a part of this, because it tells you not to evade reality or pretend. And therefore, you should be honest."

I think that is about how the virtue of honesty stands in the minds of many Objectivists. And that's assuming even that they remember the proof up to *that* point (that is, the connection to rationality, and life as the standard, and so on). I'm not putting down summaries. I spend a lot of time giving summaries; half of my lectures are summaries. And what she did is certainly okay as a summary. But the point is: If that is what you have in your mind in regard to honesty, that is not the same as understanding, not in the way that we're talking about. The statement that she gave is simply a series of very broad abstractions, with no indication of the tie to actual facts. The summary mentioned "grasping reality"—what does it *mean* to grasp the facts of reality? When you hear that, does your mind flood with examples, or does it stall, freeze, go blank at the question? What does it mean to evade? I'm *not* asking here for some formal definition. But what concretes does the term actually stand for? Why, for example, does a liar have to evade? Can't he know the truth for himself, and merely lie to others? So it's not enough to just say, "Don't evade." Why does life require *complete* honesty? Why can't you be honest *most* of the time, but occasionally lie? That doesn't mean you're evading all of reality. Can't you still live and function and be happy? In other words, there is a tremendous gap between that brief abstract summary statement and a real, concrete, overwhelming understanding of the virtue of honesty.

In the seminar, we spent maybe five hours on this one virtue, and we're going to be trying to cover that in lecture three of this course. The summary, in short, is merely like a headline over a long newspaper article. If you know the article, it's fine to be able to state the headline. But if all you know is the summary, it doesn't do you any good.

So we need a method of processing abstractions, and the method is not obvious. Just in case you think you already have anticipated me entirely, the method is *not* merely giving definitions to your terms. This is a topic that I think has been overdone. Sometimes, of course, you need definitions. But sometimes definitions can be positively harmful to your mental process. Nor does the method consist merely of concretizing or giving examples; that's just the tip of the iceberg. These are all topics for the next lectures as we develop the method. The point is that the process of digesting ideas is not self-evident. It has to be learned as a deliberate assignment.

No human skill is automatic. Each has to be learned. Whether you're talking about walking, or typing, or making love, or cooking, it doesn't make any difference. There are no innate ideas. You can compare learning in order to understand philosophy with learning how to cook. Nobody would think that you could read a cookbook or attend a course—even one with exciting demonstrations—listen intently, and then emerge knowing how to cook. You could come out with a summary, but you would not be an accomplished cook. I'm certainly not putting down lectures on cooking; I've gone to them, they're very interesting, and you can grasp a great deal this way. That's the only way, basically—in some form of reading or listening—to take in all the earlier thought and knowledge on the subject. But if all you do is read or listen, it's soon going to fade; you're going to forget your lectures just as if they had never taken place. What do you have to do? You have to cook. You have to enter a kitchen. You have to make things. You have to make the theory that you learned abstractly a part of you. You have to see it in connection with the reality around you. And in that case, your kitchen is the reality. For instance, you may have heard a lecture on saucepans, on all the types and what you should use for what kind of soufflé. Then you come into reality, your kitchen, you look at your own pans, and you have to decide, "Can I make this recipe with this pan or not?" What was the reason that you needed X size? You have to work it out and try. You have to connect your theoretical knowledge to your concrete kitchen. You may have had a whole lecture on a food processor, and you were told to press the button to start it. But now you look at it, and one way is "Pulse" and the other is "Steady"—which way do you press it? There are millions and millions of questions in order to pass from the generalized knowledge of even a brilliant lecture on cooking to the actual reality-connected knowledge of an accomplished cook.

Philosophy is the same, only more so, because the abstractions are so wide. You need to actually philosophize in order to make the material part of you. You have to enter the philosophical kitchen and work with the material from the books and the lectures. Now we can drop the analogy and just say it straight. The real goal has to be to learn to derive your philosophy from reality as though you were the first creator of it. Having heard the lectures and read the books, you have to then forget all summaries, all the lecture notes, and go back to reality and learn to grasp the philosophic idea from what you directly perceive and what you know about yourself.

Obviously, this is how Ayn Rand had to get Objectivism. She didn't get it from reading *Atlas*, nor from attending my lectures. To her, it was like seeing the truck; it was the result of her perception of reality (obviously not on just one day). There's no substitute for this. Her summary in her works is the beginning of the quest—it's like a map, or a traffic guide, but that's all. You still have to travel the same route. Of course, the map makes it a lot easier. But you still have to take the journey.

There are many, many complexities involved in this journey. To give you just a sort of advanced, anticipated idea: How do you get philosophy from reality directly, without the intermediaries of other people's lectures and books? Take one obvious difficulty: Philosophy, you know, is hierarchical; it's a whole structure, with one idea resting on another and another, and so on. So most of it seemingly can't be gotten from reality directly. You need to have a whole fund of philosophy already established to pave the way for whatever you're studying. So how do you grasp that whole fund to begin with, and then, how do you hold it in your mind to get to the next idea without having that fund of abstractions swamp you, overcome you, detach you from reality? That's a big problem. We need a method for condensing all of the background of a given issue into a simple unit that is still based on reality, so that you can hold it all easily, yet without drowning in ideas at the expense of reality. That's a technique that has to be learned.

Another example of the problem here: You have to concretize, but when, and how? Sometimes, concretization is just the wrong thing. If you overdo it, if you give too many concretes, what sets in? Who can guess? The crow epistemology. (I'm assuming you know that by the "crow epistemology" we mean you can hold only so many units in your mind at a given moment; the mind is limited in what it can absorb; if you give it too many units, it just goes blank and loses everything; that's what we're summarizing as crow epistemology.) You're trying to grasp something, and it's delicate and complicated—so if you give it too many concretes, you just obliterate your understanding. Of course, if you give it too few, it's vague, it's empty, it's unreal. Well, how much is too much?

I've indicated, as another point, that you need to know when to rely on definitions and when to say, "No, this is not the place for a definition." Another point: You need to know when to ignore polemics, all criticism from other people, and just follow a progression in the privacy of your own mind; and, on the other hand, when it's important to turn around and play devil's advocate, when there is really something you have to face and answer.

It's a whole complex process, which Ayn Rand herself called "chewing"—on the obvious analogy. And the way she thought of it was like this: First you hear or think of an idea—that's like taking a bite of food into your mouth. But then comes the chewing, the breaking it down, the ripping it into its elements, establishing its reality tie in detail. And the result, of course, is digestion—you can assimilate it, your system can use it. That's the purpose of the first half of the course: It's the theory and practice of chewing ideas, and thereby making them digestible. Without this, your ideas will be generalized, unconvincing, and ultimately unimportant to you. With it, your ideas should be like "two and two is four" or "the sky is blue"—lucid, convincing, reality-based.

One reason that people don't know the method of chewing is that it's not taught. It needs to be discovered; it needs to be communicated as a separate skill. We're going to do something on that in lectures two to six.

I now want to go to the last major topic for this first lecture. There's a *second* reason that people do not know this skill of chewing or digesting ideas. There's a particular philosophic error, very widespread even among good, sincere Objectivists, a very widespread error that stops people from grasping the right method. And that is really the subject of the entire second half of this course, but I want to introduce it in a general overview now. And that error is the mind/body dichotomy.

In my opinion, this is actually the most important issue in philosophy. I don't know whether I'll stand by that in five years, but at the moment, it is certainly the most important issue in philosophy that I can see. And it's the real killer of good people, the thing that wrecks their mental processes.

Of course you know from lectures and books in general what this is about, and I'm not going to rehash it in much detail. This is the idea that there's a basic dichotomy running through human life affecting every vital area. Everything, in effect, is divisible into the mind (or the soul) versus the body; the spiritual versus the material or the physical, with the idea that you have to choose one or the other.

There are all sorts of variants. I once made a list of twenty-eight different variants, of which I'm going to name a few, just to give you an idea of the tremendous scope of this: theory versus practice, love versus sex, the moral versus the practical, pure science versus applied science, reason versus emotions, art versus business, concepts versus percepts, rationalism versus empiricism, the analytic versus the synthetic, happiness versus pleasure, art versus entertainment.

I don't want to imply that any of these variants is unimportant—each of them is somewhat different from the next—but in my view, three of them stand out above all the rest. All the others are forms or derivatives, but there are three that I would single out as the real heart of this dichotomy of the mind versus the body. (I'm here focusing on how it would be a problem to Objectivists.) The moral versus the practical, reason versus emotion, concepts versus percepts. Let me elaborate those three.

I want to put each of them to you from one perspective, and I want you to see if you can identify a common denominator uniting all three (obviously something beyond the fact that they are all instances of the mind/body dichotomy. I'll give you the three in condensed form.

1. The moral versus the practical. This is basically the following problem: how to do right and succeed in the world
   as it actually is. The moral versus the practical is a problem of *action*; it's a problem of *what to do*. And as it stands
   in the mind of the person who holds to the dichotomy,
   there's a conflict. He feels, "I have my own standards in
   my own mind, but I'm confronted by an alien world that
   does not necessarily adapt to my standards, so that if I act
   on my standards, I'm going to be led to destruction or
   failure in the actual world; what should I do?" That is the
   problem of the moral versus the practical as it stands in
   the minds of good people.

2. Reason versus emotion. Here, the problem is how to follow
   reason while feeling. This is basically a problem not of
   action but of emotion or feeling. And here, the conflict in
   the person's mind is: "I want to follow reason; I want to be
   true to my own intellectual conclusions. But I'm confronted by alien, nonrational thrusts from—" From what?
   He might say from his body, or if he's an Objectivist, he'll
   say from his subconscious. But it doesn't make any difference, because his subconscious in his mind, at this moment, amounts to his body, his brain, his automatized
   mechanism—something outside of his conscious mind
   now. He feels, "I get these feelings. Some of them don't
   conform to my thoughts. I want to follow reason, but I'm
   confronted by these alien thrusts—the emotion, some of
   them at least." What to do about them?

3. Concepts versus percepts. This is basically a problem not
   of action or of feeling but thinking—that is, how to think
   correctly, how to use your mind. And here the person has
   a conflict as follows: He wants to use concepts, he wants
   to think abstractly, he wants to connect ideas by the use
   of logic, but he finds himself confronted by sense data,
   facts, observations from reality that simply do not adhere

to his conclusions, which contradict them, even though his reasoning in his own mind seems impeccable to him. What is the name for the type of person in philosophy who clings to concepts and says, in effect, "Facts may contradict my concepts, but if so, it's tough on the facts"? A "rationalist." Rationalism has dominated philosophy (at least the better philosophy) through the ages. Starting way back with Parmenides, who gave an argument as to why change is impossible, and then saw things change in front of his eyes, and said, "They're not really changing, because that simply does not agree with my unanswerable argument."

What is the common denominator in all three cases, the moral versus the practical, reason versus emotion, concepts versus percepts? In all three cases, it seems to the person that there is a conflict between the internal and the external, between the inner world and the outer. It's your own standards versus the uncontrolled world of other people, so therefore you can't be sure that your own standards will lead to success. Or, it's your standards versus uncontrolled responses thrust on you. Or, your standards, your inner proper method, versus uncontrolled facts that leap out at you and smash your standards. So it seems to people as though the alternative is to have your own standards, remain in inner control of your life, by means of cutting off, minimizing, turning away from the external, *or* give in to the external, conform to it, and therefore abandon your own inner integrity and standards. That would mean: Have moral standards, give up the quest for practicality; have rational self-supervision, give up feeling; have logic and conceptual system in your thought, forget about facts; *or*, take the other side—deal with practical situations (feelings, facts) as they come up, but do it without method, standards, or your own inner control.

This is a terrible dilemma if you have any part of it, a really terrible dilemma.

If the person chooses morality—chooses principles, ideals—he will come out a "tortured idealist." On the other hand, the "body" side, if you make the choice of practicality over morality, what are you? A pragmatist. If you choose the mind side regarding feeling—you say, "I'm going to remain in control, I'm not having any truck with these things that are thrust on me that I can't control"—what is a name for the "feeling" division under the "mind" side? A "repressor." And if you choose the "body" side—you say, "The hell with logic and standards, I have feelings, and I'm going to act on them, and that's it"—then you're an "emotionalist"; that's the best name for it. Regarding "thought," if you're on the "mind" side, and you cling to concepts at the price of facts, that, we've already said, is a rationalist. And there is the opposite in philosophy, too, under the "body" side—if you cling to facts and are scornful of concepts, that's called empiricist.

Of these three dichotomies, all forms of the inner versus the outer, the one I regard as the most basic is rationalism versus empiricism. The others, to some extent, take care of themselves if we grasp that issue.

If you have any part of this problem, on either side of the dichotomy for any one of these divisions, the chances are very strong that you have succumbed to rationalism or empiricism in some way. If I've learned anything about people or philosophy, it's how fantastically widespread this dichotomy of rationalism versus empiricism is. It is applicable to much more than technical philosophers; it is very, very common among Objectivists.

Objectivists tend, for obvious reasons, to the mind side. They're staunch idealists, repressors, and rationalists, if they're going to go for this dichotomy at all. There is an exception: There's a certain type who's on the other side. I really hesitate, but for what it's worth, with tremendous qualifications and reservations, this is not a universal truth, simply a *tendency*. I have noticed a more pronounced inclination of Objectivist males to go for rationalism, and females to go for empiricism. Obviously this is not a sexual phenomenon—I have known rationalist women, and also women who don't have either of these; and I've known empiricist men. But there is a certain reason—you might even guess it, because you see that rationalism is connected to repression, and you know that there's sort of a culturally different expectation for women and men with regard to emotions.

I want to just conclude by tying these mind/body issues into the anti-philosophical arguments that we started with. There's a one-to-one correlation between the three main dichotomies and the three main arguments, as follows:

Take the argument for the uselessness of philosophy in daily life. It rests on the idea of a disconnection between abstractions and concretes. It implies that abstractions are irrelevant to the reality that you live with and deal with. The idea of philosophy as a system of ideas without connection to daily life comes from rationalism. And this, I may say, is one reason why students have so much trouble digesting Objectivism: They try honestly to understand it, but they have unwittingly, subconsciously absorbed a rationalist idea of thought, and that controls implicitly the function of their minds. It defines, without their even knowing, what constitutes understanding, logic, order, and so on. It warps their whole approach to philosophy, *unknown* to them. And so they struggle and struggle, and they can't see why they never get the clarity they're after. Thus, rationalism becomes a self-fulfilling prophecy: Not knowing that they hold it, their ideas remain disconnected, however they struggle, and they end up feeling philosophy is useless.

Now take the argument for philosophy versus the self. That really comes down to philosophy versus your inner feelings or desires—that is, the conclusions of your mind versus your emotions. So if a person feels that philosophy squelches the self, that means the choice, as he sees it, is philosophy versus the self, your thought versus your feelings, reason versus emotions. And if you are on the rationalist or mind side of the dichotomy, then of course you will be especially prone to repression when you're confronted with this dichotomy. And that will give color and plausibility to the idea that you have to choose: It's yourself or your philosophy.

As to philosophy versus the world, that's obviously your own standards versus getting along with others; *your* view of right and wrong versus what works when dealing with other people. It comes down to the moral versus the practical. Again, if, as an Objectivist, you're shunted onto the moralist or idealist side of this dichotomy, you end up feeling malevolent and gloomy about your chances in the world.

All of the issues we started with tonight are forms of the mind/body dichotomy, and couldn't exist without it. And I think that's what basically predisposes people to them—people come to Objectivism committed, without knowing it, to the mind/body dichotomy in all kinds of unidentified forms. They accept Objectivism sincerely, but they do so through the filter of this mind/body issue. Deep down, they still accept the dichotomy of ideas versus reality. They still hold ideas in a rationalistic form, even without knowing it. The result is that they end up as malevolent repressors. Or they can't take that state and they then rebel and say, "To hell with philosophy." They jump to the other side and become emotionalists and pragmatists (which is just the other side of the same dichotomy, the body side of the issue).

To summarize, there are two things that enter into creating a disillusionment with philosophy: (1) Lacking knowledge of the method, an individual's ideas are unchewed, therefore dissociated from reality; and (2) instead of grasping that this is wrong and correcting the deficiency, the mind/body dichotomy takes over and makes him feel "Such is life. This is the way philosophy has to be. So the only solution is to regain contact with the actual by dropping philosophy."

What is the answer to this twofold problem? First is to learn the right method, and then get rid of the mind/body dichotomy, especially its three leading forms. And if you can do that, the result will be to reestablish your own thought on a reality basis, and thereby establish harmony between your thought and yourself, or your emotions, and a harmony in principle between yourself and the outer world. It is not necessary for an Objectivist to feel that his self is being throttled. It is not necessary to feel that the world, even today's world, is hopeless. These are errors that are caused, in part, by lack of method, and in part by an insidious mind/body dichotomy. And the purpose of this course is this twofold attack, one half to one, one half to the other.

I want to stress that I regard the whole problem as honest, so far as we will deal with it here. It is not evil or immoral as such. Rationalism is not an issue of moral default; I insist on that, because I wrestled with that problem for many years in a tremendously acute form. Many very virtuous people do it, often out of conscientiousness. You're left in the dark with no idea of how to deal with ideas. And you end up automatizing wrong ways of dealing with ideas. You end up in a position of despair: You can't live with philosophy, or without it. And that's exactly what we want to deal with head-on in this course.

Lecture One Q & A

Q: Can we expect as difficult a struggle in learning Objectivism as we would with, say, learning typing or the violin?

A: That depends. The way I would put it—how much chaos do you start with, and how much mastery are you after? Those are the two variables that will determine how much trouble you're going to have, and how much of a struggle. If you're untouched by colleges, it's easier in a way, because you don't have rationalism and the defacement of concepts bombarded into you with every breath. But if you were subjected to it, and your mind is really corroded by it to some extent, and/or you hated it so passionately that you've gone to the other side and said, "To hell with all proof, it's just a waste of time, it's just talk," so that you have a real animus against analysis and so on—if you have the rationalist or the empiricist predilection, then you're going to have a lot of trouble, because you're going to have to think while fighting the automatized method of thinking. And that is a lot of trouble; it's a lot of work. It also depends on how much you want. Do you want to get it clear? Remember the spiral theory (the idea that you learn in layers)—how many layers do you want to get? Up to a certain point, you only have to go as far as your action and knowledge require. You do not have to have the kind of knowledge of every point that involves eighty-seven hours of polishing and chewing every comma; that's unnecessary unless you want to become a Ph.D. So how much struggle depends on what you're after. But there is a reasonable level for a person, a human person, that does not involve being a super-understander, and also is clear and tied to reality. And the question also asks, "Must it always be darkest just before the dawn?" That depends on how many errors you start with; that's all. If you start more or less tabula rasa, it shouldn't be that hard, with a clear idea of method. And there are people that tell me (and I have no reason to dispute them) that they didn't have any trouble. I did. So it depends on what you start with.

Q: Would you like to say something about the difference between a serious Objectivist and a professional-philosopher Objectivist?

A: That is a good question, because there is a certain implication that since this course was offered for serious Objectivists—and yet there are a lot of technical or professional philosophic issues involved—do I make a distinction or do I think any serious Objectivist has to know everything that I come out with week after week? And yes, I do make a distinction— you do not have to be a professional philosopher in order to be serious about philosophy. I would say a serious Objectivist is one who understands the ideas within the context of his own life's concerns and actions. He has some degree of the material chewed and integrated; it's not entirely a floating abstraction. He's not serious if it's just mouthed generalities with no relation to reality. But it doesn't have to be that kind of exhausting thing where you take every proposition and you relate it to every other and you concretize it in excruciating detail and you discuss its hierarchy and its spiral and so on, and you spend a huge amount of time on every sub-aspect of honesty and its context and its implications and its applica- tions; you do not have to do that. Where do you draw the line? I would say you draw the line according to your own inner clarity—do you see sufficiently for your own actions? If you do, don't do any more. The pur- pose of this course, the moral of it, is not that you have to do what we are doing on every idea. Because you wouldn't have the time or the strength. I would rather reject a philosophy that would give an assignment like that; I mean, it would make life miserable in principle. You should do it on those ideas that trouble you, to the extent of the necessity. When you yourself feel, "This is unclear, I don't really get it; I'm espousing it, I'm acting on it, but I don't really get it"—when you have that, then do a little more chewing. But there are degrees of application. So the idea is a pro- fessional philosopher spends his whole time doing this, but you can't be expected to do that and still be serious. But the reason for going into a few examples in excruciating detail is to give you the idea of what to do in smaller amounts as and when your own life and context require.

Q: Is it possible to understand Objectivism without intensive study? Did Ayn Rand understand it before she developed it?

A: She understood, very young, some very broad generalities, which were very crucial to enable her to go on and get the next stage and the next stage. So in a way, the whole philosophy was implicit. When she rejected God and said, "There's just this world, and my goals, so to hell with God and the state"—that's not the same thing as the knowledge that's contained in *Atlas Shrugged* or *Introduction to Objectivist Epistemology*. And I venture to say if you asked her at that stage is her viewpoint objective or subjective, what is her theory of definition, and so on, she wouldn't have a clue at twelve or fifteen. She understood certain things, and then she developed it from there. So can you understand it without intensive study? Up to a point, in a generalized way. But if you try to live by it, particularly in a hostile culture, I think that without this kind of study—up to a point at least, to some extent—it simply won't stay with you, because it's too abstract and people cannot keep it.

Q: You said you struggled against rationalism for fifteen years, and you had the advantage of an association with Ayn Rand. Will your course make it possible for us to grasp Objectivism in less time? And if so, what's the difference?

A: The one advantage you have is the benefit of my struggles and grief. A lot of these points that I'm discussing, and the whole issue of rationalism, was simply not known—I mean, except as an issue in the history of philosophy—but as an issue actually affecting people's mental processes, this is a comparatively recent discovery, as far as I know. No one had ever heard of it as applied to inner mental processes. And I'll tell you what the actual thing was that led to the whole topic, at least as far as I know anything about it. I had done a chapter for my book *The Ominous Parallels*, many years ago. And I was very pleased with this chapter. I showed it to Miss Rand one evening, and asked her opinion of it. She read it, and she said (not exactly tactfully, but forthrightly), "I haven't the faintest idea what you're talking about; this is completely unintelligible." And we looked at each other across an absolute abyss. Because, in the past, I knew whether something I did was a little shaky and not too clear. But this was really clear. This was exactly what I wanted to say. It was really right. And she wasn't just partly confused; she thought it was completely from another dimension; she didn't know what I was talking about. That was really the turning point as far as my grasp of the issue, because little by little it began to unravel. How was this written? From what perspective? And how was she understanding it, from what perspective? It took many, many months. And I ended up taking a thirty-page chapter and writing a two-hundred-page analysis on what was wrong with the approach of this chapter. And that was the first actual discovery (at least to my knowledge) of how rationalism takes over a mental process unknowingly, and in what ways it takes over. And then my assignment to myself came to be to fight this until I got rid of it, which, gradually, little by little, I was able to do. And so hopefully it will take less time now if you have it, because now, maybe not everything is known, but a lot more is known than ever was. So in a way, it's an autobiographical course.

Q: There's a problem that's been disturbing me for many years ever since I began my study of Objectivism, and that concerns the issue that knowledge is essentially contextual, and that one should not need a great deal of specialized knowledge in order to be particularly highly educated, in order to be able to think about philosophical terms, and to integrate them into one's life. This usually takes the form of the truck driver, for example, who was not particularly highly educated, but nevertheless was thoughtful about the knowledge that he did possess. Is it true that Objectivism holds that this individual should be able to integrate Objectivism into his life, and how does that jibe with the issue that you said of the difficulty, especially the intellectual difficulty, of even grasping the methodology?

A: It is still true that to digest the philosophy, you have to go through a complex method; the fact of just getting a few generalities is not sufficient. So it comes down to this—what does the truck driver get out of a certain type of philosophy? And that depends on what kind of world he lives in, and what kind of action he engages in. I would say this: If you lived in an Objectivist world, and you were bombarded with Objectivist ideas all the time—you know, the way today you're bombarded with anti-Objectivist ideas, and you absorb them through your pores—it would not be the kind of work that it is now, where you're going against the mainstream, where you have to digest a tremendous amount that's alien to everything you hear, and alien to the way you were brought up. A truck driver in Atlantis, let us say, who was born and brought up there, would not, I don't think, have to go through that complex a process. Particularly if he was honest, his actions were commensurate with the scale of his understanding, he would have a generalized understanding—that would be fine. That is not applicable today. I would venture to say that there is such a thing as an honest truck driver even today who would read the novels, say, "This is true," and up to a point accept them and live by them—up to a point. But that is very unusual, and it depends on how much pressure the person can take from things that he can't explain outside or inside before he starts to succumb, and gradually the thing atrophies in his mind. So my considered answer would be this: In today's world, without this process of digestion, it is very hard—it is impossible, really—to keep Objectivism real in its full ramifications. I leave open some exceptional psychology, that is much more exceptional than mine, that is untouched in effect by what goes on, that can just grasp certain essentials and live by them—I mean, I can't prove that can't exist. But I've never seen it. And consequently, within the framework of what I've seen, without this process, people struggle, they agonize, and they fall. And I should add, this process is not a total mystery, so sometimes people get a certain variant of it on their own within their own context. So it's not as though this course is the key to the universe.

Q: *I'm not quite sure I'm with this point of the truck driver, so let me maybe ask the same question in a different way. Are you saying that a truck driver, or a person with a limited IQ (to use that term), cannot learn to digest or chew fully?*
A: No, I certainly am not saying that; let me correct that right away. First of all, I do not equate a truck driver with a limited IQ. It's a professional issue of what he's doing with his life, not his mental capacity. If you have

a limited IQ, obviously you are going to have trouble in philosophy of any kind. That certainly goes without saying, because philosophy is tremendously abstract. But by the same token, if you have a limited IQ, the problems that can come up are limited intellectually. So you're protected by the fact that, if you're honest, you only deal in very simple issues, so you'll never get to the stage of feeling a problem on the level of sophistication that I'm talking about. Am I saying a truck driver, or someone who is very nonintellectual by profession, can't grasp philosophy? Certainly not. There are all kinds of degrees of what you can do to grasp philosophy, from a general understanding—which is of general value, only that's all—on up to a very concretized, reality-oriented understanding, which gives you that really truck-like perception across the board and arms you in a tremendous number of situations. There is an issue of degrees. It is not the case that either everything floats or you've hit the jackpot philosophically. In fact, most people are somewhere in between. So let's add that into the thought to clarify.

■

Life as the Standard of Value

We are now going to plunge into the process of digesting
Objectivism—that is, understanding it in relation to reality. Our
method throughout the first half of the course will be to take
some key idea from Objectivism and then try to re-create the inner mental processes that would be involved in really understanding it. I have
found that the best way to do this is to have an actual person who is struggling to grasp the topic state aloud, step by step, what goes on in his mind
as he tries to understand, and then I offer commentary.

Now, our purpose is to concentrate on methodology, to get an idea of
the method of using our minds, regardless of the particular content. The
idea is to build up an arsenal of principles telling us how to function intellectually, so that at the end we have a plan as to what to do with any *other*
idea that's not in the course, in order to try to understand it. Of course,
no one can understand in a vacuum; that's why you can understand only
on some specific content. So hopefully, we get an added dividend each
time. That is to say, we actually get clear on some specific idea that we
are applying the method to. And tonight, as I said last time, we are going
to focus exclusively on the topic of life as the standard. I could have started
anywhere—the whole course is going to cover only four or five ideas. I
picked this because it's fairly abstract, but it's not excruciatingly abstract

the way something out of metaphysics or epistemology would have been, and it's the beginning of the whole evaluative branches of philosophy (ethics and politics and so on), so it's a nice plunging-in or starting-off point. But just remember that our real goal is to grasp the principles of method.

I had two theoretically alternative ways of giving you this course—I could come in with seventeen rules and give a lecture with illustrations, deducing them all from the definition of "understanding." I decided very much against that method. For a reason you will see in lecture seven, that would be a rationalistic approach to understanding, and I'm out to fight rationalism as the mortal enemy. Therefore, I'm deliberately doing this the way we're doing it, as an inductive approach to understanding; that is, we're going to actually see real-life examples of someone trying to understand something specific, and then see what they would have to do differently or better to really understand. And that way, we will see the real-life necessity of the rules; we'll see them actually arise in mental practice, as against simply giving you more theory that is simply abstract and unreal to you. This is a *skill* we're trying to learn, and using the analogy of cooking that we mentioned last time, you have to actually learn it in action, in practice.

At the beginning, I'm slightly adapting this method, because, instead of a real volunteer, I'm having a controlled demonstration. I have chosen a specific person to play the role of the learning student in order to enact specific confusions, in order to illustrate specific problems of thinking. And the idea is to organize things in the first few weeks until we are started off. For a really good inductive approach, it would be better in a way, it would be more natural, to take a raw student, unprepared, whom I have no idea what he's going to say, and see what comes up. And that was what we actually did in the seminar. Often, that was very fruitful, and a great many of the things you will hear are more or less verbatim from the seminar. But often, unfortunately, the price you pay for that spontaneity is simply chaos; there are so many confusions of such a kind that the class just looks up in the air and it's just hopeless, and/or the confusions a given person has may be so unique to him and his context that they're just not of general interest, and it's not very fruitful if he doesn't happen to pick a popular confusion. So to minimize these risks and give it a certain order and representative character, I've picked a person and actually written the script, and he is going to read it aloud, and then we'll look at what he did right or wrong.

Our volunteer tonight is Steve. I just want to stress that this is staged, that he's not responsible for what he reads. You should listen with the question, "What is wrong with what he is saying?" Let's be clear in advance what the purpose *is* and *is not*, because there are some things that you could confuse this with that will throw you off. Our purpose is exclusively to understand this idea in your own mind for yourself. Our purpose in this entire course has nothing to do with polemics—that is, how to argue with other people, how to identify their premises, how to convince them, given their context, how to get around their evasions, how to defend yourself against all possible attacks that they might launch.

Another thing: We are not concerned with perfect wording. We are trying to re-create inner mental processes. It is impossible to grapple with this material, to try to get it clear in your own mind, and at the same time utter impeccable, completely objective formulations. If you could rattle off perfect, word-for-word objective formulations, you would have understood the thing so thoroughly a long time ago that it would be way past the stage of trying to understand it. This has nothing to do with communication. If you took my course in Objective Communication, this is neither speaking nor writing. This is the precondition of both, simply grasping in your own mind. So it's not like a legal document, and in any comments I make, I'm going to try not to pay any attention to the niceties of the wording, to whether I would put it the same way, to whether the wording is misleading, and so on. We're trying to see a mind struggling to grasp the main drift, the essence, of a certain idea—however messy and groping and even inappropriate his language (or her language) becomes. Of course, if the language passes a certain point, if it becomes a complete slop, then it can't represent even a rudimentary internal understanding, so there's a limit here. But I'm going to try not to be picky, and to focus only on the main drift, let the person blurt it out, and if the gist is there, that's all we need for what we're trying to get.

Another thing about what our purpose is not: It is not to teach or communicate material to others. This is an entirely private, nonsocial assignment. It's how to get your mind into contact with reality on a certain issue, as you yourself are able to perceive it. The whole issue of communication, teaching, enlightening others, is something that is a much later development.

Another preliminary caution—you have to delimit the assignment. All of philosophy is interconnected. To understand one point completely, you would have to know *all* of the points. But the fact is you *can't* know them all at once; you can only learn them one at a time. But because each one is logically interconnected to all of the others, there is a tendency for every issue to sprawl over into all other issues. And you have to be aware of this in advance, and militantly set yourself against it. You can't let the issue sprawl into its presuppositions—into all those things that it rests on—nor into its consequences, all those things that it leads to. We want to understand one issue. We're not aiming for omniscience. Other issues will come up, perhaps other issues that you do not understand. If so, the thing to do is just make a mental bracket or note and say, "Okay, here's something else I don't understand; I'll worry about that tomorrow or next year, whenever I get around to it." For instance, we're doing "life" tonight. The question of honesty might come up. Someone may say, in order to establish life as the standard, "You have to live a certain way in order to remain alive," and that will remind you, "Honesty is part of the way, but I was never very clear why," and take you off onto that. Don't do it. If that comes up, say, "Honesty is a much different topic. I'm at the basis of ethics; I'll worry about honesty at another time, not now."

The last preliminary—try not to be too upset if you find some of this more complicated than you hoped. I had to more or less follow a middle ground here: How many steps should I break the method up into? If I simply said "focus on reality," it would be easy to grasp, because there's just one step. However, what can you do with it? If I break it up into twenty-three steps, it would be marvelously concrete advice, but who could hold it, because of the crow issue? I'm trying to get what I think is an appropriate number of points per lecture.

All right, I'm going to ask Steve to come up and give us the first one. There's one simple error in what he's about to say. He's going to give it as though he's thinking of it, and you be prepared to tell us what it is. Okay, Steve:

> Life must be the standard of value, because only living beings are confronted by the alternative of life or death, and there can be no values without a fundamental alternative, so there can be values only because of living entities who have to act to sustain themselves.

I see that's not exactly what you expected. But I had a purpose in getting that out of the way. He did not say anything wrong; every statement he uttered there is a true point according to Objectivism. So there are no fallacies in there. But why does that not fulfill our assignment? I'll remind you again of what he said, because it's brief enough to repeat—"Life has to be the standard because only living beings are confronted by the alternative of life or death; there are no values without a fundamental alternative, and therefore living entities give rise to values, and therefore that's it."

You can't disagree with that from an Objectivist viewpoint. What is wrong with that? Yes, it's too abstract and there are no examples. In fact, it is not an example of understanding, but of simply giving a summary. If that's all that stands in your mind, per se, you do not understand. That was just what I did with honesty last week—I rattled off some generalities that were true, covered the topic, but that was not an understanding. There was no step-by-step development, no definitions of any terms, no examples, no breaking it down, no chewing, raw generalities. You can think of it this way: What we are after is not the use of a telescope, but a microscope. We want to focus on details, slowly, one step at a time, ponder, think, get that point, go on to the next little point, get that, go back, and so on, with each point being very conscious of the tie to reality, to what we perceive. To rattle off this kind of generalized summary is useless as understanding.

There was a second problem quite apart from the fact that it was a summary rather than an attempt at understanding. Notice that we're talking about life as the standard, and he said, "The way you establish life is the standard is. . . ." What was wrong with the way he began? Before you get to a topic, you have to do something else that will make it possible for you to start on the topic correctly. You have to *identify a context*. Knowledge always arises in a context that conditions everything that is to come. There's only one time in philosophy when you simply plunge in: the very basic axioms—existence, consciousness, identity. You just say, "Look at reality," that's the beginning. But everything else rests on a whole complexity; you cannot get it straight from reality. First you need the background required to be able to grasp that particular point. So the first issue of a proper method is *always set the proper context*. What are you counting on? What do you already know by the time you get to this point? What are you taking for granted that enables you to study this particular topic?

Depending on the topic, the context will vary enormously in its size and complexity. As I mentioned, if you are taking an axiom, there's no context needed. If you take the validity of the senses, there's a brief context needed—just the basic axioms if you know the Objectivist argument, and then it simply is a corollary of consciousness. But if you take man's rights, there is a *huge* context required. What? Metaphysics, epistemology, ethics. You're already in politics, how the government should function, how society should be organized, so there's a gigantic amount presupposed.

Philosophy is a *hierarchical* structure. Each step is built on the preceding step. I've compared it to a skyscraper with fifty stories, and you have to know before you study any one floor or any one window how high up in the skyscraper you are.

Now we are at "life is the standard." That is the very beginning of ethics. So as far as ethics is concerned, nothing comes before it. So that makes the context comparatively easy, in the sense that there's nothing before it in that field. But there is something that our whole discussion depends upon. What basic knowledge are we taking for granted by the time we reach this? Metaphysics and epistemology. There are all kinds of issues: the axioms; cause and effect—if we didn't know that there was cause and effect, we would never have to enact a cause to achieve an effect, so the whole question of ethics would never come up; if we didn't have free will, we would have no choice, so the whole question of ethics wouldn't come up; if we couldn't trust our senses, or our concepts, or our logic, we wouldn't have any means of acquiring knowledge; if knowledge wasn't objective, we couldn't rely on anything we concluded; and so on and so on. If these bulwarks of metaphysics and epistemology were not known, the whole thing would collapse, including life as the standard. So in visual terms, how high up in the building are we if we're doing life as the standard? If it's fifty stories, how high up? Halfway up or more.

Now the question becomes: How are you going to hold that whole context in your mind while you focus on life as the standard? In what form are you going to hold all the essentials of metaphysics and epistemology, which in fact you require, if you're going to be able to deal with this question? Should you make a list of the fifteen most important issues from metaphysics and epistemology, and sort of carry it with you, and look at it every once in a while? Would that work? No. Why not? Because of the crow—you couldn't retain that many units; it would be useless to you. What you have to do—and this is going to be a general rule for all contexts—is condense the whole context into a couple of words that to you stand for the totality—specific enough to remind you of what you're taking for granted, but brief enough so that you can hold it. And one crucial skill of the method of understanding is how to word the context in your own mind so that you can count on it without being swamped.

If you had to summarize the whole of metaphysics and epistemology, the Objectivist metaphysics and epistemology, in two words that would remind you of the essence of each field, and therefore they would stand for the context that you're carrying on with you, what would the two words be? "Reality" and "reason." You may have a lot of confusions about those; that's okay, as far as what we're doing now. All you have to know for our purposes is that we've taken for granted that there's a reality, and that we're going to use reason to grasp that it's reliable. That's it. That's what we're counting on. Any details or problems with that come at another time. And this, by the way, is why I chose life as the standard this week, because it's easy. As the start of a whole subject, it's a snap to specify its whole context; you just say, "There are two earlier subjects, A and

B," and then you go on. But when you get to honesty, for instance, it's much more treacherous to specify what you already know by the time you get there, and by the time you get to the initiation of force, how to say what you already know is the whole thing, because if you could say that, you'd have no trouble at all with the issue of force. The problem that people have with understanding is that they try to understand everything in the one point, instead of realizing that you have to make a sharp differentiation between what you are trying to understand and what you take for granted.

I would say the rule here, the methodological principle, is establish the context in an appropriately economical form, in a form compatible with the crow.

All right, Steve, do you want to come up now and give us a different type of error? This is not intended as a summary, and we're assuming for the rest of the evening that he has reminded himself of the context, so that is not the problem at issue here.

> Life must be the standard of value, because being alive is the precondition of everything else. If you're dead, you can't have any values at all. So the first thing must be: stay alive.

Now that is certainly very clear; it is certainly true that if you're dead you can't have any values at all. Therefore, being alive, who could be against it? So, has he now understood life as the standard of value? Because if so, we're making a tremendous fuss about nothing.

What is wrong? It's not the issue that it's too abstract (it is, but it's because it commits a certain error). We're not talking here about being a rational human being; we're talking about the standard, not the means of achieving it, so we don't have to bring rationality in. And actually, you do not have to bring rationality in to establish life as the standard. Rationality comes later; that's *how* you should live. But "life is the standard" is prior to it.

Who could possibly disagree with this statement that he just put forward? Being alive is the precondition of everything else; if you're dead, you can't have any values. So the first thing must be to remain alive. Does that show that life is the *standard* of value? Absolutely not. It doesn't even discuss the question of a standard of value. It shows you only one thing—namely, life must be a means to some end. But it leaves open the end; it doesn't say anything about what your goal or standard or ultimate end is. An altruist could entirely agree with that argument. He would say, "Being alive is the precondition of everything else. If you're dead, you can't have any values. So the first thing must be to remain alive," and then he would say, "in order to achieve your proper purpose, which is self-sacrifice for mankind. If you commit suicide you can't do it." So he would say, "Life is not the standard; the standard is service to mankind. But remaining alive is a necessary condition." Adolf Hitler could say, "Absolutely stay alive in order to serve the Führer." This argument does not establish that life is the standard, the ultimate goal, the purpose.

What is the methodological point? You must grasp clearly—before you launch into a whole complexity of understanding and proving something—the meaning of the idea you're trying to understand. And you do this by restating it in several ways, making sure that the full content of that idea is set out before you. You're trying to grasp its relation to reality, so you need to know clearly what it says; that is your agenda, that's your goal. It's not enough to get a smattering and then rush into some kind of argument. You set it out leisurely, thoroughly, stress how much there is to this idea that you want to understand, and then you'll know, when you've achieved this, that you've reached the target. I can't give you very detailed tips on how to know when you are committing the error that Steve committed, but if you are taking a fundamental philosophic issue of such weight and importance as the standard of value, and you find that you can rattle off everything significant about it in a couple of sentences with which no one could conceivably disagree, then you have a reason to suspect you have omitted something. Fundamental philosophic ideas are almost always profoundly controversial. They are not bromides; they are not self-evident, unless it's like "A is A." They involve tremendous abstraction and tremendous complexity. And therefore, if you find that you can zip them off in one or two sentences that absolutely no one could ever question, the chances are very strong that you did something wrong, that you missed out on what this idea actually says. I'm not saying that complexity is an end in itself. I'm saying don't run too fast before you know what the idea is.

Here's another test to see if you've got the full meaning: We're trying to understand another author (in this case, Ayn Rand), somebody else's thought. If what Steve said represented a chewed understanding of it, why in the world did Ayn Rand go on at such great length? Why did she go into all those topics—the analysis of value, and the analysis of life, and what constitutes an alternative and what doesn't, and so on and so on, and then do it in much more detail in "The Objectivist Ethics," after Galt's speech? True enough, an author may be wrong. He or she may overcomplicate. Maybe you've found a simpler way than the original author. But it is not safe to assume it right off the bat, particularly if you're confused. If you have omitted vast amounts of the author's own idea of what constitutes the proof, the chances are you missed something significant.

Now I'm going to ask Steve to give another example of the same error. He's trying to understand the wrong conclusion. This time, he's *closer* to the right conclusion, but it's still not the right one.

> All right, let me try it this way. I've said that life is the precondition of everything else. So what is entailed in being alive? Life requires a definite course of action. For example, life requires that you walk on a steady surface, that you don't jump off a cliff; life requires that man eat food, nutritious food, not poison; life requires that a man think about what he's doing. So life requires a definite course of action. If you want to live, you must follow that course of action. That is, you must regard life as your end or goal, and you must select your actions according to what life requires.

That is a better argument than the preceding. He made one good crucial point that we are ultimately going to be able to use: that life requires a definite course of action, that you can't just survive any old way. But even so, it is simply a variant of the problem of the wrong conclusion.

As stated, it is not an establishment of life as the standard; this is not an *understanding* of life as the standard. Why? Can't you say the same thing for *anybody's* value, whatever it is? *Everything* requires a definite course of action. If you want to build a Nazi state, that takes a definite course of action. It can't be done haphazardly. You can't do just anything you feel like; if you inject some Aristotelianism, you'll destroy everything. You have to be very careful and deliberate and systematic. So Hitler could take the exact same wording but adapt it now to Nazism—"The Nazi state requires a definite course of action, so if you want to achieve Nazism, you must follow that course. In other words, Nazism must be your end, and your actions must be selected accordingly." That is word for word what he said, but with only "Nazism" introduced instead of "life."

Again, the whole explanation is misbegotten because it does not focus on the meaning of saying that life is the standard. The most that this argument establishes is that life should be *an* end, it should be *something* you work to achieve. But it does not establish that life should be *the* end, the one ultimate goal, the standard, by reference to which all value questions should be judged and decided. That is what we are trying to establish when we say life is the standard—not that life is a *means* to an end, not that it is just one among *many* ends, but that it is the one, the supreme, the ultimate, for which everything else is to be undertaken.

Although Steve took one element from Miss Rand's analysis, he omitted a great deal from her analysis of value and life and so on, and that would be another tip-off that it is not enough to say, "Life requires a definite course of action; therefore, it's the standard of value."

That more or less takes us through the preliminaries. Get the right conclusion, understand what we're after. We've done it enough. There are many things we could do if we wanted to go into great detail, which I would not advise at this stage. You could ask what's the difference between a goal and a standard, what's the difference between an ultimate goal and a purpose. We want to blurt out the conclusion here, and we can use all of those as interchangeable for this stage of our understanding, as long as we do grasp the full meaning of what we're trying to understand and don't water it down to something that is insignificant. Each of Steve's examples is supposed to be at least the beginning of his statement, sufficient to establish what his pattern of thought would be. And it's completely off the track.

As I said, we've finished the preliminaries. Now I'm going to ask Steve to give a substantially longer presentation. We're going to assume that he's established his context and that he understands clearly the conclusion that he's after. But he is going to make a crucial new kind of error. And this, in my opinion, is the worst type of error you can make in trying to understand a philosophic idea. Steve is going to commit a very characteristic, fatal error.

I'll start with an analysis of life. Obviously this is a crucial aspect of the issue; certainly Ayn Rand thinks it's important. She defines "life" as "a process of self-generated, self-sustaining action." "Self-generated" means that the source of the action comes from the entity itself, and not from some outside source. An organism gets its fuel from the outside, but it stores it and burns it, or releases it, by itself. Ayn Rand regards life as unique, as different from everything else, in one crucial way: Living entities confront a fundamental alternative of life or death, of existence or nonexistence, which nothing else does. They have to act with the possibility of nonexistence hovering over them all the time. Inanimate entities have no such possibility. Living entities have to act a special way to stay in existence, as opposed to inanimate nature, whose existence is guaranteed. For example, a tree must grow upward to get sunlight, must send its roots downward to get nourishment, or else it dies; an animal must protect itself from predators, or else it dies. As I mentioned earlier, a man must think and eat and so forth, or else he dies. In contrast, a stone or a saltshaker does not face this alternative. They just sit there; they cannot act. And, they cannot be destroyed. They can change forms, but whatever form they take, they remain inanimate material. The fact that living things have an alternative does not mean that they necessarily have choice. The lower life forms do not choose their actions. "Alternative" merely means that they have to act a certain way, or they die, and that they are *capable* of acting that way; they're not helpless. This obviously is an essential aspect of the argument. Because of this, life makes a unique contribution to the possibility of values. If there's no alternative, then no values are possible. Life has the only basic alternative. Therefore, life makes values possible.

Okay, that's the argument; but do I understand it? Again, life has a basic alternative that nothing else does—existence or nonexistence. But can't inanimate entities go out of existence? Take a statue, for example. You can destroy it, smash it into a million pieces, and it's gone. Its elements remain, but its distinctive essence as a statue is gone. Isn't that exactly like life? If you kill a living being, its life is gone. The elements remain, just like the statue, but its distinctive essence is gone. So where's the difference? In each case, there's an entity with a specific unique attribute. In each case, at the end, the elements are there, but the distinctive attribute is gone: The living entity loses its self-sustaining, self-generated action; it becomes inert material; the statue loses its distinctive shape and structure, and becomes crumbled material. I don't see it—where's the difference?

Did you follow that mental process? That was what originally put me on the track of this whole course, that exact mental process on this example, because when it came up at the seminar, the class fell into two groups: those who thought that the mental process was absolutely clear and had no clue as to how you could answer it; and the other half, who thought that this was completely unintelligible, what was he talking about, and couldn't make head or tail of why the person was saying this. And they just looked at each other like two halves across an abyss. And there was a complete failure, not only of communication, but it was almost like species interconnection. So that is a real-life case.

There were some good things in this presentation. He started off well—he gave a clear statement of the view that life confronts a fundamental alternative in a way that inanimate things don't, and that that's essential to the whole idea of value. He gave a definition, and notice, a definition is essential, a *certain* definition is essential. I'm going to shortly be assaulting definitions, but I am not an enemy of definitions. He could not have begun to understand this issue without some definition of "living entity." By the same token, we would not have known what he was talking about when he said it confronts an alternative if he hadn't said, "By alternative, I don't mean choice. I understand that some entities have choice and some don't, but they all have this basic possibility, in or out of existence, so 'alternative' is not the same concept as 'choice.'" And it was important that he defined the distinction.

So I think definitions are a good idea. In any given mental process, though, in any attempt to understand, you have to restrict them. You can't start defining every term, because of what? The crow. Only a few are tops in any mental process, and if you need more than that, don't try to understand that topic, because you don't have the concepts necessary. In this case, I would say it is absolutely essential to have some definition of "life," you should know what is meant by "alternative" as against "choice," you should know what is meant by "value." That's it. If you have to do more than that, you don't have the basic vocabulary to start worrying about this issue. So remember that I said that definitions are valuable, when I start attacking them.

However, granted that he did good things, what was the error in this process? What is the one fatal error? It was encapsulated in this idea: "A living entity has a certain attribute—self-sustaining, self-generated action. A statue has a certain attribute—a certain type of shape. When a living entity dies, it loses that attribute; the materials are there without the attribute. When you smash a statue, it loses that attribute; the materials are there without the attribute. So then both cases are confronted by the same alternative: Either they can keep their identity, or they can lose one of the elements, and the materials remain. So where in the world is the big difference? Why do living entities occupy some kind of exalted position that inanimate entities do not? Why make such a big fuss and say that living entities confront an alternative that inanimate matter does not? Why say, 'Therefore, life is what makes value possible, because to be or not to be,' whereas a statue doesn't, when it's the same thing?"

What is the error? The statue can't do anything, that's correct; but that does not yet tell us what the essential difference is. It tells us that the statue can't act in the fact of its nonexistence. But it does not tell us if there is a difference between the statue and life, in terms of the alternative confronted. The Objectivist point here is that the statue does not have the alternative. Not just that it can't act; it doesn't even *confront* the alternative, it doesn't even *apply* in the way that it does to a living thing. But the question is, why not?

Granted, the statue is passive, but I'm focusing on a different question: Does the statue confront the alternative of existence or nonexistence in the same way that life does, the only difference being that it can't do anything about it? And the answer is no, it does not. The essential error here is the use of a definition cut loose from reality. In this case, the definition of "life." It's the use of what you can call a floating definition. Properly, a definition is supposed to *connect* your concept to reality, but in this thinking process, the definition functions as a *destroyer* rather than an aid.

Now let me elaborate the mental process step by step that makes this confusion possible. The whole mental process rests on the following: "Living organism" equals one attribute. "Self-sustaining action," let's say, "self-sustaining, self-generated action." "Statue" equals one attribute here, a certain kind of structure. In both cases, they lose it. So what's the difference?

What is that person doing? He is equating the entity with its defining attribute. He is saying, "Life equals one attribute—namely, self-sustaining action." Is that what life equals? Have you ever seen a process of self-sustaining and self-generated action trot down the street? Obviously not. If we forget about definitions—let's suppose for a moment that we were in a blessed state (blessed from the point of view of this argument): We had no definitions, so that you couldn't focus on those words "self-sustaining and self-generated action"; if you were going to think about life you had to look at living organisms. What would you see if you looked at living organisms as against inanimate entities? Let me put it this way: How many differences would you see between the two? There is an entire science whose whole content consists of itemizing what is different about living organisms from everything else, and that is biology. And even in its current state, there are many more than fifty facts. Living organisms versus inanimate is a fundamental conceptual divide. There are thousands upon thousands of differences that distinguish them. I wouldn't even begin to make a list, but obviously you know not only the point about its own energy source; every element of a living organism is adapted to carry on its single goal and purpose. Its distinctive capacities of nutrition, growth, reproduction, its distinctive structure, its distinctive type of chemicals, its distinctive type of cellular makeup, and so on and so on.

On whatever level of knowledge, from a savage to a biologist, they are aware that this is not a case of two different statues, one red and one green, which is the way that mental process is sounding—"There are two different things, one has self-sustaining action, and one has the *Venus de Milo* shape, and they lose them both." That could only be because, in doing it, the person loses all of the richness of the actual concretes when he uses the word "life." All he has before him is the definition. If you reduce life to "process of self-sustaining action," then of course there is no essential difference between life and anything else. One attribute by itself—by itself, out of the context of the rest—is not fundamentally different from one attribute of something else out of the context of the rest. According to Objectivism, a definition is not *equal* to the entity, but is simply a formula to help your concept tie itself to the entity, so you know that it stands for plants, carrots, animals, and so on, and not also rivers and so on (the way people talk today about the death of a river). That's why you want to give a definition to a concept. But the definition is like a sign pointing you to the reality. What does it mean then to say "life has a fundamental alternative that inanimate matter does not"? It means nothing more than "there is a fundamental difference between the living and the inanimate." That's it. The alternative that a living organism has, if it dies, is that it goes over into the inanimate category. Whereas if an inanimate entity is smashed to pieces, it's still where it was. Sure, it has lost its shape; it has lost maybe its commercial value, its esthetic appeal; it is still inanimate. It hasn't crossed that gulf. So, when we say that life has a fundamental alternative, that is simply a conceptualization of the fact that there is a fundamental difference between living organisms and the inanimate, that they are altogether different, and that if they're to stay in that category, they have to do something; otherwise, they revert to the inanimate. And no such alternative confronts the inanimate. It's exactly in that sense that a living organism has to be or not to be, and has no equivalent in an inanimate case.

So it all comes back to: Do you perceive living organisms in all their richness and see that this is a *fundamental* divide in nature; or do you hold a definition as a string of words, and match it with another definition?

The mental trick in using a definition is that you have to keep it in mind as a distinguishing device, so your mind remains focused on reality. But, it can never substitute for the reality. You have to keep all of the richness, the variety, the complexity, the multiple attributes of the reality in mind before you, when you think. You must think with the definition keeping you focused on the *entities*, rather than you being focused on the definition. If you do this, this is the best single way—it's the only way—to remain in contact with reality. If you do *not* do this, then you take an element of thought, which is definitions, and turn them into the destroyer. You make them the *object* of thought, rather than a means to clarity. And this example that Steve gave is not a fictional example. It's very common. A number of times in my teaching career, I had to say to somebody, "Where did you get that definition?" And he would finally say, "It comes from such and such," and once he looks at the such and such, his original question disappears; the problem vanishes. But he actually forgot about the reality. It's hard to keep reality in mind. It's hard, precisely because the purpose of the definition is to substitute for that massive array of confusion, to give you something neat that you can hold on to. But when you do it the way Steve did it, then you have a string of words detached from reality. And that, of course, is the essence of the error of rationalism—concepts detached from reality. The example he gave may not have seemed rationalistic, in that he gave examples, he chewed it, he concretized; but it was pure rationalism, because the essence of it was focusing on a definition and trying to deduce the conclusion from it, oblivious to the actual world.

So let's summarize this point as follows: Beware of definitions. They are essential, but they cannot substitute for the reality. Beware of deduction from definitions. In order to avoid this error, always oscillate your mind. That is, focus on the definition, and then deliberately range over the actual concretes that it stands for, to remind yourself that the primary is those concretes, that those are what you're thinking about, that that's what you're working with, and that the definition is simply an aid.

Now we're going to ask Steve to give us another example of the exact same error—that is, this floating definition; but now, not on the concept of "life."

Last time I started with an analysis of "life." This time I'll start with an analysis of "value." Ayn Rand defines "value" as "that which one acts to gain and/or keep." Things like candy, knowledge, shelter, pleasure—these are all values. Now, she says, value implies a valuer, an alternative, and a standard of value. I'll break that down. "Valuer"—"something capable of pursuing a value." If there's no valuer, there can't be any value. A saltshaker cannot be a valuer; it cannot act. A river or a volcano can be said to act, but it cannot direct its actions toward any goal or value. "Alternative"—true, if there's no alternative, if everything is guaranteed, then there's no need to value, since everything will come out the same anyway. For example, a rock falling to earth—there's no alternative for it. It cannot value either hitting the earth, or landing softly, or landing in one piece. It's going to hit the earth hard no matter what, and if it smashes, it smashes. "Standard"—why does value require a standard? Where does the whole issue of "standard" come from?

Value implies a valuer, an alternative, and a standard of value. Value is that which one acts to gain and/or keep. There's nothing in the definition that says anything about a *standard* of value. Why is a standard required? Why not many standards? Why can't you live, for example, as an egoist one day and an altruist another day? Many people seem to do it. Why do there need to be any standards at all? Why not just live by common-sense rationality? Value requires a standard of value—where does this whole issue come from?

This is exactly the same error, only it is done not on the term "life" but on the term "value." This error also came up in the seminar, where the person experienced the discussion of a *standard* of value as like a bolt from the blue. He could grasp that you've got to have something pursuing a value, and there has to be some alternative—otherwise, what's the use of pursuing it?—but he blocked completely on the idea of why there has to be a standard. And the person had the actual experience as though we had said, "All men are mortal, Socrates is a man, therefore Napoleon lost the battle of Waterloo." He says, "Where does Napoleon come out of this? Suddenly you're talking about something that is absolutely not in the premises."

If you look at the definition—"that which one acts to gain and/or keep"—there is absolutely nothing about standards. You can stare at those words, you can give synonyms, you can look them up in dictionaries, you can give definitions of each word—you will never conjure up a standard of value out of that definition, which is what the person is trying to do in this case.

How do you find out that value requires a standard? Remember, we're not yet saying what the standard is—whether it's pleasure, going to the movies, whatever—we're not saying; we're simply talking about the *idea* of a standard. Presumably, we grasped what that meant when we specified our original conclusion, that life is the standard, the end, that which to everything else is a means.

How are we going to grasp in actual fact that value requires a standard, if not from the definition of "value"? And you can see that the attempt here is to do it from the definition. It's the same rationalistic error. But how *would* you establish that value requires a standard? Don't do it by trying to define "standard" and define "value" and then intersect the two; that is pure rationalism. There is only one way to answer these questions—the only way to know the difference between living and the inanimate is to *look* at the living things. And then there's nothing to do but look. And the same thing here—the only way to know what value requires is to do what? You have to look at values, heretical as it sounds.

Some observations of facts of reality led somebody to the definition "that which one acts to gain and/or keep." The definition did not come out of a dictionary. It had to come from reality at some point. How did a person ever grasp it? Take the simplest way—how would you get that definition? Somebody wanted a house. And he took certain actions in order to get it. You saw him act to gain it, and then he didn't want it to be set on fire—he not only wanted to gain it, he wanted to keep it. You saw this in a few cases that it doesn't take a tremendous intelligence to get the abstraction. But now, in the very act of observing this process of pursuing a house (or whatever it is), you see right away as part of it that there are many means to that value, many different things you have to do and acquire in order to achieve that end, which is a house—you need knowledge, you need carpenters, you need lumber—you need all kinds of subsidiary values to get that value. And all those things are values by the goal of the house. If your house is the goal, then all these things lead to it. And you observe that the person doesn't just sit and gloat at the house, and say, "Oh, how fabulous." The house in turn is a means to some end: the house gives him shelter, and so on. It is not stated in the definition of "value" that values come in means-end sequences, that each one is a means to a later end, which is itself a means to the next end, and so on. But that is inherent in every observation. It comes from the exact same source that the original concept came from, from direct observations, from the same place, the observation of value-pursuing activities, combined with simply one further observation—it doesn't go on for infinity. At some point it comes to an end. And if you look at living organisms, the lower species, everything has one end only. If you look at men, there's a tremendous number of ends. We haven't yet come to egoism versus altruism, rationality, and so on. No, we simply want to know that if something is a means, it has to be a means to an end. That's what we're looking for. What's the end? If nothing is an end, nothing can be a means to it. But if you simply take the definition of the term, drop the reality context, drop the range of concretes that give rise to it, and try to deduce means to end to another end to another end to an ultimate end out of it, you can't do it. And you end up asking, "Where did this concept of 'standard of value' come from?"

Let's put the point the following way: An entity has a huge number of attributes that are not part of its definition, but which are real, which are there, which are essential, and which you can find out only—by doing what? Looking at the *entity*. You can't get it from the definition.

In the seminar, I asked people to give me a list of anything and everything they know about values that is not part of the definition, that is not "that which one acts to gain and/or keep." And we got a very long list of nondefining characteristics. Values vary in complexity; they vary in whether they're perceptually available or they take a complex conceptual knowledge; they motivate people; they're the major things in history— you could never understand history if you didn't understand people's values; animals have them; they vary in importance—for example, from a raise to a new toothpaste, up and down; they involve emotions; they come in means-end sequences; we don't have an infinite number—there's a means to an end to an end, and then we stop; you can't go infinitely.

If you kept the full reality of what's involved in values before you, you couldn't say, "I've got a definition, 'that which one acts to gain and/or keep,' and I can't see anything about means and ends in it." You couldn't say that, because the totality of what is obvious about values would be before you, and you would see that one of the things is that they come in means-end sequences. And that's really all that is involved in saying that there has to be a standard. But, if you drop everything except what's in the definition, then you're baffled, and your only hope is to try to tortuously deduce it from the definition, and that's what leads to rationalism.

Let us sum up the problem of method here. It's like we can't live without definitions or with them. If you don't have a definition—if you merely had before you all the examples of values and a whole catalog of their characteristics—you could not retain it; you'd be in the position that it's too much to retain. On the other hand, if you take the definition and then you let it substitute for the reality, then you've detached your thought from reality and you've collapsed. So there is a real problem in conceptual thought. And of course, the more abstract, the more you're condensing by the definition, the worse the problem. You *have to* drop the concretes—otherwise, there's too much to hold; you *can't* drop the concretes—otherwise, you're detached from reality. And of all subjects, the most seductive is philosophy, because it's the most abstract. So there's a kind of doublethink involved in proper philosophical thinking. On the one hand, you must have definitions; you have to extract the essence into a brief statement, which reduces your units. But you always have to be prepared to keep the sense of an immense range of concretes around you, pressing on the periphery of your mind, waiting to be summoned to consciousness. Because these concretes are what you're talking about; they are what the definition is condensing.

This process of removing the blinders from your eyes and taking your concept back to its concretes, I call *reduction*. It is *not* definition; it is like the opposite of definition—you forget the definition, you reduce the concept back to the concretes, with all of their attributes. Therefore, reduction in this sense is an essential mental process. It's the counterpart to definition—whenever you use a definition, you must counter it by a reduction; you must go back to the well, so to speak.

I want to add one more thing to this point, a *crucial* tip, on how to keep the word (like "value" or "life") connected to *things* rather than to words. Because a definition is a string of words. Of course, you can remind yourself, you can make it a policy, but there is a crucial mental process that, if you have it and if you allow it to operate, will do that for you to a significant extent. In the seminar, we were trying to figure out why it was that half the seminar—and it was the male half—felt quite at home with this process of deduction from definitions, and even if they disagreed with one particular argument, they could really grasp it. On the other hand, the women in the seminar looked simply aghast; they couldn't figure out what was going on; they felt uncomfortable, they were bored, and they wondered, "What is this guy doing when he says, 'Life has got this attribute, and the statue has this attribute'?" We were trying to elicit what it is that they do that prevents this from seeming natural. And my wife came up with this—she said she finds this floating definition method revolting, or she used some word like this; she said that what keeps her tied to the concretes when she uses the word "life" is *emotion*. She said as soon as you think "life," the automatic connector, the thing that then comes to her is particular living things for which she feels strongly. And she gave us a list. For instance, a cat we had that we loved very much that died. And so the question was "a living thing confronting an alternative"—for emotion, remember the cat. Or a dog that she had once had. Or I think she threw *me* in there as an example. Or she likes the plants (we have certain ones in the apartment). In other words, she was saying that what was automatically the context that stood in her mind was a series of concretes bound together by a positive emotion. And therefore, "life" to her was important because it invoked a certain feeling of the things she liked. Therefore, when she heard the word "life," that constellation was present right away. And from that perspective, the idea of "life equals self-sustaining action" just simply baffled her. She thought, "This is from another dimension."

I think that is very, very helpful, because it points out that emotion can function, and *should* function, as a crucial psycho-epistemological agent, as a crucial means of keeping you in contact with reality. And therefore, it is not an accident that people who are inclined to floating definitions are, in my experience, typically characterized by a pronounced psychology of repression. They are very much on the premise of shunting aside emotion—emotions are unreliable, they're bad, they're subjective. These people feel uncomfortable with emotions. They automatize a detachment from their emotional lives. And consequently, they have cut off the mechanism that the mind provides to keep us in that kind of immediate, automatic psycho-epistemological contact with the concretes of reality. And they end up manipulating terms.

The same thing could be done, in one way or another, whether it's positive or negative emotions, with virtually any concept. For instance, with "value"—if you just think "that which one acts to gain and/or keep"—then, of course, you're just lost in the clouds. But if you think your wife, money, your house, clothes, and so on—if those are the things you like, if that's what you have emotion for, then "value" will immediately convey those concretes to you; if you have the feeling and let it function, you will have an invaluable tie to the details, to the concretes, that you otherwise won't have.

This is only the beginning of a long discussion of the role of emotions in thought and life. But I hope I've shocked you by coming out in favor of emotions, rather than against them. I hope you also see that I am not saying that all cognition is driven by passion, that objectivity is impossible, although undoubtedly there are people who think that is about to come. Emotions are not the means of justifying your conclusion—that would be mysticism or subjectivism—but they *are* essential to automatize the process of concretization, in other words, to automatize the tie to reality of your concepts.

Now we're going to give Steve one last chance.

> I want to show that life is the standard of value. There are two basic issues here: I have to understand value and what it involves, and I have to understand life and what it involves. Value—that which one acts to gain and/or keep. It presupposes a valuer, an alternative, and a standard of value. I'll break that down. Valuer—value presupposes a valuer. In order to be a valuer, a thing must be capable of pursuing a value. A saltshaker cannot act; a volcano cannot act in a value-directed manner. A living entity can do both. To sum up (per above), value requires a valuer, an alternative, and a standard. Living entities are the only entities that fulfill the above requirements. Only a living entity faces the alternative of life or death, existence or nonexistence. Only a living entity is capable of self-generated, goal-directed action. Only a living entity is capable

of having a goal. Only a living entity is capable of acting to remain in existence. The action required is a specific course of action, a value-oriented course of action. There would be no values without life. The need for values arises because living entities face the alternative of life or death. They need values to live. Values are a means to life, *the* means to life. Life is the standard.

I don't have an error in mind. I just wanted him to put it together in some way so we could see the whole thing before us. And I want to summarize what I think are some points of method. To begin with, it's a complex issue—what do you have to do to understand it? You break it into stages. Not *too* many stages, because then you can't hold it. Not too *few* stages, because then you haven't broken it up. How many is a good number? Three is a good number. Two or three, four at the outside. And in this case—because that gives you the units you can work with—I hold this in the form of three stages in my mind: value, life, therefore. The first stage to me is the analysis of the idea of "value"—value requires a certain type of entity, and then there's the whole chewing involved, an entity capable of acting in a goal-directed fashion, an entity confronted by an alternative (because otherwise, what's the necessity of such action?), an entity that has some ultimate goal, because it can't have a means to an infinite series of ends. We chewed those individual points earlier, with examples; I would go over and over until I say, "Okay, that's 'value.'" I just hold it by the word "value"—that's one word summarizing that whole discussion. Then, turn to "life." So far, I haven't said anything about "life," just "value." Now comes the biological analysis, in effect—the distinction between the living and the inanimate. Why only living entities have self-sustaining action, why only they confront an alternative versus the statue, and so on. And that I tie up in a word, "life."

You see what I'm doing—first you *expand* the topic. "Value" becomes all of its subdivisions. Then, once it's chewed, you condense it back to one word: "Okay, that's all in this word 'value.'" Then you expand your study of "life"—break it up into all the points that are relevant, and then condense it into, "Okay, that's 'life.'" And then, number three is simply connect the two together. It's because a living entity has to act to sustain itself; that's why values exist, so that obviously has to be the goal of any values; values *are* that which living entities pursue to keep themselves alive; that's what gives rise to it. Consequently, by saying that, we've already said: The standard has to be life. That's Q.E.D. That's just tying it together, the "therefore."

Again, the method is: Break it up into parts, chew each, then reduce each to a one-word unit, and then go on to the next and do the same thing, reviewing as needed.

Another point of method—notice it's important to have a structure, stages, a developed argument. If you just simply look at living things mutely, you do not come to any conclusions as to what the standard of value is. You do need step-by-step reasoning, and that's the point the rationalist attaches to, and which throws him off. But the alternative to rationalism is not to ignore step-by-step reasoning and just stare at random concretes. The point is that you have to combine a step-by-step analysis with a consistent reality focus. You have to remember that everything that you are analyzing one step at a time is there in the perceptions that you started with, that you can't get something for nothing. So your stages, your steps, when you're going to "value" and then "life," and so on, are simply stages of putting into words and making explicit what was there all the time. You're not getting something out of the blue. I already got the concept "value" by observing that life was the standard. I had to observe living entities pursuing their goals, pursuing their lives, in order to get the concept of "value." And at the same time, I had to observe living entities act in order to grasp that they were self-sustaining and self-generated. And in observing them act, I saw them act how? To pursue and sustain their own lives. So, when I come in and do it a step at a time, it is not as though in actual reality there is "value" with everything it requires, then there's "life" with everything it requires, and then there's the connection. All of that is our way, conceptually, of putting into words, in a way that we can grasp, the same one fact that is right there when you look at living entities act. All we're doing is putting into words what we're given in perception. There's a whole complexity, but "value" and "life" come down to: "Look, there is a carrot that is reaching out its roots, and whatever it is doing, that's it, that's value, that's the pursuit of values, that's self-sustaining action, that's self-generated action, that's being confronted by an alternative, that's life as the standard"—it's all in that.

The trick is to learn to combine the fact that there are discrete stages in thought with the fact that the fact exists as one unit, unbroken, in perceptual reality. And you see what happens if you can't keep that: The rationalists keep the structure, they keep the step by step, but they cut it off from the reality. Consequently, they always feel "I don't know where I am, what I'm doing, nothing follows, I can't get it out of my definitions." Remember the name we gave to the other side, the empiricists; they do the opposite: They keep the tie to reality (as we'll see), but they have no organization or structure, no step by step at all. They just look. And if he was a nice empiricist, he would say, "Well, look, there are all those living things, and that's it." "It's self-evident," he might say. He's swamped by lack of organization. He never knows what he's proved or what he hasn't.

"Life as the standard" does need proof. But the point is, what kind of proof? What is the kind of proof that is involved when you look at reality, form general concepts on its basis? *Induction.* Induction means really the process of coming to conclusions on the basis of observation. Deduction is the process of coming to conclusions on the basis of earlier abstractions. And the point here is, in philosophy, the proofs are inherent in the percepts. The proof is simply making explicit what is there all the time.

So what is the proof of life as the standard? The proof is two different things—a whole complexity of analysis ("value" and "life" and so on); but at the same time, the proof isn't any of that; the proof is: "Look, there are things. Those are living entities. That's it." There is no other proof. All that analysis is just a way of conceptualizing what is there in the data.

This is the goal you have to reach with every philosophic idea. You have to try to break it up and reduce it to the point where the steps of derivation are so clear to you that when you're asked, "What's the proof?" your automatic sense is, "Look." And then, of course, you remind yourself, "I had to go through a complex process to look and to automatize all that and conceptualize it"—but in fact, all I'm doing is pointing. All my proofs are pointing. If you really got it all (and of course, this is pretty fast; we only had an hour and a half—on an idea this important, this fundamental, and with this many complexities, you should easily take six hours; if we had three evenings, I hope you see by just projection, it would be even clearer, maybe more complicated, but even clearer than it is now, but you get the idea), ideally you should reach the stage that if you ask yourself why is life the standard, your inner experience should be, "Look—don't you see?" A lot of people say that in an improper way, because they think it's "self-evident." That is not correct. "See" means literally *see*—look at these living entities and you will see all of the distinctions and all of the facts, which are proofs simply organized.

At present, that is the closest I can describe the process of making a conceptual idea perceptual. Remember, we said we wanted to get like it was to the truck. Here we've taken a very abstract idea, and you should at least get the idea that you can reduce it down past all the verbiage to just sensory perception.

I'm not going to give you any more rules tonight. But I do want to just dictate about six rules, for those of you who are making a list. These are all rules that we discussed, but I'm just breaking it up into numbers.

Rule one, set the intellectual context in appropriately economical form. Two, identify the full meaning of the idea being chewed. Three, define a *few* essential terms, and then underscore all the rest, keeping all definitions connected to the concretes in reality, with all of their attributes. That's the process we called reduction. And just to remind you as part of this general rule or issue, oscillate back and forth from the definition to the instances. And, if you have emotions, let them out. Rule four, concretize regularly, above all, your key concepts. Five—and this is just a consequence of the preceding—if it's a major issue, your proof must be inductive, not deductive. Six, break up a complexity into stages, then alternately expand and condense each stage; in the end, the whole issue should be one unit, one word, such as "life."

Next lecture, we'll discuss the virtue of honesty, and I will give you a tip: The issue that threw most seminar people off was that of context. If the context were set correctly, there's nothing to understanding honesty; if the context is *not* set correctly, you can kill yourself and never understand why you should be honest.

Now I would like to give you an exercise that we'll discuss later. The purpose is to hammer home the issue of the relation of definitions to reality by means of a special exercise. There are three things you should be able to do with regard to any concept that you're working with. You should be able to come up with some kind of definition, and some list of concretes that are examples of it, and some list of the attributes that are *not* definitional but nevertheless true of the entity. You need a definition of the concept. Take "life," for instance—"self-sustaining, self-generated action"; some list of concretes, examples—"a carrot, my husband, my cat," and so on; and third, a knowledge of a whole bunch of attributes of those concretes that are not part of the definition. If it's living organisms, in order to keep in contact with reality, we have to remember the hundreds and hundreds of things that distinguish living entities from inanimate entities. It is not enough simply to say "self-sustaining and self-generated action"—it has to remind you quickly of a whole bunch of nondefining characteristics that were nevertheless important aspects of the entity— their cellular structure, their chemical structure, their distinctive capacities, and so on and so on. In order to combat the tendency for definitions to float, you have to hammer them into reality, and that requires providing a list of concretes and focusing on those concretes and seeing how many characteristics they have that are *not* definitional. And that's what will help keep before you the range of reality of the concretes. You don't need thousands of concretes; four or five is okay. Ideally, they should be spread across the category. If you were doing "living things," don't take five carrots. Take a plant, an animal, a man, a woman, whatever. If you were doing "man," you wouldn't take five white American Protestant males from New York City. You want to try to get the range of the category, and therefore, you can hold only four or five, but make them as different as you can within that range. It's crucial to concretize, but above all, to reduce your concepts to those concretes. This is really an anti-definitional exercise; it's to show you how much more is involved than the definition, so do not labor about getting a perfect definition with every word in place. Blurt it out—something that will tie you into reality. It's the access to the concretes that we want here, not the beauty of a dictionary formulation. Once you've got a series of concretes, pick out four or five attributes by actually looking at those concretes, attributes that are not part of the definition; and if you oscillate back and forth—try thinking of just the definition, and then suddenly looking at the whole reality, and then back to the definition—if you get that back-and-forth, that's the only thing I know to oil up the mechanism and reconnect your concept to reality. If you can find any emotions that tie you to the concretes, so much the better. We could do this with any concept; "man" is too easy; "life" we basically did. Take "welfare state," and do it with that. Now, that is two words, but we'll pretend it's one word. Blurt out a definition. Come up with five examples. And then give a list of attributes of "welfare state" that are not part of the definition, and we'll take that up in lecture eight.

Lecture Two Q & A

Q: Do you find images or mental pictures helpful in connecting concepts to reality?
A: Yes, to some extent, as part of the process of concretizing. If I try to imagine life, and concretize that, and I think of a cat or a carrot or which-ever, it's unavoidable that there should be in my mind a certain image, which helps to concretize and bring it right down to earth. It's certainly not just the word "c-a-r-r-o-t" in my mind, because that's just another abstraction, and I want as much as possible to bring it to the perceptual level. And therefore, if I'm not in a room filled with a wide range of living things, and my assignment is concretizing, I certainly find images helpful in that process. So there's nothing against images, as long as they serve a function.

Q: If one is attempting to understand any given principle, how is it that you can say that the method of understanding includes "obtain the right conclusions first" as a part of the correct methodology?

A: That's a perfectly valid question *if* you were learning something from scratch from reality; you couldn't get the conclusion before you got the data. But remember, we are here trying to chew somebody else's thought. We are not originating material. And if you're trying to grasp somebody else's thought, the first thing you have to grasp is "What did they think?" What was the point you're trying to understand? If you find you cannot connect it to reality, then you have to say, "I'm sorry. I thought Ayn Rand was right, but she's wrong. I reject this point." But in the process of trying to understand X and why it's related to reality, you first have to know what X says.

Q: Why not just say, "Value is that which man seeks to gain and/or keep; man's fundamental alternative is life or death; therefore, life is man's standard of value"? Why is it useful to form a concept of "value" that pertains to nonhuman entities?

A: Because that happens to be the way reality is. Value is correlative of life. Its root is the *living* organism, not any *specific* living organism. So if you're going to ground values for man, you can't do it unless you know this.

Q: If there is no fundamental alternative for inanimate matter, where does life come from?

A: That is not a philosophic question; this is a question for science—for biology, for physics. Philosophers have no method to answer such a question. To study the ingredients that make up life would require tremendous specialized observation, experiment, analysis, and so on, a whole life of immersion in the details of biological entities. And it's completely irrelevant to philosophy, because all philosophy says is: There *is* such a thing as a living entity versus an inanimate; a living entity has these attributes, and these alternatives, and an inanimate entity does not; and this is what gives rise to values, and so on. The physical, scientific, structural elements are outside the province of philosophy. The same is true of mind or consciousness. If you say what makes consciousness—who knows? At least I don't.

Q: If you tie your concretes to emotions, aren't you substituting emotions for concretes? Isn't that wrong, since emotions are not tools of cognition?
A: No, that's a complete misunderstanding. I did not say that emotions give you information, or tell you your conclusion. I said they function as the automatic interest-agent keeping you aware of concretes. If you let your emotions function, and you think "life," you don't think "process of self-generated, self-sustaining action." Concretes come right away that you *care* about. The emotions keep you concrete-oriented, not at the *price* of abstraction, but they function automatically that way. But you're certainly not using them as tools of cognition. A tool of cognition would be if I said, "I feel that we should have integrity. That is what my emotion tells me, and therefore, we should." That would be completely wrong.

◾

Honesty, Importance of Principles

We are going to continue our exploration of the method of properly understanding ideas, or digesting them, or chewing them (whatever terminology you want to use), and we are once again going to use the deliberately prestructured form that we did last time of having someone come up to commit a prewritten, circumscribed definite error. This will again be somewhat artificial, but it will be organized, step by step, and followable, and that is our main purpose this evening.

Our topic this evening is the virtue of honesty. Or otherwise put, "Why be honest?" We simply want to chew the answer to that question. And you will find that this is by far a more complicated topic than life as the standard, primarily because it's a topic from the middle of a subject (in this case, the middle of ethics), not from the very beginning, as was life as the standard. And therefore, there is a tremendous amount involved in establishing the context, which had no parallel last time.

Given the time at our disposal—and considering that we're giving a lot of time to deliberate detours in order to point out errors—we're not going to be able to chew this the way it ideally would require. It would take at least two, and possibly three, evenings if you wanted to really thoroughly analyze this to the point where every sub-aspect was crystal clear. We will, however, get an indication to carry us. What we're really

after, again, is the method, the steps, the rules of how to go about it, because if we get that, the actual steps on a particular content you can do
at home by yourself.

The straight man this evening is Peter Schwartz, the publisher of *The
Intellectual Activist*. And again, I stress at the outset, he is not responsible
for the errors that he is about to commit repeatedly. Peter is going to start
by committing an error that was committed last week by Steve in connection with his topic, so this is in the nature of a review.

> I have to start by a clear understanding first of what honesty
> is, so I'll know what it is that I'm trying to understand. Let's
> see. Honesty, first of all, is not telling lies. It means not lying
> to other people; it means speaking the truth to them. I guess
> more basically this amounts to facing reality, not evading, fo-
> cusing on facts, exercising your mind rather than turning it
> off, not turning to some kind of fantasy or make-believe to
> replace reality. So honesty, in sum, I would say, is focusing on
> reality by your mind, and as a result, not lying to other people.

All right, we're going to stop here. That obviously is not the whole
process of chewing, but that commits enough mistakes to get us started.

What step within the process of understanding or chewing was he
attempting in this brief passage? He's trying to simply define what "honesty" is. He's trying to specify what our subject is, in the same way that
last time we had to start by saying, "What do we mean when we say that
life is the standard? What are we trying to establish? What are we trying
to understand?" We want to know, "What is it?" We're saying that's something you should do—"Well, what?" So, as a goal, he's doing okay. But
he went off the track in his statement of what honesty consists of. There
are two different errors in his presentation. If you commit either or both
of these errors, you're lost for the rest of the evening, because you're trying
to prove the wrong thing. You could say it's too social, and that's correct.
It's too narrow. He's making it only an issue of how you behave toward
other people. But besides that point, what is wrong with his statement of

what it involves with regard to other people? Yes, he did give a predominantly negative statement; except for saying "focusing on reality," he practically didn't tell you anything except what you *don't* do. But honesty is basically a negative virtue. It's a corollary of a positive virtue, but its basic injunction is "Don't do certain things." So we're not going to discriminate against the negatives. That's not it.

No, now think of this—he's saying, "Honesty consists of not lying." That was one element in his statement. There were no restrictions, no qualifications. And since honest is something, according to Objectivism, that you should be, what immediately does the implication of this kind of statement mean, that honesty equals not lying? It amounts to implying that according to Objectivism, you should tell the truth always, in all contexts, as a kind of Kantian absolute—thou shalt not lie, no matter what. But that is not the Objectivist definition. That is not the concept of "honesty" that we're working with. And if it were, we're never going to validate it by reference to an Objectivist approach. You'd have to get that by an injunction from God or the noumenal world. Because there are cases where it's perfectly okay to lie. Such as what? Like to a Nazi who comes knocking on the door asking for the Jews, or in any case of self-defense. If you try to equate honesty with one concrete social policy, uttering only true statements to other people, no matter what the context, the consequences, the situation, there will always be exceptions; it will never be clear or convincing to you. When, according to Objectivism, is lying wrong? It's not *always* wrong. It's wrong when you're trying to get something for nothing by means of it, when you're trying to perpetrate it on an innocent person to get something from them that you are not entitled to, as opposed to lying to a killer or a criminal or a dictator. So the thing that honesty denounces is not the form of words of lying as such, but attempting to gain what? Some value by fraud, or misrepresentation. It doesn't make any difference what the value is—a high grade, a wife, a salary. So there's one error right there, in specifying just at the outset what we're trying to establish.

There's another error in his preliminary statement. Peter went on to say, "More basically, I guess, the essence of honesty is facing reality—not evading, exercising your mind." What's wrong with that as a characterization of honesty? It's much too broad; it's applicable to all virtues. It really amounts to the definition of "rationality." And rationality, as you know, is the basic virtue according to Objectivism. It's the virtue that says exercise your mind, stay in contact with reality, don't evade. And all the specific virtues are *forms* of rationality. But each of the specific virtues has to add something to that general definition; otherwise, it's useless, and just repeats what we already know. Each of the specific virtues has to concretize or specify or add another aspect that is not obvious just from the statement "Use your mind, think, don't evade." What does honesty add specifically? If rationality tells you don't evade, what does honesty add that is different from simply not evading? If we don't know this at the outset—this is the methodological point—it's hopeless to even plunge into this discussion, because we don't know what we're trying to establish. What does it add? Not facing reality. Dishonesty is a step *after* evasion. Evasion: you ignore some aspect of reality; dishonesty is making up a *new* reality to replace the one that you didn't like. If you *merely* evade, you just don't look at reality, and that is a default. You could walk around in a daze, but it wouldn't involve any specific dishonesty, just being out of focus. You're not yet constructing another fact to replace the actual fact. But if you don't look at something that you don't like, *and* you make up or pretend something unreal to replace it, that is specifically dishonesty. Like if you pretend, for instance, that you're a military veteran and you have tremendous experience when you don't, then you are making up something; that is not simply *not* looking at your past; that's making up a new one.

What honesty specifically says is, don't fake reality. Or, the way you can put this—rationality says existence is there, it exists, try to grasp it; honesty says *only* existence exists, don't try to make another one, don't manufacture the unreal as a substitute. Now you can see the two errors that were involved in Peter's opening statement. On the one hand, it was too concrete; on the other, it was too generalized. And consequently, he would be lost altogether in working with that kind of concept. Any kind of mental process on this topic would be sabotaged, because he doesn't know what he's trying to establish.

So, just to get a concept of "honesty" clearly before us at the outset: All virtues in Objectivism have two aspects—they partly involve a process in the mind, a process of consciousness, and they partly involve a certain course of action in the physical world (an aspect involving existence). In other words, something in your mind, and then a corresponding course of action. And in regard to honesty, the mental side is: Never pretend that things are other than they are, whether you pretend that for yourself or for others. And then in regard to action, never seek to gain a value by such pretext. That's honesty, the inner and outer side.

Have we finished with this aspect of grasping what it is? Yes, except that we have to remember one thing. There is one flaw still in what I've said. What is wrong with this little speech I just gave? It's all correct, and you'd have to do it, but we can't go on yet. Why not? It's too long. Remember that we have to always reduce the units so that our mind can hold these things. Understanding involves always expanding and then condensing. First you take the word "honesty." Then you break it up—"it means this kind of policy in the mind, as against rationality, and it means this kind of policy in practice in relation to other people, and so on and so on"—and after all that, we've got a whole paragraph. But we can't do anything with a paragraph. Now that we have expanded it, the next step is to put it back together into one quick unit, which will retain all of the material that we unpacked, but in a form sufficiently limited that we can go on. The purpose of a definition, which is essentially what we're doing here, is to keep our concept in contact with reality. A paragraph will not do this. You have to think of the paragraph, but then you have to press it down. Suppose I said to myself, "I really know what honesty is. 'Honesty is the recognition that reality exists as an absolute, that only one reality exists, that we must conform to facts rather than try to rewrite them; since the mind is our tool of cognition, we must exercise it rather than thwart it; and therefore, in relation to others, we must never try to gain a value by any form of fraud or misrepresentation.'" It's correct, but it's simply out of the question as a definition. That's an ethics; that's a treatise. Therefore, what we need now is to blurt out (and I say "blurt" because we're doing this just for our own mind; we don't want niceties of formulation now; we presumably already understand the idea from having broken it up), blurt out in a word, what does it all come down to so we can keep it in our mind. And I would hold it as something like this—"no pretending." That's it. Of course, that's not an ideal formulation, because it sounds like, "Fairy tales are wrong, or maybe fiction is wrong, because you're pretending it happened"—but I know I don't mean any of that. And I'm just trying to zero in on one simple peg to hold it in my mind. "Don't try to make up things," in effect. And then when I get lost, I have one simple thing to come back to. And this is a definition, now; this is not the story of honesty; it doesn't tell all the preconditions and all the subtleties and all the arguments for and all the exceptions to; it's a mental peg only—to keep it in your mind.

If you got that, let's assume that we've carried out step one and we grasped what honesty is. Now Peter is going to come back and try to validate this virtue, in the process committing an entirely different type of error, which, by the way, was *not* an error that we discussed last week, so see if you can see something wrong that's different from anything you saw last week.

> Okay, now that I know what honesty is, let me try to understand why I should be honest, why anyone should be honest. And I think I can do this best by illustration. Say, for example, you cheat your way into a job you're not equipped for. You don't have the ability to do the job. You'll be terrified at the prospect of having to do it, not being able to do it. And you know that you don't have the ability, so you'll be terrified most of the time, worried that somebody is going to catch you, knowing you won't be able to perform the way you should, the way you said you would be able to when you got the job. You'll have to fake more and more, and one day, sooner or later, you'll be caught. It just doesn't work. In general, if you lie, you'll experience remorse, you'll experience guilt. At least you will if you're a decent, moral person. If not, what's the whole point of devising a moral code for you? You don't want to go through life

feeling guilty. It's not in your interest. And we're trying to define here what course of action you should take that's compatible with your interest. Besides, it's impractical in another respect. People will usually find out. You'll get caught. Look at all the embezzlers who were caught and disgraced, even though they all thought they had this perfect scheme. Or take another example—suppose you cheat on your wife. Well, she's going to know, or anyway, even if she doesn't find out, *you'll* know, you'll know you're cheating. You won't be able to carry it off, not in the long run at least. You'll feel guilty. It won't work. I remember a friend of mine—Joe Edwards—who did this. And what happened was his girlfriend found out about it, they had a terrible fight, they broke up, he went into a depression for six months, and the net result was he was much worse off for having cheated than if he hadn't. So put it this way—it's a matter of respect for yourself and for others. No matter how horrible the truth, it's better to face it head-on than to try to evade it. For example, a doctor who tries to lie to a patient and not tell him the truth about his condition—that's not right. The patient has a right to know that, let's say, he's dying, even if it's as bad as that. So in other words, you've got to face the truth and be honest.

That is the polar opposite of the error that was committed last week. There are two distinct flaws with this particular approach, which very commonly go together. In a sense, he's reversing cause and effect by bringing up guilt. His point is not very well taken, because guilt is a consequence of doing something that's wrong, and the question is, why is dishonesty wrong? So to start off by saying "You should be honest because otherwise you'll feel guilty" begs the question. That is not, however, the point I had in mind. That is one minor logical fallacy. I have in mind an overall flaw permeating the whole presentation, although this type of fallacy is suggested. But this is more methodological, rather than logical. It sounded like he was espousing the view of pragmatism, that ethics derives from whether something works or not; he didn't intend that to be pragmatic; and after all, an Objectivist *would* say it's impractical to be immoral; so it doesn't commit you to pragmatism. But it certainly did *sound* like pragmatism. But it did so not because he was a pragmatist, but because of something else he did wrong that made his statements come across as pragmatism.

True, he gave examples without ever formulating what he was trying to show. That certainly is one point. The presentation was basically all concretes and examples, with no principle tying them together. If you took his content, it would be, "Cheating your way into a job leads to this, and embezzlers get caught, and doctors cause harm to their patients, and your wife will do this, and such and such will lead to depression," and it's example after example. As you know, it's very valuable to give concretes. And a little dose of this is very helpful to counteract the tendency to just say, "Rationality equals this, and honesty equals this," all in that world of floating abstractions. But it is of no use to just string together a whole bunch of examples without analysis, without stating a principle that unites them, without showing what it is they are examples *of.* This is like an intellectual hit and run—he gets an idea of an example, and then he drops it, and he goes to another example; and then another example reminds him of his friend, and he's off on that example; and then he thinks of a doctor, and then he's on that one. Examples are crucial within the framework of an abstract principle, and then the *union* of the two is convincing. But examples or concretes *without* an organizing principle have no force. It just raises questions in all directions—"How do you know the embezzler is going to get caught? Why should it happen to me just because it happened to Joe?" The examples just do not take you anywhere. So in one sense, this is the *opposite* of the type of error that we saw last time, when Steve just used floating abstractions; this person looks *only* at concretes.

And what is the other type of error in the approach that almost always goes along with this improper concretizing, this concretizing without an abstraction? I'd like you to lift your minds up from the specific discussion of what's wrong with his view of honesty to the broader methodological point of what's wrong with his whole method of approach, regardless of what subject it's on. And the other point is, *there is no structure to this reasoning,* no logical development, no step-by-step sequence. When you want to understand, you have to have a logic to your development—it has to be *this* point, and then you should be able to know why you're going to the next point, and why you're going to the next, and how you lead to the end. Peter's presentation just switches topic over and over, at random, without explanation. He thinks of an embezzler. Why? He just thinks of it. And then he thinks of guilt, and then he thinks of this, and then he thinks of Joe. And then he knows that he hasn't proved anything, so he says it's *usually* impractical; well, if it's *usually* impractical, that implies sometimes it's practical. So then it's okay. It's little bits of ideas, undeveloped, jumping from one to the other.

Notice that this example is the opposite, on both points, to the rationalist method. The rationalist is a stickler for structure. He starts with his definition, and it's step-by-step Q.E.D. He likes mathematics. You always know where a rationalist is in his argument; the trouble is that the whole argument is in another dimension. But you know where he is. But this person could be anywhere, or nowhere. The rationalist is contemptuous of concretes, but this person, in practice, is contemptuous of principles; he just spews out examples. So this type of error, this concretizing without a principle and without structure, is obviously the polar opposite of rationalism. And what is the name we gave to that? Empiricism. This is an example of an empiricist mental process and is typical empiricism. So you should now begin to tell: If something is off, is it off in the direction of rationalism or empiricism? We are going to be discussing this at length, but I wanted to give you just a taste of it.

We're ready now for another presentation that is wrong, but he's got the right concept of "honesty" now, and it's not going to be rationalism *or* empiricism. But it's another error.

I'm assuming we've already covered the definition of "honesty"; now I'm going to try to proceed systematically. First, I want to specify for myself the context that I'm taking for granted. What am I assuming? Well, honesty is not the beginning of ethics. It's pretty far down the road. So I'm already assuming a lot that has been established. And let me identify what it is, exactly, that I'm assuming. First, I'm assuming metaphysics and epistemology—that there is a reality, and reason is the means by which you know it. And in ethics, I'm assuming part of ethics; I'm assuming that life is the standard of value. That much at least I have to assume, or else what's the whole point of even discussing virtues, if you haven't established that life is the ultimate end toward which these virtues are the means? Then I'm also assuming something else, that life has objective requirements. It's not enough to say life is the standard; you have to say life has certain requirements; it's not true that you can do anything, that anything goes, that any arbitrary action will keep you alive. You have to do certain specific things. If that's not established, then again, there's no point in virtues, because you can do *anything* and survive. Then there's a third thing I think that I'm taking for granted—that the basic virtue, before honesty, the basic virtue is adherence to reality, conformity to the facts; it means behaving in accord with what is. Obviously, we live in reality; if we don't adhere to it, we're not going to survive. Reality dictates how you should live. This seems to me essential to getting to honesty. Once I've established this, I think honesty follows pretty easily, because honesty is a form of adhering to reality. Under the virtue of honesty, we're not allowed to make up a phony reality; we must adhere to the real one. So it's obvious, from that context, you must be honest; it's very logical.

He started off well. He turned to the topic of establishing the context, which is very crucial. And up to a point, he did okay: He identified reason and reality, life as the standard (correct), life has certain objective requirements (and, of course, he explained why we have to take that for granted). But something went wrong in establishing his context. Something went wrong after he got past life as the standard and it has certain objective requirements.

There is something wrong with "adherence to reality" as he used it. There is certainly something wrong with saying, "To get to honesty, all I have to do is say 'life,' and it has requirements, and the big requirement is adhering to reality, and now we just go to honesty." What is wrong with saying adherence to reality is the essential context? If all we knew was that life is the goal, and some objective requirements are necessary, and on that basis we then said, "And the big thing is adhere to reality," then "adherence to reality" wouldn't tell us anything. "Adherence to reality" is a very vague generality. It's *true* that you should adhere to reality. But if we are trying to chew this topic, it is certainly not enough. Our goal here, remember, is to be convincing to our minds by seeing the full concrete reality of what we're talking about. And when we use a mere generality, such as "adhere to reality," it does not do it.

Let me give you a parallel example so you can see why this is useless. Suppose a person were discussing politics, and he engaged in this type of reasoning: He said, "Life is the standard, and we have to have certain objective requirements if we're to achieve it; the crucial one is adhering to reality. Therefore, we have to have capitalism." That reasoning is valid; I mean, it's correct. But what is the problem with that? A tremendous amount of steps are omitted. A person who would get "capitalism" from that brief of a background statement wouldn't need it; he'd already be omniscient. And so the obvious question: Why is socialism an evasion of reality? There's no indication. What does it evade in reality? The whole ethics—how does man function, that we need his productive ingenuity, that force is the antonym of mind, that capitalism is the only system that prohibits force, and so on and so on—there's a whole context of ethics that you'd have to establish before you could say, "Life is the standard, therefore capitalism." Otherwise an honest man could listen and say, "Okay, adhere to reality; but why capitalism?" And the same principle applies with regard to honesty. A person could very well say, "Okay, I agree, I have to adhere to reality. Why do I have to be honest to do that?" The person could say, "The way I look at it, life is brutal, everybody's out to cheat everybody else, it's a dog-eat-dog world, the only way to survive is to be dishonest if you have to; that's reality. You say adhere to reality, that's just what I'm doing." That is not a joke. I mean, it *is* a joke, but the point is it's not valid, nor is it not *in*valid if all you said was that generality. And the reason is "adherence to reality" does not prepare the context for honesty. It's a vague generality. It will not carry the weight of so specific a virtue as honesty.

And this is what you could call the fallacy of the *inadequate context.* The person *tries* to establish the context, but he *omits* essentials; and consequently, when he gets to his alleged point, it simply will not become clear to him, because it rests on too much that is not being stated. *Anybody* can say, "Okay, I'll adhere to reality." You know, the type that says, "I'll make up a foolproof plan as to how to rob a bank and to escape. People do it, and sometimes they get away with it. Why is it impossible even once? And if you can do it once and get away with it, then it's realistic to that extent— I'll have all the money, and I'll be able to spend all my time improving my body at expensive gyms, so it will be pro-life." Is that adherence to reality?

What is the rule of method here? It's not enough to say, "Specify the context properly," because if you knew how to do that, you wouldn't commit the error. But one way to tell that you have specified it *im*properly is: Don't let your arguments become too causal or too easy. After you give an argument, scrutinize it with a cool eye. Consider possible objections to your argument. See if it stands up to a dispassionate scrutiny.

I am *not* saying that you should become polemical and start thinking about what a whole bunch of corrupt intellectuals are going to say to you. That is not the point. I am saying that you should try to look objectively, just for yourself, but objectively, at your argument. It's possible that it's a bad argument for a good conclusion. And you can find it out for yourself; you can see if you scrutinize it that your argument does not prove what it claims. And this is a very important ability to establish: Invent an objection that could be raised—not some diabolical insane thing that you make up, but just a straightforward, commonsense type of objection, such as was glaring from what Peter said. It doesn't mean that I'm in favor of bank robbing by the fact that I created that argument. But it's simply a way of showing that this argument is deficient—there's a gap, there's a jump, revealed by an objection, a simple, straightforward objection that you couldn't answer.

We can call this "the method of the devil's advocate." And it's really just a way of trying to be fair and scrutinizing your own arguments. It's your own conscience, really; it's not a devil telling you. If you can't answer this, you yourself are not really convinced. And the trick here is not—when you start the devil's advocate—the trick is not to slip over into polemics. If you do that, it's worse than having no argument at all, because you're losing all firsthand self-direction. This devil's advocate, properly used, is an art. You have to do it completely for yourself. You take your own most cherished view and you say, "Did I really establish this?" But if you do it, you can learn to do it without slipping into the approach of your enemy. And the important thing here is to remind yourself that you want a *convincing* argument, and not just any old argument. The purpose of going through this is to make it real to you in that truck-oriented fashion, to make it really convincing, to make it a transcript of reality as you see it. To do that, you have to really scrutinize it—"Am I really convinced?" It's useless to do what the medievals used to do—"The conclusions are all in the Bible, and let's make up any argument that will lead to the preordained conclusion." That, of course, makes the argument simply worthless and useless. So you can't say, "I know it anyway via Ayn Rand," or it's "self-evident"; if it's self-evident, you don't need an argument, and if it's self-evident then it must be an axiom, and "honesty" is not an axiom.

Proof is necessary for yourself so you yourself believe it and understand it. And devil's advocacy can be an important adjunct, properly used. If you run wild and start imagining objections to everything, it's useless. But in the case that we're talking about, there was a gap that you could drive seven locomotives through; and if you're just oblivious to that, and you go on and say, "That's pretty good," that will have no more conviction for you than if you had given no argument at all.

I think we're now going to give Peter one last shot at a lengthy mental process. This commits another error, a different kind of error than any that we've had in this course, so he's going to be on longer now in order to give you a clear, developed statement of this error.

This time I'm going to specify the context better. I'm taking metaphysics and epistemology for granted. In ethics, again, I take for granted that life is the standard of value, that it has objective requirements. I need something more specific, still in ethics, than just "adherence to reality as the basic virtue." Well, what about the basic virtue of rationality? That's a little bit more specific. That comes before "honesty," and it's part of the context of "honesty"—it's the base from which you could derive "honesty." So what is rationality? That's what I have to start with at this point. Well, it's the use of your mind. It's the exercise of your consciousness to perceive facts. It means "thinking." And the opposite is evasion, refusing to see, just blanking out. For example, say you cheat on your wife. What do you have to do there? You have to evade certain facts there. You have to evade the fact that she is assuming that you're not cheating on her, that your relationship depends on a certain understanding between the two of you; you have to pretend that you can continue your relationship with her, and you can continue acting toward her as though you weren't cheating on her. So you're evading certain facts about reality. This idea of rationality, this need for rationality, is inherent in life. That is, reason is the means by which man survives; you have to exercise reason in order to live. This isn't something vague, like "adherence to reality," because I'm specifying now what this actually consists of: It's a certain mental process; it involves thought, effort, non-evasion; it's the absolute on which human life depends.

This process tells us how you go about adhering to reality—by always keeping your eyes on it. It's more specific, and more fundamental, than just this vague idea of "adhering to reality." The real issue here is the use of one's mind. If you use it properly, then the issue of adherence to reality will just take care of itself. Now, with *this* context of rationality, then the proof of "honesty" comes down to the following, I think: I have to show that dishonesty necessitates the violation of rationality; if you're dishonest, you're irrational; that it must involve or lead to some sort of evasion, some kind of anti-thinking attitude. If I've done that, then I've proved that honesty is a proper virtue. It's a very logical proof. "Evasion is evil" is my first premise. If I can then prove dishonesty involves evasion, then it's perfectly logical, it's the end of a syllogism to simply say "Dishonesty must be evil." First I have to assume that evasion is evil; that's part of the context that we're assuming. If I can prove dishonesty is evasion, I have therefore proved dishonesty is evil. Now the question is, how can I show it? How can I show that dishonesty is in fact evasion?

Well, to me it seems a little bit easier if I were to start on a *spiritual* level—that is, when it involves spiritual values. For example, say a man seeks unearned love, or unearned praise—you know, he pretends to be something to others that he's really not in order to get their love or their affection. He does not dare face the fact that, in this case, his scheme won't work if he tells himself, "You know, you're really a worthless louse; you're just pretending to others; their praise and their love are coming because you are pretending to be something to them that you yourself know you're not." Now, if you admitted that to yourself, I think then that their praise or their love would have no value. It *couldn't* have any value. It wouldn't work. To work—you know, to produce the true feeling of self-worth that he's after—he must pretend that their love for him has good reason, that it's based on something real, so that their love proves that he really is a good person, and really is a worthwhile individual. He has to evade what he's really doing. If he wants to gain anything from his pretense, he has to evade reality. Well, then you can ask, what about emotional satisfaction? What about if he concedes, "Okay, I'm not evading, I admit that I'm pretending when I'm a good person when I know I'm a swine, but I get emotional satisfaction out of this, it's a value to me, it feels good"? Well, could *that* be a legitimate value without actually evading? No, I don't think so, because emotions can't be the basis for judging values. You can drink poison and say it gives you pleasure, but still, that doesn't make drinking poison right. It's reality, and not your feelings about reality, that are the guide to what's true or not.

Now let's take the material values of life. Let's say a research scientist falsifies some data and gets some money for it; say somebody's bribing him, or he gets a prize for some research that he in fact didn't do, or that he had to falsify. Now, can't he enjoy the money? Can't he buy real values, real goods, that he'll in fact take pleasure from, without evading? So why is, in this case, dishonesty an example of evasion? Why does he have to evade in order to do this? Well, to me, I would explain it to myself this way: He is acting self-destructively. He wants to be productive, he wants to create values, he creates these values by pursuing his work—new discoveries, seeking ever more knowledge. That's what he would normally do; that's what his life requires. But now, with his dishonesty, his life kind of becomes a self-contradiction. On the one hand, he needs to be productive to sustain his life. On the other hand, he's got to *avoid* being productive—he has to avoid doing new research, new discoveries, for fear of revealing some fact that will contradict his phony data, something that will show that he's a fraud. He's got to be afraid of this field that is his actual productive work. He has to feel fear of revealing some fact that others, other scientists, can use as a stepping-stone in their own research to come up with material that will show his research to be phony. So in fact, I would say he has to fear all scientific research, his own and other people's. Before, he welcomed other people's discoveries; he even helped them where possible; it was an aid to him. Now it's only a threat. So he will try to discourage other research. So in sum, he has to shut down his mind and close his eyes to reality.

I'll give you another fast example. Let's take, on a more mundane level, the proverbial used-car salesman. Now, he misrepresents his cars—he turns back the odometer, and he doesn't reveal the mechanical flaws, and so forth. Now, how is this dishonesty an example of evasion? He knows what he's doing. Well, I think it's still acting against the requirements of rationality. Why? On the one hand, he lives by trading with people. It's in his interest to build up his business, to create, to produce the best cars for the lowest price, to get customers; he wants the most perceptive, intelligent people to come to him, to recognize what he's offering—*normally*—people who can see the value of what he has to sell them. Now, also, he wants people who are capable of *producing* values in *exchange* for the things that he offers them. The more they know, normally, the better it is for him; the more he can exchange with them. On the other hand, if he's dishonest, he must prevent customers from seeking information. He has to fear their intelligence, he has to fear questions from them, he has to rely on stupid and incompetent people. He won't try to improve his products to expand his productivity; he'll do the opposite, because he'll try to seek people who are blind, people who are fools. However, he can't live completely off fools, or they won't know what it is that he's got to offer at all. So he has this conflict between the requirements of reality on the one hand and his dishonesty on the other. So therefore, his dishonesty is incompatible with life and with rationality.

Now that is a more real example, in that it's not as obvious, and it really is an excellent, confusing statement of a certain mental process that is really important to try to narrow down.

There are some good things in this. When he got to rationality as the contextual basis, that's much superior to "adherence to reality." It's still very general, but now it specifies a mental process, it gives you an idea of what adherence to reality consists of for Objectivists, how you would achieve it. So that's a great improvement. We've got a fairly good context now. Leaving aside metaphysics and epistemology, we've got life is the standard and that there are definite objective requirements, one of them being the virtue of rationality.

However, the first suspicious thing arose the same way in the seminar, where someone said, "I think it's easier to prove honesty in spiritual issues than in material." And then my philosophic antenna went up, because the essence of a virtue is the union of a certain mental process and a certain course of action, and if there's a mind/body dichotomy of any kind, there's something funny about the proof; there's something warped somewhere.

What is warped about this presentation? If it went on for long enough with the right context, a lot of the points he made would be relevant, would be important, would be illuminating—how the scientist has to turn against research, and how the used-car salesman has to dread being discovered, and so on, and the phoniness of this guy who has to lie to himself in order to get the approval of others, and how he's got a double standard, he has to not know what he's doing and evade. But now we're speaking of it from the aspect of: Given the context that he laid down, is this a convincing argument for honesty? That's the only question. *Not* did his individual examples or points in some other context contribute something? Obviously, I'm implying not. If not, why not? As a broad type of error, you could say he omitted from the context something about man's nature. But presumably, he would mean "the virtue of rationality," which is taken as part of the context, to be a central statement of man's nature. Because he would say—he *did* say, as a matter of fact, "Man survives by reason, that's his means of dealing with reality, and therefore, rationality is a primary virtue." There is something wrong with the context that he's counting on.

Suppose that Peter got up and said just the following (which is what it amounts to), taking the used-car salesman as a paradigm: "My only context is: Life is the standard, objective requirements, rationality. Obviously he has to be honest then, because otherwise he's going to turn against productivity. Otherwise he's going to turn against trade—instead of being on the premise of trading value for value, he's going against the whole idea of the role of productive work in human life."

What's wrong with that as an argument? He didn't say a blessed word about productivity. He didn't say anything *at all* about trade. He didn't say anything about any of those questions. All he said in his context was, "You should think, use your mind, and not evade." And with no more context than that, he's trying to figure out why this is bad. It's *true* the salesman will be led to a life of parasitism, dependence, scorn for productivity, and so on, but all of those are things of which we have not heard anything. Is productivity, the virtue of productivity—is that part of the context for the virtue of honesty? Is the virtue of trading with others value for value, you know, mutual consent to mutual profit—does that come before honesty? If it is part of the context, it would be nice to know that. If we count on that to get to honesty, that's not a little wrinkle; that's something we'd better find out.

The whole point about the error is that the person specifies a context up to a point, and then the rest of Objectivism is, in effect, all on a table before him. He went through a couple of steps—"life, rationality"—okay, and then from there, on the table, on the same exact level, equal, is productivity and trade and everything else. And then he struggles to get to honesty, and whenever he gets stuck, he drags in one of those off the table—productivity is dragged in. Now we go on, "Honesty is against the requirements of life because it's against productivity." And then we go on for a while more, back to evasion, and if he can't get there, he says, "Because he wouldn't be trading with people, and we know trade is a requirement," so he takes *that* one off the table.

What if somebody says, "But you haven't said anything about productivity? Why do I have to be productive?" What should he say? "You're thereby committed to a life of dishonesty." Then you're just going in a circle. The argument does not show why dishonesty, as a basic policy, is wrong. It takes elements of Objectivism that are not stated in the context, and it just drags them in, as and when necessary. Can you argue that honesty precedes productivity? Should you argue, "You should be honest, and therefore produce, because if you steal from others, that violates honesty"? Is that the structure? If it is, then you can't count on productivity until you've established honesty. If it *follows* honesty, you can't use it as part of establishing it. What about another possibility? Maybe productivity doesn't precede or succeed honesty; maybe it's on exactly the same level. What then? You have to establish both of them together. How do you do that? What kind of context would lead to it?

All of this is simply unclear in this presentation. And this is what I call the *anti-hierarchical approach.* Philosophy is a structure. One topic depends on the preceding, and so on. That's the skyscraper that we were talking about, the fifty stories. It is not all a heap of ideas on the same level that you can pull in what you need as and when you need it. The used-car salesman would be fine as an example, *if* we had the right context established. But here, obviously, we didn't; rationality alone is not enough to get to honesty. And consequently he's floundering and unconvincing. If we had tried the devil's advocate, he could have seen that: "What about the brilliant used-car salesman who only does it for a year, and then retires to write novels to the glory of man? Sometimes he makes a killing, so dishonesty wouldn't *always* lead to disaster," and there's no answer to that in what was given.

I want now to give you two or three more examples of this anti-hierarchical method. Someone in the seminar said, "We must be honest, because if people are dishonest, you don't know where they're coming from, what their actual basis of action is, and the result is that people become baffling and leave you in a painful mystery. Whereas if everybody is honest, then everybody is understandable to each other, and social relations are much more pleasant." Now, that's certainly true. But that is an arch-example of the error we're talking about. And it comes down to this: The reason that you should be honest is so that you'll understand other people, and they will understand you. Honesty is then validated by reference to the need of certain kinds of social relationships. What is the implication, the structure of development, as this person sees philosophy? "We have to be able to understand people; therefore, honesty is a virtue." This is completely against proper hierarchy. Honesty is a fundamental virtue pertaining to the relation between your mind and reality. It far precedes the issue of understanding other people, which is a detail at this stage of the game, where we're trying to figure out how to keep our minds in contact with reality. We haven't even laid down, in political terms, the rudiments of our domestic policy, let alone foreign policy details; and this is like saying, "We don't yet know what kind of country we're in, but the purpose of this type of country is to get along with Switzerland." You want to get along with Switzerland, but that comes much later, and you're completely lost if that's the axiom of your ethics.

Now I want to give you a preposterous example of the same error, because I want to hammer it home, so we'll go from the more plausible to the more preposterous. "You should be honest"—no one would actually think this way, but it's the same error—"You should be honest because then it will be harder for the IRS to intimidate you when you're audited, and therefore it will promote stronger fighters for capitalism, whereas if you're dishonest, you will tend to cheat on your income tax, and that will make you nervous and embolden the government to rob you." That is a complete collapse of the hierarchical approach. We're at the beginning of ethics and the relation of the mind to reality, and we're just taking for granted that capitalism is good, income tax is bad, and—by reference to those—we're going to establish honesty. Now that speaks for itself.

If you work out Peter's spiritual example (which I won't take the time to do), it comes to this same error: He takes as an absolute "I need love; how should I get it? Therefore, I should be honest, because I'll really get the love I need." That's the same way of violating hierarchy.

The methodological rule that we want to emerge from this is as follows: The context that you specify must be complete—now, "complete," remember, in the crow form; abbreviate—but it must be complete, *and* it must be hierarchical. You must know what you can and cannot use, what you have and have not established. And the fact is that we have not yet got the right context to establish honesty, and that's where the problem is coming from—we're trying to jump too fast from rationality, and that's why we keep reaching out to something else to shore us up. So the question becomes, what else is required—besides life as the standard, objective requirements, and rationality is the basic virtue—what else is required that is earlier than honesty, and would be essential to establishing the real case for honesty? What is the missing context?

Several things are presupposed prior to honesty, beyond the points we have already made. You can see the need for something in the persistence of this type of question: Most people would understand that it's hopeless to live telling lies all the time; the problem that keeps coming up is, "Why do you have to tell the truth, or be honest, all the time? Why can't there be exceptions to the rule? Couldn't the bank robber get away with it once, and therefore, it's not an absolute?" This points to an important element from the context that was not specified here, and without that element, the whole discussion of honesty is shaky and unconvincing.

That element is the need of man to live by principles, by reference to or by the guidance of principles. That is a crucial topic. It is not the same as rationality or life as the standard or honesty. And hierarchically, it precedes honesty. And without reference to that, any discussion of honesty just simply hangs there.

I have found that a lot of people don't get this point, so I'm going to discuss pure philosophy for a few minutes, just to clarify this point.

The issue of principles is not the same issue as the fact that life has objective requirements. Those are two distinct points, and together they are the reason that man needs an ethics at all. One fact is: Life is an effect—if you want to keep it, gain it or keep it, you have to enact the cause; you have to do something specific to achieve it. But that of course is true for *any* living thing; it is true for plants and animals, as well as for man, that life requires a specific course of action, that they have objective requirements that they have to fulfill. And yet there's no issue of principles for plants or animals. They don't need principles, they can't conceive of principles, and principles are not necessary the way they are constructed; they simply act according to the desire of the moment. But if man wants to fulfill the objective requirements that life requires, he has to do it by acting on principle. Why? Now we're going to take a topic that is part of the context of honesty and briefly expand it, chew it, and put it back together again. This is like a little mini topic, but "mini" because this is done within the other topic of honesty.

The first point in order to understand the issue of principles is that man has to act long-range. What do we mean by "long-range"? A person has to take account of the consequences of his action against the whole span of his life, as opposed to mere immediate satisfaction. Short-range would mean acting just on immediate, blind impulse or desire: all you see is satisfying that desire, and you don't look any further. Long-range means that first you inspect the consequences—the ones that you can see—across your future course; then you act. So if you just grab a cup of coffee of which you know nothing and gulp it down, that's short-range—you're thirsty, you swallow, that's it. But if (let's assume that you had some practical context to justify this), you analyze it first for arsenic, you take diet into account—will the caffeine jazz you up, and so on—you take into account the long-range consequences. And that's obviously applicable on all choices on all levels, from coffee to career selection—do you jump into this career because everybody is doing it, and you just feel like you want to, or do you take into account all its consequences, the financial remuneration, its relation to your interests, the opportunities of that type of work?

We haven't gotten to principles yet. All we've said is that man has to act long-range, whereas no other living thing does. *Why* does man have to act long-range? Man is *not automatic*, in the way plants and animals are. He is not automatically set to pursue what his life requires. An animal does not have to plan its course; it doesn't have to figure out, "What's going to be the long-range result of what I'm doing?" because it's automatically self-sustaining. A man has to consider any potential actions, contributions to, or effects on, his life. After all, he's tabula rasa; he has no innate reactions. Therefore, the only way he's going to ensure that his actions pursue and enhance his life is by deliberate study of the results of what he does. He has to consciously select, of course, as opposed to simply act on the desire of the moment.

This point would be true no matter what the ultimate goal was, even if it weren't life. As long as you're talking about a being like man, who is not automatically set, so that his desires don't automatically lead to that goal—whatever goal you pick, a being like man would have to be long-range.

Take a preposterous example—suppose the standard of value were the maximization of bananas. That's what all of existence is about, to have as many bananas as possible. Then, if there were a species that was an automatic banana maximizer, it wouldn't have to be long-range; it could follow the whim of the moment in any direction, because it's built in such a way that that whim will always maximize bananas. But, if man is *not* an automatic banana maximizer, and that is the thing that *counts*, then he would have to say before he decides on an action, "Is that going to lead to this, or away? I know I'm capable of destroying my fund of bananas. I know I can add three today, but by doing something that would cause all of them to rot next week. I have to know the results, because I'm not automatically foolproof." And it's the same idea: If you have an automatic pilot, then you don't have to worry; you can just sit back and let it steer itself. But if you have *not* got an automatic pilot, and you just get in and drive as the whim of the moment strikes you, that is impossible if you actually say that you have a goal. You would *have* to be long-range, because there's no other way to get to the goal.

Life (which is our standard of value) requires certain specific actions, and those are not automatically built into it; therefore, we have to figure out what they are; we have to decide before we act, "What are the consequences going to be?" We have to be long-range.

Going on to the next step—being long-range is the first step, because we're not automatic—now you have to think, "How do we get to be long-range? How do we know the future?" If we had revelations from God and we could count on it—we prayed the right way or faced Mecca—we would then find out that the consequences are so-and-so, and this is what to do—then there'd be no need for principles; we could still be long-range by getting the information by that method. But here we are counting on reason and reality as our context. By what method do we know the future?

We don't know it by sense perception, which can only know the present, and then you can remember, so you can remember the past. We can know the future only by *concepts*, by taking all of the sensory perceptions in a certain category and putting them together, by grasping that *every instance* of a certain type of action will help life, and *every instance* of a certain type will harm it—that is, by applying a concept to a rule of action. And that's what a principle is; that's *all* a principle is.

A principle, therefore, is not a luxury of highly moral people. It's not like the icing on the cake, and it makes you a very nice person if you act on principle. It's the essence of man's way of dealing with the future consequences of his actions, of knowing what they are, and thereby not leaving his long-range goal to chance. Principled action is action based on man's means of coping with reality, conceptual means, understanding it, achieving his end. And this is the root of the need for principles.

We can put the same point one other way to try to chew it one more step. Why not be a pragmatist? A pragmatist is the archetype of an anti-principled person, and that's his "principle," that's his philosophy. Why not say, "Yes, life is the standard, and it has definite means, but I'll find out in each case as I go. There are no absolutes. The way to find out what advances life is try and see—tell a lie, see what happens; if it's bad, don't do it, and then tomorrow try again, maybe things will have changed." This is the essence of pragmatism, and of abandoning principles. What is wrong with this method? Because the pragmatist does find out, let us say, when he swallows arsenic, he definitely finds out that this was anti-life (if he swallows enough of it). But when did he find out? After he died; it's too late; he finds out after the fact by perceptual means; he is necessarily blind by this method, because the only means of vision is a general principle that tells you in advance of acting what the consequences are going to be, and principle is exactly what he throws out when he says, "Let's test it in each specific case by its consequences." So acting on principle is simply man's method of acting consistently to achieve his goal.

To summarize, we have two roots of the concept of "principle": (1) metaphysically, cause and effect—life has definite conditions that must be enacted; (2) epistemologically, man is the conceptual being; he can't know these conditions except in the form of principles.

That's my quick discussion of the topic of principles. I would have liked to have had a long time to give examples, but at least you get an indication.

Have we established honesty? No. I haven't given any *content* to our principles yet; I merely said we have to find them and live by them in order to achieve our goal. But what we *have* done by this discussion of principles is establish this much: If honesty is a *principle* of human survival, then you can't ask out of context, "Why not lie in this situation? Maybe you can get away with it here." Why not? Because if it is a *principle*, then what follows? It is self-destructive to contradict your principles if those principles are mandated by life as the standard. When you take a course of action, you always have to ask (given what we just said), "What does this course of action do to my whole life?" *not*, "What does this concrete out of context do?" as though this concrete implies nothing else. And the crucial point here is this: When you violate a principle, you are throwing it out as a guide. And when you throw it out, what situation are you then in? You're either reduced to acting on blind, short-range desire, because you have no principle guiding you (which is inherently self-destructive), *or* you've substituted some other false principle for the one you've thrown out (such as, for instance, "I must always obey my mother; I must always obey authority"). In any particular case, the violation of a virtue may be very limited, and the damage that you actually do may be small (it may very well be the case that if you tell a specific lie, you're not going to suddenly die, or lose everything, or go into a panic, or destroy yourself); but the important point here is that aside from whatever damage you cause in the particular instance, you are committing an even greater harm of reducing yourself, by that violation, once more into the short-range, blind state of having no guidance.

The whole purpose of ethics is to discuss what principles man should live by; that's what the subject is. So somebody who comes in in the middle of a discussion of honesty and says, "Oh, why can't I violate it in this particular case and do what I feel like just because I feel like it?"—that person is denying the very nature of ethical action, which is *principled action*—those rules of behavior that will tell us how our actions will redound to our long-range benefit. This is an essential part of the discussion of *any* virtue—honesty, productivity, even rationality. Until you grasp that man has to live by principle, you have no means to go on and say, "What principle?" You're constantly vulnerable to the feeling, "Okay, this is good some of the time, but why can't I get away with it? What if I want to do it? What if somebody does such and such in this particular situation?" If you try to go from life to honesty without "man having to live on principle" being clear to you, your mind will sense a lack. And the problem— what Peter was struggling with—is trying to do two jobs at the same time; he's trying to discuss honesty, while at the same time trying to smuggle in the understanding that we have to live on principle. And those are two different topics. They cannot be done together. And a difficulty with philosophy is that if you do not have a clear understanding of the hierarchical structure, people plunge in with a specific topic, and then, as they get lost, they try to establish something else at the same time, and then they completely diffuse their effort, and then they are lost. First we have to know that we must act on principle, and then we can turn to *what* principle.

Let's review what would be the proper context for honesty: life—it has objective requirements—those requirements include principles that we have to act on—that is, universal laws. But what next? So far we have "life, principles." What next is required? The basic principle, which Peter has already indicated—the virtue of rationality would come next. First you have to establish that, which is essential to the context because honesty is just one application of it.

Let me ask you a funny question: Is rationality a concrete or an abstraction? It's actually both. If all I've said is "Act on principle," in relation to that, "rationality" is a specific; it's a concrete; it's telling you one particular principle as against many other possible ones. But in itself, "rationality" is a giant abstraction in relation to all of *its* subdivisions, its sub-aspects and applications. So you see, we're getting down more specifically as we go—from the need of principles to rationality. But once we get to "rationality," we have to chew that one, and make sure that's clear to us before we can go on to "honesty." But basically, Peter gave some indication of what it is; he concretized it.

I just want you to get the method—principle, principle requires rationality because that's our means of survival.

Up to a point, we can simply focus on rationality by itself as a virtue: what it is, some examples. But at a certain point, we cannot keep on just focusing on rationality. Why not? Because it's very general. And our minds are necessarily asking, "What would this consist of?" We say, "Think, use your mind." Okay, but what would that be concretely? Let's try to imagine what an example of thinking and using your mind would consist of. You see somebody really trying to understand an issue, exercising his own firsthand judgment, not just blindly obeying others. That's obviously an example of rationality, but it's also an example of independence. Or you see someone thinking, working, studying, learning a whole science and skill (say, medicine), someone else who's just a bum on the park bench, living on handouts, his mind idle. One is exercising his mind and one isn't; and that is, therefore, rationality. But that is also productivity. Or you see someone insisting, "I saw this fact, I know it's true, I'm not going to pretend otherwise," as opposed to somebody pretending, lying, faking—this is committed to his mind, as opposed to the other, but this is *honesty*. So, in the process of chewing "rationality," you first have to do it in the general way to get your guideline. But as you start to look to reality, lo and behold, there is honesty side by side with a whole bunch of other virtues, all together. So our pattern is life as the standard, the need of principles, rationality in general as the basic principle, and then a whole code of virtues developing at the same time with honesty as one part of it.

All of these subsidiary virtues—independence, productiveness, honesty, and so on—in reality, is one of them before or after the other? No. They are simultaneous. They are all simply expressions of rationality. But of course we have to develop them one at a time in our thinking. Why? Even though they are simultaneous in reality, what prevents us from developing them all simultaneously in our mind? We'd lose our minds. You'd have to have one half of a sentence on honesty, and one half on integrity, and one half on justice, and they'd just completely swim all together. So even though all these subsidiary ones are simultaneous, we've got to do them a step at a time, in stages—first this, and then this, and then this— but we have to remember that they all come at the same time hierarchically, so when we get to honesty, it's part of the whole way of life inherent in rationality, and you can't prove it in isolation from all the other virtues. At a certain point as we are chewing rationality, we zero in on honesty, and we can give a proof. But that proof by itself can't produce full conviction, because we're looking abstractly at one aspect of a whole totality. We have to see honesty as a part of the whole way of life, described by rationality, as involving all the other virtues, and as *being* involved by them all, as being part of one principle, which is rationality. So if you ask me, "Is there a specific proof of honesty that Objectivism offers?" the answer is a resounding yes and no. There is, but there isn't. There is in the sense that I can focus abstractly just on the aspect of rationality that is honesty. I can give an abstract argument, and I can give examples. But that is not intended to be convincing or foolproof by itself, because the foolproof would have to specify the relation of that virtue to all of the others.

What would a specific proof of honesty be? You'd have to say in effect—I don't want to take the time here to repeat what Miss Rand says in her discussion, but it amounts to—a form of living up to your own perception of reality, the refusal to sacrifice your own knowledge, your own view of facts, by pretending the opposite. It's a way of remaining true to reason by refusing to invent a dimension or some alleged fact above reality. And you could easily establish as a principle that we live in reality; you could not endorse the principle of manufacturing an unreal one; you couldn't do it successfully as a principle, because the unreal is the unreal; so however you pretend, A is A, you're going to have to be defeated ultimately. That is a specific argument for honesty. It shows that honesty is not just a gratuitous, arbitrary addition to rationality but an actual, important consequence. But is that the full case? No. It's extremely abstract in those terms, very, very generalized. What do you need to do now with it to make it convincing? You have to concretize. You have to take some actual examples and see how the argument applies. And here's where a good dose of empiricism is very important. If you're interested in honesty, you have to kind of make it a hobby; you have to collect concretes from real life. You have to give yourself a standing order: "Wherever an example in real life comes up—in my reading, in newspapers, in my friend, in my boss—I'm going to analyze it from the point of view of my abstract argument, to see clearly why my general argument for honesty applies in this particular case." You don't have to do it forever—otherwise you'll spend your whole life doing it—but you have to do it for a couple of weeks, or a couple of hours—at least five or six examples.

As I was preparing this lecture, I was trying to come up with a whole list of examples. Unfortunately I have time to give you only one, when the whole trick here is to give ten. Someone went to a meeting of Alcoholics Anonymous and reported a very interesting thing to me—that the first thing they stressed at this meeting was that each person had to stand up and admit to himself and derivatively to others, "I am an alcoholic. I am not merely a social drinker. I have a real psychological problem—I can't control my drinking." And they found that as long as a person simply pretended to be a social drinker—which means he was really being dishonest with himself—he couldn't get anywhere. And by just hit and miss, they reached this method that the first crucial step is that you've got to admit the truth, you have to be honest. It's not enough just to stop there; you have to go just the one step further and hook the example up to your principle. What was your principle? Remember, we gave an abstract argument for honesty—the unreal is unreal; if you try to evade it, you're necessarily going to fail. That's very abstract. Here is an example now— he is what he is, this alcoholic. He can't change by pretending to be something else. He merely renders himself incapable of dealing with it. He can't deal with what he won't face. It won't go away. Why not? Because his pretense doesn't change reality. So he simply beats his head against a stone wall, unless he first faces the fact, "This is the way things are." So honesty is mandated in this particular example. What you need to do is keep collecting examples, including social examples—you want a broad range. With your own mind in relation to others, you might say, "Why can't a doctor, let's say a so-called greedy doctor who wants to make a lot of money, tell his patient a lie? He tells the patient, 'Don't worry about this operation; there won't be any bad consequences,' because he wants to rake in the fees, while knowing that it's actually dangerous major surgery." How would our situation apply here? The patient would then presumably have the dangerous major surgery, he'd lose a limb or a vital organ or die, and then what kind of effects would the doctor experience, from the patient, from the family, from the other patients when the word spreads, from the medical societies, from the malpractice lawsuits, from the hospital, and so on? It would be suicide to his medical practice. Again, why? Because facts are facts; pretending that they are something else doesn't change them. We haven't said *anything* about what it is going to do to that doctor's own development, the psychological effects on him; he's abandoned the principle of honesty, the whole way of life. If you take a real example, it's very hard to get a self-contained example in which the only thing that he does bad is be dishonest. Why? Because in real life, all the aspects are interconnected, for the same reason that all of the *virtues* are interconnected. So as soon as you give an example, as soon as you chew it one step, you're plunged into the thicket of all of the other virtues. You say, "Don't lie, because then you become dependent on others"—you're right away in independence; "Don't lie, because then you're a hypocrite"—you're right away in integrity; "Don't lie, because it's going to lead you to a life of parasitism"—you're right away in productiveness. You see why I think the best way to present this is in a novel, because you give all of it at once. Ayn Rand doesn't have one chapter on integrity, and the next on something else; it's all in everything, and then at the end, she says, "To summarize."

We come back to the point that if you are to really ground your knowledge of one virtue, you have to see its connection to the rest. You have to see the connection not only in theory, like "Rationality leads to honesty," but concretely, because theory that's un-concretized is no good. So what you should ideally do, and this is what would take about three hours—and I did this once with Miss Rand. I must say, I didn't grasp this issue on this example of honesty; I really wish I had recorded it, it was about a three-hour discussion. She said, "I'm going to take one example only, but I'm going to really show you how to analyze one example, and I expect you to be able to grasp honesty from this." And she took an example and she showed what, if the person had been dishonest in this one instance, would be its effect on his rationality, the functioning of his mind, his independence, his productiveness, his general relation to people, his chances of success, his self-esteem, his happiness, the works. It wasn't just the inner psychological, nor just the outer practical; it was the totality. And it really took hours. But by the time it was over, I had the idea of honesty, that actual truck-like vision. Wherever you looked, it seemed like the overriding imperative was, "God, don't lie, because there's catastrophe in all directions." And this is what we're ultimately aiming for—to bring philosophy to the point where you see it in everything. And you see how much is involved to get to that stage.

Let me give you a general rule here: Integrate the topic at hand with other knowledge. This simply means connect it. You can't do this at the beginning, obviously. Until you have some idea of what honesty is and how you would establish it, you can't start bringing in independence and integrity. First isolate and get an issue clear on its own terms. But then connect it to the other things that you know—for example, honesty would have to be connected to the other virtues.

Why is integration important? I hate to quote Hegel of all people, but he had one sentence that I really envy, which I think is a really marvelous sentence. It's typically Germanic, but it really captures something. And that sentence is "The true is the whole." And giving a generous interpretation of what he meant by it (he actually meant you couldn't know anything until you knew everything): in reality, all our principles are simultaneous; it's not true that honesty becomes true on Monday, and Tuesday productivity enters, and so on. The problem is, because we use a conceptual method and can deal with only a limited amount of material, we have to break up this whole, this simultaneous whole, into little bits and fragments; we have to analyze it one step at a time. And that's fine; we have to do it that way. But the analysis, the separation, is a distortion, unless *after* we analyze and separate, we put it back together again. We must remind ourselves that it's part of a whole in reality, it is not an isolated thing, it does not stand by itself; and to really grasp it we have to connect it to the other essentials that it belongs with. So the process is really taking apart and putting back together, or in the venerable terms, analysis and synthesis. And the Objectivist term for "synthesis" is "integration"; that's all we mean by integration.

You will find that if you always make a mental note to yourself as you're thinking or analyzing, "I'm pulling out one thing, to focus on it, but I will not really grasp it until I connect it back afterward"—if you do that, you're way ahead of the game. You will find that every time you make this connection to other ideas, whatever clarity they already have will spill over to the new idea, and/or whatever clarity *it* has will spill over to them. They will mutually reinforce each other, and things will become sharper and clearer in your mind, because there will be more and more reality behind each idea. That is what is meant by a *system* of philosophy. The ideal is to get to the point where every tenet of it is so interconnected to the rest that if you rejected one, you would see that everything goes, the whole totality. And in this respect, philosophy is like mathematics. You understand that a person couldn't say, "Down with 'two and two equals four,' but I want to keep all the rest of arithmetic," because that would wipe out and destroy all of mathematics. The same thing is true in philosophy. It's a system, but it's much more work to see the system in philosophy, because it's not just one isolated aspect like mathematics—it's all of reality encompassed in a few broad abstractions. So there's a crucial element of constantly chewing and breaking down the connections—you have to do it a point at a time, but you have to keep it connected. And if you get to the stage where you could say, "If I give up the virtue of honesty, I have to turn against everything," then that is what we call a chewed, reality-connected, potent grasp.

You may wonder how much of this you need to do—since you have to include all of reality and all of your other knowledge. When do you say, "Okay, that's enough"? The crucial thing that comes in here is the *spiral theory of knowledge*. You must always remember that. The spiral theory is simply that first we learn a given idea; then we leave it, we move to something else, we learn other subjects; then we encounter the original idea again, but now with more knowledge, with a deeper context. You must have had this experience—you come back to something that you understood, but now you come back with fuller knowledge of other issues, and you suddenly feel, "Gee, now I really get that. I thought I understood that before, but I didn't really." Well, yes, you really did, except that what's happening is you're getting more integration, more connections to other ideas, and therefore you're seeing it from the perspective of a broader context. And then you go on to something new, and then the early point comes up again, and then you feel, "Now I *really* see, this is really tremendously clear," and it is, but it will be still clearer, and so on. You can't bite off too much at any given time. The hierarchy we're talking about is not like a building that you just literally go straight up or straight down and that's it. This is where the spiral is—you go up, and then back to touch the base, and then up, and then back to touch the base, and so on. That's where it got the name; if you draw it, you'll see a spiral.

We were spiraling here tonight, if you want a small example. First the issue of principles—we need to grasp that point in order to appreciate why we need virtues. But "principles," as such, is very vague and empty, unless we give it some content. So when we get to rationality, that retroactively makes the need of principles clearer. And rationality paves the way to get to honesty. And when we get to honesty, that makes rationality more specific, and it's now more convincing than if it's just the general "Use your mind," and so on. When would it be a hundred percent, absolutely chewed? On your deathbed. Because the true is the whole.

So there are degrees of chewing. What should determine how much you do at any given time is determined by your cognitive requirements. Nobody has to do more than he sees a need to do. If it really strikes you as clear in your context, that's okay; don't suffer and agonize. As and when it strikes you as *un*clear, *un*convincing, *something* bothers you about an idea, that's when you work, and you continue within your own framework. Each new step, each new example, will clarify your principles further; each new principle will clarify the other principles further; each new principle will clarify other concretes further; and it just keeps getting better and better.

Lecture Three Q & A

Q: Suppose that someone asks you if you will be going to some function, and you reply that you can't afford it. The person who asked you believes that you can't afford it financially, and you know he thinks that. But you can't afford the time or the effort, and you prefer not to explain further. Am I being dishonest?

A: Yes, as worded. But I wouldn't say this is the kind of dishonesty that will wound your soul and destroy your life. Technically speaking, you're misleading a person for no reason. There's absolutely no need to give him a side comment like this. He just asked if you're going to the function. You could just say, "No," that's it. "I'm too busy; it's too much trouble." Or just "No." I don't want to make a Jesuitical case. There's always a way of wording that does not commit you to these falsehoods—but we're talking about the essence of your relation to reality, not that type of thing. But remember also that there are contexts in which it is justified to lie to a person who is not threatening the use of force. Remember, we're not saying that lying as such is evil; we are saying that it's evil to lie in order to gain a value by fraud. But suppose there are contexts in which you know something that is entirely private, let us say about another person, that they have told you in absolute confidence, and some busybody comes in who has absolutely no right to get that information, and starts grilling you, "Did she really sleep with him?" and so on, and it's a context in which, because of your relation, you can't say "No comment" without it implying the worst. You have every right in that situation to lie. You're not trying to gain something from this person; you're trying to prevent him from appropriating a value that is yours apart from him—namely, the privacy of this information.

Q: In the process of concretizing moral virtues, isn't it crucial to see and be convinced of the relationship of a virtue to my own personal happiness, not merely my personal morality or goodness?

A: Oh, absolutely, as long as you understand the Objectivist view of happiness. But if I take this question straight—when you are integrating honesty, for instance, if you want it to have concrete, reality-oriented force, you have to see how a policy of dishonesty would sabotage your happiness. After all, this is an egoistic ethics; it tells you the purpose is to pursue *your* life and happiness, and of course, happiness is the corollary of life properly pursued, according to Objectivism. And therefore it is crucial to integrate every virtue to the effects on your happiness. The only reason I didn't stress that is that I don't want to inculcate a subjectivist slant at the outset. You have to be sure you know what happiness is, and that you can't say that if something leads to momentary or temporary frustration, "That interferes with my happiness, therefore I shouldn't do it." But taking happiness in the proper way, absolutely I agree with this question.

Q: You've demonstrated that it isn't self-evident how to validate the virtue of honesty. However, is there some sense in which it is self-evident to be honest? When I encounter a liar, I don't think to myself, "Poor fellow, he's never heard of the Objectivist proof."

A: The best answer I could give to this is the spiral, and that would be as follows: Taking civilization at the stage that it's reached now, we have a large context of knowledge of what is lying, what is honesty, that civilized people tell the truth to each other, that decency involves telling the truth, and so on. And most people today are brought up in a general way to accept this. Therefore, in this context, they see it—it's not a matter of faith—they see it in very simple terms, or if they say this isn't so when it is, they know that it isn't so. So on some level, you can say, well, it's obvious that you can't get away with making up something that isn't so, because you can see that it doesn't change things. To that extent, you can say yes, the person has enough knowledge, or *could* have enough knowledge, to understand that he should be honest. That is not, however, what we are talking about here, because in today's context there is also a tremendous amount that could confuse an honest person—for example, the claim that there are no absolutes, and then he'll be given a lot of concrete examples of the seeming practical necessity of dishonesty that the most honest person would probably find it difficult to answer. And the whole idea that you should sacrifice for others, which honest people can accept, with all of its implications, including sometimes you should tell lies to make other people happy—there's a tremendous constellation that could confuse a person. And from this point of view, I would say, "Poor guy, he *has* never heard the proof." Therefore, for him, it's a matter of what he can put together from what he was brought up with, how much temptation is put in his path. It is not the kind of clear, luminous, full, convincing understanding that makes honesty a part of his soul. The most it can be is a sort of socially ingrained habit. That's okay. You can blame people for lying. I do not want the moral of this to be, well, if they haven't heard this lecture, how can you expect anything more? But it wouldn't be as great a betrayal to lie if all you know is a few social generalities, than if you have studied it in depth, it connects to everything, and then you *still* do it; it's a much more massive corruption. So these things exist in degrees.

Q: You stated the context for honesty as "life, principles, and rationality." Do the other virtues have different contexts, or is the application of the context different for each virtue?
A: All the virtues have the same basic context: life, principles, rationality. But, to some extent, you have to prepare each one differently because each one focuses on a different aspect of rationality, and so to set it up, you need a different focus. So you couldn't say the context is absolutely the same. For instance, if you turn to productivity, you will have to stress the relation of mind and body to the role of material values in human survival, in a way that you would not have to for honesty; it would be implied, but that wouldn't be part of the immediate focus of your whole discussion the way it would for productiveness. Or if you turned to justice, you would have to focus on the relation of other men to you, why they are a value, and why moral judgment of them is very important, which is a very different type of consideration to what you would need, for instance, if you were going to validate honesty. So each virtue has, to some extent, its own unique nature and requires its own specialized context. But the basic context remains the same regardless of virtues, which one you're doing.

Q: I agree with the need of man to live by principles, you have to live long-range, and so on, but I don't see how it applies to dishonesty. You agree that in any given instance, the existential harm to the dishonest person may be negligible, and the reward enormous (like you could get a million dollars). Why can't I make a distinction in principle between those dishonest acts that are likely to be harmful to me and those that are not? Why can't someone say, "I accept the absolute need for principles and long-range thinking; but, since not all dishonest acts are very harmful, I will adopt the principle that I will act honestly when and only when I judge that it will benefit me"?

A: Let me put this in my own words. The person is saying, "My principle, which I'll follow faithfully, is that I will be honest when I judge that it benefits me, and I won't when it doesn't. So I'm still being principled." Then he elaborates on that as follows: "After all, values obtained by fraud are nonetheless values. Why can't I, therefore, on the question of honesty, rationally weigh one value against another, what I gain by being dishonest versus what I lose, and decide which course of action is preferable?" Obviously, you can see that this would apply to anything—it could apply to any virtue of any kind. So you've got a new phenomenon here—we've got a principle (at least, that's what the claim is) that's supposed to be a long-range conceptual guide, and we decide in each particular case by whether it's beneficial or not. And the first obvious answer is, well, this is what ethics is supposed to do, just what you say: You're supposed to act when something benefits you; you're supposed to weigh when it is a gain, when it is a loss; it tells you the standard by which to judge—namely, life; and it tells you, in those cases, where honesty is harmful to your life (for example, telling a robber where your money is), go right ahead, lie your head off; that's what ethics does tell you, absolutely. In *this* sense, the questioner has one valid aspect—principles are contextual. That is, they are defined by reference to a standard of value, a goal, and they can be applied only within the circumstances where they lead to that goal. Within the proper context, we say there is a principle that is absolute, it has no exceptions, and that is "Securing a value by fraud is wrong, as such, flatly and without exceptions; it is always harmful." Why? Because in any situation where it occurs, it amounts to making an alliance with unreality. Survival, we argue, requires allegiance to reality, and dishonesty, in this context, always means counting on unreality, putting something above reality. I would have one question: By what standard are you judging what will benefit you? How do you decide? The questioner says, "You weigh one value against another." How? By what means? If I give you an apple and an orange, and I say, "Choose according to the greater value," well, on that crude a choice, don't you have to have some operative standard? Don't you have to have some principle to tell you? Are you pursuing taste? Are you going by cost? Size? Freshness? What? If you're going only by life, you don't know; both an apple and an orange can help life. On the other hand, both can cause an upset stomach. So out of context, you're completely lost.

This questioner gives us an example, "What about a used-car salesman who, by one fraudulent deal, could make enough money to retire for life?" I'm simply saying that it is *not* self-evident that a trillion dollars is worth more than the harm that a lie does. Would five hundred thousand dollars be worth more than a mutilation to get it? Are there no other factors to take into account? What about a man's inner life, his mental processes, the types of other actions that this choice will commit him to, his emotional life, and so on. I'm not going to go into all that at the moment. I'm saying simply that no choice of that kind can possibly be decided by "what I judge." How are you going to judge? By what means are you going to judge? You have only two ways of judging: You're either going to judge by the feeling of the moment, "I want the retirement in Florida, to hell with everything," and that is avowedly a nonprincipled approach; *or*, you're going to judge how? By a principle that says, "This is how man must act, and this is how he must compare and evaluate choices." And if you have that principle, you cannot say, "My definition of a principle is 'if I judge that it will have good consequences'"—you just don't have a principle anymore. A principle is the only thing that can decide what to do when you have a choice. The whole point of principles is to enable us to make choices, to enable us to judge which is more important. Here this person comes along and says, "My principle is I'll do it if I like the results." Then that's the complete evisceration of principle. Since he can only judge the results by a principle, he's in a complete circle. And it ends up, practically speaking, as what? Pure pragmatism—whatever you feel in any given circumstance.

I find it very illuminating that this confusion could take place. So I want to read one more paragraph, because it makes another major error about what a principle is. He goes on to say, "I could have a principle of 'Don't go out in the rain without a raincoat, rubbers, and umbrella, because I might catch cold or even fatal pneumonia.' Still, there are situations in which I could rationally choose to go out in the rain without proper protection (say, if I have an urgent appointment, and going back for an umbrella would make me late, and so on). So it's not that I'm abandoning principle for expediency when I go out in the rain; I'm just applying a different principle and weighing the relative risks—the chance of getting sick—against the benefits—the chance of getting a new job. Why can't we do the same in regard to honesty? It's just like going out in the rain—sometimes it works, and sometimes it doesn't."

Now let's try to grasp what is meant by a principle when we talk about it in morality. A moral principle is a fundamental universal essential of human life. It has to be involved in every action, because the principles on the level we are talking about define the whole nature of human action, in everything, of which going out in the rain is a drop in the bucket. Honesty is involved one way or the other, in every mental step, whether you focus on reality or pretend. It doesn't apply only when it's raining; if it applies only when it's raining, it's not a principle; at most, it's a far-removed application. What is, then, the difference between these ideas? What would you call this thing about "go out in the rain," or that you should go out in the rain without an umbrella? That's a rule, if you want to call it that; that's a concrete-bound rule. And morality does not provide that; reality does not offer any such thing. This is that particular person's interpretation of a principle, "You should act in such a way as to protect yourself from the elements." But now, how does that apply in the rain? Reality will not tell you whether it means rubbers, an umbrella, both, or neither. So if we really grasp what a principle is, there are not that many principles; but they are at such a level of fundamentality, and they are all established by reference to the essential requirement of man's means of survival, and they're involved in every single issue. If you violate one of those, you are subverting the whole mechanism. You're not simply, in a concrete-bound way, making an ill-advised choice; you are simply wiping out the whole principle; and thereafter, if the principle was right that Objectivism advocated, you are just plunging into the morass.

LECTURE FOUR

■

Force and Rights

We are going to continue digesting Objectivism. Our topics, however, are not life as the standard, and not honesty, but force and
then rights. We have two people who are going to chew force, the
evil of the initiation of force, and then one who is going to do the topic of
validating individual rights. These are *real* people tonight. That is to say
I did not write their parts; I have no idea what they're going to say; they
are going to do their conscientious best to re-create their mental processes
when they try to understand these topics. And at the end, I will summarize *my* understanding of the topics, so as to (theoretically) add some clarification. Perhaps that's unnecessary if the volunteers do it. In any event,
try to listen intently, but listen primarily methodologically. What steps are
they using? Are they omitting some crucial thing? Don't just listen from
the point of view of whether you agree or disagree with their view of force
and rights. This is primarily an exercise in *how* to understand. Of course,
we have to actually understand something to get the methodology. But
our focus is on methodology.

I want to start by asking you to tell me what is wrong with this as a
chewing of the topic of the evil of force. This is what we actually got on
this topic in the seminar, and I think it reveals a type of error that we've
covered already several times, but it's worth hammering home again,

presented now as the inner process of chewing the topic of the evil of the initiation of force.

> We have to start with existence exists, existence has identity, consciousness is the faculty for perceiving it. Since everything is something, man must be man, that means he requires a specific course of action to survive, and that course involves him having to think and to work in order to achieve the values his life requires. Thinking is not automatic, it's volitional; so therefore, he is not born with any automatic course of action, he has to choose the right alternative course. And that is the purpose of ethics, which is a code of values to guide human choices of action, and rights are guides indicating what man's essential relation to others in society should be. Force is the only way to violate man's rights. And therefore, the threat of force really destroys man's means of survival. It really defies reality. Force negates the law of identity, because it doesn't let man live by his nature; and it negates the law of causality, because it doesn't let man keep the results of his effort. Therefore, the initiation of force is evil.

There is, in that whole process, nothing I said that is wrong. But you do not have an understanding of the topic of force at the end. What is wrong? Not only did I bring up the subject of rights before I established rights, I brought up a *lot* of subjects before I established them, so rights isn't the only one. It's a *summary* of Objectivism. That is not chewing the topic of force. There is as much time given to the metaphysical base, the ethics, and so on, as is given to the topic of force. In this presentation, force was a couple of sentences at the end, and metaphysics was a couple of sentences at the beginning, and ethics was a couple of sentences in the middle.

This is not what we're after. We *do* want to quickly scan the context on which the idea we're focusing on depends. But our goal is not to recapitulate that context, not to give a whole song and dance of the whole issue from the beginning; otherwise, we violate the purpose of the assignment, and we violate the crow epistemology. When we set the context, we don't want to start with existence and work step by step all the way down, because our minds will be blown by the time we get where we're focused on. We want to pick a few high points, and the operative word is *few*, as a reminder of what we already know, an orienter of what we can take for granted, and then focus all our attention on the one topic that we are really trying to understand—namely, the evil of the initiation of force—and chew that in detail. So there should be a tremendous difference between the hit-and-run reminder of the context—which you are not here chewing or trying to understand; you're just reminding yourself of it in a few little words—and then the detailed, intense focus on one idea that you're trying to understand.

We know, as far as the context is concerned here, that we're way past metaphysics and epistemology, so we take for granted reason and reality; we know that we're way past the beginning of ethics, so we take for granted life as the standard and rationality as the basic virtue. So it's almost unnecessary. If you want a quick reminder, you can say something like, "Reason, reality, life, rationality," but it's too much already—we're way up. It's like we're now on at least the fortieth story of this fifty-story building, so we don't even want one proposition for every ten stories. Just pull out the few that will orient us to the topic that we're going to. What are they? That, as a matter of fact, we're going to hear now from the first volunteer.

But just before that, let me give you a checklist. This is nothing new, but this is the checklist I am using to listen to these presentations to check the methodology. These are all points that we have already covered. And I have it on the sheet, not in whole sentences, but just in a few words:

1. Right conclusion—is it the right conclusion?
2. Context hierarchy—have they set the right context hierarchically? In other words, in the right order.
3. Definitions oscillate—are they defining whatever is absolutely essential, and are they keeping that tied to reality by reducing it to the concretes?

4. Concretized.
5. Inductive—as opposed to that rationalistic deduction.
6. Stages—if necessary, is the argument broken up into steps?
7. Devil's advocate—are there some objections that the person is just blithely passing by, that are blatant?
8. Integration.

That basically is what we're looking for. Not every point will be equally applicable to every topic, but in one form or another they will all come up, and it might be a help to scan. But with that, I am now going to introduce our first volunteer, Fred. With the understanding that I might possibly interrupt you or not, depending on how it goes.

Let's begin with these premises kept in mind, and limit it to these: number one, metaphysically, A is A. We know that. Reality is what it is. But specifically, reality for man, for anything in this universe, is not determined by arbitrary social convention. Second, man, specifically to survive, must be free to use his mind; he must depend upon his mind for survival. And third, the standard of what man ought to do in life is *his life*— what advances his life as a fully rational human being. Now consider three examples, a couple of them historical. One, Adolf Hitler announces that he's going to take over as much of the world as possible. And in each instance, when his armies march into another country, he is ready with a pretext: that he is only acting in defense of the German people. The second example would be, in 1967, the State of Israel, anticipating, by means of military intelligence, that they were about to be attacked on all sides, attacked first and blew up the opposing air forces, and claimed that they did that in self-defense. And my third example would be a man, an individual, in a car, who is stopped at a red light and is confronted by hoodlums who are menacing him with gestures amounting to "Pay or die," and doing what he thinks best, he runs one of them over and heads for the nearest police station. I would say if you take all those examples together, you can work out inductively a definition, a workable definition, of what force is and why it's evil. I would say force is either the use of physical compulsion or willful deception to achieve an end, to acquire a value from other people that one could not or would not otherwise acquire. In other words, you take or compel them or convince them to give you something that they would not give of their own free will if they knew what they were doing.

Why is such an action wrong? From the standpoint of individual aggressors, in order to achieve whatever it is he or she has in mind to achieve (whether it's the acquisition of territory or material goods), they have determined that they can't achieve these values on their own—can't or won't—and therefore, they're going to take it from someone else. In order to take something from someone else, you must do two things mentally—you must obliterate your awareness of what it means to be a human being, as far as *their* being a human being is concerned; and you must obliterate your own conception of *yourself* as a human being; you have to look at yourself as a gun. If you're willing to do that, it means you're contradicting the basic needs of your *own* life from the start. And therefore it's not surprising, in fact it follows logically, that you will violate other people's existence as human beings. This, by definition, and by direct observation practically, is anti-life. What comes to mind, the two problems that I need to answer for myself, are, at what point is a person provoked to violence by the actions, the overt physical force or the threat of physical force, of other people; at what point, if a person defends himself or herself, is that really self-defense, even if he or she acts first (as is the case with Israel); or, for that matter, in the case of the individual whom I described in the car, who runs over a prospective mugger or robber.

In reality, in a court of law, we might find that person guilty of an excessive use of force, given the nature of the law and the way it is. But in fact, if the person acted, if their motivation was to defend their life against someone who by his or her actions refused to recognize what it means to have a life, specifically a human life or any life, then the person acted rationally. The person who was willing to use force, from the instant they conceived the action, was in a state of irrationality, and was acting against life as soon as they carried that thought into effect, into action. Now, in practice, an entire community, a nation, can act on that premise that their needs are such that they must take something by force. If that premise is acted upon by a sufficient number of people, you have a state of anarchy and brute terror. It is no more possible to have a community of nations that are not self-destructing on that premise than it is possible to have a small group of people in a small community acting on that premise, or for that matter, to even be Robinson Crusoe on an island by yourself and learning cooperation with Man Friday. The numbers don't matter; the premise is the same.

That's excellent to get us started, because it is a mixture of good things and certain things that are not completely adequate.

What was good about this? The examples he used? No, I think that is a problem with the presentation, because what is the purpose of examples? It is to try to make it as clearly tied to reality as possible, to connect your broad abstractions to clear-cut instances. Interjecting what is excessive force in self-defense mixes a very difficult question of detailed application within a governmental-legal system with the broad topic that we're trying to discuss. So it's out of hierarchical order. If your goal is "Why is force evil?" that is a big general topic. First you would have to address yourself to that. You would have to choose your examples, your arguments, and so on, all from the point of view of understanding that, while knowing that once you've established that, there is still a tremendous amount of detailed application needed. For instance, the initiation of force versus self-defense, but what about borderline cases where there's self-defense but too much force? That's already a question of detail way late in the game that you cannot inject back into the topic, "Why is force as such evil?" That would be exactly like, on the topic of honesty, our basic question was "Why should you be honest?"; if somebody then took a really tricky question, like, "I'm up against a government bureaucrat, and my partner doesn't know," and started with that as an example, it would constantly deflect his thinking from the essence of the issue to one very specialized application. So the rule here is, *do not pick controversial concretes*. Pick a nice *range* of concretes. But when you're trying to understand, the examples should be simple and straightforward. Then, when you grasp it, you can take up trickier cases. So it is a bad idea to combine concretizing with devil's advocacy. I learned this teaching elementary logic, and I thought I'd get two birds for the price of one, and in illustrating a certain fallacy, which is a simple fallacy to understand, I threw in an argument for political isolationism, and the example aroused the class, and it became so controversial that they began to challenge the logical point involved, because they disagreed with the political point. And I lost the entire logical issue on the example. I learned from that that examples cannot be controversial; they have to be illuminating.

But there was a very *good* thing here, and that is the fact of examples. I was happy that he did not start by saying something like this: "Rationality is the exercise, and so on; force is the so-and-so; and therefore"—that rationalistic model of deduction from definitions. This was certainly not a rationalistic presentation. He started with some examples—leaving aside the Israel one, which was inappropriate for the reasons we just mentioned—but Hitler is certainly a good example on the topic of force; and the hoodlum pointing a gun and saying "Pay or die" is a perfectly good example; those are clear-cut. If we're talking about force, those are just the kinds of examples we want—a nice homey one that would happen on Madison Avenue, and then a world-scale one. So he had, in his intention, a concretized, inductive approach. I'll give him a virtue in his intention, to that extent, and one problem in implementation.

He was clear; you knew what he was doing at each point. What about structured development of the argument? He had an intention, but I did not see that that was fully yet developed here. Don't confuse the fact that he was organized—he didn't just get up and say, "Here's an example, and that reminds me of my mother, and so on"; he had a definite logic—but that's not the same thing as saying that he exhibited the essential points that we need to understand this.

He said that force is anti-life, and that's very important. The ethics rests on life is the standard, so ultimately everything has to be validated by either being for or against life; that has to be the ultimate peg. So that was good as an intention. Why wouldn't it be enough to say, "We know life is the standard. If you use force on somebody, that obliterates the humanity of the victim and of you yourself, and therefore, it's a twofold assault on life, and it contradicts your own requirements, your requirements being, presumably, the point that you depend on the mind for survival." So it's against their mind and it's against your mind, and therefore, it's anti-life.

All right, now take this just as a statement, because this is good and yet inadequate, simply in terms of expressing your own understanding. Let me give you that argument again, and just consider this now as the argument against force. "Man has to survive by his mind. Force obliterates the mind, both of the victim and of the perpetrator. Therefore, force is anti-mind, and therefore, anti-life." That argument has stages; it's clearcut. It starts with the right idea, and in fact, the essence of that argument is correct. And that is basically what Fred said. But there is something inadequate with that argument; that does *not* represent an understanding. We're assuming that we can take for granted that man depends on the mind for survival, that life is the standard, that rationality is the supreme virtue; I'm not criticizing him for not elaborating any of that. But now he wants to understand why force is evil and says, "Force repudiates all this; it's *anti*-mind, therefore *anti*-life." And he illustrated—"Look what Hitler did." So what's wrong? It's true, but what's the problem? He has to show that force interferes with man's perception of reality, with his reason, with his mind. But he said that. He said force obliterates your human means of survival. So what else is required?

Let's try this from the devil's advocate point of view. We don't know anything about Objectivism, and somebody comes in and says, "The initiation of force on someone is evil, because it obliterates or destroys their mind and your own." On a commonsense level, what would be the obvious objection to that? There are many obvious cases where that does not seem to apply, if you take it in the way it was stated. How many times have people been mugged but still have the same IQ after as they had before? Their minds were not obliterated. They were the victim of force. It could even be brutal force. As it was presented, it's as though force is like a lobotomy—once you use force on someone, it obliterates his mind, he's finished. But how? If it's a torture chamber and you're shooting electricity through his brain, that type of force would do it. But in the ordinary course of affairs, the victim does something he doesn't want to do—but does he lose his mind? Or how does the perpetrator lose his mind, for that matter?

It comes down to this: What was omitted in this presentation is the central argument connecting force to rationality. It was simply taken for granted that the evil of force is that it attacks the mind, it assaults reason. And then there were examples, definitions, context, and so on. But the main thing we want to do in chewing it is chew the connection to the context. In other words, we need a context. We want to see, through a microscope, how this particular idea connects to that context. It's not enough simply to say, "We already know that rationality is essential for survival. The thing that's wrong with force is that it's against rationality." *How* is it against it? What is it about the nature of force and the nature of rationality that are inherently opposed? And to be able to do that against a background of examples, so that it's still inductive—that would be the crucial thing. And that is what Fred hinted at, but he did not actually show the essence of what the understanding of it would consist of.

He basically set the appropriate context. I don't think it would be necessary to say "A is A" there, because I just take reality for granted; we're way late in social ethics now, so I don't see that much is gained from that. You may want to make the point that it's not an issue of social convention, that force is objectively wrong; but it's too late at this stage of the game to make *that* point. As I said earlier, by the time you get to force, you have to have established that there is a reality, knowledge is objective, truth is not a matter of convention—that's all taken for granted—and then, there's an objective standard of value in ethics, and so on. By the time you get here, if you still have in the back of your mind, "There are people out there who are subjectivists, so the first thing I want to say is, 'This is not a question to be decided by social convention,'" you've already lost the hierarchy. Because if you're still worried about those people, you're on a different topic. By now it should just be yourself and your own mind, as we've taken for granted all of metaphysics and epistemology, and the whole basis of ethics.

Now I'm going to ask Phil to come up and do the same assignment as though from scratch.

> I'm going to start by stating the context that I'm kind of taking for granted here. Basically, all of metaphysics and epistemology, that life is the standard, and that, in a way, I'm taking for granted that reason is man's means of survival. I'll explain that in a minute, because I'm not fully taking it for granted. Also, egoism—that man is an end in himself—and that man must live by principle, what we discussed last week. My proof, however, is going to chew one of the things I said I was taking for granted, which is that reason is man's means of survival. Basically I'm going to discuss in what way and how that is true, what does it mean for man to survive by reason, in some detail. First of all, the purpose of this discussion is to prove that the initiation of physical force is wrong. So briefly, to review the definitions of some terms force involves: some examples would be somebody who robs somebody else, commits fraud, obtains something from him by fraud, some material value, kills him, or threatens to do something to him (such as, if he doesn't register for the draft, they're going to put him in jail). In all of those cases, what you're doing is you're interfering, you're taking a value from him without his consent; you're interposing yourself between his reason and its acting to achieve some

value. So far, when I said I was taking for granted that reason is man's means of survival, I mean that what I'm taking so far as established is that reason is a tool of human survival, as opposed to the way that animals survive. Man does not survive automatically. He uses reason to identify; it's the process of identifying the evidence of his senses, the things that he sees out there in reality—forming concepts, drawing principles, drawing conclusions, and acting on that basis to pursue his survival.

Now I'm going to go into the proof. First of all, we can consider a man whom force is initiated against, and what can happen to him in those cases—he loses something: he loses his life, his values; his reason is prevented from acting to achieve what he considers to be to his survival. So I think it's pretty clear-cut, the examples that I discussed—robbery, fraud, killing, and so on—that these things all are opposed to his survival. But I did want to establish that, that the person whom force is initiated against, is acting against his survival.

The more difficult area is the initiator. If the person whom it is initiated against loses something, doesn't the initiator gain something? And if so, why is force destructive to his survival, and to his pursuit of values? I'm going to start with an extended example, and I'm going to then try to draw some conclusions. The example is somebody's life, and sort of how he uses reason to pursue his values in the course of his life. Take somebody who ends up pursuing the career of an engineer. Let's just sort of follow his life span and see how he uses reason throughout it. When he's a baby, we see him trying to learn, trying to learn about reality; he first has to work on the perceptual level, and then he has to eventually learn to focus, and to walk, and things like this. And at a certain point, he forms his first concepts. One thing we notice is that he's enjoying the process of using his mind. Later on, this child gets into school, and he goes to college; at some point, he decides he wants to be an engineer, and that's a long-range goal he has to have. And he realizes that it is not done in one step—he has to build his knowledge, and he has to build that career step by step through the work he does, the choices he makes, the abstract and practical knowledge he acquires. When he gets out of college, he then becomes a starting engineer, and again he's also working for certain things in the future—he wants to get more interesting assignments, and so forth. So he's working—"long-range" is a crucial concept here. Eventually, later in life, he becomes more advanced in his field, whether it's engineering or whatever it happens to be; and he does that by building on his work and his knowledge, and so forth; and by doing that, he builds tools that enable him to pursue wider values. He gets new knowledge, new assignments, more practical benefits—a better salary, things like that.

What we see in this whole example of somebody pursuing through his life and using reason to produce is that he's being productive, to produce the values he needs for his survival—he builds up, by doing this successfully at each stage, he builds up a certain self-confidence in himself with regard to reality. He learns that he's able, through these steps, to deal with reality, and get more and more, and get what he needs. We see him operating long-range; we see that, to achieve the goals that he wants—to be an engineer, to have a better salary, maybe to have a bigger home later on—he's got to plan long-range, and he's got to build on his past. And he finds that as he does these things, his success is proportional to the above things—to his self-confidence, to his enjoyment, to his building, to his operating long-range, and so forth.

Now suppose that at a certain point in his life, he decides to rob a bank. He decides, for some reason, that money, there's so much money here that he could just reach out and grab it easily, and it becomes an overriding value for him. What does this do to him? I would maintain that it throws out a lot of these things that he's been building over time. It throws out his confidence;

I mean, he has to, in some sense, not have confidence that he could have gotten as much money as he needed through not using force, so this confidence that he built up that he was capable of dealing with reality is sort of thrown out by this action, by adopting a policy of force. He throws out his independence—he's implicitly saying, "I no longer can independently, through my work, produce what I need. I have to get it by depending on somebody else to have produced it, and then seizing it." He decided that the material, the money itself, was subordinate to other things, such as job satisfaction. He's now throwing that out, and in a way, he's throwing out the work that he has done and the choices that he's made. He is throwing out his whole policy of step-by-step building and investing in the future, in terms of money, and so on. And he's throwing out the policy of cooperating with other men, that his relationship to other men is a cooperative one. Instead, he's adopting an adversarial relationship—he's going to prey on them. One thing that does to him psychologically is that, in the process of building up his self-confidence and his skills, he learned to, in this case, admire other men for having these qualities, and now he's got to sort of turn against that, because their perceptiveness now becomes a threat. The virtues that he's built up and that he's turning against become a threat to him when other men practice them.

He loses control of his life. He has fear. He throws out control of his life. He's not growing and building anymore. He's like at an animal level. He is living by feelings over principles, because his principle was to go through his whole career and so on, and now he's saying in some cases, if the bank is out there, I'll just grab it. So he's violating the fact that he has to live by principle. The materialism of values—he's taking values at a materialistic level. He's reducing himself down to saying, "Money is the important thing." And you can see this in people who initiate force. For instance, a Mafia hit man is not somebody who you'll find at a ballet or the Metropolitan

Museum; his pleasures are drugs, gambling, casual sex, and fast cars. So he's reducing himself to the animal level. All right, so what I'm saying is that force is evil because, in actual practice, to survive by reason means to build self-confidence, to grow, to live long-range, to be independent, to have a cooperative relationship with other men, and not have values all be at a materialistic level. That's it. The only thing that I want to say in conclusion is, you asked us to say, "Have I proven this?" and I think I have some points, but they're all sort of floating together on the same level.

We are extremely fortunate because that illustrates different points than Fred did, and between them, we've got a great demonstration. If you can name what's good and what's bad about that one, you're really in business as a digester.

Phil really did a lot of good things. He was focused throughout on concretes, and there was a nice range of concretes—robbery, murder, the draft—but there weren't too many. They included political, extreme cases (murder), lesser ones (like crime against property), and so on. It seemed to be clear in his mind what force was. And he was not using some very abstract definition deduced without examples. So it was not floating, and it was certainly not rationalistic.

What else was good about this? He said using force is a violation of living by principle. He *also* said that using force is a violation of self-esteem or of self-confidence, that it was a violation of independence, that it contradicted the whole living long-range, that it put you on the animal level, that it contradicted the life of productiveness and achievement, and that it was the exact opposite of everything required to build up and develop yourself from the time you were a child.

So he made a great number of points about the relation of force—to what? That's the point. That's the virtue, and the problem, of his presentation. And that's why he felt at the end that he could go on indefinitely that way, adding more and more, but somehow he hadn't nailed it to the wall; and yet he had a wealth of material and it wasn't floating, so there's only one thing that he didn't do right. The key is, what is it that he focused on the relation of force *to*? Not only psychological well-being; he included existential actions—that the criminal is no longer independent in practice, that he was no longer productive—he didn't make it just "This will curdle your soul if you use force." No, it wasn't that. He took many different aspects of the Objectivist ethics, all of them being various forms or expressions or applications of rationality, and he showed that force would conflict. He took each very briefly as an example of the case of the engineer. And he said, "See what this will do to self-esteem. And what it will do to productiveness, and what it will do to independence and to acting on principle." What exactly is the name of that process, which is a very essential process (which is the *conclusion* of understanding, not the *essence* of it?) When you connect a topic to all the other things that it belongs connected with, and thereby cement all your knowledge together? *Integration.* The main flaw is that he took the topic of *integration* with the rest of his knowledge as the *essence* of understanding this one topic, when it's not. Integration here is the cherry on the cake. He omitted the same thing that the first speaker omitted. What is the essential principle of why force is wrong? To grasp it, you first have to grasp it as a principle. What is it about force that makes it wrong? Sure, it's anti-reason—*why*? You have to grasp it in principle, because if all you hold is, "It's anti-reason because it's anti-independence and it's anti-long-range and it's anti-principles," it's like the crow epistemology—you cannot retain it all—and consequently, what you feel in your mind is, "I have a whole bunch of arguments against force, but they're all sort of like each other. They don't jell into one insight, one clear grasp, '*This* is force, and *this* is why it's wrong.'"

What you properly want to do is first grasp, in a nonrationalistic way, why force is wrong *in principle*, and *then*—if you stop there, of course, that's no good—*then*, you concretize *and* integrate with all the other aspects of the system. That way, the principle gives you the direct essence of the principle to retain in your mind, and all the integration then is tied on one central trunk in your mind, and it doesn't just lie there like six or eight or twelve different arguments that you don't know what to do with.

So, I would say that he was good on examples; he was very good on integrating, but the integrating was premature. Instead of focusing on the *essence* of the evil of force—he touched on that, he hinted at it—but I listened to that, and I thought, "Oh, if only he would stop here and give me a speech on this one sentence that he uttered, really chew that one point until the principle is clear, then he could go off onto concretes and integration with other points, and there would be no problem." But that's what he didn't really do.

Now let me have a few minutes to give you an idea of how I would go about this. Please don't take this as a criticism of the other two speakers, because they did very well under these circumstances; they did not have it all written out, the way I do. What I want to stress here is what I think was omitted, which would be the peg, the principle.

I would start: According to Objectivism, there are two fundamental ways of dealing with others: by reason or by force. I know that Objectivism holds, in some way, that force is anti-mind, anti-reason; somehow, it's destructive of the mind. But how or why? That is what I'm trying to understand. That much. It would not satisfy me to say, "Because the mind requires productivity, or the mind requires self-esteem," because I'm changing the subject from the mind in its essential functioning to some derivative or application, and I want to directly connect force with the essence of the mind, if I want to really grasp this in principle. The way I would do it is to imagine that things were different; I like to sometimes rewrite reality, to change one thing, because that helps to highlight the way things really are. So suppose that reality was different in one way—let us suppose that the wielder of force could actually change your mind by using force. Suppose a dictator had that power, like from *The Twilight Zone*. For instance, you were an atheist, and, if somebody pulled a gun on you and said, "Start believing in God, or I'll shoot," you were able to do it. Suppose you could say, "Okay. After all, my life depends on obedience to this guy, so now I'm going to start believing in God." I would say that if you could do that, there's no argument against force. You'd just have a different conclusion, that's all. Then the only thing we'd have to ask is, "If you're going to use force, try to do it on behalf of good ideas." The fact is, the *crucial* fact that nobody brought out—but that's the essence of how the mind operates, and therefore, is going to lead us to the essence of why force is anti-mind—is that you *cannot do it*. You can, of course, *say* to him that you believe in God, but you cannot literally make your mind do it. And the key point here is that, in this sense, your mind is out of your control. It will not obey an injunction to believe, not even if you know that your life depends on it.

Why can't a mind be compelled to accept a conclusion? That takes us back to what the mind is. It's one thing only: a *cognitive faculty*, a faculty for grasping knowledge, a faculty for perceiving reality. And if you know epistemology, you know it has to do this by a complex process of thought, evidence, coming to conclusions, and so on. It has to observe facts, judge, connect, and the result is either knowledge, or at least an honestly held conclusion, even if it's an error. But if a mind avowedly defies facts that are within its awareness—if it says, in effect, "Forget reality, the truth is irrelevant"—the faculty literally cannot function; it would stop dead. There's no way for the person within the confines of his own mind to proceed. The crucial point is that we are not saying it's *bad* to force a mind, because to say it's "bad" would imply that you can do it but it's wicked. The fact is, you cannot do it, not in the sense of forcing it to come to an opposite conclusion to the evidence it itself sees. To try to force a mind to accept such a conclusion against its own judgment is like saying, "Accept what you know is not true." It's like saying, "Try to believe that red is green, or that two and two is five." And you can't make a man believe such a thing, George Orwell to the contrary. You can drive him crazy, but you can't make him believe it. If somebody says, "Your money or your life," you can give him the money—the gun will make you give him the money—but it won't make you believe that it's his money, and it cannot make you believe that, not the mere act of the gun being held.

So what then does the forcer accomplish? He cannot force you to think a certain way. What is it that he *does* accomplish? He forces you to *act* a certain way. What way? Against your judgment. He doesn't *change* your mind (this is the essence of the situation)—he makes it *irrelevant*. It is removed from life. To the extent of force being initiated against you, your mind has nothing to say about your action. Since force cannot make you think differently, all it can do is rupture the tie between thought and action. Force makes thought inoperative, inapplicable, pointless.

We have a context established in which we have two things—neither of which we're supposed to be chewing here; we've already gotten to them—number one, man survives by the use of his mind, and number two, all ethical issues must be determined by principle, because man has to survive long-range, and that's his only method. If we have only those two established in our context, what are we entitled to conclude? If man survives by the use of his mind, and we have to decide issues in principle, and the essence of force is to make mind inapplicable to life, what inexorable conclusion do you have to come to? Force is in principle anti-life. It has to be evil in principle, because its essential function by *its* nature and by the nature of the mind is to remove the mind from any relevance to action. In its very essence, it is something aimed at man's means of survival, by the nature of that means of survival.

That is what I call an argument in principle. But it's not enough. I haven't yet chewed it; I haven't concretized; I haven't integrated. I have given a central peg, a central argument that does establish in principle what the essential connection is between this point and my context.

If we grasp this in principle, we do not have to say, "What about the perpetrator?" Phil said—and I've heard this time and again from people working with this issue—"It's easy to see that force is bad for the victim, that it's against his life. But it's more difficult to prove that force is evil for the perpetrator." And this is absolutely not true. Why not, just on the basis of the way we've set it up so far? Why can't you say, "We still have the problem of the perpetrator"? If you grasp what it means to think in principle, and that ethics is an issue of principle, you cannot say, "I've established that this method is destructive of man's means of survival. I know it's bad for some people, but why not for others? I know it's bad for the guy on one end of it, but why not for the guy on the other end?" If man has to live by principle, and if he has to survive by his mind, that, in itself, is sufficient to establish, just as much for the perpetrator as for the victim, that he is violating the essential principle. So it comes down to this—is the context really clear in your mind? Do you grasp the necessity of functioning by principle, coupled with the necessity for *rationality* to be the principle? If you grasp those two, then as soon as you see that force is a violation of rationality, it's wiped out for everybody, the perpetrator or the victim; it's no more difficult for one than for the other.

This is just the beginning. I have to concretize this, because so far I am talking abstractly, which is good, because otherwise one gets lost in concretes. But you have to know that when you state a general argument like this, it is like a promissory note, like an I.O.U., and now it's called in for collection, and the payment is the concretes. But the concretes have to be concretes illustrating this point. So if I go at this stage to, "It violates independence," then I'm talking about something different, I'm talking about the applications of rationality. I want actual concretes showing that force makes the mind irrelevant. That was my argument. I want to concretize that exact principle.

Let's take the mugger. He says, "Your money or your life." How does that make your mind irrelevant? That's very simple. It doesn't make your mind irrelevant in every single question of your entire existence, but by the same token, the mugger is not initiating force on every aspect of your existence. He's initiating it on your money. So what question does he make your mind irrelevant to or removed from? "What should I do with my money?" Your conclusion now is irrelevant. What you think has no effect. His gun, of course, doesn't change your mind, but it makes your mind inoperative in that issue; it's as simple as that. If his will is dictating what you're going to do, your thought is simply beside the point. Of course, if you live in a society where that man is recognized as morally wrong (and the government is on your side), this is a very delimited interference with your mental processes, because you're free to go on thinking, and you act accordingly as soon as he leaves the scene, and you're even free to go on planning how to spend the money when the police force recovers it, on the assumption that the government hunts down the criminal because they believe that the initiation of force is evil. But if the government is on *his* side, if all of your money were expropriated, then you couldn't think about the material side of life at all; it would be completely beside the point. For instance, under complete socialism, where the government tells you everything that you can and can't do with material property—what has to be built, how, where, and when—on all those issues, then, your conclusions are simply irrelevant, inapplicable. In fact, thought is for one purpose, and that's for action, to guide value achievement.

If the action is pre-dictated, then thought is unmotivated and not possible. Of course, even under socialism, you can think about how to escape, if you can do it. But Leo, for instance, in *We the Living*, couldn't find any way, and just gave up; he quit thinking altogether. Even within socialism, you can think within the frame of the possibility of action. For instance, if they give you toothbrush coupons, and there are two colors to choose from, red or green, you can decide which one you want. But the point is this: Insofar as force applies, mind does not. That's the issue. Mind versus force—in principle, they are opposites. And if we wanted to take the time, you'd see there's a whole spectrum of degrees from mugging through the Southern black slavery—there was not much point for the slaves to think about their values or goals; they had more short-range-despair goals, basically, an unthinking way of life because there was no possibility of doing anything with their thought—on through complete totalitarian socialism, where *every* action is controlled in principle, and the result is whole societies with no science, no invention, no art, no ingenuity, and starvation—a large-scale example of force across the board. That's the principle of the mugger across the board; and the result is the extirpation of thought across the board. The utter extreme of this was the concentration camps. The concentration camp is the only example (as you know, I make the point in *The Ominous Parallels*) of absolutely consistent totalitarianism, where force rules every moment, and absolutely nothing is left to the discretion or judgment of the individual, literally nothing, so far as that's possible. Even to the point where people tried to prevent themselves from perceiving what was happening before their eyes, unless the guard said to do so. And you know that the result of that was mass death in an unprecedented way in history—mass zombies and mass death. That was the unavoidable result of this type of condition. Except for those people who could project another way of life and could keep alive by remembering or anticipating a world in which they *could* act; they were able to keep themselves functioning to that extent, by trying to think of a nonforce world.

The purpose of concretizing would be to take it across the whole gamut; to the extent that force exists, it makes thought useless. If you go by principle, then you have to say it's anathema.

A few last points, just to finish off on force. What is the context? Life, principles, rationality—those are the main ones. But is that enough, even with the concretes that we've given? It's a *partial*, it's an argument in principle, and it shows that that principle is not floating. But what have we still omitted? We've omitted the complete richness of the argument, all of the aspects that it encompasses, because rationality is not *only* the exercise of the mind to grasp truth; it's all the expressions of that, including independence and integrity and honesty and productiveness and so on. Now that we see the essential relation of force against reason, it's at this point that what Phil did becomes crucial—integration, which consists now of tying it, point by point, to all of the other topics in the ethics.

Let me make one point here on the question of induction versus deduction. Why couldn't I simply argue as follows: "Rationality requires the perception of reality; force interferes with the perception; therefore, force is anti-reason." Therefore the whole thing is a strictly deductive argument. Why is that invalid, if that is the essence of what you have to say? Even though that is a key point, why is it not enough? You could say that you have to know what you mean by each concept, and you have to be able to answer particular cases so you can deal with examples, but you have to have been able to have formed these concepts to begin with. How, for instance, do you think the concept of "rationality" is formed? A person doesn't just sit down one day and say, "Let me see, I'm going to give a name to the use of the mind. I'm going to call that 'mentality' or 'rationality'" and then go on from there.

How would Ayn Rand have reached her concept of "rationality"? She would have to have observed a tremendous number of actual instances of human behavior, and say, "Here is a person working, here is a person being a parasite, this one is using his mind, this one isn't; here is a person acting on his conclusions, when this one is a compromiser, so this one is following his mind and this one is hypocritical and betraying; here is a person holding a gun on somebody, and therefore he's using force and not mind, and here is a person who's working independently," and so on. In other words, she'd have to *observe*. Reality doesn't come in any order; it doesn't bring you all the examples of honesty on Tuesday or in January, and then on Wednesday or February, all the examples of integrity, and then six months later all the ones of force; it's all mashed together. She would have to observe instances of force *along with* all the other instances of irrationality, in contrast to all the different forms of *rationality*, and then she would connect them all up and she would say, "What is it that's common to all of these instances of force, dishonesty, and so on?" and she would form a concept of "rationality." In other words, she reaches that fundamental concept only by a long induction, which requires her to be attentive to the actual facts, including the issues and concrete examples of force. So first you observe reality, and you form your concepts, including the concept of "rationality"; that is an inductive process. In forming the concept, you are implicitly saying, "This excludes criminality; that's the opposite of it." And then when you systematize it, you state the principle why. If a person enters at that stage and merely hears the deductive arguments, it sounds like rationalism. But the point is to grasp that the operative concepts *come from reality*, and the theoretical argument is simply an organization of material, once you originally get it from reality. You have to observe all the evil effects of force—criminality, dictators, and so on; after all, Ayn Rand majored in history, and she did it for a reason—she wanted to know what the actual result was of certain principles in human life. And she found that wherever she looked, certain types of behavior led to disaster, and other types didn't, and she was able to grasp from that, "There is something wrong with force." And then she was simultaneously working on her idea, "How should man live?" And then she connected the two—force is anti-mind. But there was a preliminary period of simply gathering the observational data. In reality it's all simultaneous. Our process has to be *in*duction to reach essential concepts, and then deduction therefrom. The further we go, the more we chew, the more we integrate, the higher on the spiral, the clearer we finally get.

We're going to do one more topic tonight. Obviously we cannot give
it the detailed attention we gave the last topic, but we'll at least give it a
stab as one more example of the process. And that is the topic of the
validation of individual rights. We're not yet saying what is the relation
of that topic to the initiation of force; we're just taking this topic by itself.
And our volunteer is Donna.

> I already know all the things I did wrong. The validation of
> rights, why rights are right. I'm in the realm now of political
> philosophy, and rights tie in ethics to politics. Rights are moral
> principles defining and sanctioning man's freedom of action
> in a social context. What does that mean to me? It would be
> how to act, the right way to live with other men. So now I have
> to think, "Hmm, life—what is life?" It's self-sustaining, self-
> generating action. I think the operative word is "self"—what
> I have to choose, what I have to decide, for *myself.* I'm going to
> give some examples of that. The example that first came to my
> mind was abortion—do I have the right to choose for myself
> what I want to do with my body? Does society, or anyone—
> government, anyone—have the right to tell me what I must
> do? Another one is gun control, guns—do I have the right to
> bear arms? Do I have the right to have a gun without getting
> fingerprinted, without having to register that with anyone? Do
> I have the right to protect myself? To follow that up, it's the
> new example of children being fingerprinted now, and the gov-
> ernment saying the reason they are doing that is to protect those
> children and their parents so that they can find them if they're
> lost. That's the reasoning beyond that—protection. And then
> the third example is when government intervenes in businesses.
> I'll use the airlines, decontrolling the airlines or controlling the
> airlines, and the difference later on when it was decontrolled.
>
> I'll tie those in in a moment, but I want to discuss the source
> of rights—where does it come from? And it comes from the law
> of identity—A is A, man is man. In order to live, I have to use

my mind. I have to act on my free judgment. I have to make choices for myself. And in order to live, I have to work so that I can get the values that I want, and keep those values. In the case of all three examples of choice and protection and being able to work—I am lost. Dr. Peikoff says when you're lost, say you're lost.

Let me go back to life, liberty, and the pursuit of happiness. That's in the Constitution, and that's basic rights. The right to my life means that I have a right to freedom and the right to pursue what I want, so we'll take it back to work. In a country like Russia or China, you are told what kind of work you will do. You have no choice; you have no right to do what will make you happy, that which will let you live and pursue your life. In the case of an abortion, you don't have the right to your own life; you're now told that you have another life to look after, that you must do that; it stops you economically from working; you now cannot achieve certain values that you want to achieve. And in the case of businesses where government tells you that you must have certain controls, that you have to charge certain prices, again, you're not allowed to work; you're not allowed to gain, produce, and to keep what you produce.

One thing that I haven't brought up, which is very important, is that the only way to protect individual rights is in a capitalist society. The government was set up only to protect us against physical force. They're not there to dictate to man what is right and what is wrong. Individual rights means subordinating society to moral law, that moral law comes first; society doesn't tell us what is right and what is wrong.

The right to support your life by your own work does not mean that others must give you a job, must support you. You have the right to pursue your values, and to work for yourself. A man, we do not have to give a man a job, give a man a home; that's not a part of producing, productivity. The last thing I wanted to say is there are no other rights—there aren't economic rights; there aren't any other rights but individual rights; those are the only rights.

There were again some virtues and some flaws. It was not rationalist by virtue of two definite features. It was a much more empiricist presentation. Why? What were the features that made this empiricism, two outstanding features? The structure was not there; it was not well structured. Now that's not a criticism. You have to do what you understand, but I'll just show you on some points how you could organize your thinking a little better. What was the other point that was obviously not rationalistic? A large number of concretes, too many concretes, more than we could deal with; it outweighed the abstractions, which also indicates empiricism.

Let me give you one example of a lack of structure. You started by giving a definition—you said rights are moral principles sanctioning independent action, and then you asked, "What does that mean? It means, how I should act in relation to others." Which, you said, you were just going to blurt out your simple understanding. But unfortunately, having put it that way, it made the issue of rights synonymous with any question of social ethics: How should you behave in dealing with others? Should you tell the truth to them, should you be just to them? All of which are questions of ethics, not of politics. So you left it pretty vague. And that was my first sign that this is not a rationalist presentation, because a rationalist sits on the definition lovingly and elaborates it, because his whole thing is then to extract his conclusion from it. And you gave it a perfunctory look—you went through the whole discussion, then at the end you said, "Now I have to make clear what I mean by 'rights'—they don't mean rights to economic handouts and so on; they mean rights to action." Which, if you were going in a systematic way, since that was your original definition—"a sanction of independent action"—you would have clarified right there: "What do I mean by 'rights,' and what don't I?" That was the tip-off that this is definitely not a rationalist presentation. That's an example of lack of structure—instead of trying to get the conclusion clear first and then going on, you said something, you went on, you got lost, and you threw in a little more about what you mean by that conclusion.

To have a proper structure, what is the first thing you do after you say what you're talking about, what your conclusion means? The first thing you do is to set the context. Donna did *include* the context, but where? At what point? First of all, she went into a number of examples. So when we approached those examples, all we had in our minds was a general definition of "rights" that wasn't really clear, and now we rush right into examples; we had no real way of knowing what we are supposed to be taking for granted. In her own mind, Donna had no real way of knowing. She didn't separate the issue into two parts: the context that I'm taking for granted—"This is not my assignment today, this is what I'm counting on"—versus "This is now what I'm focusing on." And that's why, when she plunged right in with examples, and then said, "Life requires that we use our mind and make choices and work," she stopped dead and got lost. The reason she got lost is perfectly logical and unavoidable, because, since she hadn't said what she was taking for granted, her mind was confronted with these big generalities—"We have to live by the mind and work and so on"—and you knew those are not self-containedly clear, so one part of her would say to herself, "Let's start thinking about why you have to use the mind, and why you have to make choices, and why you have to work," and on the other hand, her mind said, "I'm supposed to be doing life, liberty, and the pursuit of happiness, not this other stuff," so she just stopped dead. And the reason is that she did not create a division of labor.

Chewing has to be very, very uniquely focused on one topic. If you're going to focus on rights, you have to first say, "I am *not* going to discuss the following: so-and-so and so-and-so; I'm taking this much for granted. If you don't understand this, that's a different matter. But for now, I'm saying *assuming*"—and Donna gave us the perfect lead-in to it, because she said, "This is political philosophy." I thought she was just going to go now off into the right statement of the context because we're taking for granted now the *totality* of ethics. And the whole of ethics tells us what? How a man should live, what principles he has to follow in order to live. And we're taking *all* of that for granted. So, this should be really a breeze then. By the time we turn to this topic, we already know everything about how a man should live. We're just making an obvious application of what we already know—for example, that life is the standard, and rationality is the means of achieving it, and every man should live for his own self-interest, and he should live by principles, and he should be honest and independent, and so on, and he has to be productive—all of ethics is taken for granted. We've already proved, presumably, in ethics that if we violate any of this, that's anti-life and that makes it impossible for us to survive. Once we know all that, it becomes a relative snap. It's like a little tiny application to go to this topic, as I'll show you in a moment. But Donna did not. She *said*, "This is politics," but she didn't really live up to that, because she said, "This is politics," and partway through she said to herself, "Gee, there are really a lot of ethical points here that I'm not too clear about." Once she thought that, she should have said good-bye to politics—"It's just useless to talk about rights, and if I don't really get this, I'm not going to waste my time on politics. Why? It comes much later," and she should have said, "I'm going to change my assignment, to hell with rights, let's discuss so-and-so," or whatever.

Donna, do you see by the way you approached it why your mind would have to stop? You're trying to understand, but you do not delimit what you're trying to understand. Every one of us could learn more about any broad principle; that's what chewing and the spiral consist of; so if you don't delimit the assignment, as soon as you say one of these generalities about "Life requires work," and if your only assignment is "I must understand," then your mind thinks, "I've got to understand then, why does it require work? I can't remember." And it dredges up "work"—"What is work? It's achieving values, choices." And then you think, "What am I doing? I'm getting nowhere near life, liberty, and the pursuit of happiness, so I've got to drop that," but you feel dissatisfied and confused, and then it becomes chaos. So this is the best I can do to dramatize for you why you have to set a context and then say, "I will not discuss this context in this thought process. If I'm not clear about it, I'm going to change the thought process." That's what I call an example of structured thinking—"What am I trying to show? What am I counting on that I will not think about now? And now, what is my specific topic?" But you didn't do that; you sort of jumped around, and that's an example of lack of structure in a number of different ways.

Now let's take the issue of your examples. You gave us a lot of examples, and that's good; we want a lot of examples. But your examples, unfortunately, were not ideally chosen. You picked *interesting* examples, but what is the one problem with these examples from the aspect of what we are trying to do? These are examples on the same order as Fred's example of Israel: they are controversial, complicated, difficult. For instance, if you say about abortion, "How can the government tell me what to do with my body?" that by itself is not really convincing. Because a famous libertarian said to me once that he believes in absolute liberty, and if a typewriter is his property, he should be able to throw it at another person. "How should the government be able to say what I can do with my property? If it's my typewriter, I can drop it on somebody else's head." So to say, "I can do what I want with my own body" is not true. You can do what you want to do with your body, *if* your body stays out of the way of other bodies. But that raises the issue of the anti-abortionists: "But it's murder! This little embryo is another human being; you can't use your body to kill it." That's wrong, but it nevertheless is a complication—it's not a clear-cut self-evidency. But clear examples are what you want when you're trying to understand. Gun control is also a very complicated issue, because guns are lethal weapons; the government does have a right to restrict force in a society (that's its essential function), and therefore, it's a very debatable issue; you can't have an H-bomb in your front yard and say, "It's my yard." Who is going to draw the line, at exactly what point, and say, "You can have a pistol, but you can't have a submachine gun"? Those are really tricky questions. You first have to understand the issue of rights thoroughly, and then try to untangle all the complexities of that particular concrete. So for rights, I would want straightforward examples like slavery or robbery or murder. *Then*, after I understood that, I would go to the interesting, complex applications.

The other problem with Donna's concretes is they weren't connected clearly to a principle. Concretes that don't illustrate a principle are correspondingly not of much use, because the idea is the union of the principle with the concretes. Otherwise, there's nothing to tie them to-gether, to enable you to hold them, enable you to see why these concretes are important, or what the issue is. The closest you get is to say, "The source of rights is the law of identity: Man has to live a certain way, and rights are that way." That's true, but it is a little too generalized. You could give us one step more of breaking down why you have to have certain rights, and how that relates to what we've already established in ethics. It's just too general to say, "Man has to live a certain way, and rights are that way." *How* are they that way? Not just concrete examples, but in principle; it's the same issue we were asking with regard to force. What is the principle of connection between the ethical principles of how man should live and the topic of rights? You hinted at it; you suggested it; you said things that, if I played the Socratic interrogator and kept asking, I would have finally elicited from you. But as stated, it was fragmentary.

There is just one other problem I wanted to point out here, which is that you violated the principle of the hierarchical structure. Because what topic did you bring in as very important, which should be in this discus-sion but comes later? Government and capitalism. Government, according to Objectivism, is the agency that protects rights, so we don't discuss gov-ernment until we have rights in the picture. So in validating rights, you can't say, "We know this is what the government is supposed to do." You're anti-hierarchical then; you're using something later to establish this. And capitalism is way down the line. When we get to capitalism, we validate it by saying, "This is the system in which the government performs the right functions, which is protecting rights." Capitalism is the end of politics, and we're at the beginning of politics. So you had an anti-hierarchical element.

Let me try, in about five minutes, to indicate to you a few things about how I would approach the issue of rights. I would begin by stating the context: This is the beginning of politics, the way that "life is the stan-dard" is the beginning of ethics. And the question is, what should be the relation of the individual to society? Are there any immunities, any pre-rogatives of other people that society has to respect, or not? Is there any limit to what it can do to the individual, or not? This is before we get to the discussion of government.

Let's stop and ask why this whole question of rights is necessary. Just because people talk about an issue doesn't mean the issue is worth discussing, so what would be wrong with the following? "Let's just get rid of rights altogether. The whole topic is otiose." Why not just say, "We've already established in the first half that the initiation of force is evil; therefore, the government should bar it because it's immoral, and that's it. The government should prohibit robbery; it shouldn't initiate force; we've already established that force is evil—that's it. Who needs all this life, liberty, and the pursuit of happiness, and rights? This is unnecessary, just a big complication. We should just go from 'the evil of force' to 'government bars force because it's immoral'; that's it." These are the types of questions you should ask if you're trying to understand. If it's not really clear to you why something is an issue, you should ask, "Let's get rid of it and see where we would be then; does it really answer something? Is it an important question, or can I get along without it? Does it raise some new aspect?"

In fact, you could not just go from "force is evil" to "therefore the government should ban it." Because there are all kinds of evils. The fact that something is evil or immoral does not mean automatically that the government should ban it. If that were your argument, the implication would be that the government is the upholder of morality, and anything we've established as immoral the government should stop—it should prevent people from being dishonest, from being compromisers, from being unjust, and so on. That would be totalitarianism. You would think to yourself, "Maybe I have to modify and say the government should prevent immoralities only if they affect others." But obviously that is insufficient, because in some sense, *every* immorality "affects others." If you lie to a friend, you affect him; if you're unjust to an employee, you affect him. But those don't belong to the government. Why? There are a lot of things that people can do that are bad and that affect others, but that's not what we're talking about. We're asking one specific question—is there an absolute minimum necessary if society is to be possible? Are there some conditions on which this society has to be organized, if it's to function at all? Are there some things without which human beings cannot live together? And that's exactly the topic of rights—what, if any, are those conditions? So it *is* a necessary issue when you get to politics. You cannot simply say the government should prohibit whatever is immoral.

I agree basically with the analysis of what rights are. I think that's covered in the literature, so I won't go into that further. What I want to do is indicate how rights are derived from morality, the essential abstract argument. Because it's really very straightforward. Rights take for granted the whole of ethics. And the principle relating ethics to politics is simply this: *What is moral in ethics must be possible in politics.* The way of life that we define in ethics as the good, as that which man's life requires, must be possible to live in society. Therefore, all we have to know is what that way is, and how others could prevent it. Then we'll be able to read off: Those are the things they can't do; these are the things you have a right to. In other words, society has to institutionalize the conditions that enable man to follow morality. You look back to the ethics, and we tell each man that the fundamental goal is life—act so as to sustain your life; your need to act a certain way is what creates values to begin with. And when we come to politics, what do we say? The fundamental principle has to be, *you* act in such a way as to sustain your life, and if other people interfere, they are violating the crucial condition of human existence and coexistence. The fundamental value in ethics is life, and the fundamental right is the right to life. In morality, we hold that you can achieve your life only by using your mind, your reason, and so on, and acting accordingly. What does that come out to in politics? Liberty—the right to act according to your judgment. So liberty is simply the sum of those virtues—rationality, independence, integrity, thinking by your own mind, acting accordingly, and saying that in society no one can prevent you from doing that, not if life is our goal and our purpose is to have a society in which you can practice the principles of human survival. Ethics tells us that productiveness is a central virtue. Politics tells you to keep what you've produced and use it to sustain yourself; that's the right to property. Ethics tells us pursue your own well-being—that is, egoism, which in politics entails the right to the pursuit of happiness.

These are all one issue: Ethics is simply "life is the standard" and all it requires; politics is simply: to achieve life in an organized group, this is what they must leave you alone in, these are the areas they cannot touch; they have to let you do the basic things that human survival requires. So what then is the context of rights? I would say the totality of ethics, but I would keep it in my mind with four words: life, rationality, productiveness, egoism. I picked those four because I want to get the four rights, but those are the four issues of ethics, which are the context after which you can simply rattle off the conclusion in politics. So this is easy if you keep in mind the context. But if you're not clear on the need of rationality or productiveness or egoism, then you will be stuck in politics.

Is this inductive or deductive? Because in a way, all I'm doing is deducing from the principles of ethics how they have to apply in society. So it looks like deduction, right? Except that you could not have reached those principles without observing many things in reality, including governments around the world. You could not have reached the issue of rights if you didn't observe the whole history of man, the correlation between standard of living, progress and freedom, on the one hand, versus stagnation and so on with slavery or violation of rights. You couldn't do it just by deduction from "rationality." You have to observe a tremendous amount of history, concretes, facts to reach the conclusion on an inductive level. A certain type of government facilitates human life, and a certain doesn't—it contradicts it. And then you say, "What do I know about man and the mind that would explain this?" And you tie that in to what you have established. You integrate it to your knowledge of the need of the mind and productiveness. At that point, it is deductive. So like all of philosophy, it's inductive to get the essential material, and then deductive as organized and presented as an argument. And the flaw of people is to come in without all the earlier observation, and think that all you do is churn out conclusions from some definition.

I want to ask one last question, and then we will leave this topic. This is a question of hierarchical order as a kind of anticipation of what we're going to be focusing on in the next lecture. If you had to take three topics and arrange them hierarchically—the issue of force, the issue of rights, the issue of government—what order would you put them in? Obviously government has to come after rights, because government will be the last. But would you say "force, rights, government," or would you say, "rights, force, government"? I think you can definitely prove that force precedes rights, that the evil of force precedes the validation of individual rights. And I'm going to give you that just as an example of hierarchical reasoning, and then you apply it to the rest of the material for homework.

Force, the evil of force, is part of morality; it's a basic principle of how to live. It would hold true even apart from any organized society. If there were just you and one other person on a desert island, the evil of force would apply. Remember, our standard is man's life. And that means man's life qua man, as against qua animal—qua thinker, rather than qua forcer. The evil of force is built into the essential, defining what is the proper way of life. Then you get to rights when you reach politics. You say, "All right, now that I know all this, how should society be organized?" And then you work out the various rights. You see that the only method of violating these rights is the use of force. What principle applies here? The spiral. The basic principle is now appearing in a political context, and you're now seeing a further confirmation. Just as the evil of force is part of the essence of ethics, so now, it's the fact that force is the antonym of rights, and that's the thing the government has to wipe out, that simply confirms further how force is anti-life. If you do it in reverse—if you argued that rights come first, and that force is evil because it violates rights—it would imply that force is evil only on political grounds—that is, that force violates the proper social arrangements. It would amount to saying that force is wrong only because it violates the right structure of society. And yet the actual evil of force is much deeper than that. The evil of force is that it violates the essential requirements of man's mind, and the very essence of his method of survival. That is more basic. It's like a metaphysical issue pertaining to man's nature and his relation to reality. It's more basic than the details of how society should be organized. And rights, in that respect, are just a detail; a *crucial* detail, but from the perspective we're here talking about, a later application.

I don't want to hammer this point to death, because actually, in reality, everything is simultaneous. But it is true that your thinking will be helped if you keep clear what comes before what, what is a fundamental and what is an application.

Lecture Four Q & A

Q: *In discussing the topic of force, isn't free will a necessary part of the context? Shouldn't this already have been chewed before a chewing of the evil of force?*

A: Of course, free will is a prerequisite, not only of the topic of force but of *all* ethical questions, because there can be no advice as to how to value if we have no choice. But the questioner here implies, "Isn't free will something you have to focus on in order to really understand force, the evil of force?" I don't think so. But there's absolutely nothing wrong with saying, "The mind doesn't work by force, because its essence is the choice to focus or not, and if it doesn't make a certain choice and see the facts on its own, it can't be force." If you bring in to the discussion of the impossibility of forcing a mind the fact that it is volitional and has to be controlled and regulated by the owner, the mind itself, that's fine; I would not fault that; it gives you an even fuller focus on it; it's helpful. But my principle is Occam's Razor—entities should not be multiplied beyond necessity. When I want to understand at the beginning, I try to strip to the bare minimum, the absolute minimum, required of the context to get to this point. And from that point of view, I could imply free will, but I don't have to focus on that so long as I focus simply on the fact you cannot do it, the mind is a cognitive faculty, it operates a certain way. I don't have to go all the way to the root in order to grasp this one issue of force. Of course, to grasp *everything* about the issue of force, I *do*. But the idea of chewing is to restrict your range. So I would never say that's wrong. If you understand free will that clearly, that to you volition means a certain way the mind must operate and therefore you can't force it, terrific; that's a better integration still than the way I suggested. But I tried to indicate to you why I strip it down as much as possible in trying to understand it.

Q: Would a complete argument on the evil of force cover the claim that one should at times force people to act a certain way for their own good?

A: Definitely. It's a very widespread confusion and might stand in your mind as, "I understand force to destroy life, but what about force to preserve life?" Man survives a certain way, and force is antithetical to that principle, and therefore it is evil in principle. It is just as true in this case as in all the other cases that you are paralyzing the mind of the individual to the extent of the initiation of force, even if, in any particular concrete case, the particular thing you give him helps him. You are still initiating a principle that is at variance with the requirements of his long-range, principled survival. If you advocate the idea, "I can initiate force when I choose, and I can violate his mind, his conclusions and his judgment, so long as in my opinion this is for the long-range welfare of the person," that is the end of being opposed to force, because there is no way in which you could prevent that same pretext being used for anything—mass robbery, on the grounds that people have to learn to live in difficult conditions (that's what the ecologists are saying—that is, they're doing that for your own welfare, for your own benefit). They burned people at the stake in the Inquisition for the benefit of the victims, so the soul could go on to the next dimension, and so on. Once you start injecting my opinion of what's good for his life, as a separate issue aside from what it does for his mind, that's it; you've wiped out the principle.

■

The Hierarchy of Objectivism

Let's now turn to the issue of hierarchical structure and the logical structure of Objectivism. I want to give you the theory behind this (or at least remind you of it). All knowledge is built on a hierarchical model. We build knowledge on knowledge. We acquire knowledge in a certain order, certain steps being the basis for the next steps, and new knowledge at each stage of our development is made possible only by the earlier knowledge. That's a simple statement of what it means to say knowledge is hierarchical. Putting it negatively, knowledge is *not* a grab bag of disconnected items that we could take in and grasp and know in any arbitrary order. It has a logically necessary order. That's what's meant by "hierarchy"—a logically necessary order of dependence, each level resting on an earlier one, and that on an earlier one, and so on, back to the foundation, which is whatever is given us directly and without any reasoning in sense perception. That's what we call the "self-evident"— that's the very beginning, and from there, everything is built on that.

So when you have the hierarchy of any item of knowledge set out before you, you know the anatomy of how you acquired that item of knowledge. You have its cognitive pedigree—where it came from, what it depends on—and thereby you are able to grasp its proof, how you know it is true. Once you set out its hierarchical base or roots, you can then say, "So and so and so, the earlier points are the things on which it depends, and by reference to which it can be established." You want to prove this item? Then this is what you have to first establish, because that's what leads to it. You want to understand this item? Since this is the point at which it arises, all these earlier points are its *context*; that's what you must assume and that's what you must count on when you are trying to chew it. This is true of any item in any field.

We are now going to do it in one specific field, and that is *philosophy*. Like all knowledge, philosophy has a hierarchical structure. To prove any particular item within philosophy, you must discover what it depends on. And to understand it, to chew it, you must know what context you are counting on.

Our continual question in trying to grasp the hierarchical structure is going to be, What comes before what? What do we have to know to know X? This is straightforward, simple, but we must make some preliminary clarifications. Here are a few just to get us oriented.

First of all, in reality, all philosophic truths are simultaneous. There is no hierarchy in reality. Hierarchy is an *epistemological* issue, not a *metaphysical* one. For instance, suppose I asked you the question, "Which comes first in reality, A is A, or man is a rational being?" You couldn't possibly answer that question because "man is a rational being" is the statement of one specific identity, and "the law of identity" is merely the general statement that everything has a specific identity; the law of identity has no content apart from all its instances, and its instances are instances of it. You couldn't possibly say that specific identities come first in reality, and then a month later, the law of identity comes, or vice versa; they are simultaneous in reality, metaphysically. But, if we want to grasp these two propositions, then we have to grasp the law of identity *before* we grasp that man is a rational being. Why? Because in order to grasp that man is a rational being, we must first have some knowledge of the basic principles of logic, in order to guide our thought. So we have to—not necessarily explicitly, but at least implicitly—grasp the law of identity close to the outset in order to be able to go on, form concepts, form definitions, and so on, and one day rise to grasp the definition "man is a rational being."

Here are two propositions that name facts that are simultaneous in reality, but they have a hierarchical relationship in our knowledge, and one of them, the *knowledge* of it, is a precondition of grasping the other.

A second clarification: There are many options when we set out a hierarchical structure. It is not true that every step is inexorable, that no variation in sequence is possible. In broad terms, if you take the overview of the whole development, the order is logically dictated; there are no options. But in many cases of detail, there *are* options. And don't let this bother you. I'm going to explain the deeper significance of this issue later. But just as an unexplained teaser, I want to point out that this is going to be a very important issue in distinguishing Objectivism from rationalism and empiricism. The rationalist *hates* the idea of options; he wants everything to be like geometry. An empiricist hates anything that *isn't* an option; he wants any order of any kind as he feels. The key to Objectivism here is a logically necessary structure in principle, *plus* many options in detail and application. For now, don't worry about this issue; I'm just giving you a broader motivation to appreciate the issue of options. For now, we just want to try to grasp the respect in which there is logical necessity and no choice, and the aspect where there is a certain option. And we'll discuss that and its roots and its meaning in subsequent weeks.

To give you an example of what I have in mind here: Suppose we get to ethics, we've established "life as the standard," we've established "the virtue of rationality," and then we have, let us say, two virtues glaring at us—independence and integrity—and now I ask you to arrange this whole process hierarchically. Both of these virtues, independence and integrity, are concretizations of rationality as we know it. They're on the same level; neither one necessarily precedes the other. Depending on your particular order of reaching and treating these questions, depending on the topic that first comes to your attention, you have a choice whether you go from rationality to independence to integrity, or rationality to integrity to independence, and there are many other possibilities. As we've said before, we have to develop *all* the lesser or derivative virtues together ultimately, as aspects or specifications of one overall way of life. So there is no necessary order on a question of relative detail such as this; there are options. But suppose we take as two ideas "life as the standard" and "integrity as a virtue." On the question of the relation of these two, there is no option. What is a virtue? A means of achieving a value. What is a value? How do you decide that? By reference to some standard of value. Until you know the standard of value, you can't know values, and until you know values you can't know virtues. So you must know a standard of value before you can turn to virtue; there is no question of an option there. There is a basic necessity of overall structure, with options at various levels.

Now I want to clarify a third possible confusion: Don't confuse this issue of hierarchy with the issue of your childhood development. They are two different things. The steps by which you grew up are not what we're talking about. For example, as a child, thanks to the existence of other people, you may learn about integrity before you ever think of the standard of value. Your mother may tell you, "Don't be a hypocrite—if you believe something, you should act on it"; and she may tell you that at a stage where you've never *dreamed* of such a question as "What is the ultimate value?" You are, in this example, the beneficiary of mankind's accumulated wisdom; you are getting a piece of data without its hierarchical base. And that's fine, because, presumably, in time, you'll rise to the point of grasping its roots. But the point now is, don't confuse this sort of thing with what we are trying to do tonight. If that child wanted to *prove* that integrity was a virtue, he has to say more than that his mother told him; he has to go through something like what we went through on honesty. So hierarchically, "integrity" still comes after "life as the standard," even though he got to it before. The issue in this is *not* childhood psychology; this is adult epistemology. We are trying to organize our knowledge logically, regardless of the haphazard order in which we acquired it. We are trying to show objectively how we demonstrate a given point, what it logically depends on, what you need to know to prove it. And therefore, we are arranging our knowledge in an objective order: axioms first, then what they directly make possible, and so on, ending with the most remote issues of politics or esthetics that might require a whole philosophic system before you could even ask them.

UNDERSTANDING OBJECTIVISM

I want to try not to be dogmatic here. There are a lot of technical disputes possible. I don't say they have no answer, but they certainly are tortuous questions of infinite detail. These are not essential to our purpose. Harry Binswanger and I, for instance, have argued sometimes for hours on whether a given tenet in technical epistemology precedes or follows some other one. And it can be extremely complicated. But that is not our purpose here, and I'm asking for the license in advance to ride roughshod over those types of questions. We want to get tonight a broad grasp of the total structure in essential terms. So I just say at the outset for fairness, not every Objectivist professor of philosophy will necessarily agree with every detail of what I say; some of the details are arguable, and ultimately, we could only establish the detailed hierarchy by some technical, full-fledged volume; that someday will come, but we do not need that in order to understand Objectivism.

So this is the frame of mind: We're adults, we have a wealth of philosophic ideas, and now we want to systematize them logically. Where do we start?

Here is the exercise on the hierarchical relation of the ideas in Objectivism. I have distributed a sheet [see below] with twenty different statements or topics, deliberately in an utterly random, senseless order. I want you to number them logically from one to twenty; the more fundamental, the more primary, the smaller the number. There are options. There are certain cases where you have a choice, which is one of the significant things in this exercise, which we want to point out in contrasting Objectivism to rationalism. I made this relatively easy. I left out a lot of tricky ones, and after we go through the order of this twenty next time, I'm going to throw them at you one new one at a time, and you tell me, would it go between four and five, or nine and ten, or whatever, where would it go? And we'll get more and more tricky as we go, until hopefully you'll have a real sense of the hierarchical structure.

[The exercise distributed to the attendees two weeks earlier:]

Capitalism as the only moral system.
Romanticism as the conceptual school of art.

A is A.

The virtue of independence.

The evil of the initiation of force.

Knowledge as objective (versus intrinsic or subjective).

The senses as valid.

Existence exists.

The virtue of honesty.

Concepts as identifications of concretes with their measurements omitted.

The integration of man's mind and body.

The validation of individual rights.

Consciousness as the faculty of perceiving that which exists.

The nature of art, and its role in man's life.

Reason as man's only means of knowledge; reason versus mysticism.

Reason as man's means of survival.

The proper functions of government.

Rationality as the primary virtue.

The law of cause and effect.

Man's life as the standard of moral value.

I picked twenty at random there; there may be five hundred, and
depending on how you break it up, five thousand. And I'm going to ask
for volunteers to simply say what they would take at a given point, and
briefly why. What would come first here?

[Audience member:] *Existence exists.*

Yes, there is absolutely no choice about that; "Existence exists" is
number one. It's not that it's the broadest generalization. It's because
until we have existence, there's no other question—there's nothing to
study, there's nothing to know, there's nothing to organize, there's nothing
to think about. If there is no existence, we're wiped out completely—us,
the question, and the subject matter. So you can't get away without starting with existence. As an abstract formula, you don't get "Existence

exists" until very late in life, and a lot of people never get it; but implicitly, it has to be grasped at the outset; the fact of reality has to be grasped through the act of opening your eyes. And until you have that, you simply can't go anywhere. That's the unavoidable starting point.

All right, now it gets a little more interesting. Where do we go from there? What is number two?

Consciousness as the faculty of perceiving that which exists.

Yes, because if we don't have a faculty of awareness, if we have no means of grasping existence, then right away we're stopped completely again; there are no longer any questions of development or order or knowledge. If we are unconscious, we have no faculty of awareness, that's the end of all cognition, and there's no such thing as hierarchy. So before you can get a step off the ground, there has to be something and a means of being aware of it. Why couldn't we have started with consciousness as axiom number one, and then existence as the second? What philosopher did that? Descartes. His whole catastrophe was a wrong hierarchical order. He started with consciousness as number one. But by that very means, he made consciousness a self-contained entity that depended on nothing earlier. So it was something other than the faculty of perceiving existence. And then he spent meditation after meditation trying to dredge up existence, and he couldn't find it. And that led to centuries of what's called "idealism" philosophically—only minds exist—and they couldn't find any physical world. You cannot start with consciousness.

What comes after existence and consciousness?

A is A.

Yes, "A is A" would be number three. Why? It's a corollary of existence, of the fact of existing as such. "A is A" is like the basic law defining what is reality, what it means to exist—"To be is to be something." So right away that raises a question. If this is a direct corollary of existence, where a corollary is like a restatement from a different angle, but an obvious implication—once you say "existence," that implies it's *something*, and

"A is A" just makes that explicit—why couldn't we go from existence to identity, and then to consciousness? I wouldn't make a federal case if you did that; that's not a disaster if you do that. But you could make a case against going from existence to identity to consciousness: In order to know anything, you first have to have consciousness—"A is A" is already an item; it's like part of the content of knowledge. So the way I would look at it is first, the bare minimum you must get in is that "There's a reality and I have a means of being aware of it; *now* let's see what we can find out."

But in your description, you said that "A is A" would be true even if there was no consciousness. Doesn't that then put it in front of a perceiver?

The first part is correct. But they are all simultaneous—"A is A" is independent of consciousness for its truth, but it's not independent of the existence of consciousness to be *grasped*. Remember, this whole hierarchy exercise is an exercise on what depends on what, what point do we have to know in order to *know* the next point. And I'm simply saying that if you set out the pedigree of knowledge, before you could say "I know" *any* content, you have to have a faculty of cognition. You could argue in reverse—before one can know, there has to be something definite for one *to* know. They're all simultaneous, and in fact, you could argue, "Existence exists" is really a blanket statement. Remember the way Galt puts it—"Existence exists, and the act of grasping that implies two corollary axioms, that something exists which one perceives, and that one exists possessing consciousness, consciousness being the faculty of perceiving that which exists." And the "something," of course, means "identity." So they really are all together. But just to get us started, I think it is a perfectly logical order. Where do we go from there? There is also an option, but I have a preference.

The senses as valid.

No, I can't agree with that; I think something has to go before that. I'll tell you when I would get to the senses, after one other point first.

The law of cause and effect.

That's possible, but I don't think preferable. Possible on what grounds? You could argue that cause and effect itself is an application of the law of identity to action. Cause and effect says that since everything has an identity, then a thing must act accordingly; in a given set of circumstances, it can only express its nature; therefore, the cause is the nature, the effect is what it does, and the same cause will lead to the same effect. So it's simply the application of the law of identity to action. And there is no further proof of the law of cause and effect except: "A is A, and actions are actions of entities," and then you just put them together.

Even though you could make that case, I prefer, for the reason that I preferred consciousness ahead of identity, to go in another direction—because I'm very conscious of the fact that if we are establishing philosophic knowledge as adults, we want to validate our knowledge step by step as we go. The crucial philosophic realm is epistemology; the crucial thing we have to know always is how do we know we know; and therefore, at any point where there is a choice, I'd say that in order to establish something philosophically, to establish the philosophical hierarchy, go to the epistemological issue of how you know. You can't do that before you establish reality. But once you do, then I'd go right away to, "And we have a means of knowing it—consciousness." Then, of course, we need "A is A," because that's going to be the guide to all of our knowledge. Once we have "A is A" in the picture, we have a stable reality that is what it is; again, urgently pressing is how we are going to know anything, including even the application of the law of identity to action. And from that point of view, therefore, I go now to a whole epistemological sequence. We've already had one element of epistemology—the faculty of consciousness. But that does not yet tell us how we know; it just says we have a faculty of knowledge. What crucial piece of information do we need at this stage in order to bring in the next element from within epistemology? Something that will tell us, "In principle, this is how to acquire knowledge." In other words, we need epistemological guidance to enable us to go on. We don't want some minutia or detail; we want some overall principle at this point,

where we can say, "Now we're going to use this to validate all our further
knowledge, including the details of epistemology." That's why I wouldn't
start with the senses here, which are a detail. What do you a think I would
go to?

Knowledge as objective versus intrinsic or subjective.

No, I wouldn't go there until substantially later. "Knowledge as objective versus intrinsic or subjective" means one particular theory of knowledge versus two others; and it involves a whole bunch of questions—what
are concepts like, how do the senses function, and so on—we wouldn't be
able even to explain what we meant by "objective" versus "intrinsic" or
"subjective" until we had a whole theory of epistemology. So that comes
much later in the picture, as I mean it here. I hasten to say that if you define
"objective" in a much more simple way, not in contrast to the intrinsic and
the subjective, not as a whole theory of epistemology, but just as "It's crucial
to focus on reality to get your material," that's what I had in mind; but I'm
using a different wording for that here. What wording am I using that
would then come after "A is A" and be *the* principle of epistemology?

Reason as man's means of survival.

No. "Reason as man's means of survival" comes way later. We don't
even know that man is a living being yet; we don't know that he has a
conditional existence, that he needs a special method of survival; we don't
have any clue to biology and life. All we know is that there's something,
we have a means to being aware of it, it is what it is, and we want something to guide us to how to acquire knowledge.

"Reason is man's only means of *knowledge*"—in other words, the issue
of reason versus mysticism. That would be number four. That would be
the basic principle of epistemology.

Of course, to know fully what you mean by "reason," you need a whole
system of epistemology: Reason is the faculty that starts with the senses
and forms concepts and uses such and such a method, and so on. That
does not invalidate this point. You can still know that reason is your only
means of knowledge in a general way sufficient to guide you to reach those

details. And here there's an exact parallel to ethics—just as in ethics "Life is the standard" is the base, and then, how do you know what "life" means? You say "man's life," but what *is* man's life? All of the virtues help you to define it—man's life means rationality and independence and integrity and so on. But this doesn't invalidate the hierarchy, and it doesn't mean you start with "honesty."

The same thing is true in epistemology. First you start with the principle, "A certain use of your cognitive faculty as against mysticism," and then you break it up and find out all the steps that it involves. So you could ask, "What then, in essence, does 'reason' mean to you at this early point, before we know all the details?" I would say, in essence, it really tells you, "When you come to conclusions, base them on facts, without contradiction." That's it. It tells you those two things—go by facts, as opposed to feelings, revelations, and so on; and, remember that A is A; therefore, any time you have a contradiction, you're wrong. Those are both issues we've already established—there's a realm of facts, there's reality, and A is A. "Reason," at this stage, amounts to saying, "Follow your early axioms. When you acquire knowledge, acquire it always not by feelings or revelations, and so on." This is the basic principled rejection of mysticism, of the idea that you just take any emotional content that occurs to you, but that you must find some way of focusing only on what is, and on prohibiting contradictions in your thinking.

So you see here a certain pattern. In metaphysics, we have a fundamental—existence—and then later a corollary (identity), and then later yet another one (causality). The same way in epistemology—first there's going to be a fundamental (reason), and then its detailed analysis.

It now becomes pretty simple to figure out where we go from here, within terms of what we've been offered as options. What would have to be next, after "Reason as man's only means of knowledge"? We've got to find out what it is.

Knowledge as objective.

No, "Knowledge as objective" still cannot come at this point. I'm going to give an entire lecture on that next time, the objective versus the intrinsic and the subjective. And that is the conclusion of a whole system of epistemology; you could not even define that, let alone validate it, except by reference to a whole detailed theory of what reason consists of. I will say this—if all you mean by "objective" is "focus on facts, don't go by feelings," I've already covered that, because that's what I'm meaning by "Reason is man's means of knowledge." But if you're speaking more specifically—and that's why I put "versus the intrinsic and subjective"—that does not come here.

We need something that will tell us what reason consists of. We want to anatomize, to break up reason; just as the law of identity specifies existence, what it is, now we want something to tell us what reason is.

The senses as valid.

Yes, "The senses as valid" comes next. You can't know anything about reason unless you know that we have to begin with what we perceive; that's how reason operates; the first is the sensory evidence. And then the next one right away would be—"Concepts and so on," or the nature of concepts. Those two in that order. And then we have grasped what reason is, what this process is that we earlier said is focusing on facts, obeying the law of identity, and now we see the process in much more detail, starting with sensory observation, integrating it into concepts by certain methods, and so on.

At this point we are now ready to stand back and take a summarizing overview. We are still in epistemology, which precedes any of the topics about how man should live and act. We are now strictly in how man acquires knowledge, and there's one more purely epistemological proposition in the twenty. And it would have to go exactly at this point. This is the last epistemological proposition left. And it would have to come at this point, because it presupposes all the others, and it, in turn, is presupposed by all that comes. Not "Mind and body," which has to do with man's nature and the relation of thought and action; that comes later. "Reason as man's means of survival" does not come here. Survival tells what man has to do as a living being; we are still regarding him only as a cognitive being; we first want to get the method of acquiring knowledge, and then we'll say, "A being who acquires knowledge this way, and who is also a living being, who has to struggle to remain alive, had better take such and such an attitude." But we're not there yet. We don't have man as a living being yet, just as a cognitive being; we're still trying to secure how we know; we've given a principle and broken it up into some details, and now we're prepared for "Knowledge as objective." That is a summarizing overview, and it depends on the knowledge of what knowledge is. It's a *conclusion* of epistemology. Before you could say "objectivity," you couldn't even define it, except by saying, "'Objectivity' means forming concepts a certain way and being able to reduce them to sense experience." But you have to have the senses and concepts before you can even have such an idea as "objective" versus "intrinsic" versus "subjective." So that is what I would call a summarizing overview within epistemology.

So you can see epistemology as like three aspects: the fundamental, the details that chew it, and then the generalities that summarize it. And I think you'll find, basically, in every branch of philosophy, that same hierarchical structure. In politics, for instance, the fundamental would be *rights*. And this is from the Objectivist viewpoint. What would the details be? How do you implement rights? What does the government do? And this means a capitalist system with a free market. And then what would be the summarizing overview, the conclusions we come to politically on the basis of having set out this much? Capitalism is practical; the weak have a terrific chance under capitalism, and so on. All those generalities that rest upon a detailed knowledge. In ethics, what would the fundamental be? Life as the standard, and I would throw in there rationality as the main virtue. And then all the details, chewing it—honesty, integrity, and so on. And then what would be the summarizing overview that we can then take as a view once we know the details of what the virtues are? The moral is the practical; first we'd have to know what the moral *is* before we could connect it. Virtue leads to happiness; we'd have to know what virtue *is* before we could get to that. So in every branch, there is a base, a series of chewing it in details, and then an overview that is a vista that opens you to a general conclusion that required those details. I hope that gives you a clear idea.

Just to finish, before I go to the practical branches of philosophy, I would put "The law of cause and effect" in here. I've finished off epistemology, as far as this sheet gives me the chance to do it, and now I would finish off metaphysics; that's the last metaphysical proposition. As I said, I don't think it would be wrong to put that back with "The law of identity," but I put it as number eight because I'm highly conscious that the essence of philosophic organization has to always carry "How do you know what you claim you know?"

Now that we've finished metaphysics and epistemology, we turn to what topic? Does ethics come next? No, it does not. There is an area of philosophy that comes at this point, that rests on metaphysics and epistemology and prepares the ground for ethics and politics as kind of the link between the two, and it itself is not pure metaphysics in the sense of the nature of reality, nor is it epistemology. It's the first application of those very broad abstract subjects to something specific that will then pave the way to ethics. I would say if we had a fifty-story skyscraper, this is about twenty-eight or twenty-nine now; we're getting up into the middle ranges. What is the general name, not the proposition, but the general name of this subject matter? Not metaphysics, and not epistemology. It's also not metaethics, because metaethics is how you validate value judgments, and we're earlier than the issue of value judgments. Rather, this is *the metaphysical* or *essential nature of man.*

We've said a lot about man's nature by implication—how he acquires knowledge, that he's part of reality—but now we have to address ourselves to certain essentials that will make clear what type of entity he is in total, which can then be our guide to how he should live. And what is proposition number one of this branch, that serves as the principle for the metaphysical nature of man?

Integration of mind and body.

No, I would put that second. I'll tell you why in a minute. That is, of course, an issue of man's metaphysical nature. But what could be argued is even more fundamental than that?

Man's life as the standard of value.

No, "Man's life as the standard of value" is already a value judgment; that's ethics and comes after where we are now. You couldn't raise the question "What is the right value for man?" until you know what is man.

Reason as man's means of survival.

Correct. "Reason as man's means of survival." How does that differ from "Reason as man's means of knowledge"? Are those two the same issue? No. One is pure epistemology; it doesn't say anything about life or non-life; it says simply, "If you want to acquire information, this is your means of access to reality." Now we come to, "Here is an entity, and we're going to prescribe a code of action for him." What kind of entity is he? He's a living entity. Every living entity has a means of survival. The only way it can survive is in accordance with that means of survival. What is *man's* means? Whatever it is that gives him the means of coming into contact with reality, that will be his means of survival. If we know already that his means of knowledge is reason, then when we come to what is his means of survival, it must be that faculty. So now we are applying epistemology to the nature of this entity in order to prepare the ground for ethics. And that's why we would have to have "Reason as a means of survival" here.

Why would that precede "The integration of mind and body"? Here there's a certain option. It depends how you interpret "mind and body." So, it wouldn't be completely wrong to put "Mind and body" first, because it depends entirely on what you interpret that to mean. "Mind and body" subsumes many different issues, depending on how you break it up. Some of them are merely direct consequences of basic metaphysics. If you say to me, "How come you as an Objectivist don't believe there's a fundamental clash between mind and body?" what would my answer be? "Mind is consciousness; consciousness is nothing but the faculty of perceiving that which exists; so if you grasp the relationship of consciousness to existence, that would obliterate the whole idea that there's some kind of war between the two." So if I took it on that broad metaphysical level, then obviously this is purely metaphysics. But I didn't interpret it this way. In the same way, you could say the relationship of the senses and concepts is an issue of mind and body, because the senses are reality acting on the physical body, concepts are our mind's way of organizing the data, and therefore, the relation of the two is the physical and the spiritual, and the outer and the inner.

But I wasn't taking "mind and body" here in this very broad sense as including all of metaphysics and epistemology. I had in mind a specific thing—the integration of thought and action, or theory and practice. I'm trying to lay down the idea that this is the type of entity for whom thought is actually practical. When we say reason is man's means of survival, we mean it; reason is not just some disinterested abstract activity that someone pursues at cocktail parties; it actually governs his behavior; he's a union of mind and body. From that point of view, the mind/body issue is simply a specification of "reason as man's means of survival." It's a way of chewing, clarifying, bringing down one step further the basic issue of "reason is man's means of survival."

Okay, since we've been doing most of our chewing on this last half, it should be pretty straightforward from here. What comes next? "Life as the standard of value," the base of ethics. "Rationality as the primary virtue," number twelve. What is the difference between four and twelve? What is the difference between "Reason is man's only means of knowledge" and "Rationality is the primary virtue"? When you say, "Rationality is the primary virtue," "virtue" is a term out of morality; you're saying, "This is good, this is right, this is how people ought to be, this is the basis for deciding everything else about their character." When you say, "Reason is man's means of knowledge," there is no value judgment. That is not an ethical proposition, not a statement of how you should live. It's simply, "If you want to acquire knowledge, this is your faculty." And then because of that, much later, when we get to life as the standard, we say, "The thing you have to cultivate is that faculty," and that's where "Rationality as the primary virtue" comes in.

We now have a clear-cut option in the next two of what would come next. A pure option—you could go in either direction. And what is that option?

The virtue of honesty, and the virtue of independence.

Yes, "independence" and "honesty" are on a par; we've already discussed that, so it could go either way. I put "independence" first, simply because it's not quite as negative as "honesty." But there's no law that you have to do that.

And then what would come next? We've already discussed this in the class last week. What would come next?

The evil of force.

"The evil of force," right. I put that after "independence" and "honesty" because it's a more social consideration. "Honesty" and "independence" still set out what your basic relation to reality has to be. And then, on that basis, we say, "If this is what your relation to reality should be, then you can't do certain things to others." So it's a much more derivative and purely social virtue than "honesty," which defines the essential relation of your mind to reality.

And that takes care of ethics, as far as it is represented on this little sheet, and then we can name the rest. Now we have a choice.

The validation of rights.

That depends. "The validation of rights" *if* you go to politics now; you can go directly to esthetics. Esthetics does not presuppose politics; politics does not presuppose esthetics. So the best way to think about philosophy is like an X, with five points on the crossbars and in the center. The two branches at the top are metaphysics and epistemology; they're on the same level, and they both point into the center, which is ethics. And then from there, you can go down either leg to politics or esthetics. Normally we could do politics first, simply because people are less interested in esthetics. But if we did politics, you're right, "The validation of individual rights" would come next. And what would come after that?

The proper function of government.

"The proper function of government" would have to be next. And only then could you get to "capitalism as the only moral system," because only then would you be in a position to say, "This is what the government should do, and in capitalism this is what the government *does* do, so capitalism is proper."

And now, if we take the esthetic leg, I want to give you two choices there, and I think it's pretty clear which of those two has to be discussed first. Which?

The nature of art.

First "The nature of art"—what it is—and then, of course, your theory of what is good art, and that would be "Romanticism," which I'm putting as number twenty.

[The "corrected" list, put in proper hierarchical order:]

1. Existence exists.
2. Consciousness as the faculty of perceiving that which exists.
3. A is A.
4. Reason as man's only means of knowledge; reason versus mysticism.
5. The senses as valid.
6. Concepts as identifications of concretes with their measurements omitted.
7. Knowledge as objective (versus intrinsic or subjective).
8. The law of cause and effect.
9. Reason as man's means of survival.
10. The integration of man's mind and body.
11. Man's life as the standard of moral value.
12. Rationality as the primary virtue.
13. The virtue of independence.
14. The virtue of honesty.
15. The evil of the initiation of force.
16. The validation of individual rights.
17. The proper functions of government.

18. Capitalism as the only moral system.
19. The nature of art, and its role in man's life.
20. Romanticism as the conceptual school of art.

This has been a reasonably straightforward exercise. It gives you a kind of overview from the beginning. Now I want to throw at you a few propositions, and ask you to number them for me; if it goes between one and two, call it 1-A. "Emotions as consequences of premises." Your first concern should be what section it comes in—is it ethics, is it epistemology, what is it? And then, since you have only a few, it shouldn't be too hard to tuck it in somewhere. What branch is this? This is not epistemology; emotions are not means of cognition. This is the nature of emotions, which are a crucial faculty of man, and what their source is. I'm not telling you how to get knowledge; I'm telling you something about man's essential nature. So this goes in "Man's metaphysical nature." Where does it go? 10-A is correct. It is a specification of the mind/body issue. First you put down "Mind and body are integrated to form a unity," and then against that background you say, "Look at emotions, and you'll see an instance"—we're chewing that principle. So it's the same thing again—each successive level, relative to the preceding, chews, concretizes, breaks down. Again, I think there's a certain option here. You could say something like "Reason is man's means of survival." And then, "What about emotions? Well, emotions are simply consequences of it." And then, "Now I'll draw the broader principle: Just as emotions follow from premises, so mind and body." But I think it's pretty artificial and awkward that way. I think it's much more natural to follow the rule that the principle comes before its details. And here, "Reason and emotion" is a detailed implementation of the mind/body issue.

All right, here's another one: "The primacy of existence," by which we mean facts are independent of consciousness.

After "Knowledge as objective."
No, that's not correct. This is not epistemology. This doesn't say anything about how we acquire knowledge. This is an analysis of what it

means to exist. This is a breakdown, a chewing, of what it means to say something is real. So it belongs to what branch of philosophy? Metaphysics, so it has to be somewhere very early. It couldn't be 1-A, because it says facts are independent of consciousness, so first we have to know about consciousness. I don't think it could be 2-A, because how do you know existence is independent of consciousness? Because it is what it is, it's something; it's not the amorphous nothing that we can make whatever we want. This is just a corollary of "A is A." Therefore, I would say 3-A.

I now want to jump through a few others here. What about "egoism"? And I mean by that the Objectivist view of rational self-interest. That's something we haven't discussed at all in this course. How about at 11-A—that is, right after "life as the standard of value"? But how would you argue for egoism if all you have is "life is the standard of value," and you do not yet have "rationality as the primary virtue"? How could you theoretically argue for "egoism," simply by reference to "life as the standard"? You could argue that a standard implies a purpose. And you could also argue that the essence of life is the achievement of values, not their sacrifice or destruction, and therefore, inherent in a living organism has to be self-sustenance. So you could make a general case. But, I still wouldn't do this, because even though it's very crucial to get the purpose in as close to the beginning as possible, if we're specifying the Objectivist concept of "egoism," essential to that is *rational* self-interest. So from that point of view, I would make it 12-A. I would see as the structure of the base of ethics: "life, rationality, egoism." In other words, "Such and such is the standard, this is the method, and this is the beneficiary." And then the rest is all details of how to carry out the method to reward that beneficiary. The essential Objectivist argument for selfishness, the deepest argument, is that thought requires selfishness, that the integrity of the mind requires selfishness. And from that point of view, it's a *consequence* of rationality; it can't *precede* rationality.

Here's another one to place: "Free will," or "Volitional consciousness."

I would put it as 8-A, the same category as "Cause and effect." Why?

Because free will is what human beings require; it's the effect of the cause of what makes a human being rational.

You mean that free will is a consequence of a certain type of brain, and so on, so it's an instance of cause and effect? I would never look at the question that way, because you do not have to know that to establish free will; you don't have to establish free will by inference from the law of cause and effect. Talking hierarchically, what do you need to know to know a certain proposition? And here, I think you can definitely show that free will is much earlier than cause and effect, as we have here located "Cause and effect." It comes way before "Cause and effect."

I'd say 4-A.

Right after "Reason is man's only means of knowledge"? I think that's a very respectable choice. I'll just tell you frankly, that was my first view, and after a long argument with Harry Binswanger, he convinced me that it should be 3-A. I really could not answer his argument that it was even more basic than "Reason as man's means of knowledge," because it was the precondition of even *having* a means of knowledge; if we were determined, if we had no choice, we would just simply enact whatever came through our consciousness. So the necessity of such a subject matter as "How should I use my mind?" "What principle should I follow, reason or whatever?" presupposes choice, and therefore the need of guidance. So I agree with that; I was converted. And I moved "Free will" up to the status of an actual axiom of epistemology, the precondition of the entire subject.

What about "Atheism"? Here you have real choice. It all depends on what you take God as being. If you're very smart, 1-A. That's pretty fast, though. I would put it at 3-A as about the earliest. First of all, I want "The law of identity" before I start polemics. But if you saw God as the antithesis of the law of identity, it would be a side note after 3; if you see God as essentially the issue of faith or revelation, it would be a side note after 4; if you see God as essentially a miracle worker, it would be a side note after 8. Since this is a fantasy that we are rejecting, it has no intrinsic logically necessary place. It's like the statement "There are no ghosts":

When do you get to that? You don't get to it if nobody brings it up; and since there *are* no ghosts, they can be anything that anybody says. And that's just to indicate to you that when something is that completely non-hierarchical, it's not an intrinsic part of the development, and you just tuck it in anywhere; it's a polemical thing, and you have to separate that off from the actual, essential ideas.

What about "Man is a being of self-made soul"? Here I think it's clear-cut that there are no options, given what we have already got on the chart. This idea depends on at least two roots. Number one, it requires free will. If we have no free will, then we're just automatons reacting to forces acting on us. But what else does it require? Your soul, in the context of that statement of Galt, is your character, your ways of acting, your desires, your emotions. So until you know where your emotions come from, you cannot make this statement that you are a being of self-made soul. "A being of self-made soul" is a summary that rests on "My emotions come from my ideas, and my ideas are within my choice." And therefore, this can't be stated until after "Emotions as consequences of premises." So if that was 10-A, I would call this 10-B.

I want to give you one last one: "Knowledge as hierarchical." That's the whole exercise that we're doing. At what point in the hierarchy can we grasp that knowledge is hierarchical? And here there is one option. What branch of philosophy is that in? Epistemology. Is that a fundamental principle? No. What would you have to know to get to that? You'd have to know an awful lot about how you acquire knowledge—that man is a conceptual being, that concepts are built on earlier concepts, and we can make them wider and wider or subdivided and so on—so where does this have to come? Either 7-A or 6-A, both "knowledge as hierarchical" and "knowledge as objective" are summarizing overviews within epistemology; they are conclusions about knowledge based on the detailed breakup, and there's nothing to say that this has to come before or after "knowledge as objective," as far as I can see.

I want to correct an error that I made—I gave you two 3-As. "The primacy of existence," I said, comes right after "A is A," and "Free will" comes right before "reason is man's only means of knowledge," so I gave them both the same number. Logically, it should be 3: "A is A"; 3-A: "the primacy of existence"—you include the basic thing of reality, it is independent of us; and then 3-B: "Free will," we have a choice about how to get to know it; and then 4: "Reason." So it was incorrect to call "Free will" 3-A; I had forgotten that I had already assigned a 3-A.

I want to march right on, and I want to do a brief spiral exercise. This is, in a way, the reverse of the hierarchy exercise, so it will either clarify everything to you or confuse you. The hierarchy principle says you have to know the earlier first to get to the later, but the spiral issue says you don't know absolutely everything about the earlier one the first time you encounter it; when you go on to the later, that helps you retroactively with the earlier; it enriches it; it concretizes it; as you go, you get a fuller context of knowledge, which redounds backward and makes even clearer and fuller to you the very pieces of information required to get to the later stages. So there's a twofold relationship here: The earlier points pave the way for the later, they show you how to establish things; the later, in turn, enrich, clarify, concretize the earlier. So when do you really have it all? The true is the whole.

Now I want to do the reverse. Up to now, we've been asking only, "Does A precede B?" Now I want to take a B that definitely comes later than A, and see if, retroactively, it sheds some light, some clarity, on A. And you'll see that the unit of philosophy, therefore, is not an isolated proposition, but the whole system: The earlier is required to get to the later, but the later is required thoroughly to understand the earlier. So the only time you get a complete understanding of *any* element is when you know *every* element, and that is what it means to say it's a *system* of philosophy, an *integration*, and not simply a series of discrete items. So in this exercise, I'm going to give you two ideas, one early, one late, and then ask you how the late one helps with the first one, how it helps give us a fuller grasp of the early one. So it's like the reverse of what we were asking before.

Here are two ideas. The early one is the primacy of existence—things are what they are independent of us. The later one is cause and effect. How does cause and effect, when we get there, help us retroactively to get an even fuller idea of the primacy of existence? The primacy of existence is very generalized, right? When we get to cause and effect, we have something more concrete, more specific; we now, in effect, have the idea "An entity has to act a certain way, given its nature, no matter what your desires, your wishes, your hopes, your fears. The identity of things is inexorable; you can't get around it, because an entity acts according to its nature." So the later, which is "cause and effect," helps to chew what is meant by "Facts are inexorable, they're independent of us," by applying it to one category of facts, how entities act; and by doing that, it specifies, makes it more real, more concrete.

Now I'm going to give you a much more difficult one. This is not an easy exercise, primarily because you have to really be at home with these ideas so thoroughly that you can pull two of them out and compare them, but since we have to kind of revivify each one, it's a tremendous strain on the crow epistemology, because you first have to hold one, and then another, and they're both, however concrete, very abstract, and then intersect the two.

So let's just say "the virtue of honesty," which is a derivative virtue, and the point that "emotions come from premises." That emotions come from premises is man's metaphysical nature, and that's much before a derivative virtue like honesty. And yet, when you finally get to honesty and think through what it involves, it retroactively heightens, clarifies, strengthens your understanding of emotions as consequences of premises. Is that too tremendous a jump? I just want to give you a sense of the possibility, you see, of the later retroactively helping to clarify the former.

I think a sense of honesty provides you with some feelings about what emotions were, or are.

In a way. If you focus on honesty from the aspect of its relation to emotions, in clarifying what honesty is, you'll be reaffirming from a new perspective what you learned about emotions coming from premises, as follows: What does honesty involve in relation to emotions? I'm going to be aware of them and their sources; I'm not going to just take them as axioms that I act on, because dishonesty involves saying, "I'm going to put an emotion above reality, I'm going to take it as a primary, I want something regardless of reality, and therefore I'm going to fake it." So dishonesty involves placing an emotion above reality, which implies that an emotion can be treated as a primary. As against what? Merely a consequence of the faculty of thinking and perceiving. So full honesty, in effect, is saying, "I reaffirm that my perception of reality is paramount, and that I won't place my emotions above it, because emotions are merely consequences of my ideas." We had to know this to reach this virtue, but when we reach it and analyze it, we see another angle on the very thing we established about reason and emotion.

Here's a dramatic example: How does Romantic art help to clarify or enrich existence exists? That's number twenty going back to the beginning, the end to the very beginning. And somebody at the seminar actually worked out the following: "When we grasp Romantic art, what that type of art is, it includes the idea of projecting the world as it might be and ought to be. Therefore, it gives us a new angle on the metaphysical versus the man-made—it contrasts what *is* open to man's choice with that which is there irreducibly, about which we can do nothing whatever. So, Romantic art, by stressing what is man's area of choice, implicitly leaves as the residue that which is untouchable: existence, which *everything* has to adhere to." If you ever read a Romantic Realist novel from that point of view, you see, it's art, and it's the last derivative, and yet it gives you a different angle on this generality "Existence exists."

In the seminar, we tried to take two propositions at random from the hierarchy and see whether you can do it, but it became so fantastically stretched that it actually degenerates into rationalism. For instance: We took "The weak have their best chance under capitalism" and tried to show how, when we actually grasp that (which is way late in the game), that helped to clarify "the validity of the senses." And after a lengthy discussion, we concluded that is simply too big a jump. We could take "The weak" back to "Reason," because they survive thanks to the system making the men of reason free; but when you start getting down to "The senses," it gets to be incredibly stretched. Someone said, "Under capitalism, men use their senses, and that enables the weak to survive," but I don't think that adds much.

So when do you fully know a thing? By what stages? First you have to grasp its context, then you have to go beyond it, and that will retroactively clarify it even further. And then you're just going beyond, going up the hierarchy, which is what we've been calling integration with other knowledge, showing how it relates to the other things within your overall structure.

Lecture Five Q & A

Q: Is the use of the hierarchy purely deductive reasoning, and in that sense rationalism?
A: No, absolutely not. We do not just sit there with "Existence exists" and say, "Therefore consciousness, therefore identity, therefore this, therefore all the way through life, therefore"—absolutely not. As we said when we discussed those things, you cannot deduce rationality from life as the standard; that requires observation of man's nature and his means of survival. That is inductive. You can't deduce honesty from rationality. You have to know what does honesty consist of, and what does perceiving consist of, before you can even reach "rationality," and so on. There's a tremendous amount of induction in reaching all of these abstract philosophic principles; the hierarchy is simply a way of relating them logically once we reach them, a way of showing what depends logically on which; but we do not get from one level to the other by deduction.

Q: If metaphysics comes first in the branches of philosophy, then why do the first ten items hierarchically shift between metaphysics and epistemology?
A: Because metaphysics does *not* come first. Metaphysics and epistemology are simultaneous—what exists and how we know it are the foundation that starts together. And that's why the very first axiom is "Existence exists, and the act of grasping this implies there is something, and we have the faculty for being aware of it." And thereafter we shift back and forth, "We have consciousness," "A is A," "Existence is independent of consciousness," "We acquire knowledge by reason," and so on. The two are completely intertwined.

■

Objectivism Versus the Intrinsic and Subjective

We are about to plunge into the most abstract lecture of the course, the first and only topic from fundamental philosophy—from metaphysics and epistemology, rather than from ethics and politics—and we are going to chew that topic. It is the topic of the objective versus the intrinsic and the subjective. I picked this topic for several reasons: partly because I wanted to give you an idea of how we apply the methods of chewing that we've been discussing to *fundamental* issues, and not simply to ones from ethics and politics. And this present topic, although it is certainly much more complex than any of the ones we've taken up so far, is not inconceivably technical. For instance, if we had taken the theory of concepts and had to go into measurement omission, that would be much more technical and complicated. So this seems reasonable for a one-evening task. In addition, in content, this particular topic is extremely important for our present course; it is the actual foundation of being able to understand Objectivism versus rationalism and empiricism. That's why I'm covering it tonight, in preparation for the next three lectures, which are devoted to that issue. There are a great many direct practical results of this topic on all of the issues that we are particularly interested in, and which will constitute the climax of the course: on emotions, repression, judging other people, and so on. If I generalized from Objectivists I have known across the years and had to pick one issue that they have confusions about that is the source of their trouble with Objectivism, it is the failure to grasp the Objectivist view on this issue. I will be chewing this topic myself, step by step, trying to make the issue clear, with lots of examples from real life. I think you'll see that this is going to be relevant to the topic that we're going to discuss at some point on the role of philosophy, and of Objectivism, in actual daily life, because Objectivism in daily life, in very significant part, means objectivity as against the subjective and the intrinsic.

In my experience, part of this issue is clear to most Objectivists, so I think we can deal with that part quickly at the outset and then set it aside. And I mean the issue of objectivity versus subjectivism. I'd like to read a couple of paragraphs where I cover subjectivism in my book *The Ominous Parallels*:

> In metaphysics, subjectivism is the view that reality (the object) is dependent on human consciousness (the subject). In episte-mology, as a result, subjectivists hold that a man need not concern himself with the facts of reality. Instead, to arrive at knowledge or truth, he need merely turn his attention inward, consulting the appropriate contents of consciousness, the ones with the power to make reality conform to their dictates. According to the most widespread form of subjectivism, the ele-ments which possess this power are feelings. In essence, subjectivism is the doctrine that feelings are the creator of facts, and therefore, man's primary tool of cognition. If men feel it, declares the subjectivist, that makes it so.
>
> The alternative to subjectivism is the advocacy of objectiv-ity, an attitude which rests on the view that reality exists inde-pendent of human consciousness, that the role of the subject is not to create the object but to perceive it, and that knowledge

of reality can be acquired only by directing one's attention outward to the facts.*

So subjectivism says, in effect, that the subject—that is, mind or consciousness—creates the object—the world, reality. Feelings—whether your own, if it's the personal version of subjectivism, or some group's, if it's the social version—feelings as the omnipotent element. If you or we or they feel it, that makes it so. As against objectivity, which says A is A, reality is there, it's unaffected by our feelings—in other words, the primacy of existence, on which view the only way to know reality is to study it and try to conform to the facts, rather than try to change them by means of our feelings.

Examples of subjectivism are everywhere. For instance, in the Middle Ages, they thought that the Earth was flat—"For them it was flat"; now we feel it's round—"For us, it's round." In the ancient world, they thought the Earth was at the center—"For them, that was the truth; it was at the center"; now we feel the sun is at the center and so on. If you've ever heard a dispute between an atheist and a theist, both of whom are subjectivists, they'll fruitlessly hash it back and forth for a few minutes, and then the one will say, "For you there's a God, but for me, there isn't." The typical subjectivist takes various disagreements and says, in effect, "There is no one correct answer; there's no universal truth; what I believe becomes true for me; what we believe becomes true for us." The same approach applies to value questions. Altruism versus egoism? I've had many people argue with me and say, "For you, egoism is right; for me, altruism is right; for the Russians, Communism is right," and so on. Whether it's on the level of facts or values, the viewpoint is that there is no such thing as *the* answer; there are only varying opinions applicable only to the consciousness that holds them, for so long as it holds them. Therefore, the theory is, you can't know reality, only your own viewpoint about it, only your own consciousness. The "truth" has to be defined as "whatever the

*Leonard Peikoff, *The Ominous Parallels* (New York: NAL Penguin, 1983), p. 62.

appropriate consciousness decrees." As to "reality," subjectivists vary in their technical views. Somehow or other they all say, "Reality will take care of itself. You pay attention to the controlling consciousness, and reality will take care of itself." Some of them say, "We never come in contact with reality, so who cares?" Others say, "There is no such thing as reality, period, so let's just forget it." Others say, "Yes, there may be a reality, but all we ever know is the reality that we affect; therefore, reality, practically speaking, bends itself to our feelings, it molds itself, it becomes what we want. So if we believe something, reality becomes that." Of course, there are many realities on that view—you have your reality, and I have mine, and so on.

Metaphysically, therefore, subjectivists dispense with reality as a factor to be reckoned with; and epistemologically, they say look inward for all guidance; the only thing you have to consult is some consciousness.

Notice a couple of points here. Subjectivists insist that consciousness has a nature, that it's something, that it has an identity. In fact, they make that one of the pinnacles of their viewpoint, because they say, "Each of our consciousnesses has a very definite identity; it's something, it has to operate according to its particular nature; so how could we ever jump outside our consciousness and see reality as it really is by itself? All we can ever really know is reality as it goes *through* our consciousness. And therefore, all we can ever know is the world that we ourselves subjectively interpret, or in other words, subjectively create." That's Kant's philosophy. He is really the modern father of subjectivism. His argument, as he presents it, rests on the idea, "Our consciousness is something very definite and specific, with a definite nature; therefore, we're cut off from any true reality. All we can know is the reality that we create." And that is subjectivism.

Notice also that the subjectivist on the street makes a big deal out of the fact that people disagree. To him, the most obvious thing to convert you to subjectivism is to say, "You think this and he thinks that," as though that's then self-evident, "Who's to say?" The obvious implication is that there's no automatic way of getting the truth from reality. And that's true—disagreement does prove that there is no automatic way to get the truth. We can all expose ourselves to reality and come up with different answers. The subjectivist concludes that if there's no *automatic* way, there's *no* way; no automatic answers, then there are *no* answers; so we'd better give up reality and take refuge in our own consciousness.

We have not yet said a word to *validate* objectivity. I just so far have tried to give you a preliminary idea of how it contrasts with subjectivism. But the main topic we want to get to tonight is the *trichotomy*, if I may use that word. There are three different theories on this question. Subjectivism is one, to which Objectivism is obviously opposed, by its very name. But it is just as opposed to a third viewpoint, and Ayn Rand actually coined the term for this third viewpoint—*intrinsicism*. And that is what we want to start looking at.

Now you may think, "The way to express the Objectivist view is simply to say, 'Adhere to reality in your thinking.'" That would capture our opposition to subjectivism; the subjectivists dispense with reality. But it would *not* capture our opposition to intrinsicism. If you said to an intrinsicist, "The crucial thing is to conform your mind to reality, obey reality," he would say, "Wonderful, I couldn't agree with you more. I'm one hundred percent in favor of obedience to reality." An intrinsicist really means that, yet his viewpoint is just as wrong, just as disastrous, as subjectivism.

What we want to do is to form a concept of the objective that will contrast at once to the subjective and the intrinsic. So we'll have to steer a proper line and not fall into either of these views.

I'd now like to have a little exercise for about two minutes, and that's what I would call a "blurting out" exercise. We're trying to learn the method of chewing, so we want to plunge in and get an idea, "What is this idea of the objective?" If you try to, at the outset, rattle off some formal definition, your mind will simply reel. It's not prepared; you don't have all the data before you that led to that definition; there are too many points in any proper definition to be able to retain. And therefore, if you started chewing this by saying, "Miss Rand says 'objective' is," and then repeat one of those sentences, even if that's the briefest sentence that could capture it, it's like a body blow to your mind (if I may mix metaphors). You can't approach a subject this complicated, when you are unclear, without some kind of anchor or guide or peg that you can rely on as your basic mental guide, your organizer, your compass. And this is applicable to more than just the topic of the objective, although this is how we're illustrating it. "Honesty" wasn't that tricky a concept. But this one is tricky. If you don't have some kind of guide to help you delve into the subject, you will simply drown in a mass of qualifications and details that you cannot hold.

This guide, once you have it, is only a general orienter. It's just the first step. You then need to expand it, to work out the details, the aspects, the formal definitions, the chewing, and so on. And so if I could give you an analogy, it's like this: If you want to get to Los Angeles from New York, you have to have a basic direction; you have to say, "I'm going west." That's what you blurt out, so to speak, to keep you oriented. And then you can have maps and you consult highway signs and topography and so on for the details of the road. And if ever you get lost and can't make heads or tails of the map, you come back to, "I know I'm going west, so I'll go to the garage and ask him which way is west."

What we need is some kind of very crude thing like that. To go west will not take us to Los Angeles, but at least if we follow that, we will not end up in Rhode Island. And at this point, we want to get that kind of basic anchor. And the only way to do it is to blurt out in a few words a clue as to what objectivity would consist of. It's like a simplified, inelegant, sloppy, super-super-essential definition that no one else would understand. Obviously, if it's too blurry—it's like saying, "I'm going west, but 'west' covers everything from Mexico to Canada"—it won't take you anywhere. As I'm going to show you at the end, you could blurt out the essence of the concept of the objective in two words. It really would be clearer at the end. So, what are some possibilities? How about "consciousness of reality"? An intrinsicist will say, "Certainly consciousness of reality; the whole thing of knowledge is consciousness of reality." How about "form of knowledge"? This is trying to suggest the idea that knowledge is held in a certain form. And that is on the track, but again, an intrinsicist could say, "I'm aware of knowledge, so I hold it somehow, in some form." With the subjectivist, it's not too hard to blurt it out; you could just say, "Obey reality," and that would certainly distinguish you from the subjectivist, but it does not distinguish you from the intrinsicist. How about "perception within my context"? But that suggests the possibility of subjectivism, because the subjectivist would say, "Sure, that's just what I say—you can't get out of your context; when you perceive, your whole context is brought to bear on it, and the result is you never see things as they really are."

The whole trick with this is to grasp objectivity in such a way that you don't slip into the subjective on the one side or the intrinsic on the other. You can't distinguish objective from intrinsic until you know what the intrinsic theory is. So I want to forget about the objective for a while, and go at some length into intrinsicism, which is a much more complex theory for people to grasp. And by the way, philosophically, intrinsicism has been much more influential than subjectivism ever dreamed of being.

The intrinsicist says, "Reality is crucial; reality is all there is; reality is the sole factor in cognition. Consciousness contributes, essentially, nothing to the process. Consciousness is only an empty mirror. It has no nature of its own, no effect on the process of cognition. There's no process it has to go through, no particular method it has to use. Consciousness is like an emptiness on which reality writes. In the same way as an object strikes a mirror and the mirror does nothing, it just reflects what's there, consciousness is like that." On this view, consciousness is passive in two fundamental senses. It's passive metaphysically—it can't change or alter the nature of reality. That's the primacy of existence, which intrinsicists are strong advocates of. And, consciousness is passive epistemologically—it doesn't do anything to acquire knowledge; it just has to expose itself, wait, and then get the illumination.

There *is* a form of human cognition that does live up to this model: sense perception. With sense perception, there are entities out there— tables, chairs, and so on—they act on you, on your sense organs. Your mind, at least as an adult, does nothing; you just turn your eyes, wait, expose yourself, and you're struck, that's it; there's absolutely nothing you have to do. You open your eyes and look and you see my face. There's no mechanism, no methodology, no process; it's pure passivity on your part. And if I say to you when you look at me, "How do you know I'm here?"

you would say—precisely because it's a completely passive thing—"Look. I can't say any more about it; it's obvious, it's self-evident." Which, in fact, it is. And that's all you can say about percepts.

If you wanted to haggle, you could say that there were physiological processes our brains had to learn to go from sensation to perception when we were infants, and there is a certain issue of focus involved now—if you let your eyes blur, you won't see me clearly—but leaving aside those technicalities, it's true that sense perception is an example of pure passivity. There is no method of seeing; you just open your eyes.

Since this is obvious to anybody, this is *not* what is involved in the discussion of the intrinsic versus the objective. The trichotomy does *not* apply to sense perception. I would not call sensations "objective," nor would I call them "intrinsic," nor would I call them "subjective." None of those terms apply. The issue arises only on the conceptual level. On the perceptual level, at least on this point, there is no debate; you just passively expose yourself, and that's it.

But the point of the intrinsicist is that the conceptual level operates just like the perceptual level. Reality operates on our minds just as directly, he thinks, in the *conceptual* realm as in the *perceptual*. There are certain entities intrinsic in reality (thus the name, you see, "intrinsic," entirely apart from us) that act on our minds; not on our senses, but on our minds. And all we have to do is turn our minds to those entities, and then they strike us, we're illuminated, we know. And if you ask a person, "How do you know?" he gives exactly the answer on the conceptual level that we would all give on the perceptual level. He says, "You just know, it's obvious, it's self-evident." There's no more he can say to you than, "Look, look with the eyes of the mind, not with your physical eyes, and you will discover that there are special nonsensory entities out there, acting on you, leading to all crucial knowledge." An intrinsicist, therefore, feels no need to base knowledge on sense experience. Why not? For him, conceptual conclusions are arrived at independently of perceptual conclusions, simply by these intrinsic entities acting on his mind. And it's just as obvious on the conceptual level as it is on the perceptual level, when you come to a conceptual conclusion that it's true merely by looking at the entities involved in reality. Usually they think the senses are invalid, but in any case, even if they *did* think they were valid, they would say, "Sensory knowledge is completely independent of conceptual knowledge; we don't have to discuss it to discuss concepts."

A subjectivist says, "Consciousness is the only factor in knowledge; reality is irrelevant." The intrinsicist is the exact opposite: "Reality is the only *key* factor; consciousness contributes nothing but passive receptivity. Some kinds of entities intrinsic in reality act on you and create knowledge. Therefore, no work is required for cognition." And no such course as this one would be possible. There's no chewing required to understand; there's no laborious process of concretizing and integrating. Reality does all the work for you. Of course there could be no course on perceiving objects, because you just do it automatically. And the intrinsicist view is: Reality does the same thing on the conceptual level. Or we can put his point this way—"Reality alone tells you how to follow it. All you have to contribute is not to resist. But if you leave yourself open, reality will sweep you irresistibly to the full truth."

That of course is very abstract so far, so let's try to concretize the intrinsic as it comes up in daily life. We'll take a person who has an intuition of what horse is going to win in the sixth race at Belmont. You ask him how he knows: It came to him; he feels that he just knows. Of course, a subjectivist could *also* say he feels it, but to keep his union card, he would have to say, "For me, this horse is going to come in, but for you, maybe not." And even after the race, the real subjectivist will say, "You never can tell who won. You think he won, but I don't," and so on. The intrinsicist also has a very strong feeling, but he thinks, "My feeling is really right. There's one reality, and I know it. This is the real truth, and anybody who disagrees with me is wrong—number four is coming in." So it is emotionalist, but it is what we can call a *righteous emotionalism*—it's still the idea of a feeling as a tool of cognition, but it's a feeling that he definitely believes gives him the one correct answer. If you ask him *how* he knows, that's the whole point—he has no method, no process, no steps. He just knows. It carries a powerful conviction to him, just like sensory perception; and he's *annoyed* if you ask him. He may say, "I don't know, I just know." Or, he may say, "I have a special access to these things that you don't. Only certain people get these messages. Something out there told me." Something intrinsic in reality takes the total burden and acts on him, and he just waits, accepts, smiles, and then of course loses his bankroll the next day.

Take another example: Somebody is offered a job, has seemingly great advantages, but he has a premonition of disaster—"Something is going to happen. It's just not good to take this job. I just know there's going to be trouble." Of course, in actual life, there can be many different subconscious factors, observations, and so on that were fed to him and that caused him to have this feeling of disaster. Maybe he perceived something that he hasn't identified. But you would normally say, "We need to analyze where this comes from. Are you really grasping something that is important to discover? Maybe your feeling is right. Or maybe you are afraid of this job, and the whole thing is rationalizing; you're grabbing on something out of context." But that, of course, is not the intrinsicist viewpoint. His viewpoint is that no analysis is necessary. He's struck by this powerful sense, "Disaster is going to happen, I know." No analysis, no process, no steps, nothing. He may call it intuition; if he's religious, he may call it revelation; if he's a Nazi, he may call it the prompting of his blood. There are a thousand names for it.

All of parapsychology is based on this approach, because the key to the parapsychologist is: Some kind of events intrinsic in reality act on you, and you know them just like perception, without any method or process, but it's *not* perception; they insist that it's *extra*-perception. It's a *mental* perception, not a *sensory* perception. This is squarely the intrinsicist viewpoint. And that's why all they can say is, "I just know." It's not subjective, they say; when they have their so-called precognition, they really "know," they think. But they know without any method of awareness. Parapsychology is just the intrinsicist position rewritten to apply to psychological phenomena without an overt reference to God or religion.

I think you can see an obvious tie-in with the intrinsicist position and with mysticism. Intrinsicism and mysticism are not the same, but they're related. Mysticism is the view that knowledge can be acquired by means other than the senses or reason. A mystic believes that knowledge is possible—he's not a skeptic; he thinks he has the real answers—but the essence of his theory is that no process is necessary to validate one's knowledge, no analysis, no proof. If you say that you have a means of knowledge other than the senses or reasoning, what *is* that means of knowledge? When you strip through all the terminology, it comes down to, "I just know, and you don't see it." You know the famous expression, "to those who understand, no explanation is necessary; to those who don't, none is possible." In either case, they don't explain. Intrinsicism, therefore, implies mysticism. I don't mean to say that all intrinsicists are mystics, because I have known intrinsicists who are truly motivated by the desire to conform to reality; they want to adapt their minds to reality. And they think that there are only two choices—either you're a subjectivist or you say, "My consciousness will simply obey reality and contribute nothing." And so their motive is not mystical; they want to uphold reason. But what I've tried to show is that *by* their basic approach, they are led ultimately to mysticism by implication, because they are led to the idea of accepting conclusions without any processing or proof.

Philosophically, intrinsicism is more basic than mysticism. Intrinsicism is like the metaphysics of mysticism. Intrinsicism is one basic theory of the relationship of consciousness to existence. That's as fundamental a topic as you can get. And it says, in effect, "Consciousness is nothing; existence is all." And then, on that basis, mysticism becomes the appropriate epistemology—"Then accept whatever strikes you." There would be no way to justify mysticism except on this view of intrinsicism as its foundation. If you ask a mystic, "How do you know?" his answer has to come down to, "Reality told me." And if you say to him, "But what did you do to validate your view?" he'd say, "I don't have to validate. I just exposed myself; reality acted on me." So intrinsicism is the model underlying all mysticism. So the way I would put it is: All intrinsicists are potential mystics, and all mystics are implicit intrinsicists.

I want to note a few points just on these examples to help develop the theory of intrinsicism. What is the intrinsicist idea of the nature of consciousness, its distinctive characteristics, qualities, and so on? In a word, the intrinsicist view is, "Consciousness has no nature; consciousness is a pure empty mirror." And in fact, the intrinsicist philosophers agree with Kant and echo his point repeatedly; they say, "If consciousness *did* have a nature, then it couldn't know reality, because then we would be trapped in the nature of our own consciousness, and we could never get out and see true reality. And therefore," they say, "the only way to say that we know reality is to say that the mind is nothing but pure receptivity—it adds nothing, it contributes nothing, there's no such thing as the distinctively human consciousness." I regret to say that Aristotle implied the acceptance of this viewpoint in the *De Anima*, and the whole Aristotelian tradition has upheld this as the only answer to subjectivism.

You can see why the intrinsicists are led to this view, if we take an analogy of the stomach. Suppose somebody advocated on the level of eating, "You can take in anything, swallow anything, in any quality, any quantity, any order. Just pour it in your mouth and let your stomach take it in—nails, roast beef, Kleenex, bedspreads, rotten tomatoes—just pour it all in." Your immediate answer would be, "The stomach is *something*; it has to digest what it takes in, and it can't digest what you have just enumerated. It has to go through *some* process, and that implies there are only *certain* kinds of ingredients, in *certain* quantities, in a *certain* order. A is A, a stomach is a stomach." The intrinsicist takes that first view of consciousness. He says, in effect, "You can pour any idea into a consciousness, any idea, in any order, in any quantity. No processing is necessary; no digesting is necessary; you don't need to do anything to assimilate it; you just toss it in." How is it that we're able to absorb that? "Because our consciousness is nothing but absorbing. And therefore, it contributes nothing, it puts down no requirements, there are no necessities—anything can be tossed in, because it has no nature."

Be clear that intrinsicism is an issue of the method (or lack of method) that a mind uses. It has nothing to do with its content. For instance, if I tell you a man is a socialist, could you tell me from that whether he's an intrinsicist, a subjectivist, or an Objectivist? No, you could not, not any one of those three. Because what if the person, for instance, thinks it's arguable and it's provable—even if he's wrong—he thinks you can give arguments that objectively establish that socialism is true? That would still mean to that extent he's within the objective approach. What would make him an intrinsicist? If he says what? "It's self-evident. I don't have to argue this question. I don't know how I know; I just know." What would make him a subjectivist? If he says, "Socialism is true for me."

Intrinsicism means automatic illumination on conceptual issues. How would this apply to questions of value judgments, morality? It's the same. On this viewpoint, moral or evaluative questions are also self-evident: You merely expose yourself to reality, and some kind of intrinsic entity acts on you and produces illumination; you simply automatically infallibly know what is the good, in the same way you infallibly know what is the true. How do you know? You just know. No method, no process, no steps. Sometimes advocates of this view say we have a special moral faculty that is like the perceptual faculty, and it's attuned to goodness or rightness. Sometimes they call it the "moral sense," and sometimes they call it "conscience." But whatever the terminology, the idea on the value level is: Reality writes on you; the good out there simply acts on you.

Many people who never heard the word "intrinsicism" hold this view. For instance, "We need to help the poor." If you ask people why, a lot of people will just look at you and say, "What do you mean, 'Why?'? It's obvious, that's the good." And if you ask them, "How do you know?" they'll say, "What do you mean, how do I know? That's self-evident." A subjectivist would say, "For me, you should help, while for you . . . ," but that's not what we're talking about. We're talking about people who say this is the right thing to do. If a person gives an argument, "We have to help the poor because—" and he gives some reasons, then, to that extent, that's not intrinsicism; he's trying a process of validation. But for most people today who believe this type of view, they simply think you just *have* to be this way; something in reality mandates it, and you just know it. Or take pacifists. Pacifists are typically intrinsicists, because their attitude is, "Killing is wrong, *intrinsically*." How do you know? "Just inspect the act; just look, and you will see that an inherent attribute of the act is its evil; it just leaps out at you." These people make no distinction between killing in self-defense and a war of initiated aggression. Who kills whom for what with what result—all of that's beside the point. Killing has an inherent attribute, which is badness, and you just attune yourself to the act, and you grasp it; it's self-evident.

Or take egalitarianism in its commonest interpretation. "Differences in income are bad; inequalities as such are unjust." Why? Some people give whole complex arguments, but the typical egalitarian says, "That's obvious." It doesn't make any difference what the cause is of the inequalities, or the effects; it doesn't make any difference in what they are unequal; it's just intrinsically bad. I took a philosophy class many, many years ago, and the professor put before the class this situation: "Imagine we have one society where there are tremendous differences in income from the lowest to the highest, and in another society where everybody has the identical income, which is, however, lower than the lowest one in the first society. Which one," he asked, "is the morally superior society?" And I was the sole person in the class of about fifty who voted for the first society. The rest of the class—and this was a graduate course in ethics—considered this simply out of the question, "Equality is intrinsically good, and therefore, it's much better that we all starve as brothers."

You hear this kind of thing all the time. Bigness is bad. Extremism is bad. There's no question of what kind, what effects, what causes, what context, nothing—it just has an attribute in it that it's bad. And how do you know? "Anybody knows." Violence is bad. What's violence? Is it self-defense, is it the police arresting a criminal? Whatever it is, it's bad, and everybody knows it. It's the idea that goodness or badness is like a little nugget that resides inside actions or states, apart from human purposes, apart from the causes of their actions, apart from the effects.

I think the most eloquent philosopher to subscribe to this view was John Stuart Mill. He was the champion of the greatest happiness of the greatest number. One of his arguments was, in structure, like this: "Pleasure is the good. Therefore, the more pleasure, the more goodness in the world. Therefore, we should live for the greatest pleasure of the greatest number, because the more pleasure we bring into the world, the more goodness, and what more can you ask of an ethical man than to bring a lot of goodness into the world?" If you said to him, "Good for whom?"

he'd say, "What do you mean, good for whom? Goodness isn't good *for* anything; goodness is just goodness." He would say, "When you say something is a rug, do you say a rug *for whom*? You say a rug, that's it." And if a rug was the thing that was important, we'd heap up as many rugs as we could. Pleasure has got this little attribute goodness in it. So it doesn't make any difference *whose* pleasure; we just have as much pleasure as we can. The philosopher who first formulated this view—goodness as an entity out there in the world, pure goodness that acts on us and causes our conclusions as to value judgments—was Plato: the Form of the Good, which is pure good. And of course, you couldn't possibly ask Plato, "What is the Form of the Good good for?" He would be scandalized at that question. He would hear that question exactly as you would hear, if somebody said to you, "What is reality real for?" and you'd say, "What do you mean what is it real for? It's real." And Plato would say, "What do you mean what is it good for? It's good, and it's out there, and it just acts on us."

There are three points in particular that I want to mention here about intrinsicism in value judgments. They're all implied in what I already said, but they're going to come up over and over, and I want to introduce you to them in a general way now.

First of all, *an intrinsicist regards human purposes as irrelevant to value judgments.* For him, you cannot say, "Good for what?" On the Objectivist view, value is of value to whom and for what; value implies a goal-directed action, an ultimate goal that becomes the standard of value. But, in fact, the intrinsicist thinks that if you set up an ultimate goal, if you introduce a purpose and a beneficiary, you become subjective. It's like saying, "True for whom, true for what? The true is true, and the good is good, period." So we have the idea of value apart from purpose, and therefore, apart from valuer, apart from beneficiary, apart from results; and this is defended as the only way to be nonsubjective in the value realm.

A second characteristic of intrinsicism in value judgments: Not only is purpose irrelevant, but *context is irrelevant.* And this, of course, follows from the point that purpose is irrelevant. Let me first, by contrast, indicate to you what the correct approach would be. Assuming you have a purposeful approach to ethics—for instance, you say life is the standard—then that purpose defines good and evil. And then when you come to evaluate an act like killing, you say, "I can't give you a flat answer, 'Killing is good' or 'Killing is bad,' because there are two very different kinds determined by their different relations to my standard, my ultimate goal. Killing the innocent is anti-life, but killing the guilty in self-defense is defense of life against its destroyers. So, by reference to my ultimate goal, the allegedly same one action really comes out as two very different actions." And so you would say, "I can't say killing is wrong flatly. It depends on the context. It depends on the circumstances. It depends on its relation to the ultimate goal in that type of situation." By "context" here, we mean all the relevant facts that have to be brought to bear in order to tell whether the action is right or not. Since, for the intrinsicist, certain actions have an in-built goodness or badness, the circumstances and effects are simply beside the point. And that is why the Bible says, "Thou shalt not X, thou shalt not Y." It doesn't say, "In these circumstances so-and-so"; it doesn't even consider context. That's, of course, the Ten Commandments, which are ten intrinsicist rules of ethics without any context. This is not, of course, restricted to religion. I'll give you an "Objectivist" example—that is, not actually, but one I've heard many times from Objectivists. It goes like this—it's usually said by a college student—"I know you mustn't be dependent. Therefore, if I depend on my parents for funds to go to college, that's dependency, and that is therefore evil, flatly. Dependence is taking a value from someone else, not earning one's own way, and that's bad." This is an intrinsicist approach to Objectivism. Because what would you say in fact? Whether you should take money from your parents for college depends on many factors: It depends on the circumstances; it depends on the *context*. I could certainly specify contexts in which it *would* be dependence and *would* be improper—if you're a lazy bum, you're coasting along, you never do any work, you're in your forties and you're still going to high school—that is certainly against the requirements of life. But, if you're a teenager or in your twenties, your parents can afford it, you're working hard, you're in a difficult situation because the economy has been wrecked, so you're preparing yourself for self-sufficiency, nobody has to sacrifice—in that context, it's perfectly pro-life.

The same single action—taking money from your parents—in different contexts can come out as either good or bad. But for an intrinsicist Objectivist (which is a self-contradiction), all he retains is, "If it's independent, it's good, and if it's dependent, it's bad, and that's it." This leads to the approach of dogmatic absolutes. By "dogmatic," I mean without specifying any context or circumstances; it's simply "Thou shalt not take money from thy parents." And since it's experienced as self-evident—"I just know that this is true"—there's no sense of the need to analyze it. There's no inner sense guiding the person to say, "You have to break this up and say, 'Under these circumstances, what is the principle, how does it relate to my basic values?'"—all of that is gone.

Another example: "You shouldn't sanction evil," and he absorbs that like "Thou shalt not kill"—"Thou shalt not sanction evil." How do you apply this generality in a particular case? In what context does it lead to what kind of action? Does it mean that if you're at a job and your boss comes in and utters a political opinion that you are opposed to, you are obliged to stand up, punch him in the mouth, and say, "This is an outrage, and I'm not going to sanction evil"? If so, that's incompatible with life as the standard; you can't go on living. Obviously, it doesn't mean *that*. It would take a half an hour to specify what are the contexts in which that comes up, how should it be applied, what is the principle, and so on. But if you're an intrinsicist, you just get emblazoned on your mind, "Must not sanction evil, must not be dependent." And that is an Objectivist version of intrinsicism.

Let's go to one more point in regard to an intrinsicist on value judgments. Purpose is out, context is out, and the third thing that's out is *choice* or *options*. An intrinsicist finds choice or options anathema; to him, that's the foot in the door of subjectivism. His view is that everything is dictated by reality; consciousness contributes nothing; therefore, if you inject your preferences, that is a scandal—you are mucking up the direct grasp of reality by this kind of inner element that's utterly out of the picture now. If you said to him, in regard to mathematics, "I prefer the Pythagorean theorem to a different one," you would realize that that, of course, is ludicrous. And he takes all value questions as just like that—either reality said it, or it didn't say it; if it said it, then you must accept it, and if it didn't say it, then you can't accept it, and that's it. So there is no choice on value judgments, no options.

Again, I have heard budding Objectivists take this view, and do it in the name of objectivity. For instance, I don't know how many times I've gotten this one—"Why doesn't every Objectivist have to be a philosopher?" At first I didn't understand that, and then I had it explained to me as follows: "Miss Rand said that we should have productive careers, and a career is supposed to involve the fullest use of your mind. The fullest use has to involve the widest abstractions. Philosophy involves the widest abstractions. Therefore, everyone should be a philosopher, and all other professions are inferior." Leaving aside the gross *non sequiturs* in that argument—whether they think philosophy's at the top, or fireman, is irrelevant—what they think is: Reality dictates careers, and therefore, you just sit back and study it, and the right career will be dictated by reality; and you have no more right to a preference in your career, or in your wife or husband, than you have in regard to geometric truth; facts are facts; expose yourself and you will know.

So we have value judgments without explanation, without purpose, context, or choice—because they're just self-evident. This is a very widely held view of ethics, and the effect on people who take this view, in the short run or the long run, is that they come to think that value judgments are utterly arbitrary (which of course they are by this view, because there's no explanation), they think value judgments are detached from life (which of course they are on this view, because they have no effects that are relevant, no purposes that they serve), they think that value judgments are just dogmatic absolutes that half the time you follow and half the time you resent, they think you have to repress your own desires in order to follow value judgments because there is no room for choice, options. So what typically happens with this type of intrinsicist is that he starts off as a fervent moralist, and partway through he just gets sick of the whole thing, and he ends up as a subjectivist, and he says, "To hell with all that stuff, live it up. Take anything you want; it's good for you; that's all you need if it leads to what you feel you want at the moment." So he sinks to the idea that *everything* is a choice.

I've illustrated these points on value judgments, but all of the same points are applicable on purely intellectual issues also. And you will see that intrinsicism on the purely intellectual level is also the idea that purpose is irrelevant to the pursuit of truth, that context is irrelevant, that choice or options are irrelevant, inapplicable; and you will see that, even where value judgments aren't involved, an intrinsicist is against purpose, context, options, on all questions.

Now I'll give you an example of intrinsicism in regard to politics, in particular, property rights, and this was the question put to me: "I swim up to a desert island that is owned by somebody, it's his property, and the guy says to me, 'This is my property, keep off, just tread water until you die.' What do you say I should do? Am I not obligated to leave? After all, he's got a right to his property." Of course, my answer to that is, that's the theory of *intrinsic rights*, so that somewhere in the island, if you dig it up, you'd find oil, and beneath that is the right to it. But that's ridiculous. Rights depend upon a whole context of organized society; they are the conditions alone in which men can coexist, where every man has the chance to live. But if you have a situation like this where it's his rights or your life, it's finished as the end of rights; the context is gone, and you kill him before he kills you. And yet, here was a person trying to be faithful to the idea of rights, but as a complete dogma.

The most common, institutionalized form of the intrinsic view is religion. God is the entity intrinsic in reality that is claimed to be the revealer of truth, and in morality he gives you commandments. That is the essence of the intrinsicist viewpoint (although, as we've seen, it does not have to take a religious form). Historically, the real author of this is Plato, because his universals, or Forms, were the intrinsic entities out there that acted on our minds, and then what happened historically is that Plato's universals moved into God's mind; but that merely changed the name. This is so widespread today that if you say to somebody, "Such and such is an absolute," they automatically equate that with a dogmatic, contextless, arbitrary, religious absolute; they can't *conceive* of an absolute that is not the same as a divine revelation. And consequently today, you have got only two people in the field: those who say, "Yes, there are absolutes, which come from God," and those who say, "That's ridiculous, there is no God, it's all a matter of opinion; what's true for you isn't true for me." If you want a perfect formulation of the intrinsicist view—I think it was from Numenius—"All knowledge is the kindling of the small light by the great light that illumines the world." The great light that illumines the world is God, the small light is your mind, and he just sets fire to it (I don't mean in the sense of destroying it)—he illuminates it and you grasp. That's it; that's the absolute intrinsicist view of knowledge.

After religion began to atrophy, the same basic approach to knowledge was adopted in secularized form. The same idea was implanted in people's minds: that something external was supposed to act on you and illuminate you with the revealed truth, but as God began to fade from the picture, what replaced him as the external entity intrinsic in reality that gives the revelations? The Führer, the government, the bureaucrats, the president, the Princeton Institute of Advanced Studies, the Harvard professor, and so on. Intrinsicism breeds authoritarianism, because something outside of you has to act on you to give you truth. Your role is passive, it's simply to be illuminated, and in practice that means you have to wait until somebody else fills you up, sets off that fire. In the past, it was the priest, and now it's the government. But it's the same basic philosophy. You can also see it in regard to computers. How many people say, "The computer said this, so it has to be true; it was on that screen"? I don't have to refute that. You know GIGO, "garbage in, garbage out."

I'm still chewing the intrinsic. You see in how many different ways you can advocate Objectivism, and yet out of a desire to be faithful to reality and not be a subjectivist, you can become an intrinsicist. I gave examples of moral dogmatism. Another example would be the overuse of the self-evident—how many times have you heard somebody think Objectivism, or half of it, or one-quarter of it, is literally self-evident; therefore, anybody who disagrees is necessarily dishonest. Why? Because if only he looked at reality, he'd know; it takes dishonesty not to grasp it; everybody other than Ayn Rand was simply dishonest, and her contribution was only that she was honest. That is the model that some people operate with, and that is intrinsicism, and that, of course, is a complete corruption of the self-evident. The only self-evident is the *perceptual* level; no philosophy is self-evident.

I want to give you another important category in which Objectivists, despite themselves, have a tendency to intrinsicism. This is what I would describe as *improper self-criticism in the face of error.* Consider a case where you're playing poker, where, in a given situation, the most rational thing to do is a certain move, for instance, not to draw a card. You follow the right rule, but you lose by doing so, and you see when the cards are finally turned up that if only you had done the opposite of the right method, you would have gotten an ace and you would have won a fortune. I'm sure that you've all had this experience. There's no way to have known; it's a freak; it was just simply bad luck. But, if you say to yourself in that situation, "I *should have* drawn the card, how stupid," that is intrinsicism. Why? Because you're condemning yourself on the basis of having had limited knowledge and following a definite method. You're saying to yourself, "I should have known in a case where there was no possible means of knowledge." So you're implying, "Means should not be necessary. I should have had a revelation. I should have ignored my human method of knowing. Since I went by the objective evident, I was no good." This is condemning yourself for being objective, and implicitly holding the intrinsic as the model, the ideal of knowledge.

Take a ludicrous example. There are two forks in the road, and you study the two and which one you should drive on, and on the left you find that the bridge is out and it's suicide, while on the right it's perfectly safe by everything you know—you take the right, and you're hit by a meteor. Now would you say, "You see, I'm so stupid, I should have taken the other one"? Obviously not. You would say you went by the evidence, you should have done exactly what you did in that context. But, if you feel "I should have known" in a case where it is impossible for you to have known, that implies holding revelation as your model of knowledge, and criticizing yourself because you didn't get it. And that is taking intrinsicism as your cognitive theory.

Here's one last example of improper self-criticism, what I myself have been guilty of and unfortunately sometimes am to this day. I'll write a section for some article or book according to an outline that I thought was appropriate, then I find in the process of writing that the last point should have come first. And I think to myself, "Oh, stupid, I should have started with that point." That's the same thing, because in actual fact, I could not have known to the best of my ability that that particular point should come first until I tried actually organizing it one way, and then I realized logically it required a different structure. The abstraction is this—and you can fall into it despite your knowledge just by lapsing on your awareness—if you castigate yourself for an error, that is generally intrinsicism, because the theory leaves no room for fallibility. The intrinsicist approach is that there is nothing to be done to get the truth but look at reality, so if you didn't get it, you must be guilty; you just didn't attend to the message reality is beaming at you. "It was a stupid error on your part." Now there *are* stupid errors, but that means when you're sloppy, when you're out of focus, when there are known facts and you just disregard them. The point is: Not all errors are stupid. But according to intrinsicism they are, because, in effect, everything is self-evident on this view, and so if you don't know, you are stupid for not knowing.

Now let's look at intrinsicism in relation to subjectivism. (We still haven't reached the objective yet.) The subjectivist doesn't grasp that existence exists, that we have to conform to it. And that's an obvious error. What is it that the intrinsicist does not grasp at root? What's the source of all the other mistakes? One thing. He says, "Yes, we have to conform to reality," but he leaves out one crucial word—"We have to conform to reality . . . somehow." That's it. Reality does not do it for us; we have to engage in some kind of process, or call it "method," call it "steps," call it "rules"—something we have to *do* to conform to reality that's up to us to do, and simply passive exposure will not give it to us. Where do these steps or this process come from? Obviously, they have to depend on our form of knowing, our method of functioning mentally, our minds, our particular consciousness. Intrinsicism ignores the fact that our consciousness makes a critical contribution to cognition. It is *not* just a passive mirror; consciousness is *something*, it has a definite identity, and it has to function accordingly; it can learn only by expressing what it uniquely and distinctively is, and our knowledge, therefore, is going to be affected through and through by the identity of our minds; we're going to see the marks of our minds everywhere, stamped on every item of knowledge. Anything we know as knowledge is acquired *by us*, by minds such as ours, which have to go through a certain process.

"But," you might ask, "isn't this subjectivism? Isn't this what Kant said?" No. We grasp reality by our minds, and what's important here is the conjunction of the two—reality and our minds; that is the essence of objectivity, the union of the two. Let me say it again in a little more detail: The objective approach says: we have to adhere to reality, our conclusions have to correspond to facts, *but*, for a conceptual being, this is not a matter of passive exposure; it requires the exercise of deliberate effort that we have to choose, not simply waiting for reality to imprint itself on our minds, but following a deliberate method of cognition, obeying certain definite procedures, steps, rules. The rules, of course, depend on our particular consciousness; they are the way our consciousness has to operate to gain knowledge of reality, given our specific identity.

Knowledge has to reflect the nature of our consciousness, but that does not make it subjective. Just because it reflects our consciousness, that does not mean it ignores or flouts reality. And if you grasp that, you will have no temptation to swing from intrinsicism to subjectivism and back again. The method that we use to acquire knowledge has to have a *dual* source, if you want to put it that way. The rules that we follow have to be based on two things: our minds and reality. Knowledge is not a fantasy or a subjective reflection of our natures apart from reality. We have to find some kind of method of knowledge that will be in accord with facts out there *and* our mode of cognition, that will reflect reality *and* our way of grasping it; and the result of such a method will be an awareness of reality achieved by certain means. That's what we call "objective," as against intrinsic or subjective.

"Objective" means adherence to reality in cognition—by following certain rules of method, a method derived from facts and appropriate to man's form of cognition. That would be a formal definition. You should understand the need for every element in that definition. Let me make it briefer, because it's necessary to get it as brief as possible so that you can retain it. Objectivity is the systematic effort to correspond to facts by using a human method. Or let's make it even briefer: We have to conform to reality somehow. Or briefer still: Correspond somehow. That's what I would call "blurting it out." Subjectivists deny the first: They say you don't have to correspond; intrinsicists deny the second: they say there is no somehow. Objectivism is the union—reality and our mind's way of grasping it. So you could have said, "Correspond somehow," "facts by method," "reality by consciousness"—anything like that that would capture the two sides, with the subjectivists denying one and the intrinsicists denying the other.

This takes us some of the way, but it's still too abstract, because there's one crucial point we have to chew. And that is: What does our consciousness actually contribute to knowledge? Here I'm making a big fuss about our consciousness, its nature; it dictates a whole lot of things about what we have to do—we have to break this down. I have taken eight points at random—and there could be many more—about the nature of our consciousness, and I want to go through them with you. And I'm always asking this question—what does our consciousness contribute to knowledge? What about its identity affects knowledge? And at the same time on each point, I have to show that even though it does contribute that element and that that element originates with us, that does not make our conclusions subjective; they still correspond to reality. So knowledge is a marriage; both reality and consciousness are involved in every aspect. And we have to be able to chew this in order to finally break down this idea that consciousness is just a passive mirror. If you wanted a full discussion of what consciousness contributes to knowledge, how that affects how we acquire knowledge, and why is knowledge still knowledge of reality despite this contribution, that would entail a whole course in epistemology.

Let's assume for this discussion that the senses are our only means of contacting reality, because the issue does not involve the senses. We're interested in what happens *after* the senses.

A. *Conceptualization is necessary to acquire knowledge.* Organizing perceptual material according to similarities and differences, reducing all the concretes in a certain category under a given symbol that becomes a word in our mind that stands for an endless number, and then wider and wider abstractions. This is all described in *Introduction to Objectivist Epistemology.* This is obviously a human process, not a process of gazing at Plato's essences. *We* have to organize, *we* have to categorize, *we* have to abstract, *we* as human beings introduce a special perspective on concretes in order to be able to hold a whole cluster as one unit; so it's *our* form of functioning; *we* bring that into existence; reality does not. But does it therefore distort reality? No, it does not. We drop measurements—I'm assuming that you're familiar with that aspect of the theory—but the fact is that when you *do* omit the measurements, the concretes involved are the same; once you omit the measurements, the concretes involved have the same attributes in a given class. So it's *only* a human perspective when we classify them together, and yet it's a human perspective based on reality. As you know, the fact that we have a conceptual consciousness imposes a whole series of rules: how to conceptualize, when to form concepts, what kind of similarities are enough to justify a concept, what you do with a concept, how you keep it tied to concretes, when a definition is necessary, and so on. A whole series of rules for how to use concepts. How do we validate these rules, what dictates them? The nature of concepts. The nature of reality, the facts of reality. It's reality that we are organizing. And that gives us a whole series of rules contributed by us, based on *it.*

B. (All of these are intertwined.) *To do all of this thinking, we need some method.* We're constantly drawing conclusions on the basis of earlier data; the conclusions aren't self-evident; we need some method to tell us how to get from one thing to the next thing, how to get from an observation to a conclusion. And the method of reason is logic, the art of noncontradictory identification. Is this a human method? Absolutely. Logic is the way our minds have to operate in order to get from certain observations to certain conclusions. It's a way of connecting the information available to us—because we learn it a step at a time; that's the kind of consciousness we have. If everything were self-evident, we wouldn't need logic. If we were omniscient, we wouldn't need logic. So logic is definitely "only human." Does that mean it's subjective? No, because the essence of being logical is obedience to the law of identity, which is the central law of reality. We're *only* following a human method, and yet the essence of that method is our way of adhering to reality. That same pattern is always true—our consciousness contributes the need for a certain way of functioning, but if we do it properly, that way of functioning is our way of grasping actual reality. So it's neither intrinsic nor subjective.

C. *We have choice*—that's part of the identity of our consciousness; that's inherent in a conceptual consciousness. We have choice as to where to focus on reality, at what exact point to contact reality. For instance, in forming concepts, nobody could possibly say, "You've got to form 'table' before 'chair,' or vice versa, or 'dog' before 'cat.'" There is absolutely nothing that anybody could tell you mandating that one has to come before the other, because they're on the same level. It depends on what strikes you; it depends on how you exercise your choice. You're confronted by this vast array in reality—where do you choose to zero in on, to the dog, the cat, the chair, the table? It's up to you; reality has nothing to say about that. Of course, in a different context, reality has a lot to say. Before you can get "man," for instance, you can't get "justice." So there is a certain definite structure. But, on any given level of the hierarchy, there's tremendous option. *Why* is there so much option? One fact only: Our consciousness is volitional; that's the kind of consciousness we have. Which means that our mode of contacting reality depends on our choice. This element of volition redounds throughout our knowledge. When we were discussing the hierarchical structure of philosophy, we saw on a broad level that there was a logical necessity, but there were many options. We'll see in ethics that there are many options, many different preferences, all in accordance with reality. There are many options in organizing material for an article; there is no such thing as the one right organization for an article; that would be an intrinsicist view of "right." But choice does not mean subjectivism. Our choice is only this much: In what order should we focus on reality? In what order should we organize the data? In what order should we pursue certain goals? If we are rational, we're still completely oriented to reality. The issue is only how are we going to use our choice to come in contact with it? So it's still reality, but reality as grasped by our consciousness. Options are going to be a crucial element in any objective knowledge, but not everything is optional. Because there is reality that we're using our options to correspond to, it will be only those options within the framework of adherence to reality; that is what will distinguish the *obj*ective from the *subj*ective.

D. *Context*—this is a fact of our consciousness, that we build knowledge on knowledge. And that, of course, is an aspect or a consequence of being conceptual. Our knowledge is limited, each step conditioning and making possible the next. It follows that there can be no out-of-context revelations. You always have to be able to specify, "This is the knowledge on the basis of which I came to this conclusion; this is my context; these are the relevant pieces of information I possess." A fact about your consciousness dictating a rule about how to acquire knowledge. Does that make it subjective? Not at all, because your context is not an invention—you still have to adhere to reality—it's reality as grasped by a special kind of context, as against an intrinsicist revelation.

E. *We can grasp only so much at a time* (the crow issue). That's a fact. Does that dictate a specific method? Absolutely, the spiral method, among other things—you go up to a point, then leave and go to something else, and then come back, in a special, specific order. You have to do that because of the nature of your consciousness. If you didn't have that limitation, you could say, "I'm going to study honesty tonight and finish with it tonight, that's it. I'm fed up with this topic. I'm going to do it once and for all and never go back to it again." But you can't do it. You have to acquire knowledge a different way because of the type of consciousness you have. There's another form in which the identity of consciousness conditions how you have to acquire knowledge, and in what form you hold it. But still, it's knowledge of reality. It's simply how *much* of reality you can hold at a given moment.

F. *Integration*—the necessity of integrating a conclusion with others. We discussed that in connection with force and honesty. Why can't we connect it to everything right off the bat? Our consciousness has a certain identity—first it has to grasp, and then it can connect. Is this ignoring reality? Nonsense. It's all information about reality, but we have to put it together a certain way.

G. *Consciousness is goal-directed, it's purposeful*; that's part of its essence. And this introduces an element that runs throughout knowledge. There are dozens of areas where, before

you can function cognitively, you must know your purpose; you must know your goal. Why? Because that's the
kind of consciousness you have. You have a purposeful
consciousness, a consciousness that can function only by
aiming to achieve a certain end, and until you know the
end, you can't get it operating. To an intrinsicist, this is
scandalous, because if you introduce your purpose, then
it's just what *you* want to achieve, and it's subjective. But in
fact, you cannot escape purpose. If we are defining a term,
to take just that one process—"I want to define 'man'"—
well, for what purpose? You're trying to distinguish that
concept. From what? I want to be able to understand man,
as against these things around me—dogs and cats and so
on; that's my goal. On the other hand, suppose a scientist
wants to define "man" in a way that will distinguish him
from ten thousand other closely related physiological
structures possessed by animals; his purpose is different,
and consequently, a definition that will be satisfactory for
that purpose will be completely different from the child's
definition or the general definition. Does this make definitions subjective? Absolutely not, because we can achieve
our purpose only by looking at the actual facts that distinguish "man" from the other things in question when we're
giving the definition. So you see that purpose is not restricted to value judgments. It's not only the good that's
good "for what"; purpose is built into consciousness as
such, and therefore, it redounds through the life of the
mind, and it does not imply subjectivism. Let me take a
ludicrous example just to show you that consciousness is
really *something*, therefore it has to function a certain way,
therefore intrinsicism is wrong, but it doesn't mean subjectivism is right. Here's the example: Human beings get
tired. That's a fact inherent in human consciousness. If
everything else were the same, but we never got tired, we

wouldn't have to worry about certain things. But there are special rules that take into account the fact that we get tired, such as: Watch how long you work; review, when you work too long; double-check; only do so much and then take a rest; don't get stale; don't over-stare. Another example: We are emotional, we have emotions. That's as much of a fact as concepts, context, and purpose. Does that imply anything? Absolutely. For one thing, as we mentioned earlier in the course, it implies that you have to use those emotions as one of your automatized ways of contacting concretes, to prevent your concepts from floating. For another thing, you have to monitor your own state of emotions. Since you know you can be overcome by emotion, and that overcoming can disconnect you from reality, you have to keep one eye on them—"Am I hysterically frantic right now? If so, this is not the time to come to a decision." That's a special method of cognition, or rule, derivative from the nature of consciousness, and it would not be applicable to another type of consciousness, but *is* applicable to us; so intrinsicism is nonsense. On the other hand, it does not detach us from reality; it's *our way* of staying in touch with reality.

We could go on indefinitely, but that's just by way of trying to chew this idea for you. Our consciousness as a complex, detailed identity is conceptual, volitional, contextual, purposeful, emotional, and all of this will be reflected in our knowledge; all of this will have effects. First of all, on *how* to acquire knowledge, on the right procedures; and second of all, on the form in which knowledge is held in our minds, because the form in which we hold it is dictated by the method by which we acquired it. If you acquire knowledge by logic, integration, you're going to hold it in the form that is logically related, concretized, defined, and so on. This course is intended to help you hold philosophical ideas chewed rather than floating.

We can summarize. In one sense, all of cognition reflects only our consciousness. Intrinsicism, if you think about it, is simply nonsense. Knowledge is fantastically "creative"—it's all created by our minds. But immediately, the other shoe has to drop—our consciousness is the faculty for grasping reality, so our knowledge is not subjective. Every facet of our consciousness injects an element into knowledge, but it's still knowledge of reality. That's the essence of the objective viewpoint.

What then is the basic validation of the concept of the "objective"? It comes down to two axioms. One, consciousness is the faculty of perceiving existence (that's as against subjectivism), and two, consciousness has identity (that's as against intrinsicism); and that one, by the way, is just the union of "A is A" and "consciousness." There is no further validation of objectivity; it's simply a corollary of these two, and they are both axioms. But it's so abstract at that stage that it doesn't mean anything. You first have to chew in detail what the contributions of consciousness are to knowledge—senses, concepts, and so on—and then only at the end can we give some content to the idea of why it's the objective versus the intrinsic. That's why on the hierarchy sheet I put it at the end of epistemology, rather than the beginning.

So what is the context for understanding objectivity? You have to know all of metaphysics and epistemology. But if we restrict it down to the bare essence, it comes down to: "Existence is there independent of us (the primacy of existence), and we only grasp it by a certain kind of conceptual process." Once we know all that, we just draw the general conclusion, "Therefore, we grasp reality somehow."

There are three basic viewpoints on this question of consciousness in relation to existence. You could take the view of consciousness turned in on itself, ignoring existence—that is subjectivism, and it leads to skepticism in epistemology, the idea that you can't know anything. The other side—there is consciousness effacing itself, considering itself as nothing but a passive gazer with no nature—that is intrinsicism, and that's the base of mysticism. And then there is consciousness as the grasper or perceiver, with a complex identity, and therefore a special method; and that is Objectivism, and that's the base of reason. So you see, this issue of the trichotomy is really the *metaphysics of epistemology*, the basic metaphysical relationships that give rise to the whole approach to knowledge.

I think you can see why the concept of the "objective" is necessary. At the peril of repeating this one more time, from a slightly different aspect: A conceptual consciousness is volitional; it's not, therefore, automatically focused on reality; it has to do so deliberately, by a specific method and policy. It can't give up reality (that would be subjectivism) or expect reality to do the work for it (that would be intrinsicism). So a special concept is needed to designate how consciousness would deliberately, volitionally take the steps necessary to stay in contact with the object. That's exactly what is meant by "objective." The allegedly opposing schools, the subjective and the intrinsic, while in many cases flatly opposite of each other, really agree in one essential: They deny the need for a special volitional method of corresponding to reality. The subjectivist says, "We all disagree; there is no automatic agreement; therefore we're lost." And the intrinsicist comes in and says, "There *is* an automatic way—reality automatically will write on us and give us the uncontestable truth, so we don't need a special method." And the subjectivist says, "Oh, if only that existed, it would be terrific, we could know, but unfortunately there is no such method, so we're lost." To put it even more simply, the intrinsicist says, "Knowledge is possible only by revelation," and the subjectivist says, "True enough; unfortunately, there's no revelation." Or, in ethics, the intrinsicist says, "If there is no God, anything would be permitted" (Dostoevsky's contention), and the subjectivist says, "True enough, that's why everything is permitted." In other words, they're on exactly the same model of knowledge.

If you want to look at Objectivism this way, you could say we agree with half of each and disagree with half of each. With the intrinsicists, we agree that we must correspond to reality, but we disagree regarding the idea that we must do it by a specific method. With the subjectivists we agree that consciousness has a nature, there is no automatic correspondence, we must follow our minds, we can't jump out of them, but we disagree that this detaches us from reality.

Before we leave this topic, I want to touch on a couple of the topics that we've already discussed and see if you can integrate this topic with some of them.

Let's take rights. Because it's so fundamental, this trichotomy affects every other issue in philosophy. On every issue, there's a subjectivist view, an intrinsicist view, and an Objectivist view, and after a while you start to recognize it. What is the intrinsicist view of rights? Where do rights come from? They're self-evident; and what feature of reality creates them? What intrinsic feature is their source that lets us know they're true? The American founding document—"All men are endowed by their Creator with certain unalienable rights." This is the idea of rights as a product of some factor out there endowing you with rights. According to the intrinsicist view, rights are self-evident—"We hold these truths to be self-evident"—and they truly are self-evident; you just look and you grasp. There's nothing dishonest about this, but it's simply mistaken. That's the intrinsicist view—rights as the consequence of a supernatural entity and it's simply self-evident; that's an attribute all men have. As against that, there are the moderns who swing all the way around, and in rebellion against intrinsicists, their view is, "Yes, there are rights," but rights are created how? By social conventions—by the legislature, by Congress— rights are whatever Congress says they are, so long as Congress says they are. And then when they decree new rights, those are new rights. The Objectivist view is neither of those; the Objectivist view is, "Given a certain goal—life—given certain facts of reality as our context, then, in a certain situation, we must respect certain principles of behavior that have nothing to do with an outside revelation or a dogma, and that have nothing to do with any acts of Congress or anybody's preference." And we were counting on this objective model entirely in opposition to the dominant themes.

Or take the issue of honesty. What is a subjectivist view of the virtue of honesty? "Honesty is a matter of what I feel like. When I feel like being honest, that's right for me; for you, you don't feel that way, that's wrong." Or, "In Western civilization we've been taught to be honest, and for us, that's good; but on Samoa they love to lie, and therefore for them, dishonesty is good"—that's the typical modern view of honesty. You don't have to be that crude about it. You can say, "Honesty is okay if it works." Who determines whether it works? The essence of pragmatism is: "Consult your own goals, or society's goals." And how do you validate your goals? "You just have them. If you want certain things, that's where you start." Now that is a pure subjectivist interpretation of honesty, and it completely annihilates the idea that honesty is mandated as a *principle*, regardless of your feelings. But that makes it sound like an absolute, and then as an absolute, which it is, we're pushed into the intrinsicist view of honesty. They certainly have a view, typically, "Thou shalt not lie, period." That is an intrinsic dogma; in Kant's terminology it's a "categorical imperative"; it's a religious commandment; and according to his viewpoint, if you are a babysitter and you have this young baby upstairs and a drooling maniac comes to the door and says, "Do you have a kid here?" you absolutely have to look at him and say, "Third door on the left." Maybe you might remain silent. If you speak, you've got to tell the truth. That is honesty as a dogma—no context, no purpose, no effects are relevant, no method, nothing. That's what people think is meant by saying honesty is a matter of principle, and that's why the two schools are: honesty as dogma or as subjective. And what do they omit? Everything that we've been discussing with all the examples—honesty is a principle, dictated by a purpose, applicable in a context.

Every topic involves this trichotomy, because after all, this trichotomy applies to the relation of consciousness to existence, and it involves everything—you can't get away from existence, and unless you're asleep, you can't get away from your consciousness, so no matter what you do, some model of this is going to be operative. And I think you see why I chose this as a good example to work with, because it truly is everywhere, and it gives you a clearer idea why Miss Rand chose the term "Objectivism" of all the terms, even over reason—because this is the core distinguishing concept that leads to the Objectivist view of reason and all the rest of it.

Lecture Six Q & A

Q: In the history of philosophy, can you name any intrinsicists who try not to be religious?
A: Despite his basic approach Aristotle has definite intrinsicist elements that he inherited from Plato. And the only other one that I can think of offhand is Spinoza, who was an atheist; if you call him religious, he's an atheistic pantheist. Typically there has been an alliance throughout the history of philosophy—Plato being the archetype—of intrinsicism and religion, or supernaturalism. As supernaturalism faded, then philosophers become unreligious and subjectivists, and that's the modern period. So it's only as an anomaly that there is one of those without the other in the history of philosophy.

Q: Could it be argued that intrinsicists are dishonest, because sometime in their life they must remember doing something in a rational manner, such as learning a musical instrument, learning mathematical tables, or a part in a school play? Surely they must see that they had to work at this, it didn't jump into their head. Why do they disregard this information?
A: I definitely disagree that an intrinsicist has to be dishonest. The ones I'm most familiar with were motivated primarily by a revulsion against subjectivism. And they held to "We have to adhere to reality," and their intention was to beat down the wave of modern subjectivism. Why didn't they grasp this? The questioner is overlooking the fact that it's a tremendous jump between commonsense observations and a philosophic theory that integrates them. It takes a genius to state abstractly what everybody knows in some concretes. "A is A," for instance, as an abstraction, was self-evident when it was named. But for how many millennia did human beings go through not grasping that contradictions are wrong, even though they knew that this was this and that was that? They hadn't reached that abstract level. That's why Aristotle was a genius, to be able to conceptualize the self-evident. How many people know, and *have* known, that you have to pursue your self-interest or you can't live? In concretes—you have to go to a job and earn money, and so on.

Q: Why do you say that intrinsicism has been more influential than subjectivism?
A: For a simple reason—a subjectivist says, "Go by your feelings." Where do the feelings come from? Feelings are not primary. The subjectivists *treat* them as though they are, but in fact, they are not. So if you take these subjectivists, where did they get their feelings, passions, desires, and so on, which they claim are the criteria? They went to church, they went to school, they heard all the dogmas, they got them from somebody who took it on himself to give out standards (which the intrinsicists do), they absorbed those standards, they programmed themselves, and then they threw up their hands and said, "I'm just going to follow my automatic conditioning." A subjectivist cannot generate a value judgment, because he's looking to his own consciousness, which is empty. So he's got to get it from somewhere, and the only two places are from reality or from an authority. And the only authority that stands up and says, "This is the truth, this is what you must accept," if he's not an Objectivist, is an intrinsicist. So what it comes down to is that it's religion that has programmed all of the subjectivists, because religionists are the dominant intrinsicists. So there's no doubt that intrinsicism is much more influential. In my opinion, intrinsicism is even superior, given that you could make a choice among two profound errors. Maybe I'm just reflecting subjectively my own background, but I would much rather have a conversation with an intrinsicist (especially one that hasn't gone completely mystical yet) than a subjectivist, because he still retains a respect for fact, reality, and you still can argue with him about his method. Whereas a subjectivist is like the destruction of all communication, "Oh, that's just your opinion, it's true for you," and so on. You can't get one step.

Q: You said that consciousness has identity, as against intrinsicism. As I understand it, intrinsicism merely says that consciousness is irrelevant to cognition. I don't see how this prohibits it having an identity.
A: No, it does not say that. Nobody could say consciousness is irrelevant to cognition—if you didn't have a consciousness, there'd be nobody to know. So even an intrinsicist grants that you have a faculty of awareness,

you have a consciousness, it's not irrelevant. But what is irrelevant is its nature. It contributes nothing except being a blank, indeterminate mirror. The essence of it is not that its existence is irrelevant, but that it has no identity.

Q: You spoke of the intrinsic nature of the Bible.
A: Let's clarify that—*every* book has a nature. So it's not true that every time you use the word "intrinsic" that it's intrinsic*ism*. *Atlas Shrugged* has an intrinsic nature—there's so many pages, so much paper, so many words, and so on. That has nothing to do with what we are here talking about. The intrinsic view is not that nothing has a nature, but that over and above the perceptual level, there are entities intrinsic in reality that act on our minds and cause knowledge or value judgments. That doesn't mean that this lamp doesn't have an intrinsic nature, or this cup, but they are perceptual entities. Obviously the Bible has an intrinsic nature— that's just the law of identity.

Q: Isn't it true that within the same religious text (the Bible), there are the words, "An eye for an eye, a tooth for a tooth"? I have two questions. Is this not the opposite of intrinsicism? Does this then represent religious hypocrisy? And second, since one seems to be at least in certain cases an alternative principle, then the pure intrinsic nature doesn't apply.
A: The questioner is saying, in effect, "There are some good ideas in the Bible, so doesn't that mitigate the fact and make it so that you can't say it's an intrinsic approach?" Intrinsicism is an issue of *method*, not necessarily of content. The Bible can have individual points that are perfectly correct; there's nothing to say that in content an intrinsicist always advocates wrong ideas. The point is he has no way of telling right ideas from wrong ideas, but sometimes he comes up with right ideas. Not every one of the Commandments is wrongheaded, and the same for "An eye for an eye." The point is this: What makes the Bible intrinsicist is that when you ask, "How are these Commandments defended, what is their objective basis?" the answer is simply, "God said so."

Q: Does man's form of consciousness contribute categories to his conceptual form of awareness, like Aristotle's categories? Is there a specific set of categories, for example, substance, state, action, place, time, relation, and so on?
A: No, I would say not. This is apropos of "What does consciousness contribute?" The so-called categories, as Aristotle presents them, pertain to the *nature* of reality, not to our method of grasping it. And consequently, they are not a product of consciousness. They are, as Aristotle presented them, the broadest abstractions applicable to anything that exists, the so-called *summa genera*. That is not part of what consciousness contributes.

Q: In ethics, is the so-called deontology versus teleology debate an example of the false dichotomy between intrinsicism and subjectivism?
A: Yes. That is a very good application, if you are a philosophy major. Deontology includes those philosophers like Kant who say there are certain absolutes that you must follow regardless of their consequences and apart from any goal to which they lead. And that is clearly the intrinsicist view. Teleology in ethics is the view that we validate virtues by reference to an ultimate goal, but the way most teleologists hold it, that goal is arbitrary. There's no way to validate the goal; you simply have to say, "*If* you want to achieve it, follow this method of action, but if you don't want to achieve it, something else." So that comes out as being the subjectivist approach. Therefore, as these are commonly construed, they are exactly this dichotomy. You *could* argue that Objectivism is teleological in that it starts with a value, an ultimate goal, and validates everything by reference to that. So it repudiates the idea of "Thou shalt" or "Thou shalt not" as out-of-context absolutes. But today, teleology is almost completely dominated by subjectivists, so practically speaking, this is a good application that I did not cover in class.

■

Rationalism

We have covered some essentials of the positive approach to understanding Objectivism and how to chew it. Of course, we could multiply the issues; we could have an entire course, and more than one, just on what we've been doing, but the idea was to give you an indication of a method. Now I want to turn to the negative, to errors, basic misconceptions and wrong approaches toward understanding Objectivism and toward understanding philosophy as such. So we have a two-pronged attack, what's right and what's wrong by contrast. And the first thing we're going to do, which is our subject for this evening and may spill over a little bit into next week, is *rationalism*.

Rationalism is a method of approach to ideas that, more than any single other error, wrecks intellectuals, particularly good intellectuals, because it operates by corrupting them via the best within them. It attaches itself to a man's desire to be rational, to go by reason, to go by logic, to be objective, and using that, if he commits this mistake, it warps his thinking at the very root. So, more than any other error, in my knowledge, rationalism has negative effects on good people who go into the intellectual world. At the same time, it utterly alienates nonintellectuals and makes them decide that the intellectual world is a bunch of hot air, a bunch of floating talk that has nothing to do with life, and consequently, it has the effect of keeping those people out of the field altogether, so it becomes like a self-perpetuating monopoly of poor thinking.

Although rationalism is a profoundly mistaken method, it's not in and of itself evil or immoral. And I want to stress this at the outset. If it's applicable to you or your acquaintances, it is not an issue of moral default to commit this error. I think I've indicated that I wrestled with this for many years, and I have every reason to believe that I was thoroughly honest in the process. Many highly virtuous people do it out of conscientiousness. Rationalism is an automatized, imperfect way of coping with confusion; it does not reflect on your seriousness or on your character. Particular rationalist philosophers may be dishonest, but people in this room, I feel safe to say, are not. What it comes down to is: How to deal with ideas is a special skill that none of us is taught, and people flounder when they get thrown without any guidance into something as abstract as philosophy. Rationalism—and also empiricism—are two ways of floundering, of trying to cope when you don't know how to cope. They govern you without you even knowing that you subscribe to them. What happens is that rationalism operates to define for you implicitly what you take as logic or understanding or reality; you don't even know that that theory is setting those definitions; and therefore, all you know is, "I'm trying to understand such and such, but I don't understand"—you don't realize that the very concept "understand" that you're using is influenced by this particular theory. So when you are influenced by rationalism, you do so most often without even knowing it.

I'm using "rationalism" not exactly the way the term is used in the history of philosophy. As you know, there are two broad schools in the history of philosophy, the rationalists and the empiricists. The rationalists are those who advocate reason, in essence, and derogate the senses. The empiricists are the reverse; they advocate observation and derogate reason. But as I'm using "rationalism," it's a method used not only by avowed rationalists, but also by most of the official empiricists in the history of philosophy. So, the method of rationalism is often used unwittingly even by people who claim to reject all the tenets of rationalism. It's used by those who call themselves empiricists, and it's also used very often by Objectivists.

The best way I know how to handle this is to treat it as a syndrome, a collection of symptoms, and I'm going to enumerate a list of symptoms of rationalism.

Number one—this would be the descriptive essence of rationalism—*ideas above reality*. The rationalist regards ideas as a realm over and above reality (by "reality" I mean here the physical world). He sees ideas as a private world different from reality and superior to it. This means that he has a completely different concept of "ideas" than an Objectivist would. He does not regard ideas as a means of knowing the physical world; he regards ideas as essentially sundered from, separate from, the physical world. What philosopher is the archetype of rationalism? Plato. His world of Forms, or world of Ideas, which is a world of abstractions existing independent of and superior to this world is the true philosophy of rationalism, and is accepted even by people who claim to oppose Plato. It's a world of *floating abstractions*, and by "floating" we mean disconnected from concretes, from the things in this world.

A rationalist is all in favor of abstractions. He is a highly conceptual person. He likes broad abstractions. And to that extent, he has a great virtue. But he has an essential error in his view of what an abstraction is *for*. He doesn't see concepts as a means of grasping percepts. He sees two worlds, the world we *per*ceive, and the world we *con*ceive, and they are entirely sundered.

Many people have individual floating abstractions simply by default. For instance, many people on the street have no clear idea of what they mean by "freedom," and if you ask them, they're all in favor of freedom, but "freedom" to them stands for some dissociated image of running along the beach at night and positive emotion and a few things like that. They have no clear idea what actual governmental measures would advance it or detract from it. That would be a single floating abstraction. And if you have just one, that does not make you a rationalist per se; that could just be a default of chewing, a failure to connect that one concept to reality. A rationalist goes beyond this—he has a whole world of floating abstractions, a whole dimension that he goes off into, made entirely of abstractions disconnected from concrete reality.

I don't want this to be a floating abstraction, so I'm going to give you a perfect example from an actual historical rationalist, the German philosopher Leibniz, in the late seventeenth century. I'll give you just a bit of his philosophy. Leibniz starts (or the aspect I'm going to look at starts) with, "The world is full of things that are compound," like tables, rocks, mountains, and so on. By "compound" he means a thing consisting of parts. That seems very innocuous, right? The world is full of compounds. Who could possibly deny a proposition like that? But from this point we're going to see what this supposedly entails. If we keep breaking a compound up, Leibniz holds, that will be broken up into parts, and if we break the parts up into parts and so on, we can only go so far, and ultimately we must reach *simple substances*, substances that have *no* parts, the *ultimate* parts. And we have to reach this; otherwise, we have an infinite regress. So if there are compounds, ultimately there must be simples, things that have no parts. And those simple substances he calls *monads*, from the Greek word for "one." So the universe is made up of monads, and now he's going to see what those monads would have to be like. The first thing we can infer is that they can't possibly be material or extended, spread out, three-dimensional, because if they were extended then they would have to be divisible, they would have to be capable of being broken into parts, at least in thought; if they were spread out in space, even if they were only an eighth of an inch long (for instance), we could separate the left side of the monad from the right side, so that would give it two potential parts, and it would no longer be absolutely simple. And yet we proved that there must be simple entities comprising the universe. Therefore, these ultimate entities cannot be extended; they cannot be material. If they cannot be material, then they can't be in space, because only material things are in space. We've already found out that the essence of the universe is not material, but it must have *some* nature, these monads. What could they be—if it's not material? There are only two things that we can conceive of that the ultimate elements of the universe be: matter or mind. If it's not matter, they must be minds, right? What do minds do? (You see, we're just all doing this by a process of reasoning.) Minds ultimately can only be aware; minds can only perceive things. So these monads must perceive. What do these monads perceive? And since monads are all that exist, the only thing they could perceive is other monads. If all of them are doing nothing but perceiving all the other monads, what is the difference? The only two ways that a mind could differ is in what it perceives and how it perceives; but what it perceives is the same, so they must differ in *how* they perceive. And how *could* they differ? Well, some of them must be clearer, and others blurrier.

Now then, we go on and on, and we finally reach the idea (I'm leaving out a lot of steps), the most confused monads are the ones that we call "tables" and "chairs," and the clearest one is God, and so on and so on. I've just given you a taste; we could go on indefinitely (and Leibniz does). But you see the method. I've just given it to you in structure. "There are compounds, and if there are compounds, there must be simples; if there are simples, they must be indivisible; if they are indivisible, they must be nonmaterial; if they are nonmaterial, they must be nonspatial; if they are nonspatial, they must be mental; if they are mental, they must be perceivers," and so on. That is a perfect example of rationalism. It's not just one term detached from reality; it's a whole series of them, a whole world of concepts, and when you enter into it, they have definite relations to each other. It's Leibniz's world, like Plato's, and it has a whole complicated structure and rules on how you get from one to the other, absolutely none of it at any point connected to what we observe in this world. And if you tell him, "Look, here's a table, and here's a chair, and it looks material and to be in space," he'll say, "That's ridiculous. I've *proved* that if it's compound it must be simple, and so on, so all of this is illusion. We have another world, and I get to it by this series of concepts."

It should be clear to you that you can do exactly the same thing with the right ideas. This is an issue of *method*, not of content. Leibniz happens to be what's called an idealist; he doesn't believe in matter. But you can be an Objectivist and get all your ideas from *Atlas Shrugged*, and then approach them this same way, in which case you are a rationalist in exactly the same way.

Let's take the example that we used before, the type of Objectivist who says it's wrong ever to take money from your parents to help you in college, and see how that would be reached by this same Leibnizian or rationalistic method. And the way I've heard it structured is like this: "If there are to be values, life must be the standard; if life is to be the standard, rationality has to be the supreme virtue; if rationality is to be the supreme virtue, independence must be a virtue; but since mind-body integration is an essential metaphysical principle, independence must apply both intellectually and materially; but parents are responsible only until maturity, and I am past the age of maturity; therefore, taking money from them would be anti-life." That is the same thing as Leibniz did, only using more plausible ideas, Objectivist ideas. But it's a whole series of inferences starting from what is supposedly an obvious foundation, with no references that point to the actual situation, context, or concretes; no reference to whether he is working hard in college, needs help legitimately, has a long-range plan or is a bum, whether his parents have to sacrifice—all of those questions are simply dismissed as being completely irrelevant. He's got a series of abstractions, and then, in a void, a conclusion to which they lead, without any perception of concrete reality.

To give rationalism its due, there is a good element here. The rationalist wants to be logical, he's appalled at the idea of going by emotions, he wants to be objective, he wants to have proof, he's very conceptual, he loves broad principles—"If there are compounds, there must be simples; if life is the standard, you must be rational"—he loves that; he revels in broad abstractions. And that's good, up to a point. But the trouble is he goes astray in his love of concepts. He goes astray because he doesn't realize what a concept is. It's true that if you're going to be conceptual, you do have to be selective in your focus. A conceptual mind does have to be selective. What do we mean by "selective"? While it's abstracting, a conceptual mind has to drop out of attention certain actual facts of reality. For instance, when you put together all the different tables under one concept "table," you have to deliberately ignore the fact that one has four legs and one has five, that one is brown and one is white, and so on. You do have to drop out of attention many actual facts of reality and just focus on the common denominator. So it is true that inherent in a conceptual mind is selective focus, actually ignoring certain elements of reality.

The rationalist, unfortunately, goes one step too far—he drops reality as such. As a continuation of this same selectivity, he drops concretes altogether. Of course, in a way, you *cannot* focus on concretes when you think abstractly. This is what, in the nature of the mind, gives rise to rationalism. The essence of a concept is to enable us to hold a countless number of concretes without focusing on any one of them. The purpose of a definition is to enable us to focus on *one* attribute, and *ignore* the dozens of others that the crow epistemology couldn't hold. So we *do* have to ignore many facts of reality when we think abstractly. But the essence of a proper method is to ignore while keeping the concretes implicit, potentially alive in your mind. The crucial necessity of proper thinking is: Focus selectively, drop the irrelevant facts, but always remember that they are there, they have to be capable of being recalled at a moment's notice, and your abstraction is no use except as a means of bringing you in touch with data about these concretes. But the rationalist drops the concretes and just cuts them off. He doesn't keep them potentially alive in his own mind. He enters his own world of abstractions, just like Plato, a world of universals.

You can do this very innocently by the very nature of what you do when you form concepts, if you're not aware of it. And this is particularly true if you are young, you have no guidance, and you are exposed to a whole system of philosophy for the first time. You will then find that you have a mass of ideas you cannot digest, you do not know what to do with them, they're whirling in all directions. Especially if you take a course or read a book where you're given a dozen definitions and a thousand principles and a hundred arguments, and it's just spinning in all directions, and you have a desperate need (many people do) to simplify, to make it graspable, and so they latch on to something that's clear to them, in the same way that Leibniz latched on to "If there's a compound, there must be a simple." That much he knows, that becomes his anchor, and he's going to hang everything on that.

That is understandable if you're eighteen years old, plunged into a whole philosophy, including Objectivism—the sheer weight of it overcomes you, so you start to deal with a floating realm of principles untied to life. That's why the only antidote to rationalism is detailed digesting in a proper way. If and when you can grasp the ideas in connection with reality, then there's no temptation toward rationalism. Of course, this chaos does not have to lead to rationalism; it can also lead to empiricism, which is another way of remaining in control. That we'll look at next time.

That is our basic description of rationalism. It contains, by implication, all the other points. But let us now name a second point, and that would be *deduction as the basic method of knowledge.*

If you asked Leibniz or any rationalist, "How do you know that your conclusion is true, that everything must be a monad?" or if you asked the Objectivist in the example, "How do you know that you shouldn't take money from your parents?" the answer will be, "What do you mean? I proved it inexorably from my starting point—if this then this, if this then this—I have a whole chain, and my conclusion is therefore inexorable." Rationalists love the expression "Q.E.D.," *quod erat demonstrandum,* "I've proved it; this is it." Their idea of what guarantees the conclusion, what validates it, what makes it incontestable, is not that you see that it corresponds to reality—a rationalist would never say that. What he would say is, "It has been deduced," and you can't beat that; that is *the* method of knowledge. And here again, it's *deduction,* not as a means of grasping reality, but as a method of connecting ideas without relation to reality.

The contrast to deduction would be *induction,* which is the process of generalizing from observation. Induction is the attempt to grasp abstractions on the basis of observing concretes, and that is the antithesis of the rationalist's whole approach. He regards induction as shaky, uncertain, confusing, disorganized. It might be helpful, like Plato says, to engage in a little induction when you're young, to give you some preliminary ideas, but once you get the ideas, you're past your baby clothes, you throw that out, and then you are just in a pure realm where you deduce one idea from another.

We saw these two different approaches on the topic of life as the standard. And you remember that the deductive approach, which I attacked over and over, would be the idea, "The way to establish life as the standard is, 'value' is defined as 'that which one acts to gain and/or keep.' By that definition, it must follow that there's something that acts to gain, there is some ultimate goal, and so there must be an alternative. 'Life' is defined as 'a process of self-sustaining and self-generated action,' and that means it must be the thing that alone is capable of pursuing goals, and which alone is confronted by the alternative, and therefore, by those two definitions, it must follow that—" and you deduce the whole thing with no reference whatever to the facts of reality. If you ask that type of ratio- nalistic Objectivist where those definitions came from, there is no answer whatever. Those are just the definitions; they strike him as okay, they're in *Atlas Shrugged*, he's got to start somewhere. And of course, you know the crisis that that leads to—the complete disassociation of those definitions from reality, and consequently such problems as how you distinguish a living thing from a statue. As against that, actual proof is not deduction, but induction; it's observing actual living organisms, and observing the countless differences between them and the inanimate, observing all of those hundreds and hundreds of differences, and then merely conceptual- izing, organizing, making explicit what your perceptions gave you. That would be an inductive approach, and completely opposite of the rationalist.

You can put the rationalist's insistence on deduction the following way: He is not concerned with the relation of ideas to facts, but with the relation of ideas to ideas. He starts with certain ideas, and then he wants to show that the next idea follows from *that* idea, and the next one from *that* idea. So his eye is always on his little world of ideas to make sure that they cohere with each other, never on the relation of ideas to facts.

A true rationalist carries this all the way. He is not convinced by sen- sory observation. He feels a need to deduce even what he directly ob- serves. And there are some Objectivists like this. They feel that if you just look at that table and say, "Therefore, it exists," that's unconvincing; how do you know the senses are valid? But, suppose you could give a deductive proof that the senses are valid, then you could accept the evidence of your eyes because you would have now validated it by reference to deduction. So, for instance, they'll say something like this: "Science has proved that whenever we have a sensory experience, there must be an object causing

218 ■ LEONARD PEIKOFF

our reaction, and therefore, whenever we perceive, we must be perceiving a real object; and therefore, if we perceive a table, there must really be an object there, and therefore, we can trust our eyes." Therefore, therefore, therefore, that's all deduction. Now observe: This type of person thinks, "I can trust my eyes because I've given a deductive proof." And if you ask him, "How can we rely on what science has proved, if we can't trust our senses? Where does science come up with its conclusions?" that doesn't occur to him. He's now incorporated the senses into a deductive framework, and once he's done that, he's happy.

We can put the point this way: The rationalist resents the real self-evident—that is, the perceptual level. He has his own substitute for it, as we'll see in a moment. Now you could easily see from this account that if deduction is the only method of knowledge, what is going to be the favorite subject of a rationalist and his idea of the model of all human knowledge? That subject is mathematics, which has been the ideal of rationalists since time immemorial, starting with Pythagoras, who said, "All things are numbers," through Plato, who, finally, in his old age, changed his universals into Pythagorean numbers, all the way through Spinoza, whose ethics was demonstrated "geometrically," just like mathematics, right on through Bertrand Russell and *Principia Mathematica*, so it's all the way to the present. Mathematics as the paradigm of knowledge.

I just want to comment here briefly that mathematics is *not* the proper model of knowledge. Mathematics is a profoundly untypical subject, and it is absolutely not typical of human cognition. It's an extraordinarily abstract subject, which focuses on a single attribute of physical entities (namely, quantitative relations), and in fact, you can even make a case that mathematics does not even really *have* a content of knowledge; it's basically a method, the way logic is.

The important thing is why the rationalist picks on mathematics, and if I put this pejoratively, it would be, mathematics is the *easiest* subject there is.* That's not a friendly description, but it's relevant to pointing out some-

---

*[From a later question period:] All I meant with that overstatement was that—as a pattern of knowledge, as a model of knowledge—deduction, however complicated, is

thing about rationalism, because the rationalist is floundering and he needs something straightforward that he can grab on to. Contrast, for instance, the typical mathematical proof with what you have to do to validate the virtue of honesty. In a real cognitive situation, you have to pick certain elements out of a vast, complicated context; you have to delimit the aspect under consideration; you have the necessity of integration facing you in dozens of directions at the same time; you have all kinds of complexities that would make your head spin to try to know what you know, and what it rests on, and what context you are using, and so on. With mathematics, however, this is not necessary. You start off with a few delimited axioms, because you're deliberately saying, "I'm not focusing on reality, only one attribute, and to hell with everything else," and in mathematics, you just churn out the conclusions from those premises; there are no traps, pitfalls, weighing of evidence, and so on.

And this demonstrates an important point about rationalists: They cannot deal with intellectual complexity, or they don't want to, they don't know how to. Consequently, when they begin to feel that everything is swimming, their method is to grab some abstraction and say, "That's my beacon, that's my starting point, and I'm going to hang everything else on this."

Periodically I get letters from rationalists denouncing Objectivists for celebrating Christmas. And they are almost invariably rationalistic. They all are some variant of the idea, "Christmas is the holiday celebrating altruism, and you're supposed to give gifts and do things for others, and so on; therefore, it's the opposite of Objectivism; therefore, it's immoral to celebrate." What I want to point out to you here is why this is an example of a rationalist mentality. The fact is that Christmas has a great many attributes. It is not simply a holiday for which you're supposed to

---

not comparable to induction. Induction requires a complexity of context and integration that has no parallel in deduction. And mathematics is deductive. In that specific sense, in no way derogating mathematics, I would still hold out for the fact that the basic method of thought in mathematics is easier than in physics, for instance—without denying that mathematics is extremely abstract, takes enormous intelligence, and is extremely important.

give gifts. There are many other things—Christmas is supposed to be a time of goodwill, it's a time when you have a tree, it's a time when you have certain kinds of decorations, it's a time of protracted absence of work, it's a time of office parties, it was a holiday begun by pagans and then taken over by Christians when they couldn't stamp it out, it's a time in which people are constantly denounced for being too commercial and in giving gifts not in the spirit of self-sacrifice but simply selfishly and materialistically and so on—now, this whole chaos is true of Christmas. The rationalist, however, decides—in this case, the Objectivist rationalist—that there is a feature he doesn't like. All the rest is irrelevant, and he's going to make his deductions on that basis.

It's true that we do have to simplify a complexity. That's why we need definitions, in order to know what we're dealing with. So we have a valid need here—we can't deal with the complex unless we simplify. But the rationalist seizes arbitrarily on something that he can deal with that makes it simple, and goes from there. So we have a world of ideas cemented by deduction, allegedly modeled on mathematics.

One corollary of this is that there is a strong tendency to *determinism* in rationalism. And the tendency comes about like this: Deduction is the proof that so-and-so *must* follow from the preceding—so a true rationalist thinks that anything he's trying to explain follows of necessity from the preceding, which follows of necessity from the preceding, and so on. This "must," in his mind, is incompatible (usually) with choice. He feels, given the starting point, the next step is inevitable, and the next and the next, and therefore, the whole thing couldn't possibly have happened differently. The perfect example of this philosophy, of a determinism implicit in rationalism, was Spinoza. Spinoza is what was called a "logical determinist." That is, he thought that everything in the universe was determined, not by atoms or by God or by Freudian desires or anything like that; he thought everything was determined by logic itself. The sheer necessity of everything flowing deductively from the starting point meant every aspect of everyone's life had to flow inevitably from the starting points, and consequently there was no choice at all.

Now let's turn to the third point—the rationalist view of the proper starting points of knowledge. And you can describe this as follows: The rationalist view is that *the starting points are purely conceptual self-evidencies.* Now let's develop this point. A rationalist rests his whole case on his starting points, so he's very high on axioms. But he does not get his axioms from observation, from sensory perception; as we've seen, he resents that whole approach. So where does he get his basic self-evidencies, on which he's going to rest his whole deductive chain? He has his own version of the idea of the self-evident. His starting points, he says, are not self-evident on the *per*ceptual level; they are self-evident strictly on the *con*ceptual level. They are self-evidencies that you grasp only when you grasp concepts, not any way of looking at reality; you simply seize on certain abstract ideas; you say them aloud to yourself, or in your mind, and it strikes you—"Sounds good," "Okay," "Obvious," "Common sense," "Incontestable," "I'll buy that," whatever it is, "Where there's a compound, there must be a simple; who could deny it?" There's no question of observing what's around you. It's just that you utter the proposition, and if it's right, it reverberates in the mind. If not, then you say, "That's no good; I want something that has that quality, and that then is my foundation."

I gave an example of this made up by Miss Rand; it's a perfect example to capture the rationalist approach to axioms. The rationalist will say something like this: "Man has only two eyes, so he should see only two things, one with each eye"; that would be an axiom. "An eye can see only one thing, one eye, one thing." That sounds okay. And then, what will follow from this will be two schools. One school will say, "We have to accept the inference from that. Men *do* see only two things; everything else is an illusion." And the other school would say, "Oh, that's ridiculous. We see all *kinds* of things, but that's because of all the hidden eyes we have." This is the typical pattern—an alleged self-evident axiom, and then two schools that war with one another on the basis of it. And this is very common. One of these letters that come in periodically denouncing Christmas started with a whole series of axioms. One of the axioms was, "A holiday is a celebration of the exceptional." That was listed as a self-evident proposition, "A holiday is a celebration of the exceptional," as against the usual or daily or common. And the rationale seemed to be,

"If it was usual or everyday or some common event, it wouldn't be a cel-ebration, and if it wasn't a celebration, it wouldn't be a holiday." If you said to this sort of person, "What about Labor Day? That's a holiday, and the purpose is to celebrate something that is common and ordinary and daily and taken for granted. What about Mother's Day?" This person just never thinks of that possibility. It's just that it sounds good, "A holiday is a celebration of the exceptional." It just never would occur to them to look at reality and see if that's what holidays are. You just infer "a holiday," and see how that strikes you, that's it. That is a typical rationalist approach.

Ultimately, since the rationalist does not get his axioms from sense perception, he has to get them from somebody else—he needs some kind of authority. So there's a tendency of rationalists to be authoritarian. When they say, "This is obvious, this is commonsense, this is incontest-able," what they really mean in the last analysis is, "This is not debatable, nobody will challenge it, everyone agrees." Sometimes authoritarianism is only by implication, and the rationalist will abandon it if you point it out to him. But sometimes rationalists are openly authoritarian. And the clearest example is the medieval theologians, who knew all their conclu-sions in advance from the Bible, and then merely concocted deductive arguments from alleged self-evident premises in order to validate what they knew in advance.

Let me now give you a different kind of example of the same rational-ist approach. Imagine a group that starts a political movement on the idea "The initiation of force is evil" as an axiom, as a self-evidency, as a pri-mary—you just know that it's evil, and that's it—which is basically what the Libertarians do today; that's where they start, that is their equivalent of "A is A," "The initiation of force is evil." This rests solely on authority, in this case the authority of Ayn Rand, from whom they filched this idea; but in her, it is a late, late conclusion, on about the thirtieth story, of an entire philosophic system. And of course, for them, they just take it over. And there, again, you see the need to escape any complexity, to grab as self-evident something that strikes them, that they can take in and hang everything on that.

The most common form of these rationalist axioms is *definitions*, so this is a continuation of point three. A rationalist loves to start with definitions. Where does he get his definitions? From the study of entities in reality? No. Definitions, to him, are simply a string of words equal to another word. "Life" equals "self-sustaining, self-generated action," and wherever you have "life," you can strike it out and stick "self-generated, self-sustaining action." Definitions are simply verbal, linguistic, unconnected to reality, as are all concepts. The rationalist's focus is only on the relation of words to words, or concepts to concepts, not to reality. And you see again in this example why there is an authoritarian element in the rationalist—since he doesn't get his definitions from observation, he can get them only from *usage*. It's society that becomes his authority.

You can do many, many things with definitions, and if you are familiar with St. Anselm (1033–1109), who was another famous rationalist in the history of philosophy, he's an extreme example of a rationalist approach to definition. Definitions to him, so far from coming from reality, *precede* reality and give rise to it, and that is kind of the perfect rationalist approach. In his famous so-called ontological argument for the existence of God, he says, in effect, "Let's start with a definition of 'God.' We don't know whether there is one, but we're going to start with the definition. God is 'the being than which nothing greater can be conceived.'" And you say, "Maybe there is no such thing." "Let's not worry about that," he responds, "it's just a definition, and definitions, of course, are not related to reality, so you can just make one up. Now let's imagine that God didn't exist. I can think of something even greater than that—namely, something with all of His attributes, but He also existed. By definition, God is the being than which *nothing* greater can be conceived, so he must have every perfection including existence. Therefore, God exists." Did you get that? It's like: Look at these two pens, the one in my left hand and the one in my right (my right hand is empty), but Anselm would argue, "These two pens have every characteristic in common—they're both six inches long, they're both blue, they're both sharp, they both have ink, and so on and so on. There's only one difference between them—the one in my left hand exists, and the one in my right doesn't. Which is better? Obviously the one in my left hand. So if the definition was 'the pen than which nothing greater can be conceived,' it would have to be the one in my left hand."

This is the belief in words as having power over reality, definitions as being primaries disconnected from reality and you simply manipulate them, and periodically something pops up as a result. And that is the perfect example of rationalism.

There is a corollary of this rationalist approach to starting points, and that is what we can call *monism,* from the Greek for "one," so it literally means one-ism. Monism is the view that whatever you're trying to prove or explain, the ideal model of knowledge is that you should begin with only one starting point. Since your starting points are vulnerable, the fewer, the better. Ideally, therefore, if you are a full-fledged philosophic rationalist, you would like to have one insight from which everything else in the universe will follow. For instance, Plato had exactly that, and he called his supreme entity "The Form of the Good," and everything followed from that. The medievals followed Plato, but they made it "God" as the single thing. Plotinus had the perfect name for expressing this viewpoint—he called his supreme single principle "the One." The important thing about the One is that it is one; you couldn't say anything about it, because if you said anything about it, that would bring in two aspects, so it was just One, and everything followed from that.

Some Objectivists have this monist mentality or approach. For instance, they cannot stand the fact that Objectivism begins with three axioms—existence, consciousness, and identity. Why should there be three? And so what they try to do is reduce them all to just one, and the way they reduce them is to say, "There's really only one axiom, the law of identity, because if you deny existence you're contradicting yourself, and if you deny consciousness you're contradicting yourself, so we can literally prove existence and consciousness. Therefore, we're just down to one, and that's the law of identity." This is completely wrong. You cannot prove existence without taking it for granted, and if you don't take it for granted, how did you get the law of identity, and what is it a law of? This is an entirely rationalist attempt to prove everything but one axiom, in this case the law of identity. But the rationalist feels that until he's got it down to one, there's something wrong with him.

I have to confess to having this idea at an early stage of my development, and I had it in the following form: History comes from ideas, ideas come from philosophic ideas, philosophic ideas come from metaphysics and epistemology, and they come ultimately from certain axioms (or perversions of them), and ultimately I thought that you could work it out that there was only one idea central in all history, and that was the law of identity; therefore, if a major philosopher attacks the law of identity, all the rest will follow in terms of cultural trends, political trends, economic trends, and so on. That is a monist rationalist approach. And it's obvious that no one error, however disastrous, will explain everything else. It's a ludicrous construct. That's what I would call "Objectivist monism."

Point four: *certainty with omniscience.* When the rationalist has completed his deductive proof from his self-evident axioms, he claims certainty for his conclusions. "After all," he says, "I've given an unequivocal proof, every step is necessitated, my axioms are not challengeable, and therefore, my conclusion is one hundred percent certain." And this is very important to a rationalist—he cannot stand probability, "It's a matter of opinion," "Who could ever know?" He really wants to know. He wants to have *the* answer, and that's one reason that he loves mathematics—because if you prove it in mathematics, it's Q.E.D., unavoidable.

"But," the rationalist goes on, "to achieve certainty on any question, we must be completely comprehensive. We must cover everything involved in that subject, *everything*, before we can claim real certainty." One sign of a rationalist is an obsessive need for comprehensiveness. For example, if he is writing an article—keep in mind that an article has to be delimited; you can only do so much; even a book has to be delimited; even an encyclopedia has to be delimited; you have to leave out a tremendous amount—but a rationalist cannot stand omitting anything. He feels that if he omits something, "I didn't prove my case. It isn't unanswerable, it isn't convincing, it is not absolutely certain." Any of you who are teachers may recognize this; I certainly have had this example. For instance, some years back, I would not have been able to do what I did in the opening lecture of this course—that is, to say, "There is a mind/body dichotomy. I'm going to look at only three forms of it even though there are twenty-two others." That would have killed me; I couldn't have left out nineteen. Of course, it would have been extremely perverse to give twenty-two; you could never have held it all; from the crow epistemology, it would have been too many units to hold. But the idea would have been: If you just touch on three, you're leaving out nineteen, you're missing out most of the key elements in the subject, you just aren't making it clear.

This can apply in teaching, it can apply in writing, and it can apply in thinking. In thinking, it takes the form, "If any one point is not fully clear to you, your certainty about the entire issue is destroyed." It's the idea, therefore, that you must know *everything* to really know *anything* about a given issue, and that's the name for point four: "certainty with omni-science."

What would explain this rationalist need for comprehensiveness, for omniscience, for constantly covering everything, which is essential to his approach? It's an unavoidable consequence of his wrong way of holding abstractions. It's because he holds abstractions as floating and detached from reality. His abstractions, as we've said, do not stand in his mind as integrations of concretes, but as ideas in another dimension unrelated to concretes. The unavoidable result of that is the feeling, "However wonderful your theory, however wonderful your principles and abstractions, they somehow miss out reality; they leave out issues, topics, facts of the world, of actual real life. And therefore, the only way to cover reality, since you can't do it by concepts, is, in effect, by a concrete-by-concrete survey, over and above your broad abstractions." The aim for comprehensiveness is really a desire to do on the perceptual level, by constant accumulation of concretes, what the rationalist cannot do on the conceptual level because his concepts do not stand as integrations of concretes.

Let me give you the same point in slightly different terms: Concepts are functioning in his mind improperly. Abstract arguments, therefore, are simply not convincing to him. He feels that they're vague, general-ized, empty, and he's *right*—as they stand in his mind, they *are* vague, generalized, and empty. Consequently he feels he has to make up the deficit, and the only way he knows—since he can't do it by abstract concepts—is to plunge in and go over every detail of the territory, try to take every little aspect or point of the topic and say, "See, I can deal with that, that makes it more convincing, and I can deal with that, that makes it more convincing, and I can deal with that," and so on. And consequently, he is unable to delimit any topic in his own mind.

Take honesty as the example. We discussed it as an abstract principle, but the principle was chewed with a few examples, a specification of the context, a definition, and so on. And we were able to say, "We understand this now, no matter what example comes, because we see the relation of the principle to reality." There were many, many things, though, that we didn't discuss, but we didn't have to, and we didn't have to feel, "We're not really sure," because the principle, as far as we went with it, was related to reality. But a rationalist, approaching honesty, would hear the abstract argument, and he would feel, "Yes, that's fine, I like abstractions," but at the same time it's not enough. It just doesn't convince all by itself. He feels, "There are so many things about honesty I don't yet see, and any one of them threatens my broad principle, because my principle," he knows, "is somehow floating." So he has this need: "Let's jump in, let's take every possible question about honesty that you could dredge up; we have to know everything." And of course, if you're going to try to know everything about *any* one thing, you have to know everything about everything. He can't delimit. As soon as you say "honesty," he says, "Yeah, I see it in theory, but what about the used-car salesman? I don't see how it would apply. What about white lies? What about social lies? What about if you're a doctor and you have a patient who's sick—how sick does he have to be, what diseases?" And there are hundreds of thousands of questions that flood into his mind with the feeling, "Until I understand this, I don't understand honesty."

The correct approach is to stay away from those examples like the plague, as we did; take the simple examples to grasp the principle, and then use the principle, if and when necessary, to untangle some of these complexities. But the rationalist can't do that. For him, the principle is simply a floating generality (and in his mind, it is), so he has to supplement it by grabbing every concrete form of lie and studying that particular one as well as he can, and it becomes an endless process of multiplying, and if he leaves one out, he feels, "I'm not being conscientious; I don't really understand; I don't have the answer to the next example; I have to write a whole volume on honesty, and even then I've just scratched the surface, because every example brings up ten thousand other concepts that I don't really understand, and those to others," and pretty soon, it's the typical rationalist syndrome, the thing sprawls everywhere, and he feels that he can know nothing.

There's another aspect involved in this point of "certainty with omniscience," a very important consequence of his approach. We've said that the rationalist ends up trying to do on the perceptual, concrete level what he can't do by means of abstractions. He's reduced to an enormously detailed concrete-by-concrete survey, without benefit of broad abstractions. But how can you hope to know all of these concretes without abstractions? How can you deal with these thousands of examples of honesty without abstractions? Obviously, you cannot. The whole idea of an abstraction is to enable us to put an endless number of concretes together into a unit. Without those, we would just be swamped; the crow epistemology would make us expire; you'd look at five examples and your mind would just wipe itself out.

The rationalist is in this exact position. He throws out abstractions when he wants to be absolutely certain, and he starts studying all the examples, but he feels completely swamped by all those examples; he feels the tremendous pressure of, "How am I going to deal with it?" His solution is: "This is just too much to deal with, so for now, I'm going to focus on just one example and forget everything else. I'm going to ignore all the other examples. I'm going to take just one detail, one topic, one point, and I'm going to, on principle, say the hell with all the rest of it, I'm just going to study that one until I really, really get it, until I'm completely satisfied. And then, when I've got that, tomorrow I'll take the next one, and I'll work just on that until I really have that," and so on. Of course, he has one problem with this: How does he get one? How does he really grasp it without concepts? The only way you can grasp what's wrong, for instance, with white lies, is by reference to the principle of honesty. But he decides, "That's too vague; now we're going to study white lies as a special subject. And I'm going to really get that before we look at black lies." But how can he do it? Well, he feels, "White lies is a huge subject. There are so many different kinds of white lies, and so many different motives, and so many different people. Maybe white lies is too broad a subject. Maybe we should study just white lies told to close relatives." And of course, that doesn't work, and so he gets more and more concrete, more and more *disintegrated*. He takes a stab at white lies for close relatives, and then a stab at used-car salesmen with Chevrolets, and so on, and if you tell him, "You're not getting anywhere this way; you've got a whole bunch of disconnected items, and none of them prove anything, because you haven't connected it all and seen the principled overview," he feels, "Oh, no, you're just taking me back into this world of generalities, and I've got to know everything."

So he is, in effect, in a world of disconnected concretes *on principle*, as a means of trying to become omniscient. And that approach we call *compartmentalization*. Compartmentalization is basically antagonism on principle to integration. It's deliberate disintegration, the deliberate separation of one item of knowledge from all others, and particularly from all wider abstractions that could explain or clarify. It's the idea of making every item a separate watertight compartment without relation to the rest of knowledge; the refusal to connect one area, or item of knowledge, to another. And the basic cause, as far as rationalists are concerned, is this (to recapitulate): First he has floating abstractions, then he throws them aside with a fervent commitment to study one narrow point until he "really gets it," and then he discovers that he *can't* get it, so he narrows his focus even more, and he ends up staring at a concrete-bound point that he *cannot* get, and then another one, and another one.

I'd like to give you an example to show you how compartmentalization is a necessity of floating abstractions. "Man sees that the laws of the government are ruining the oil industry." That takes an intelligence to observe, and to this extent, if he really sees it, he has abstractions that are tied to reality, that are not floating. "Government" stands for something to him; "law" stands for something to him—he knows what laws he's talking about in regard to the oil industry; "oil industry" stands for something—he knows what enterprises, and so on, are involved. Now, let us say, he comes to the clothing industry, or the medical field, or the banking industry, and he wants to know, "Why are the laws passed by the government bad in this field, too?" If you tell him, in essence, "Controls as such create destruction in *any* industry, whether it's oil or medicine or banking or whichever," he says to you, "That's too vague. It's too generalized, too empty. You can't talk," he says, "about 'controls as such,' because it depends what *kind* of controls. And you can't talk about 'industry as such,' because oil differs from medicine, which differs from money, and so on and so on." That is like a confession on his part. To him, "controls as such" is a floating abstraction disconnected from reality, and so is "industry as such." It's too broad, it's not connected to concretes in reality, and therefore he experiences it as vague, generalized, empty. He can keep his concepts tied to concretes up to a certain point, but beyond that level, he can't; his concepts start to float. He does not have the conceptual apparatus to tie X and Y industry into one unit. He can't grasp that the laws governing medicine, and the laws mandating price controls in the oil industry, come under one unit—namely, "controls." So he has no option, given his mentality, given the way he holds concepts, but to treat each of these industries as separate, unconnected entities, because he doesn't have the means to connect them. So, for him, the oil industry is one compartment of his knowledge, and the medical industry is another compartment. If he were to write a book, he would have a chapter on oil without any reference to medicine, and a chapter on medicine without any reference to oil.

All of us have to separate; we have a totality of experience; we can't just sit and stare at everything. We have to separate; we have to say, "I'm going to focus on this, and not on all the rest of it." What prevents rational separation of fields from becoming compartmentalization? Realizing it and being able to connect what you separated back to the rest of your knowledge. And by what means do you connect? By means of broad concepts. But they will function only if they are not floating. If they float, they cannot serve to connect. You can think of a compartment, in the bad sense of the term, like this: A compartment is a separation gone bad. Separation is legitimate, for specialized focus, but only on the premise of reconnecting it to the total by means of abstractions, which are broad enough to grasp what's in common between it and the rest. But a compartmentalizer is somebody who simply can't do that; his concepts float, and therefore he has to break things up into a compartment and stare only at that. When a rational mind separates, there's always the feeling, "This is temporary." A rational person, not a rational*ist*—feels that it's important to see the relationship, the connection, between the separated element and the rest of what he knows; but to do this requires broad concepts that actually are connected to reality.

The person with an impaired or inappropriate approach has no inner need to connect his separation, to complete it, by connecting it back to the rest. To him, separation is an end in itself; you separate out white lies and study them, and next week or next year you study used-car salesmen, and next month you study another type, and it's just a number of types, so you study the coal industry, or the oil industry, or the medical industry, or if you're not that abstract, you wouldn't even get there—if you're a newspaper columnist, you study strip mining laws, or you study strip mining laws in Tennessee, or you study strip mining laws in Tennessee in 1981, or you study foreign policy in the first half of the twentieth century, or you study the invasion of Grenada—however it is, if that is your topic, it's not just that you focus on it and then connect it; it's on principle disconnected from everything else. That is the compartmentalizer. And a rationalist is one of the real exponents of this. He demands certainty, his method doesn't enable him to get it, he decides that he must know everything, and then he plunges in out of helplessness to start compartmentalizing, and then he can't reconnect his compartments because his concepts all float. And you see the paradox—here is a rationalist, who idealizes wide-scale vision, broad concepts, general theory, and he ends up by the logic of his method being a concrete-bound, disintegrated gazer at this item and this item and this item. He reaches the very opposite of his intention. And therefore the paradox is that in practice, in many cases, you cannot tell the rationalist from the empiricist. The empiricist is busy going around studying the disintegrated concretes, and so is the rationalist. The reason is, since he loves concepts (the rationalist), but he disassociates them from reality, and therefore he's helpless to deal with reality and is thrown back. He has no alternative but to try to deal with it *without* concepts, which makes him concrete-bound. So he's led to the opposite of his ideal by the unavoidable necessity of his approach.

I want to continue with a couple of last points on the topic of "certainty without omniscience." I think you can see why a rationalist is driven into mysticism. Concepts fail for him; they don't give him the understanding he wants, so he tries the perceptual level, of being concrete-bound. But the purpose of concepts is precisely to explain what you can't cover perceptually. So the rationalist is in this position: He wants to have a large-scale vision and understanding of reality, his concepts can't do it because they float, and his percepts can't do it because nobody's percepts can do that, so he ends up necessarily with the idea, "I get this large-scale vision *somehow*, by some means *other* than percepts or concepts. If I diligently study enough percepts and enough concepts, somehow I'll have the illumination that transcends all of them." And all the major rationalists in history did exactly that. However much they were in favor of deduction from axioms, at the climax of their theory of knowledge was: You get a mystic vision, and that explains everything. Plato said that, Spinoza said that—it's throughout the rationalist tradition.

The people in this room would not, I'm sure, have a tendency to look for one all-encompassing mystic vision. You might, however, experience this issue of "certainty with omniscience," by constant swings on a given subject. And this would be a test of whether you have a rationalist problem or not. Do you find on a given topic that part of the time some aspect of it is unclear to you, and you feel, "I don't understand that subject at all; I'm simply ignorant, I don't get any of it"? And then you get the answer to that one point, and now nothing suddenly seems confusing, and you feel, "I understand everything, this is completely clear to me, I know it all"; and then a week or a month or a year later, some point comes up that you can't answer, or you forgot some point that you had known before, and suddenly you say, "I really don't get this topic, it's completely confusing to me." It's typical of a rationalist to swing from "I know everything" to "I know nothing." Properly speaking, your attitude should be that you know what you know, *even* when you realize that there are things about that subject that you don't know. For instance, if you know that capitalism is correct, and you know that in a reality-oriented fashion, you should not be shaken if somebody brings you some example from the nineteenth century that allegedly proves the evil of capitalism and that you can't answer. You do not have to be omniscient; you do not have to know the answer to every piece of concrete example or lunacy that someone could bring up, to know your principle or why it is correct. But if you feel, when you hear the principle, "Now I know everything," and then, two weeks or two years later when this example comes up, "I don't understand it at all, I'm completely thrown, I don't even know if capitalism is right," that is a rationalist idea—the goal is omniscience. So long as you feel that you have it, you're certain, and as soon as you don't have it, you're wiped out.

In the moment of feeling omniscient, the rationalist feels as though he's had the revelation. He knows everything. He doesn't need to specify, "I know it within this context, up to this point, in this framework"—none of that is relevant; he knows everything. And then, as soon as he loses his conviction, it's gone altogether: "I can't know"; he becomes in practice a skeptic. So he alternates between a dogmatist who thinks he has the absolutes without any context, and then a skeptic who's uncertain.

Now point five—*the concern with order, or system*, a very special kind of order or system. That, of course, is implicit in what we've been saying, and in the very fact that mathematics is the ideal. There is a certain virtue in this attitude—the rationalist detests chaos. He always goes in a step-by-step fashion. When you follow his thinking, you always know where you are. His thoughts are always systematically connected. And to this extent, that is good, that's a virtue. It's much better than just a hash of jumping from one thing to the other when you don't have any idea why. He's very big on logic and structure and order. But he has, unfortunately, several vices on this topic. First and foremost is the fact that the order that he cherishes is actually arbitrary, because it is detached from reality. His axioms, which are his cherished starting points, are themselves arbitrary, out of context; he just plunges in wherever he feels like (such as in the Leibniz case of "compounds require simples"), and he just yanks out of them by deduction whatever he can, and the whole thing is a floating castle in the air. Consequently, you can say that he is a staunch advocate of order, but it is order apart from reality. It is not order *dictated* by the facts of reality; it's an order arbitrarily imposed on a world of concepts. So his order is artificial, and you can see that very clearly in the fact that the typical rationalist is obsessed with things like symmetry and neatness, which is like order apart from any reality reference. For instance, Kant, who is a mixture of everything bad—he's a rationalist, an empiricist, an intrinsicist, a subjectivist. But in this regard, he certainly is a rationalist. And if you know his *Critique of Pure Reason*, he's trying to work out the a priori endowments of the mind, and he works it out to four sets of three each in each set, and he is going to have four sets of three absolutely no matter what. There's got to be three in each, and each of the three has to be a positive and then a negative and then a union of the two, which is where Hegel got his particular order of the dialectical process, which is the thesis, antithesis, synthesis, so he was another rationalist, order without reference to reality, which he grabbed from Kant. All of these people have a definite structure, but it's completely arbitrary, and you can see that in this loving attention to neatness, symmetry, there has to be just the right number of divisions. That's one trouble with the rationalist concern with system and order.

There is another quite different problem: Even though, in fact, his order is arbitrary, he doesn't recognize this. He experiences it as though reality demands the particular order that he follows, as though he has absolutely no choice in regard to the order he follows. As he sees it, there are no options in the thought process, in the writing process, in any form of cognition. There is always only one definitive pattern that you must follow. So if you are writing an article, and you are a rationalist, it is simply anathema for you to feel, "There are ten different ways that I can do this article, every one as good as every other." You will feel, "This is impossible; I want my article to be objective, and that means I want it to be dictated by reality; and reality will therefore tell me, if I really study it conscientiously, that the place to start is with X, that's the first point, and then from there will follow Y and Z, and so on—the whole thing is written by reality, the article, in effect, is out there, and all I have to do is look at the right features of reality and read them off, and that will dictate the structure."

To give you another personal example of this point, in the early stages of writing *The Ominous Parallels*, I could not figure out an outline for a chapter. And an outline, as it stood to me in my mind, was a necessary structure dictated by reality where there was no option. I had that problem most acutely on the chapter on Weimar culture, the culture of hatred, where I was covering art and music and education and literature. And no matter how I wrestled with it, I couldn't think of a reason why you have to start with art and then go to literature and education, or start with education and then go to youth movements—there was absolutely no necessary structure. In actual fact, these are all simply illustrations within the broad principle of a certain type of cultural situation. The whole chapter was inductive; it was generalizing what the culture is, as you can see by looking at this concrete and this concrete and this concrete. And in induction, there's absolutely no necessity for a particular structure, a particular order. I remember discussing that chapter specifically with Miss Rand, and she said to me at one point, "It doesn't make any difference; it's all just examples anyway. Choose whatever is most interesting to you and most eloquent in your opinion, or most dramatic." And of course, that absolutely scandalized me, because I thought she was saying, in effect, "Be a whim-worshipper." I said, "I have to have a *reason* for finding it more interesting. Why should this be more interesting just because I find it more interesting? I have to prove that it really *is* more interesting. How can you tell me to go by my emotions? You're going to make the whole thing subjective." You see, the order of a rationalist has to be a deductive order. Induction has no order as he experiences it, and that's another reason that he can't deal with it. Or to put it another way—there's got to be a *logic*, but logic to him means "If this then this, if this then this,

236 ■ LEONARD PEIKOFF

if this then this," and if it's simply a series of things on the same level, data that are simultaneous in reality, he's lost in thinking or in dealing with it. And I remember saying to Miss Rand, "How can you possibly advocate such a thing? Would you have gone to Euclid and told him, 'Start with whatever proposition is most dramatic'? I mean, you would realize that that destroys geometry altogether; that makes it completely subjective." Rationalists take the idea "On every subject matter, whether writing or thinking, it should be like geometry." Reality has to dictate, by itself, quite apart from you, your interests, your purpose, your knowledge; all of that is beside the point. Reality must dictate a certain order, and you simply have to mirror it, follow the order dictated by reality; otherwise it is subjective. That's why, when we did the hierarchical structure exercise, a rationalist would like the fact that there's a certain order, but he would balk at the fact that there are options. If there are options, we no longer have any objectivity.

You see the idea that reality itself sets your mental process. That you have a theme is irrelevant; that you have a purpose is irrelevant; that you have interests is irrelevant. Something inherent in reality is the sole factor relevant, and you are supposed to simply mirror it with no contribution from you. You can guess what view of knowledge and the relation to consciousness to existence underlies this.

So we have this paradox that the rationalist order or system is in fact detached from reality, but he experiences it as dictated by reality, by a reality beyond him to which his desires, his interests, his selfish concerns, his feelings are simply irrelevant. And therefore, it is very difficult to argue this point with a rationalist. If you try to explain to him that his order is arbitrary, he says to you, "I can't grasp what you mean by saying that my order is arbitrary; it's dictated entirely by reality; it's deductively necessary; I contributed nothing to it."

Now point six, which follows clearly from what we've said so far: *The rationalist is anti-emotion.* As soon as he hears the word "emotion," he right away says, "Subjective, you're destroying everything. Don't bring personality into the question. We want to be neutral, factual, impartial, objective, concerned only with reality—emotions are out. They have no role whatever—no role in grasping the data, no role in organizing, no role in presenting." Desires are simply irrelevant. Your *interests* are irrelevant, because your interests are motivated by your values, and that is simply a "subjectivist" point of view. So when you go to acquire knowledge, you eviscerate yourself of all interests. You are supposed to be an empty mirror mirroring reality. If you have a personal interest, a personal involvement, that of course is going to distort and detach you from reality, that is wrong. And of course, if you told a rationalist that there is a psycho-epistemological need to keep your emotional life alive in order to keep your abstractions concretized, he would simply be aghast at that. In effect, the way he puts it is, "You have to follow reality, however boring it is to you personally. You have to be selfless." In actual fact, if you are writing and are bored, that is an unfailing sign that you're doing something wrong, that you're trying to write something either that you don't understand or that your subconscious is not convinced is important, and that will stop you more than any other thing. The only way to get out of that is to stop and to ask yourself what you actually want to say, what actually interests you. And—if you can get the answer—that is, all the considerations integrated by your subconscious that led to this desire—that is what will enable you to write. You may be wrong; maybe what interests you is mistaken, and that's not relevant to your assignment; but you'll never know until you get it down on paper; you'll never know by saying, "I can't go by what interests me," because then you simply stop yourself dead. But the rationalist feels that to say "I want" is a confession of guilt. You're not supposed to say, "I want"; you're supposed to say, "This is what is required," and you simply have to repress—if you have a want, wipe it out, push it aside, get it out of there, because that is interfering with the neutrality of your presentation.

Therefore self*less*ness is inherent to rationalism: *your* interests, *your* values, *your* desires, *your* concerns, simply have to be wiped out. You can project from the Objectivist view of selfishness as a virtue that it has to be pro-emotion, not in the sense of emotional*ism*, but in the sense that it has to be opposed to rationalism fundamentally. I'm saying that because I'm conducting a campaign in this course in favor of emotion to counteract a certain tendency, and here is one very important aspect that we are going to be elaborating when we get to the later lectures.

To conclude this point about emotion: A rationalist is actually ambivalent or inconsistent about emotion, because on the one hand he is repressed and prides himself on being repressed—he thinks that's a virtue—but on the other hand, in actual practice, how does he choose his alleged axioms? "If you like them." So in actual practice, he's an errant emotionalist. Of course, he doesn't admit that, because he thinks he's getting it by direct revelation from true reality. But nevertheless, in actual practice, he's going by his emotions, not by his perception. So, as on so many of these issues, he's mixed. By having the wrong attitude, which he thinks he's doing in the name of virtue, he ends up falling into the vice. He's all for concepts apart from percepts, and he ends up being concrete-bound. He shuns emotions, and as a result he's an emotionalist. He cannot get away with these one-sided distortions, and in order to function, he ends up as the opposite of what he purports.

Point seven: A rationalist on polemics—"polemics," as you know, simply means the method of arguing with opponents. *A rationalist feels a tremendous need to engage in polemics.* He feels extremely vulnerable when people disagree, and as a result, he feels a tremendous passion to convince them, to change their minds, to get them to come around to his viewpoint. Why does he feel so vulnerable? Because he doesn't feel secure about his own ideas; he's not really convinced, whatever his deductive structure, because in fact his ideas are floating; they are not tied to reality. Hence in his own mind, they seem shaky (which, in fact, they are). He can't, therefore, be content simply to present his ideas to someone else and let them stand or fall with their honest judgment. If you are secure internally, with your own mind, you can tell your view to others and take the attitude, "If you see it, fine; if you don't, that's your problem." But if you are insecure, if you feel shaky, and then they say, "I don't see it," that is like the knife in the heart. You feel, "I have to get to them. I have to force them to accept it, to agree. I have to, in effect, hit them over the head with a Q.E.D. I have to beat down their criticism and come up with the unanswerable argument." On the direct level of sense perception, this doesn't come up.

If somebody tells you he doesn't see the table, you tell him, "That's your problem." You say, "Look, there it is; if you don't see it, that's tough." But, for many people, if the question is life as the standard, or the evil of force, or the desirability of honesty, they do not see that as blatantly as they see "Here is a table." There's some fog in their own minds, there's some floating, there's some disconnection from reality. And therefore, they feel threatened, they need to reduce the insecurity, to batter down their opponents. And if they take the rationalist way out, they start constructing allegedly impregnable proofs.

The motivation of these proofs varies depending on the rationalist, but generally speaking, the purpose of the deduction is "Have to coerce others" and "Have to convince themselves." It's partly polemical and partly personal. Now you see another reason that the rationalist fears and dreads induction: You cannot coerce somebody by induction. You simply have to leave it to his judgment, to his honesty, to his knowledge, to his integration. You cannot get from ten thousand examples to: "Therefore, you *must* conclude this." All you can do is point out to him, "Here are the examples, here's the context, here's the indication of the integration—go home and chew it now." You can't force it on him. But you see, by deduction, you can allegedly overpower the guy. You can get him to say, "If this then this, if this then this, and so on and so on, therefore you must." And this is another reason why rationalists hate induction—it just doesn't work as a social weapon.

This need of the rationalist for deductive proof is often manifested in a multiplication of proofs. For instance, first a rationalist will give a proof of some point. And then, because, of course, his proof isn't really a proof, he's not satisfied, so he picks the proof apart and breaks it up into two more-detailed proofs, taking one sub-step, and he gives a separate proof of that, or finds some new objection in the new proof to counteract that— he's like an engine constantly multiplying proofs, and it's like if you come back a year later or five years later, he's created a mammoth set of proofs, and he's still trying to construct new ones to close new things that have sprung up. It's like plugging holes in a dike, and there's this obsessive need to have proofs of the details of proofs of the sub-details of proofs, and so on, and it's a desperate attempt to armor himself against the fact that the court of last appeal is observation, and since that's no good, he's got to build these incredible structures.

Lecture Seven Q & A

Q: Is there really no proof for induction? Then how do we use it? I do feel comfortable using it, but I feel as though maybe I should not be if it isn't proved. Is this rationalist thinking?
A: No. Induction requires a validation. That is not the same as saying it has a deductive proof. You cannot convert induction into deduction; you can't make it a species of deduction; it is something different. That doesn't mean that it can't be validated, and in fact I'm going to say something about induction in lecture nine to give an indication of how it would be validated. That is not the same, though, as equating "proof" with "deduction." There is inductive proof and deductive proof, and they can't all be reduced to deduction.

Q: Can you give an example of a philosopher giving up abstractions and focusing on concrete-bound points? Isn't this anti-philosophy?
A: Yes, certainly it is, but that doesn't stop it. The best example would be David Hume, who said you can know nothing but the sense perception of the moment that goes by you. He was the arch-empiricist; he is to empiricism what Plato is to rationalism, the perfect Platonic example. But he thought all you could do is observe as the little color patch goes by; you couldn't even know when it came by the next time that you'd seen it before, let alone get to such a wide abstraction as "redness," or to such a thing as the cause of it, which was unknowable, and so on. Bertrand Russell is an arch-example, as is the whole modern analyst movement, which says in essence, "Integration is a mistake; connecting anything to anything is a mistake; the only way we can know is to take some little item and focus on it out of context." Bertrand Russell is famous in epistemology for a theory of "the." That's it; that's the level on which they operate.

Q: Can modern philosophy (twentieth century) be described as empiricist in content and rationalist in method?

A: Yes, that I would think is a good summary formulation. They preach the slogans of empiricism, but in actual approach they are completely rationalistic. Symbolic logic is a gigantic rationalistic construct invented by Bertrand Russell and the empiricists, and it's a whole series of incredible arbitrary rules for how to connect arbitrary concepts together. The whole of modern philosophy is extreme rationalism in its approach.

LECTURE EIGHT

■

Rationalism and Empiricism

I n this lecture, we'll continue our discussion of the improper methods of thinking, of dealing with ideas in philosophy. I want to conclude rationalism, the substance of which we did last time, and then turn to its seeming opposite—namely, empiricism.

The rationalist syndrome includes two distinct points about polemics. For one thing, the rationalist feels a very strong need to engage in polemics. He feels insecure, because however many deductions he has gone through from however many allegedly infallible axioms, and however much he claims to have modeled his argument on mathematics, in fact it's detached from reality, and some part of him senses this. Consequently, he feels driven to convince people who disagree with him.

Second is the characteristic *method* of polemics—what does the rationalist do to try to refute his opponents and bring them around to his side? He bases his entire argument on ferreting out internal inconsistencies in his opponents. He tries to trap his opponents in contradictions. He tries to show them, "You said A, and now two paragraphs, or two pages, or two volumes later you're saying non-A, so aha, you have to abandon your viewpoint." That's what's called "internal inconsistency," showing a man that even accepting what he says, he is not following it out logically. Why doesn't the rationalist try to refute people by pointing out facts of reality that their argument overlooked? Because that is not his realm; facts are not his domain, not sensory-observational facts. His realm is always ideas detached from reality, and therefore, if he finds an idea that he wants to refute, he can't do that by matching the idea to reality, only by relating it to another idea. And in this case, he wants to show his opponent, "Given this idea, this other idea doesn't cohere with it."

As a characteristic method of functioning, he accepts the basic premises of his opponent. He does that as a matter of course. He says, "Okay, I'll accept your premises, but even so, I'll show you that you can't get away with this again with me, because you're involved in a contradiction." This is, by the way, the method staunchly advocated by professional philosophers of *all* schools, and the only method that they typically recognize in any form of argument. You cannot challenge anybody's foundation; you can simply show him "If," then he's committed a contradiction.

What is wrong with this method? There's nothing wrong per se with pointing out to someone that he's committed a contradiction. After all, rationalism has no monopoly on being opposed to contradictions, so it's perfectly okay to tell someone in passing, "You know, you just contradicted yourself; you said A, and now you're saying non-A." But if that is your characteristic method of argument, it is very dangerous, because you are no longer looking at reality. You now have your eye exclusively on your opponent, on his ideas. Your whole focus is on, "How can I trap him, while accepting his premises?" The first thing this does is to make you lose all sense of what is even worth refuting. No matter how insane your opponent's claim, if you are a rationalist, *nothing* is that insane, because there's no reality by reference to which to judge. So your first thought has to be, "Okay, if you say that, what about such and such?" So your opponent could come in and say, "Reality is made of Campbell's soup," and it would not occur to you as a real rationalist to say, "But look, there is no soup." That would simply be a vulgar irrelevancy. You would say, "If it's a soup made by Campbell's, then Campbell's has to be the authority of reality, but if Campbell's"—and then you deduce, and you go into this whole thing. This is not an exaggeration, unfortunately. The rationalist attitude is: Anything that is asserted with which he disagrees must be refuted because it's there. And you have to refute this because somebody said it. That, of course, is already devastating on your mental processes. It means you lose all sense of what is worth investing mental effort in, and what is ridiculous. You get completely detached from facts, knowledge, cognition, reality. Any fool can come in and say anything, and that sets your mental agenda, and gives you your mental assignment.

Beyond this problem, it is a very impractical method: it does not work. Because, inherent in this method of polemics is that you accept your opponent's basic premises; you accept his essential approach. And once you do that, in the long run you are lost. The only way to argue with someone is to challenge him at the core, as we'll see when we get to the Objectivist approach to polemics. But that is the exact opposite of the rationalist. He plunges in, he accepts the foundation, in order to have something by reference to which to demonstrate a contradiction, and then, of course, he is at the mercy of the opponent. He never gets anywhere, because he's given in on the foundation. A typical example is a rationalist atheist arguing against a theist. The theist comes in and says there's a God. The rationalist doesn't ask, "On what basis, what's your evidence?"; right away he wants to find a contradiction, which is the only thing he knows. So he'll say, for instance, regarding the problem of evil, "If there's a God and he's all good, how do you account for earthquakes and diseases and all the evil things that happen in life? Therefore, that's a contradiction." This doesn't make any truly religious person bat an eye. There are *dozens* of answers to the problem of evil, and it comes down to, in effect, "God's definition of 'good' and 'evil' is beyond our ability to grasp, but someday in the hereafter we'll see that all the things that we think are evil are really part of His plan." What are you to say in answer to that? Can you say, "This is invalid"? No. If you accept the idea of God, then you have to accept the idea of something that is beyond the power of the mind, and then you are completely lost; you're just tinkering on the surface with trivia; you've already given up. It's okay to show contradictions in your opponent, but it can always be only as a sideline. After you attack the essence, by reference to reality, you can make him squirm by pointing out a few contradictions, but it has to be just the trimming on the cake; it cannot be the substance. And yet that's what it is for a rationalist. So of course, since it doesn't work, but that's his only method, he does it more and more and more, so he becomes a maniacal polemicist.

And now my last point about rationalism: What is its essential philosophic base, the metaphysics and epistemology that it rests on? In a single word, intrinsicism. The rationalist's idea of a realm of dissociated concepts that has no connection to sensory observation would be possible only on some kind of Platonic idea—that is, that there's a world of real universals, real Platonic forms or essences, that are out there intrinsically in reality quite apart from our minds and concretes, and which act on us and yield the awareness of conceptual information. If concepts were nothing but our abstractions from sensory data, you could never possibly have the idea of a world of separate concepts. So the idea of ideas above reality implies that there are some kind of ideas intrinsic in reality that act on us.

And you can see intrinsicism in many other aspects. The rejection of any choice or option. The rejection of emotion in any aspect of cognition. The rejection of personal evaluation as having any relevance. All of that implies that our consciousness can contribute nothing to cognition. We have to be an empty mirror on which reality is to write. And that, of course, is the essence of the intrinsicist view: "Something out there acts on us. We contribute nothing."

Another example of this is the rationalist rejection of context. The only way you could know *dogmatic* absolutes—that is, without reference to context—would be absolutes that you learn without reference to human consciousness. Because consciousness would not contribute to knowledge, knowledge would simply be reality out there acting on you and producing this conviction like a bolt from the blue. So the model of the rationalist would be, "Expose yourself to reality, contribute nothing—not context, interests, purpose, values, method of organization, nothing—you just expose yourself and reality writes itself on you." And that's why I say that all rationalists are intrinsicists—at least by implication; they may not know the issue, but they would endorse it if they grasped it.

However, the reverse does not necessarily hold true. You can be an intrinsicist without necessarily being a rationalist. For instance, an overtly religious type who is not interested in reasoning or in deduction, and is quite content to just have mystic revelations, would be an intrinsicist but not a rationalist. Rationalism is a *specific* consequence of intrinsicism. You take intrinsicism, and then you add in a conscientious person who wants to be rational and logical, who wants to think step by step, who does not want mystic revelations—he will end up as a rationalist. So it's like the best an intrinsicist can end up. An intrinsicist with a commitment to reason ends up a rationalist. An intrinsicist without a commitment to reason can end up a mystic.

Let us now turn to empiricism. We can be a little briefer, because in many cases, all we have to say is, "It's the opposite." Empiricism is less common among Objectivists. In my experience, within the Objectivist world it's more common among nonprofessional intellectuals, nongraduate students, and as I've said with no pejorative inclinations, among women, although that's not an absolute. But it is by no means restricted to women. In fact, there are certain areas in which men characteristically think in empiricist terms. There are many men I know who are rationalists in one area of their lives and empiricists in another; it's not the case that if you are one of these in one area, you have to be that in every area. And I've frequently found Objectivists who are highly rationalist in their approach to philosophy, abstractions, and theoretical ideas, but then when they think about their personal lives or their personal concerns or their emotional lives, they are very empiricist. So, consider the possibility that it might be applicable to you in some other realm of your thinking.

In a general way, empiricism appears to be the complete opposite of rationalism on every issue. The empiricist, like the rationalist, is also (if we give a generous interpretation) confronted by chaos—swamped, confused, swimming amidst a complexity of ideas, and he needs some method for dealing with it. In the face of this, the rationalist tries to seize on some overriding concept or principle that he can see clearly in the midst of it all and to deduce everything from this. The empiricist also seizes on something that he can grasp in the midst of the chaos, but it is not an overriding concept or principle. *An empiricist seizes on familiar concretes*, and often also on *emotions*. And that gives him a sense of a tie to reality and a world he can deal with, a world that he recognizes, a world that he cares about. So as a general description, if you take the best version of empiricism, the empiricist is committed to reality, to fact, to observation, to values, but at the expense of concepts.

Now let's just go down some specific points and compare empiricism to rationalism.

Point one on empiricism: *the emphasis on reality apart from abstractions or concepts*; reality above or against ideas. The empiricist might *use* ideas, but he always feels that ideas are suspect. They are somehow detached from reality. They are "academic," sterile, theoretical, unreal. They are talk. Often, of course, this attitude is generated by sheer reaction to rationalism. The rationalist looks like the champion of ideas, he puts this whole imposing castle of ideas in the air (the way Leibniz did), and the empiricist says, "Throw the whole thing out, back to sensory observations. Perceptual concretes." The extreme examples of this in the history of philosophy would be the Greek Sophists, who simply denied abstractions outright, and David Hume, who denied everything except the empirical datum of the moment. Empiricists like empirical data, which means something you can point to, some perceptual concrete. They care less about how it's related to some other concrete, because that involves concepts and connections and abstractions. But to point to some concrete and say, "Here now brown," or whatever it happens to be (some of the more ambitious ones get to "Here now tomato"), that is for them intellectually satisfying, that's real, that's convincing, that's clear. Sometimes this is done out of helplessness because they simply do not know what to do with concretes, and when they get into concepts, they start a-swimming. Sometimes, however, it is very militant, and it is a principled method of functioning, a principle of being opposed to principles or opposed to concepts.

Examples in real life will convey this better than simply a description, because few real-life people walk around saying, "Here now brown." So I want to give you some examples from an arch-conservative who I believe is employed by a right-wing foundation to advance capitalism, and this is from a paper written on how to prove that man has property rights, which he is in favor of. I'd like you to focus on how this is an arch-example of the point we're talking about:

> A few defenders of property base their defense on the right to life. They point out that a person cannot eat without at least implicitly establishing property rights over the food he consumes. Similarly, a person would have trouble keeping warm without some property rights with respect to clothing and shelter. Here is an argument that, as far as it goes, is compelling. But certainly a person can eat without the rights to sell, trade, mortgage, let, give away, or bequeath his food. In addition, this argument applies only to consumer goods. What about the main concerns of socialists, the raw materials and capital goods which constitute the means of production—why should anyone own *them*?*

The idea is that you can't base property rights on the right to life. What does he construe the right to property as? What does he immediately reduce the right to property to? Does he say "the right to use and dispose of material wealth"? Absolutely not. Because if he said that, it would immediately establish a connection to life: Since life requires material wealth, you have to have the right to create, use, and dispose of it. What would he say if you said "the right to use and dispose of material wealth" as the right to property? His immediate reaction would be, "That is so incredibly broad, 'the right to use material wealth,' that is so vague, that is so incredibly generalized. 'The right to use material wealth' would include the right to eat, the right to chew, the right to swallow, the right to regurgitate after you swallow; then the right to clothing—how much clothing?—the right to sweaters in winter but not in summer, and what if you live on the island of Bali? Then you'd have no right to a sweater by

---

*Brian Summers, "The Moral Foundations of Property Rights," *Lincoln Review* (Fall 1982).

the nature of the right to life; and the right to shelter, what kind of shelter?; how many rooms do you need? And then of course after we've got eating and shelter, there's the right to sell, the right to trade, mortgage, give away, bequeath. How much can he bequeath, to whom? How can you discuss the right to property in terms of one abstraction formulation?" To him the abstraction simply blurs the reality. So the first thing his mind has to do is say, "Property is too vague. Eating I can understand." But then the moderns would say, "That's ridiculous, because we can break eating down into all its steps." Of course, once he breaks it down to eating, he's completely lost, because why, then, any amount of eating versus all the rest of the things? And if you said to him, "How could you have the *right* to eat, the *right* mind you, without the right to produce?" which he says production of goods is a separate question, "How could you have the right to eat—where is the food coming from?" He doesn't ask that question, because he's not concerned with where it's coming from; he's asking the question "Do you have a right to it?" That's the concrete he's focused on now. That's a completely separate question from "Where does the food come from?"

This is, of course, completely hopeless. You could never establish any rights by this method. The only way you could establish the right to property, the right to eating, is by the right to man's need of material goods, and because man has to produce those goods by the use of material means of production, it has to be man's right to material wealth. You have to take it on that abstract a level; without that, you're completely lost. But this is, you see, a true empiricist. And it simply strikes him as just talk. "It's just abstractions; what has it got to do with the real concretes that we see in reality? Nobody ever sees 'disposing' of goods. All you see is writing a will, or swallowing, or whatever it happens to be, so we have to take each of those concretes." This is what empiricism is like in practice. This man probably never studied empiricism, but from the way his mind works, this is what it means to prefer concretes to abstractions.

Now, here's something from another conservative. The man is defending William James, who was an arch-empiricist. (Pragmatism is simply a modern form of empiricism.) And he writes the following in a letter to some publication: "William James understood that anyone can argue from 'principle.' All it takes is a little well-chosen doubletalk." It is much harder to mask the actual consequences. The consequences of an action are concretes. Therefore, the way to judge an action is not by some abstract formulation—"Does it conform or not to this principle?"—but by looking at what happens when you do it. Then you actually see—you open your eyes and the concretes strike you. That is the pragmatist version of empiricism. It is simply concrete-boundedness, with insistence that the concretes that count are the *consequences* of an action, so it's just a modern form of empiricism. You see here the tremendous skepticism about concepts—all it takes is a little well-chosen doubletalk to argue from "principles"; anybody can allegedly prove anything; he just has to rig his words and come up with some deduction, the way rationalists do. Therefore, any discussion of principle is completely to be dismissed. And so he concludes: "I think a conservative just *has* to be pragmatic, that is, judge policies, people and ideas by their consequences, rather than by the pious principles they may claim."

How are you to judge the consequences? How are you to know what consequences mean what about what action? Recall that we had a long discussion about honesty some lectures back, and whether the used-car salesman was dishonest, and why the only way to judge the consequences is by reference to principles that conceptualize the long-range effects and how that relates to your standard of value. So this viewpoint is the absolute reverse of the truth. It is only principles that enable us to gauge the consequences. But here, we're supposed to use concretes *without* reference to principles. How are we to decide that? It comes back to feelings, which is all that empiricists have. Simply whatever strikes them directly, and they don't even make a distinction usually between emotion and perception, because they have absolutely no means to go by anything except their feelings.

I'll give you one more example of empiricism in practice. This is also a militant empiricist, but he's on the left now, not on the right. This is from a letter received by *The Intellectual Activist* in response to the advertisement that it took out about the Soviet shooting down of the Korean

Airlines passenger jet.* *The Intellectual Activist* denounced it and explained in what way this is intrinsic in the whole Soviet approach and why we should boycott the Soviets. This is a letter from a full professor at a leading university in this country. I'm going to quote certain excerpts, because he argues very articulately, and thoroughly, empirically, against the act.

> You say that Soviet citizens "may not get jobs or travel or read newspapers or rent apartments unless the government approves" [quoted from *The Intellectual Activist* advertisement]. Could you please be more specific? American citizens cannot travel beyond the country's borders without a passport—that is, without government approval. In what respects is the Soviet system more restrictive? American citizens who hold government jobs cannot change jobs without government approval, if their jobs require security clearances. And no one can be appointed to a government job, country, state, or federal government, without government approval. In what respect is the Soviet system more restrictive? American citizens cannot read newspapers that call for the violent overthrow of the American government by force, or newspapers that print names of CIA personnel, or newspapers that provide instructions for making nuclear bombs, and so on. In what respect is the Soviet system more restrictive?

For this individual, traveling, reading a newspaper, renting an apartment, getting a job—those are floating abstractions, and thus much too broad. Who can deal intellectually with such an immensity as getting a job? You can't compare two systems in terms of the principle that governs getting a job in one versus the other. You can only compare concretes. You can point to a concrete in the United States where you need government approval, and a concrete in Russia where you need government approval, so what's the difference? Is it just a quantitative issue of how

---

*The advertisement appeared in the *New York Times* on Sunday, September 11, 1984.

many jobs? What's the difference? It's still the same—for every concrete in one, there's a concrete in the other. Do you see why this is empiricism? You couldn't argue with this person, because suppose you gave him fifty examples in Russia against only three in the United States, what would he say? "That was under Stalin." You can't talk about the nature of the system, and the principles, and so on. You just collect concretes.

In case you think I'm exaggerating, I'm going to quote one more brief passage from this letter:

> You say that Soviet officials "exhibited the same savage behavior every day toward their own citizens," that they exhibited it against the passengers of the doomed airline. Can you cite examples of such behavior from yesterday, or the day before that, or on any of the previous thirty days (to take a convenient period of time)?

On the crow epistemology, you can hold concretes for up to thirty days, and that's all he's got. All the rest just recede into the past. So you can't make these incredible generalizations—he calls it "dangerous hyperbole"—of this kind; you can just itemize concretes. Now this is what you call an empiricist.

This gentleman teaches at the University of Minnesota, he's a full professor of philosophy, and his specialty is epistemology.

Now let's turn to point two. What is the primary cognitive process according to empiricism? It is certainly not deduction. Empiricists tend to dismiss deduction as antique, insignificant; they tell you that your conclusion in deduction is already implied in your premise (which is really true; all that deduction does is apply to a new case what you knew in principle all the time anyway). They actually derogate deduction too much, but I wouldn't fight with them profoundly here, because I'm not a great champion of deduction either, simply because I'm emphasizing the opposite right now to counteract the balance of rationalism, but of course, deduction does have a place. Nevertheless, for the empiricist, *the primary process is observation*. If they are extreme empiricists, like David Hume was, they will reject induction as such; there is no such thing as generalization; it is simply too conceptual. But if an empiricist is not that extreme, he can countenance induction. The rationalist finds induction very unconvincing, very tenuous. He says that induction gives you only probability at best, and the empiricist comes in and says, "Absolutely right." (But he wouldn't say "absolutely.") He would say, "You're right, induction leads only to probability, only to the tentative. There are no absolutes and no certainty." He's content with induction, so far as it's heavily based on concrete enumeration, on examples. He likes the narrow focus, the specifics. But the more general the induction, the more distrustful he is. When he hears some generalization, his instinct is always to try to find some counterexample that will shoot it down. His sense of it is "A generalization is an abstraction; an abstraction is dangerous; it's shaky. It's probably unreal, unjustified." Therefore, when he hears a generalization, his mind goes right away to "Try to find some example that will shoot it down." And here you can see a difference between the rationalist and the empiricist: Both the rationalist and the empiricist sometimes experience the sense that there's a clash between theory and practice, or between abstractions and concretes. Confronted with that feeling of a clash, the rationalist says, "Down with the concrete, it isn't real, and follow this concept," and the empiricist says, "You see, I always told you that concepts are unreliable, so throw them out; we have to go by the concretes."

As a reformulation of this same point, empiricists are very suspicious of principles. They do not like the idea of broad conceptualizations that insist that the same consequences will accrue from the same course of behavior. For instance, if you showed an empiricist that government controls will lead to disastrous consequences with regard to medicine, he would be suspicious if you showed him that it also applies to the oil industry. He'd think, "That's too easy. You're trying to rig things. You're trying to put it all under one abstraction, and reality happens to be stubborn. It's intractable, it doesn't fit your neat little schemas." So he is against integration on principle. Instead of trying to connect what he learns in one realm to another realm, he positively tries to *dis*connect, because connections to him smack of over-conceptualizing. And of course, if you're against concepts, you have to be against integration, because integration is what you do with concepts.

So the empiricist is a compartmentalizer, too, on principle. The narrower his focus, the more he shuts off everything else, the happier he is. As part of his hostility to integration, the empiricist hates the idea of system building. By "system building," we mean the idea of integrating your views in philosophy so that it's all part of one total proceeding from certain basic principles. Rationalists are the great system builders. Empiricists like to think of each thing as a separate issue. To them, a system is a confession of weakness. So, one of the things that an Objectivist approach would like about, for instance, Objecti*vism*, would be precisely the tremendous systematization and integration: Sex is connected to metaphysics, economics to politics, education to esthetics, and so on—they're all united. To an empiricist, this is not a virtue but a scandal. And what is the word he uses for any broad concept that attempts to integrate and clarify and unite diverse data? It's "simplistic." "Simplistic" is the empiricist tag to derogate integration and conceptualization. An empiricist would say that my whole lecture today was a travesty, "Because," he'd say, "you're trying to present empiricism as a systematic approach involving a definite view of A, B, C, E, and this is ridiculous. We don't have principles governing our method of functioning. We do whatever seems appropriate in any given concrete situation." And therefore, empiricism ends up being completely self-destructive: it won't even stand for empiricism. At the very end, empiricism is just like modern philosophy, which is completely empiricist and has self-destructed altogether: They won't connect anything to anything, and the result is they do not any longer know even what to talk about. That's the dead end of empiricism. In today's philosophy, of course, they also lovingly focus on concretes, but the concretes are words. Not concepts, but the words that people utter, and you have seventy-five descriptions of how people utter them. Being excruciatingly over-detailed is a mark of an empiricist.

Does that mean empiricists throw out abstractions altogether? Oh, no, certainly not. They have to talk, they think, they have theories; they don't just grunt and point. But their abstractions are dissociated from observational reality, from concretes. They are floating. They are just like the rationalist abstractions, and they would *have* to be, because the empiricist says that you can't connect concretes via abstraction. So when he uses abstractions, he feels perfectly happy to let them float. Just as the rationalist (the champion of floating abstractions) ends up being concrete-bound, the empiricist, the champion of being concrete-bound, ends up with floating abstractions. And philosophical empiricists are very open about this. If you look at David Hume, for instance, he said very clearly, "There's two types of knowledge, two types of ideas." He called them "matters of fact" and "relations of ideas," and what that amounts to is that one was the concrete-bound form and one was the floating abstraction form, and they had nothing to do with each other. And that is a true empiricist, and that, of course, is one of the roots of what later became in philosophy the analytic/synthetic dichotomy, which is the floating abstraction versus the concrete-bound. So it's just one expression in technical philosophy of this same approach.

We're still presenting various aspects of the insistence on observation, as against deduction or even induction, so what would be the favorite subject of an empiricist, the way math is of a rationalist? Not just science, but a specific science. He wants some science where there are no clear principles. Theoretical physics is already much too abstract for him. He wants something "complex, dense, obscure," where there are masses of data, where nobody knows what they're doing and no one could begin to accumulate it all, and you immerse yourself in it. Sometimes empiricists like history, because they think there are no principles governing history. Or statistics (as misused in the social sciences), or increasingly today I've noticed they like psychology, because they think psychology is all just studies of isolated trivia that have no connection to any other studies, and to be a psychologist is just to memorize and accumulate these masses of data, and so that to them is the ideal.

From their emphasis on deduction, rationalists tend to be determinists. What about empiricists? Since their view is "Who could understand anything?" they tend to be *indeterminists*. An indeterminist is not simply anybody who is not a determinist. An indeterminist is somebody who says,

"Anything is possible. There are no laws; there is no cause and effect. Who knows what's going to happen tomorrow?" So you see, again, another false alternative on this issue. The rationalist says, "Everything is inevitable; we can explain every drop of the universe by reference to certain principles, nothing could be different," and the empiricist says, "That's ridiculous; this is a universe ruled by chance, chaos—who knows what's coming next?" Which is just what William James and the pragmatists said. And all of this follows from a certain method of thought. The more you study these methods, the more you see that people like James and Dewey are not as peculiar as they seem when you first study them, because there's a very definite logic, and all their central tenets cohere, fall together, from a certain epistemological approach. The problem is that they don't tell you what that approach is. It takes a long time to figure it out. But when you do, you can read philosophers with much greater understanding.

Let's take one more point about empiricism: What is their view of the proper starting points of knowledge—that is, of axioms? What do they think, for instance, of the rationalist idea that there are self-evident conceptual truths that are the basis of all knowledge? Anathema. The empiricist finds the whole concept of "self-evident" repugnant. He says, "All kinds of sins have been committed in the name of the self-evident; we have to get rid of it; there is no self-evident." What does an empiricist think of definitions as your starting point? They're okay if you want to play around with floating abstractions, but if you're talking about real cognition, absolutely not, because *definitions are simply conceptual relationships detached from reality*—they're just social conventions, they're just linguistic, they're just people saying, "We're going to use *these* words instead of *this* word." They're like linguistic abbreviations, and therefore, when he wants to think about something that he considers real, an empiricist has no particular interest in definitions. He might rattle off a few, but it's like a perfunctory social duty. A rationalist has a fervor for definitions, because he's going to hang everything on his definitions, so he will lovingly elaborate his definitions. But an empiricist says, "If you don't like this, start with some other. What's the difference? Definitions aren't that important."

Rationalists and empiricists have the same basic view of definitions in terms of what they are—namely, the relation of one concept to other concepts detached from reality. But, for that reason, an empiricist tends to derogate definitions.

But if his axioms are not definitions and not so-called self-evidencies, what are the empiricist's so-called axioms? Where does he start his thinking process? You just start with whatever you're interested in. There is no beginning. As pragmatists say, "We are enmeshed now in the total of human knowledge—who could start as a baby and say, 'This is where I begin'? You just start, you plunge in. There's no special reverence for this idea, which is a so-called fundamental, as against this idea, which is a so-called derivative." Some pragmatists even say, "That's an elitist approach to knowledge; that's undemocratic. Why should some ideas be commanding and all-powerful, and others be just little corollaries way down the line?"

When we discussed the rationalists, we said that their insistence on axioms usually resolved itself into one axiom, so they became monists. What do you think an empiricist becomes? With regard to methods of explanation, methods of understanding, do you think he takes the view that we have to have one base, one starting point? Absolutely not. Monism is to him anathema. What do you think his attitude is? "The more, the better." That's called *pluralism*. That is, "the many as an end in itself." Because, you see, pluralism is what you're left with if you have no conceptual framework. It's only concepts that can unify a complexity, that can take a whole multiplicity and make one principle out of it. If you don't have concepts, you like the multiple *because* it's multiple. Thus, the empiricist is the type who writes history books using a method that usually puts off most decent people to history altogether, because you come to the Civil War and there will be five causes of the Civil War, or twelve causes of the Civil War, and you just have to memorize them—"The cost of grain and the Northern industrialist attitude to this, and the abolitionists to this, and John Brown's body here, and this one there"—and it's just a whole catalog, some fundamental, some derivative, some concrete, some abstract, this person's theory, "and there's no more expanding frontier," this theory, and he just memorizes the twelve causes.

That is a typical pluralist approach. If you want another example, the very last sequence of my book *The Ominous Parallels,* where I quote a typical scholar on the cause of Nazism. He says there have been something like five different theories of Nazism put forth: that it came from the politics of Weimar Germany, or that it came from the economics, or that it came from the German psychology, or it came from whatever, socio-this, and so on, and he says, "I have no quarrel with these. We have to say there is no single-line interpretation. It's a little of all these things, and a dozen more, too." And you can read my analysis of that. That is a true empiricist. That method, in its own way, is much more hopeless to deal with than that of a rationalist, because a rationalist will say, "The explanation is capitalism"—I mean a bad rationalist who's a left-winger, he'll say, "The explanation of Nazism is capitalism"—and you can *argue* with that, you can say, "No, it wasn't capitalism, Germany was more anti-capitalist than any other country"—it's possible to have a discussion. But the kind of person who says, "I don't care *what* your explanation is, one explanation is wrong," you can't deal with him. He's opposed to concep-tualizing phenomena as such. And I have gotten much more hostility to my book on that ground than on any other—that is, that it is a monist interpretation. Which, if you want to call it that, it is, because I say there's *one* explanation—philosophy.

In this regard, the rationalists are the theoreticians of the human race, and they are typically monists, even if their theories are detached. The empiricists are the eclectics; they don't come up with theories; their idea of knowledge is to combine everybody else's theories, which they think is a big improvement. So they take five concretes and twelve rationalist theories and come up with seventeen explanations.

This approach is advocated today in psychology, which is a thor-oughly empiricist domain. There were certain major theoreticians, whether you like them or not, in psychology—for instance, Watson with behaviorism, or Freud with psychoanalysis. And they put down a definite monistic view, if you will, one theory of the nature of man. And however wrong those were when I was a student, *now*, it's an intellectual feat to get a professor to reduce back to one of those, because he will say, "Why do we have to choose between Freud and Watson and Skinner and seven other types? It's a little of everything." You can't do anything with that mentality, and that is what they now regard as sophisticated. That's pluralism in psychology. In architecture, Ayn Rand satirized that in John Erik Snyte in *The Fountainhead*, because he had all the different architects, and Roark was modernistic.

I think from here we can now run down fairly easily the other characteristics of empiricism, and they will be pretty clear. Number four would be the empiricist attitude to certainty, which we've actually already covered— *they reject the idea of certainty, of comprehensive answers, of definitive, final answers.* The empiricist approach is to stress how much is still unknown, all the limitations on our knowledge, the impossibility of saying, "This is the truth." There's a constant push in the direction of skepticism. Just as rationalism has a constant push in the direction of mysticism, empiricism pushes toward skepticism.

Five is the attitude toward order or system, which he's against as such. As he sees it, the choice is reality *or* system, order, structure in your thinking. Essentially, he's committed to an unstructured thinking process, with little logical progression or development. He feels free to jump from anything to anything, very often by association. What is his view on the question of does man have choice or options? "*Everything* is options. You can go anywhere you want, in any direction." So it's the same basic idea as rationalism—namely, thinking is a system detached from reality. And one side says, "Do it," and the other side says, "Nonsense, overthrow it, let's not have this system." Or putting it in terms of another terminology, the rationalist says, "We must follow logic; to hell with reality," and the empiricist says, "We must follow reality, to hell with logic. Logic is just a game, it's just a way we put propositions together, but it has nothing to do with real reality, which," he says, "is not logical." It's "dense, opaque, complex, irrational, nonrational, brute facts." Does this mean that empiricists shun logic? Not at all. Empiricists developed modern symbolic logic. For instance, Bertrand Russell was an empiricist (part of the time). But what is the thing that is the mark of the empiricist in regard to logic? In effect, you could call it "polylogism," many logics, but that's a consequence; the central attitude is *logic as a convention*, logic as a game, logic as something other than a principle for grasping reality. And this is an expression of his view that "Concepts are floating; therefore logic is floating." All the modern conventionalism in philosophy—that logic is just a matter of the way we use words, and so on—is empiricist.

It's important to understand that when we say empiricists are opposed to order and system, this does not mean that they cannot write a decent paragraph. An empiricist can write a book, and very often they're easier to follow than the rationalists. They can write clearly, lucidly; there's a certain plan to their writing. So don't think in some kind of superficial way that I am saying that whenever you see chaos in writing, that's empiricism; that could just be ineptness or ignorance of how to write or inexperience or not organizing your thoughts on a particular subject. An empiricist can be a professional writer, lucid and clear. That does not change his opposition to order and system and logic in the sense we are talking about. When I say opposition to order and system, I mean opposition to *hierarchy* in your presentation or acquisition of knowledge. The opposition to distinguishing fundamentals from derivatives; the opposition to the idea that there are certain points you must take, and they lead to certain others. It's *that* that he opposes, the principle of the hierarchical structure of cognition. But within his nonhierarchical way, he may be very organized and clear. In fact, since he stays on the level of concretes, he's usually easier to follow than the rationalist, who has these enormous floating abstractions. Although not today, because the empiricist has discovered symbols, so they don't like to just talk about concretes; they put it all in symbolic terminology now, so it's just all a bunch of floating letters.

Number six, the empiricist attitude toward emotion. Here again, he's the diametric opposite of the rationalist, and we've already covered it. *Pro-emotion, freely feels, and passes value judgments.* He does this out of the essential nature of his approach, because, given that he just has disconnected concretes and sense perceptions, how is he to know what to do with it, what conclusions to come to, what actions to take? Since he doesn't have conceptual guidance, what can he rely on ultimately? His feelings. Once you cut off the conceptual level, you have to rely on the automatic functions. And the automatic functions in this case are what you want, what you feel, what you fear, what you loathe.

The rationalist says, "Watch out for feelings—they will take over, you won't be in control. These alien thrusts will just come, they won't be part of your neat system, you'll lose control." What is the empiricist answer? "Who ever had control? Who wants control? We can't be in control. This idea of control is a rationalist myth. We simply have to go according to the way feelings strike us." He may not say it always in the form of "go by feelings"; he may merely say, "I don't believe that. I say go by what works," which is what the pragmatists say; Dewey insists that he is not an emotionalist, that we should go by what's practical; but when it comes down to how you determine what's practical, it's by feelings, so it's essentially one step removed.

Number seven: the empiricist attitude to polemics. *The empiricist characteristically also feels vulnerable in the face of disagreement.* He feels uncertain, because his view is "Nobody can be sure." What does he do if he tries to convince someone, to the extent that he would? Sometimes he will give examples; sometimes he'll point to concretes that he thinks support his view. But, of course, that is not very satisfactory, because it's very hard to prove anything by examples, and somebody else can always find other examples, and usually he's arguing with the rationalist, who dismisses examples, so that doesn't work well. Sometimes he clings to his feelings, because that to him is a source of security, and he says, "I know that this is true, I feel it." But that's not very typical of him, because even stronger than his reliance on feeling is his idea that you can't really know. So typically, an empiricist confronted with someone who disagrees with him does *not* try to convince the other person, not after a certain preliminary, more or less feeble, attempt. You can't, you see, convince on the concrete-bound level, so he doesn't try to coerce his opposition. His typical approach is to say, "You disagree with me, you're no better than me anyway, we're all in the same boat—that's your opinion, this is my opinion, after all it's a democracy."

This doesn't mean, by the way, that he will not engage in theoretical arguments with a negative motive or a polemical motive. He's happy to refute rationalist arguments. He loves to pick apart flaws and show that the conclusions don't follow, and every argument that he demolishes gives him the feeling "another blow against the enemy," in this case, people who think that they can prove something by conceptual manipulation. Sometimes the empiricist tears down arguments by trying to show what's wrong with them logically, but more characteristically, he finds counter-examples. He will hear a whole imposing argument and just zing in one concrete, feeling no need whatever to refute the argument. Now you can understand a person who would say, "Here's a concrete that refutes your argument." An empiricist typically does not feel the need to address an argument as such. He brings in his concrete, and he just dismisses the argument—"Anyone can argue anything, so what the hell, arguments aren't even worth discussing," he sometimes feels. He's the exact opposite of a rationalist, who would say, "Concretes aren't worth discussing. Who knows what concretes are? Anybody can prove anything by concretes." So when a rationalist and an empiricist talk to each other, there's tremendous dissatisfaction. Each thinks the other comes from Mars, each thinks that the thing that is convincing to him is unintelligible to the other, and it's very unsatisfying.

To summarize empiricism, the valid elements are the desire to focus on reality, concern with concretes, with perceptual observation, with facts, and the recognition of some role of emotion, of choice, of options, but the fatal flaw is that all of this is sundered from concepts, from logic, from structure.

Now the last point, number eight. *The philosophy at the base of this approach is not intrinsicism but subjectivism.* "You can't know anything. We have no means of grasping reality," according to this view. "All issues are decided by consciousness ultimately apart from reality. We go by *our* choices, which are not determined or based on reality, but *our* emotions, which determine *our* personal starting points, whatever interests us personally—we can never get out of our consciousness." So it is simply the expression of the idea of subjectivism translated into a step-by-step methodology.

Here you see the paradox of the philosophy of empiricism: The motive, so it is claimed, is to focus on reality, not the floating world of rationalist concepts. But it ends with the idea of complete disregard of reality and absolute entrapment in consciousness. And that's what has to happen because of a wrong method: Since man can't know reality, only on the concrete-bound level, when you try to restrict cognition to that, you drop out reality, and you end up trapped in your subjective consciousness. So each of these schools leads to the opposite of its intentions. Here we have an alleged commitment to reality ending up as being based on an utter disregard of reality.

That is the false dichotomy of rationalism versus empiricism. If you go back to lecture one, you can see in what way this is an illustration of the mind/body dichotomy, the dichotomy between the inner and the outer, standards without reality or reality without standards, control by giving up the outside or the outside by giving up control. The rationalist wants control, standards, principles, reason, so he gives up facts, emotions, reality, and he treats it as his inner world. The empiricist says you cannot give up reality, so he gives up control, principles, concepts, standards. To see these two arguing is, as I've indicated, a really horrendous thing, particularly if it's in the form of a man and a woman who very often are in love with each other, and find this particular thing simply indecipherable. One side, the empiricist, finds the rationalist irritating, exasperating, boring, otherworldly, full of hot air, and consequently asks, "What is he talking about?" (I am, for convenience, using the sexual stereotype, which is not always true.) And the other side says, "She is so disorganized, arbitrary, sloppy—what is she talking about?"

Here again I want to remind you that you do not have to have one consistent psycho-epistemology. You can be rationalist in one area and Objectivist in another; you can be rationalist in one and empiricist in another; you can divide it up in many different ways. In my own case, I was very rationalist in writing but not in teaching; I had a completely different attitude toward teaching than toward writing. Rationalism didn't tempt me in regard to teaching. And that is definitely possible if your psychology works a certain way. So if you're trying to apply these to yourself, don't assume that you're going to be the same thing in every area necessarily.

Now a few concluding remarks about these two, just so we'll have a clear understanding of where they fit in the total framework of the human mind. Rationalism, empiricism, and Objectivism (which we're getting to next time), those three do not exhaust the mental life of man. Not everybody is a rationalist, an empiricist, or an Objectivist. There are several other significant categories. For one thing, you can be nothing. By that I mean you have *no* systematic method or approach, not in *any* field. You may be eclectic, you may have no definitions of the proper method, you have no particular tendency to any method. Maybe the person doesn't deal with ideas, or just simply accepts other people's views with no particular attempt to think them through by any means. This sort of person, usually an unphilosophical person, not interested in philosophy, will simply pick from various camps, whatever happens to strike him. For instance, he can mouth an empiricist bromide such as "That's simplistic" one day, and the next day say "God is the only explanation of everything," and have no sense whatever that these come from two entirely opposed schools. You've seen this phenomenon in ethics, in politics—it's not true that everybody in politics is a capitalist or a communist or anything; a tremendous number of people are nothing in particular; they just mix a whole bunch of different slogans; they have no even dominant tendency.

Let me put it to you this way: Rationalism and empiricism are already an achievement of a certain kind. They are a certain definite methodology, albeit flawed—a definite way of dealing with ideas. And you have to reach a certain intellectual level to have that, just as, for instance, in regard to ethics, to have a wrong view is already one step above simply an unreflective, unexamined hodgepodge of slogans, where you couldn't say that this person is an altruist or an egoist or a pragmatist or anything. So you shouldn't try to pigeonhole everybody.

Then there's a type of phenomenon that's very different from what we've been talking about: Both rationalism and empiricism take a valid element in human cognition and then distort it by separating it from a necessary other half, and that's what leads to all their confusions and chaos. But nevertheless, each does have, at least in its motivation, an element of validity. But that is to be contrasted with the position we can call outright irrationalism, which is the open, deliberate rejection of reason *and* experience, of concepts *and* percepts. For instance, the real medieval mystics, such as the Church father Tertullian (ca. 160–ca. 220)—he was not a rationalist, and he was not an empiricist. He said, "It is certain because it is absurd, not because I see concretes which defend it, not because I see arguments which defend it; it's absurd, you *can't* defend it." That's a different phenomenon again.

Or take the modern nihilists, who delight in demolishing everything— "Our senses are no good, our mind is no good, nothing exists, nothing can be known, nothing is of any value"—*that* is a different phenomenon. It's not the *implicit* mysticism of rationalism, or the *implicit* skepticism of empiricism, but the gleeful, joyous, ecstatic mystics and skeptics who love to obliterate everything. That is a different phenomenon. To take a simple example, Adolf Hitler was not a rationalist or an empiricist or an eclectic.

And there are still many other possibilities; this is not offered as a map of the human potentiality. I'm sure that if we were to make a study of savages in the jungle, they're not rationalists, empiricists, Objectivists, they're not eclectic mixtures of these, they're not irrationalists in the sense of nihilists out to destroy. They're something altogether different: They're completely undeveloped; they have no method and no discovery of any control over their minds yet, so they're imagistic, pre-conceptual, which is not the same thing as being anti-conceptual; they're tremendously fear-ridden, emotion-ridden, but that's not the same thing as what we're talking about; that's a primitive type of mind; they haven't yet discovered reason or experience as definite items of method. A baby would be like that for a while, or an animal. Or you could take psychotics, and there again, depending on the type of psychosis, you have a completely different type of mind, at least qua psychotic, which is in part like savages. It has some elements of being concrete-bound, and has some elements of floating abstractions (certain schizophrenics will build castles in the air), but still they are crazy, and Leibniz wasn't. So that's a whole field that I do not presume to know or to be commenting on. So this trichotomy of rationalism, empiricism, and Objectivism is offered not as an exhaustive survey of the possibilities of the human mind, but simply as the dominant mistaken methodologies characterizing Western civilization at this time as a result of the history of philosophy being what it has been. And that means that it is very widespread, but it is not a universal necessarily in every culture and period.

I want to caution you to think twice before you immediately see rationalism and empiricism everywhere. They are everywhere, but not *everywhere*, not in the exact way you would necessarily think. For instance, you cannot say blithely, "All religionists are rationalist. Religion is a rationalist phenomenon." Religion is such a broad category; it includes so many types today. Some religionists are open irrationalists, like Tertullian, the real medieval type, which still exists today, but a lot of religious people are simply eclectic—they accept some religious elements and not others, and there's no systematic viewpoint. There are definite rationalist elements in most religions of the West. For instance, if you are a theologian, you are a rationalist. A theologian is typically a person who tries to systematize the dogmas and deduce them from certain starting points, and that makes him a rationalist. Or you could say the essence of Western religion is to explain this world in terms borrowed from Plato, because Christianity is really that, too—the deduction from God—and that Platonist element in Western religion is certainly a rationalist element. So when you get to the more philosophically religious men, that's definitely rationalistic. But the way it stands in a particular man on the street—it all depends.

One last clarification and application: Can you say, "All politicians are empiricists"? No, just in the same way that you can't say that all religious people are rationalists—it's too broad a category. It's even possible to have a good politician, theoretically. But even taking them as they are now, there are usually some empiricist elements. For instance, most politicians are pragmatic, they're against principles, they're anti-ideological, and therefore, by implication, they're distrustful of abstractions; they tend to be skeptics and say there are no definite answers. They definitely tend to be pluralists and say, "There's no one thing, there are seventy-five laws we have to pass to ameliorate a given situation," but even all of these tendencies don't really make them empiricists, because most politicians have not risen to that stage. They do not have a definite methodology; they are merely mouthing a few empiricist slogans, more or less by sheer dint of their college educations. They've been burned by ideas in the past, so now they're chary of them; they've given up ideas. But true empiricism is a philosophic methodology. It comes from a definite, even if implicit, view of what is required to understand something, to make it clear, to make sense of it, to make it graspable. And politicians today typically pick up some consequences of empiricism, because it's so dominant in the colleges, but politicians are typically eclectic and nonintellectual, which is not the same thing.

That gives us a survey of rationalism and empiricism, and that leaves the last possibility, and you see a clear idea why the philosophy of Ayn Rand was given the name it was given, the perfect name for a philosophy whose whole approach is based on the objective, as against the intrinsic and the subjective, and that's *Objectivism*. On all the points we've covered the last two weeks, I'll go over them again, this time from the point of view of the Objectivist position on these questions, rather than on rationalism and empiricism. And when we do that, we will then be able to turn to one of the arguments we raised opening night, namely, "What is the use of philosophy in daily life?" Which we will finally be prepared to answer, having finally then next week grasped what it is to hold abstract ideas in a form that is not floating.

Lecture Eight Q & A

Q: When I come across an abstraction that seems unclear, I try right away to think of an appropriate example in reality. Is this approach empiricist?
A: Absolutely not. If you are confused about an abstraction, it is *vital* to be able to give an example. We've been talking about the importance of concretizing abstractions from the word "go" in this course, tying them to concretes. Empiricism detaches concretes from abstractions; it focuses on concretes. What's vital is the union of concretes and abstractions. Even

detailed concretes. For instance, if you're studying the right to property, and you define it as "the right to the use and disposal of property," you have to ask yourself, "What does use and disposal consist of?" You have to be able to say, "'Use' and 'dispose' mean 'create' and 'produce' and 'eat' and 'swallow' and 'sell' and 'trade'"—you have to list all those concretes in your own mind. *Chewing* makes sure your abstraction is connected to reality.

■

Objectivism Versus Rationalism and Empiricism

O ur subject is Objectivism, but from a particular perspective: in relation to rationalism and empiricism. Or more exactly, in *contrast* to rationalism and empiricism. I want to explain how the Objectivist approach differs from both of the ones that we've been covering, in regard to thinking in general, understanding philosophy, dealing with ideas, and writing. We're going to cover basically the same points we've covered on rationalism and empiricism, but now from the Objectivist point of view, and our stress is going to be on the methodology of thinking—how to use the mind to its greatest advantage.

First of all, I want to restate briefly, as a reminder, the Objectivist view on the mind/body question in general. As you know, rationalism and empiricism are two sides of the mind/body dichotomy. The rationalists are the spiritualists; in one form or another, they disdain the physical world—the senses, the physical—and the empiricists are the materialists, disdaining concepts, thought, the operation of the mind. The rationalists focus on the inner and dispense with the outer, with reality; the empiricists try to be outer-oriented, but at the price of dispensing with any inner standards, principles, conceptualization.

Objectivism is the first philosophy to stand for the integration of mind and body on every issue and across the board. It denies that there is a war, that there is a dichotomy, that you have to choose in *any* form. We regard the whole thing as a false alternative; there is no clash on any level, including no clash between the inner and the outer, and no need to choose.

Let me give you a brief reminder as to why, before we go through the points in order. First of all, there is no ineffable mystic soul. If we use the term "soul"—and there's nothing against it—we use it to designate an aspect of man's consciousness. Similarly, the term "mind" designates an aspect of consciousness, the conceptual faculty. The key point here is that consciousness, according to Objectivism—and we're speaking here now in the broadest sense, whether a human or animal—consciousness is a part of nature; it's a fact of reality; it's an attribute possessed under definite conditions by certain living organisms. Putting it negatively, it is not unnatural, it is not supernatural. It is through and through a natural faculty, and its function is not to attune us to a mystical dimension, but to perceive physical reality—that is, the world of nature revealed by our senses. All of this is really just an elaboration of what's contained in Galt's axiomatic statement: "Existence exists, and the act of grasping that implies two corollary axioms—that something exists, and that one exists possessing consciousness, consciousness being the faculty of perceiving that which exists." And in that characterization of consciousness, the Objectivist position is implicit, because consciousness is nothing but the faculty of perceiving the something that exists, which is physical nature. So the integration of consciousness and existence is implicit in the axiom. There is no dichotomy, and the mind-body integration is just a way of spelling that out as it applies to man. Human consciousness, therefore, is this-worldly in its essence and function, just as this-worldly as is the human body. And when the two elements (mind and body) are united, that constitutes a single, indivisible entity—man. According to Miss Rand's statement, man is a being made of two attributes, consciousness and matter, or mind and body. The function of the mind is to acquire knowledge and define values. The function of the body—in this connection in its relation to the mind—is to carry out the conclusions and value judgments of the mind. Each of these attributes, as *Atlas Shrugged* discusses in great detail, is indispensable to the other and to the total entity that is man. Without a mind, man has no means of knowledge and no way to direct his actions or preserve his life. Without a physical brain and body, we can have no consciousness or ideas at all, let alone any way of carrying out our ideas in action. The two elements are two indivisible aspects of one harmonious, integrated entity.

The task of philosophy should simply be to carry out this principle— the mind-body integration—to every cardinal issue of philosophy. I now want to take the topics—I believe we had eight that we covered from different points of view under rationalism and empiricism—go down the list, and in each case my theme is going to be that the answer to the false alternative of rationalism versus empiricism is grasping the mind-body integration.

Point one: the relation of ideas to reality. Rationalism advocates ideas above reality; empiricism advocates reality above ideas, ideas are to be dispensed with. Objectivism says ideas are the *means* of *knowing* reality. It's not one or the other—not floating ideas, not raw concrete-bound data that is un-conceptualized; the nature of knowledge is facts conceptualized, facts grasped through the medium of ideas. And this whole approach is inherent in the Objectivist concept of "concept." And that is why *Introduction to Objectivist Epistemology* is so central to the whole Objectivist approach. In essence and leaving out a lot of complexities, concepts are integrations of percepts; that's the central point from the *Introduction to Objectivist Epistemology*; they have no content other than the percepts, the concretes, that they integrate. They are a way of holding an endless number of instances, far beyond what we could grasp by direct perception, in one mental unit. And this is true of every concept, whether it's "table" or something so abstract as "honesty." "Honesty" is simply a way of holding the countless concrete acts, cases, instances of honest behavior, all the millions and trillions of times that people tell the truth, that they face facts, that they don't make up a mythical "other reality" and try to retreat to it. There is an unlimited number of such cases, and "honesty" is simply a way of retaining the sum of them in one mental unit, so that we can come to a conclusion about *all* of those instances, the great majority of which we would never dream of thinking up or actually experiencing. As against Plato and the rationalists, concepts are *not* a means of attuning yourself to another dimension. They are shorthand ways of retaining concretes in this world. But they are inextricably tied to concretes. Therefore, their whole content is the concretes that they sum up.

And, as against the empiricists, concepts are *not* subjective, arbitrary, social, without any basis in reality. Concepts are ways of *integrating* concretes, based on the actual *nature* of those concretes. They are objective, not subjective, based on reality, for purposes of our cognition. Essentially, the purpose is to expand the crow, to enable us to be able to take all those countless concretes in one unit, and thereby deal with it, whereas otherwise we could not. So they are a device of our minds, based on reality.

A major part of the secret to a healthy mental process is to keep the two dimensions going in your mind at the same time: uniting percepts and concepts, abstractions and concretes. If you have trained yourself to the right mental process, you should have a continuous dual urge: One part of your mind should always be straining in the direction of thought, abstractions, concepts; another part should be straining in the direction of percepts, observations, concretes. Whichever one you're on, you should feel the need implicitly to do the other also. It's like just a temporary division of labor—you look away from one for the moment, but the longer you look, the more it should be beating against your mind, "I'm leaving that dimension out," and vice versa.

Now let's take some cases where this would apply. First of all, in the midst of any abstract discussion, you should have a continuous urge to concretize, illustrate, apply. There should be an inner pressure to point to examples of what you are talking about in reality. You should feel that inner need growing with each new abstraction, each new general principle that is piled into your discussion, until you feel "I literally cannot go on with this discussion until I start to concretize." For instance, if you are discussing honesty, you can take an abstract argument and it's important up to a point; but after we define "honesty," we relate it to rationality, we say a few things about man's relation to reality, you have a lot of abstractions now working. You should feel a desperate need: "What does it mean practically? What would be an example? How do these abstractions actually work out?" And if you remember our discussion, we kept on giving concretes, and the same would be true for the evil of force, or the validation of rights, or any topic. On the other side, in the midst of an observation of concretes, you should have an urge to conceptualize, to integrate, to unite, to find the common denominator; because the more the concretes are multiplied, the more the crow should be rearing its head, and you're feeling "I just can't retain all this," so you will have an urge to unify, to reduce the amount of concretes, by some sort of abstraction or principle. And that's why if you get a presentation such as we got under "honesty," where you just jump from one concrete to the other to the other, your mind should begin to boggle; you just can't take it. "What do these have in common? What is the principle?"

Obviously, you cannot do them both simultaneously; you have to focus from one to the other. Whichever one you're doing, you have to remember that the other is there, and that it's waiting to be done. Both of them are crucial. They have to go along together.

Another application of this is to the topic of definitions. We need definitions. A definition consists of narrowing your focus, ignoring a huge amount about the thing you're defining, focusing on just the attribute that's going to be definitional—whether you're talking about the welfare state, or man, there are all kinds of attributes, as you know, that you have to leave out, that you have to ignore. If you just sat and looked at that huge quantity of attributes, your mind would be paralyzed. But you have to ignore them, you have to work with the definition, you have to use that, and at the same time, there has to be a pressure, an urge within you, to say, "There are a tremendous number of other attributes besides this definition; I must never constrict my concept to equate it just with the definition; I've got to have this inner need to keep going back to reality and reminding myself of all these other attributes that I'm temporarily dropping. My definition is a condensation. What does it condense? What are the other kinds of things that are involved?" So again, a twofold urge: In the midst of a survey of attributes, there's a need to condense them, to bring them down to an essence so that you can hold it. On the other hand, when you focus on the essential, you need to know what it is the essential of, what are the other attributes.

I'll give you another example, because this permeates every aspect of the thinking process. Every specialization has to be paired with an integration. By "specialization," I mean a deliberate focus on some one subject. Obviously, *all* thinking is that; you can't think about everything in general. If you focus on "honesty," you're already specializing: you're delimiting your attention to honesty, and you're leaving out all the other virtues, the rest of philosophy, chemistry, physics, astronomy—vast torrents of things. And of course, we simply have to do that. We have a finite capacity; we cannot take the totality in at once. If you think of "honesty," you *cannot* also think of "independence" and "integrity," and so on. But, the key point here is that as you specialize, there should be pressing on your mind as your future (and not-too-far-distant future) goal. "I'm looking at this separately, but I have to integrate it; I have to connect it to the other topics; otherwise I can't really grasp it. I have to see how honesty relates to independence and integrity and to whatever else is significant." There we get back to Hegel's formulation that I like: "The true is the whole." When you look at a part, you have to remember that until you see it in relation to the whole, you have not fully grasped it. On the other hand, the whole can be grasped only through its parts, in steps, in stages, by specializing and saying, "I'm going to ignore the rest for now and just focus on this." Again, there should be a twofold urge: When you survey the total, for instance, ethics as a whole, and make general statements about that, you should feel the inner need, "Do I know what the parts of it are?"; and on the other hand, when you focus on some one part, you should have a constant sense of "I have to keep this connected to the total." Compartmentalization—which I mentioned under both rationalism and empiricism—is one of the major attributes of poor thinking; it is specialization without integration. It consists of taking some one area, zeroing in on it (which we have to do), and then just leaving it separate as an entity apart from the rest of cognition. And that is disastrous.

So, in every aspect of thinking, the key to a proper methodology that will prevent you from being rationalistic in another dimension, or concrete-bound and empiricist, is a consistent union of the two by means of oscillating back and forth. That's the essence of the Objectivist methodology, the union of the two. And therefore, I think, it's very interesting that Ayn Rand preferred to write her philosophy in the form of fiction. You do not have to write philosophy as floating abstractions, but nevertheless, it's very significant that she did not want to present philosophy as a series of abstractions, even with some hypothetical examples. She wanted the actual union. And her typical novel is a whole series of concretes, which is the plot, the beginning, the whole first part of it, and then the abstractions at the end, in Kira's speech, or Roark's speech, or Galt's speech. That is the so-called empirical and the rational—more exactly, the concretes and the abstractions. And she had to write it in the form of fiction because she could not abide floating abstractions, nor could she just write a story without saying, "What does it mean? What's the abstraction? What's the principle?" (For my analysis of her literary style, with emphasis on the integration of concretes and abstractions, see my preface to *The Fountainhead* excerpts in *The Early Ayn Rand*.)

Point two. This is the issue of induction and deduction. Here again, the integrated employment of both is the proper approach. Each has a role: Induction grasps principles, generalizations, general laws; deduction applies them to the new cases. Deduction is not useless, as the empiricists say; it does give new knowledge, but knowledge of application, applying a general principle to a new concrete situation. The prime process of these two, however—while I don't want to slight deduction—is induction. That necessarily has to precede deduction; that's what gives you the generalizations, the principles that deduction then applies; that's what gives you the real meat of knowledge. The proper relation of induction and deduction was contained in our discussion of life as the standard. You'll notice it was essentially inductive—we observed certain facts about living entities that differentiated them from inanimate things. And the proof derived from that observation. Notice that we were generalizing, we were inducing. In the very act of forming the concept of "living entity," we were saying, "There is a certain type of thing in the category 'living thing,' and all living things have special kinds of attributes, a special kind of structure, special type of action—they need a special course of action to sustain them—as against all the things in this other category, the inanimate, which are different." This is an essential induction required to reach the very concept of the living versus the inanimate. Once we've done that by observation and generalization, we grasp that crucial distinction, then we of course have to systematize. If you just look at living versus inanimate, that doesn't yet give us ethics. We have to systematize, conceptualize, define "life," "value," and so on, and then set it out deductively; once we've reached the key definitions and principles, we need to organize it deductively, as we saw. So, of course the deduction is critical. But the deduction merely organizes the essential points that were reached by observation and induction. Otherwise, there's no answer to the question "Where did the definitions that we're using in our deduction come from?"

I don't want to derogate deduction. The proper role is mind-body integration. But I *do* want to take the emphasis off of deduction as the primary cognitive process, because we have to combat rationalism. Therefore, I would say, putting it in an extreme statement, the essential process of knowledge is not *from* principles, but *to* principles. So both schools, the rationalists and the empiricists, are wrong. The rationalists are catastrophically wrong on this topic, because they disdain the essential element of the process of human knowledge.

I now want to say something about the validity of induction—the so-called problem of induction, and the Objectivist solution. I'd like to point out that there *is* a solution, by the way; it is known; this is not an unresolved issue. There is nothing further to wait for as to the solution of the problem of induction. I do not say that there aren't details and aspects of the question unresolved, as induction applies to complex scientific procedures. For instance, there are tricky questions, at least tricky in my state of ignorance, on the issue of theory construction in physics—how you choose among competing theories, both of which seem to explain all the known facts. There are some tricky questions in the technical methodology of science, which I'm not going to try to address in this general lecture. But my point is this: As induction is employed by ordinary people, as opposed to by physicists—that is, in daily life *and in philosophy*—there is no unresolved problem of induction. So let me now indicate this briefly.

First of all, of course, we can dismiss David Hume, because his alleged problem is completely unwarranted. His problem of induction, as he bequeathed it, was based on the idea that cause and effect is a myth. Of course, if it were a myth, you'd really have a tremendous problem of induction: Why should the sun rise tomorrow just because it did yesterday, if there's no reason in the world why it rose yesterday? But of course, if there *are* causal laws, if there are absolute principles in reality, if entities do act according to their nature, then you can know that the entity with this nature in the same circumstances will act the same way in the future. So there's no problem with cause and effect on that level, if you have a metaphysics of cause and effect.

But that is not the total answer, because even if we grant that there are cause and effect laws in reality, the question becomes, "How do you know when you have correctly discovered such a law?" Obviously, in any induction, we cannot be exhaustive. By "exhaustive" I mean separately observe every instance under the principle. You couldn't, for example, study every example of man to determine that he's mortal; among other things, you'd have to wait until all of us died, including yourself. And what about all the men still to come? You couldn't study every example of honesty to determine that it's beneficial; first of all, there are trillions that are long gone that you could never come in contact with, and so on. You have to take a sample of instances, and then generalize to a universal conclusion that goes far beyond your sample. You must gather concretes, and then at a certain point (to use the conventional terminology) leap to a generalization; that's the so-called inductive leap, about which philosophers make a great fuss. How can you justify it? When do you know, in effect, "This leap is justified, and I really have a principle here"?

I could give my answer in many lectures, or in a shorter explanation, and I'm choosing the second. My answer to this question is two words, about which I will elaborate—*integration* and *delimitation*. That obviously needs some explanation. Now let's first take integration.

You know that in any induction, we have to begin by observation of concretes; we have to enumerate instances. We obviously need a number of instances. "How many?"—which is the way some people put the question. And I would say in answer to that, you cannot possibly give a quantifiable answer. You cannot say, "The number you need to justify your conclusion is 3,809. When you have that, go ahead and leap." In some cases, three thousand is not enough; in other cases, four is a superfluity. What determines? That is where integration comes up. Integration with what? With other knowledge that you possess. We induce in some context. A newborn baby on the table smacked by the doctor does not generalize. First he has to conceptualize; he has to observe, distinguish, separate, and so on. You have to accumulate a tremendous amount of observational knowledge and implicit definitions before you can begin to induce. Your induction has to be guided by all of the already accumulated knowledge, however primitive; it has to be integrated with what is already known. Therefore, how many instances you require in connection with a given generalization depends on the rest of your knowledge.

Take the obvious example: We see a thousand white swans, and we never come across an exception. With nothing further, you would be unjustified to generalize. It would be shaky, unconvincing, to conclude all swans are white. Why? Because if your knowledge has been developing normally, you would have presumably observed that color is generally a nonessential, that it's a superficial attribute with little connection to the structure, nature, or actions of a given species. You can see that in human beings, who range from red, white, black, and so on, and yet are all still human. Once you see this across many species, you already have a principle to guide you with regard to the swan, which is: Be suspicious. Do not assume that ten thousand cases proves anything, because it's only color. That other knowledge—if you integrate your observations of the swans to it—would undercut, undermine, jeopardize your potential generalization. On the other hand, "All men are mortal"—now there you may have observed only a thousand or a hundred. But it integrates with a huge number of other observations. You know that it integrates with what you observe about *all* living beings, in all categories—ages, animal, vegetable, plants, whatever the climate, the region, and so on. There is a powerful mass of data with which you could integrate this observation, which immensely strengthens it.

That is not, by the way, the *only* integration; you must integrate with everything you know that would be relevant. I once had an interesting discussion with Miss Rand where she said that if there were no aging process, even if everything else remained the same, she would be much less secure in the generalization that "All men are mortal." Suppose that she had hypothesized, just pedagogically, the following: Everything is the same, every man in fact has actually died, and it's true of all living beings, but there is no aging process; all we observe is that we're entirely strong, young, and so on, and then bang, for no reason, we drop dead; as against the present situation, where you see the gradual atrophy, and the gray hair, and the lines, and the stooping over—the living entity is obviously beginning to fall apart. The aging process connects the mortality that we observe to something about the nature of the entity. It's another kind of fact that we see in all of the entities that integrates with the mortality, another set of observational inductive facts that support mortality by integrating them with what we know. Observe that we're not omniscient; so there's no use in asking me, "Do you know what causes aging?" Even if the facts of aging are not yet explained, even if our knowledge is limited (which it always is), it remains true that the new integration adds weight to the fact that men are mortal. And vice versa: The fact that we observe that men are mortal adds weight to the fact that they're going to go on aging. Each one supports the other, because the two together, integrated, give us a fuller picture of living organisms and what their nature is. And of course, we could tie in further—we know that all entities, the inanimate included, wear out, that you can't expend energy in perpetuity, that machines ultimately collapse and turn into rubble, and so on; and we could make an obvious connection to living organisms. These are scientific, not philosophic, examples. I just want to give you an indication here that the solution to induction does not lie in sheer quantity. You have to have some instances—otherwise you're just rationalistically making it up out of the blue. But the crucial thing is the relation of your instances to the other information you have.

Now someone is sure to say, "Isn't the whole thing circular as you've presented it?" Because after all, I say, "The knowledge that man is mortal is strengthened, is established, by the tie-in to aging. And the conviction that aging will go on is based on, or partly based on, the observation of mortality." So don't we have an infinite regress? How can you use A to strengthen B, which then in turn strengthens A? And is not this a circle?

The best simple answer to this is yes, it is circular, but this does not mean it's a logical fallacy. There's bad circularity and good circularity. In bad circularity, the kind that is a logical fallacy, you assert an arbitrary claim, and then use it allegedly to prove itself. For instance, I say, "I am infallible," and you say, "What's the proof?" and I say, "Jim says so," and you say, "Why trust Jim?" and I say, "I know he's right, and I'm infallible." There I'm just going in a circle; I arbitrarily assert something, and I use it to establish itself. In induction, your initial statement is not arbitrary; it's based on a fund of observed concretes, which are independent of the integration—you actually observe men dying, or men aging. The second step is an actual integration; you are not simply reasserting an arbitrary claim and using it to establish itself; you are connecting what you observe to everything else that you know; you're not merely uniting it to itself, which is what deductive circularity is. So induction is circular only in the sense that each element of the total supports the others, and vice versa. There is no fallacy in this; it truly is integration—making a whole, in which each part implies the rest and supports the rest.

So the so-called circularity here is really an expression of the mutual interrelationships of parts within a whole. And this is essential to knowledge, and we have seen that throughout this course. For instance, when we established that force is evil, we didn't just quit; we then had to integrate it to all the other virtues. (Remember that whole process we went through of how you relate it to self-esteem, and how you relate it to honesty, and so on.) All of that integration strengthened the conviction that force is evil, and the conviction that force is evil in turn shed light on all of these other concretes and strengthened our knowledge of *them*. This process, if you call it circularity, is the essence of integration. If you remember our hierarchy exercise, each level led to the next and enabled us to grasp it, but the next in turn made the early one clearer, fuller, richer, more concretized. So don't be afraid of what's called "mutually propping up" knowledge—each element props up the others, and what gets carried on is the total. This occurs throughout knowledge; it's really what we mean by the spiral.

You see how integration would apply in philosophic knowledge. Take the issue of honesty. Assuming we have the right context, how many examples did we need? Not very many. We certainly don't need hundreds of thousands of examples. A few. After a few, if we have the right context, you see the principle right away—a man trying to survive in defiance of reality in a specific way—and we already have all the other knowledge, which is what our context is, that we could integrate this to. We know already that rationality was essential; we see that honesty connects to this, and it ties in to all the other things we've already established. So only a few instances are necessary to validate the induction, because the essence of the induction is then to connect it to everything we already know about the nature of man, what he requires to survive, the nature of rationality. The observations, in effect, suggest a principle; the principle then integrates with a wealth of other observations already conceptualized, all of it ultimately giving us a fuller picture of the nature of the acting entity. This, parenthetically, is why induction requires proper definitions. If you define "man" as a rational animal, that's okay. And then when you explain why honesty is necessary, it ties right back to, "This is what a rational being needs to survive." But suppose you define "man" as the entity with a thumb, which is also supposedly distinct, and then you come now to integrate your observations about honesty, there is nothing obviously to tie it to—why should a thumbed creature be harmed by disdaining reality? There's just nothing to grease the integration. Thus, the right definitions, which are themselves a product of observation and induction, become the peg for future inductions, and those future inductions strengthen the earlier definitions, which in turn strengthen the induction.

And my other point was *delimitation*—proper induction must always be delimited. Our knowledge is always delimited; it's always specific. We always acquire knowledge within a certain framework of what we know and what we don't know. What is the term for everything we already know relevant to a given item, that conditions our coming to that conclusion? "Context." An inductive conclusion has to be preceded always by the understood clause, "Within the knowledge so far acquired, within the context of what we already know, man is mortal, honesty is life-promoting, force is destructive of the mind," and so on. Our induction has to carry with it a specification, a delimitation—we are always saying, "Taking into account all of our observations, definitions, cognitions, inductions, and so on, *so far*, this is our generalization." Do we know everything? Obviously not. Our inductions are not rationalist dogmas; they are not revelations expressive of omniscience; they are not out-of-context intrinsicist bolts that are engraved in the sky. The rationalists are wrong. Does this mean, therefore, that our inductions are uncertain, as the empiricist would say? No, and I will illustrate this later. Here the point is that later knowledge never contradicts earlier knowledge, not if the earlier knowledge was acquired by the right method. All it does is specify the conditions of the earlier knowledge.

Induction is perfectly valid and unproblematic. Its essence is: integration within a specified context. More technically: "Within the knowledge now possessed, this principle suggested by concretes integrates with everything known, particularly with essentials as now defined, and contradicts nothing." And if you can say that, then the generalization is valid. "Within the context now known, this generalization—which was actually based on observed concretes—integrates with everything, particularly with essentials, and contradicts nothing"—if you can say that, it's valid.

Putting it negatively, it means that the worst thing you can do is compartmentalize, because the essence of induction is connection, union with the rest of knowledge. That is why both rationalists and empiricists are suspicious of induction: Both of them are compartmentalizers, and consequently, they have no way of knowing whether their generalizations are valid, and therefore they regard it as precarious, uncertain, unreliable. The empiricist says, "Okay, I'll go with the uncertainty," and the rationalist says, "Let's get rid of induction."

To complete the topic of induction and deduction: For rationalists focusing on deduction, the model of human cognition is math. For empiricists, the model is some sort of sprawling, unstructured science, like statistics [as misused by the social sciences]. For Objectivism, the model is what? There is no model. All sciences properly performed are in the same boat, except for mathematics and logic, which are untypical (for reasons we've already discussed). Knowledge does not consist of picking out some such subject that you feel warmly toward and then modeling all the rest of your knowledge on that. Philosophy sets the terms, the principles, to govern all cognition, but even *it* is not a good model of all cognition. Even though philosophy does unite the abstract and the concrete (induction and deduction), it is nevertheless also untypical, because it is extremely abstract and does not engage in experimentation. You cannot approach cognition by modeling it on some subject. You have to approach it by principle.

Now to point three: the Objectivist view of axioms. Axioms exist, they're important, we have to specify them—to that extent, rationalists are right, and empiricists are wrong—but, as against rationalism, axioms (according to Objectivism) are *preconditions* of knowledge; they are not the starting points of a deductive development; they are not the foundations from which we infer conclusions à la mathematics. The three axioms of Objectivism—existence, consciousness, identity—are not starting points from which you can deduce conclusions. If all you know is "Existence exists," and you sit and stare at that, you will never get any further. Those axioms are the foundations of knowledge, which means they *enable* us then to look at reality, to have actual experience that we then have to conceptualize, induce, integrate, and so on. So the rationalists are right—there are fundamentals that are important; there is a hierarchy. But the true fundamentals are not our deductive starting points. And above all, *the true fundamentals are on the perceptual level.* That's the other main difference from rationalism. The only self-evident, the only starting point, is direct perception. There is no so-called conceptual self-evidency, à la Leibniz or the rationalists. Don't be confused by "A is A," which is an abstract statement, but it's an abstract statement of a perceptual self-evidency. The rationalist poses as a champion of hierarchy, fundamentals, but in fact he starts with arbitrary starting points and ends up disregarding true fundamentals and even opposing them, as Leibniz, for instance, ended up opposing the material world. The whole idea of fundamentals in a hierarchical structure implies that we *start* our hierarchy with what we learn by observation, and that the more sophisticated is based on that. Therefore, to hammer this point home again, *definitions are not axioms*; they are not *starting* points of cognition, but *conclusions*. As we've said over and over, reasoning does not consist of starting with definitions in a void. Definitions are actually inductive conclusions; they're crucial, but they are not the beginning of knowledge.

It is very important to know when something is an axiom and when it isn't. You can take a true principle, something that is actually the case, but if you falsely take it as an axiom in your thinking, it will wreak havoc by the sheer fact that you took it as an axiom, even though it's absolutely true. It makes all the difference to how you think with that principle whether it's an axiom or itself a conclusion resting on a lot of other information. As an example of this, let's take the principle that "controls breed controls." That's true: Once a government starts controls, those controls are going to cause dislocations that they have to rectify with other controls, and so on, so the process grows forever. But suppose that in your thinking you let it function as an axiom, a starting point. "Starting point" means it does not require proof, because it's supposedly an axiom. It doesn't require a context. It's just "that's it," that's where I begin; the beginning doesn't require a context, it's the beginning, and you can't have a context as you get started. How will you start to think now with this principle that controls breed controls (which is, mind you, true)? The only obvious conclusion would have to be, "I guess dictatorship is inevitable. Because controls breed controls—that's my beginning—we've got lots of controls, so they're going to breed more controls, and more controls, and so on, and the end has to be dictatorship." If you say to such a person, "How would you explain the American Revolution? There were a lot of controls, and that bred a revolution, so you could say controls bred freedom." That will simply be inconceivable to somebody who takes it as an axiom. Or else it will plunge him in chaos, and his conclusion will be,

"You never can trust a principle; some empiricist will always find an exception." The reason you get into these kinds of snarls is because "controls breed controls" is not an axiom; it's a derivative, which means it already has a whole context, and it applies only in that context; it's not a primary. "Controls breed controls"—how, why, and in what way? Well, they lead to crises. They can lead to some people being sacrificed for others, so they have to have pressure groups, and the pressure groups rebel against being scapegoats, so they come in and demand more controls if *they're* to survive, and so on, and all of that will take place, *assuming* that nobody tells them there's an alternative philosophy, as, for instance, was said in the American Revolution. So in the appropriate context, if you see the proof, the context will leap out at you, then the principle is true. But if you start with it as an axiom, you lose everything on which it depends, and you are lost. By the way, this is why there is no context for a true axiom. You do not say, "Within the framework of what we already know, A is A." You do not say that, because until you say, "A is A," you cannot open your mouth to say, "Within the framework"—you do not know anything until you know "A is A," and that conditions all subsequent knowledge. A true axiom is just there. There's nothing whatever to say about how it applies, or when it applies, or how you get to it—you just look, and that's it. So to take something improperly as an axiom is to treat it as though it was like "A is A."

If you want another example of this, I refer you to an article by Harry Binswanger ["An Answer to 'Libertarian' Anarchists," *The Objectivist Forum* (August 1981)]; he analyzes the Libertarians, who take the principle that "It's evil to initiate force" as an axiom, instead of as the conclusion of a very long and complex approach to ethics and philosophy. And he analyzes very acutely how, if you start with it as your axiom, there is literally no way to know how to interpret or apply that principle.

When we were on the topic of axioms, we mentioned briefly the issue of determinism versus indeterminism. So let me, in a word, cover Objectivism on that. The best term for the Objectivist position is *self-determinism*. It's obviously not determinism—we believe in free will; you have the choice to think or not, and that in turn determines your actions and

286 ■ LEONARD PEIKOFF

emotions and so on, so there are laws of human psychology, there are principles we can gather. Indeterminism is also wrong—there is cause and effect; free will is not a violation of cause and effect but rather a *form* of causality. So the best way to describe the Objectivist position is not "Everything is inevitable; there's no choice," or, "There is no law; the world is chance." For Objectivism, the world is lawful, everything has a cause, but in the case of human action, the cause is certain choices that we ourselves make, free choices, which govern the resulting stream of events. Everything about us is determined by our ultimate choices that we ourselves make.

Point four—*certainty*. And here the Objectivist position is: certainty yes, omniscience no. Certainty within a context. Let us now look at the point that induction can yield certainty, if you delimit and specify the context. Take the issue of the cause of history. The thesis of *The Ominous Parallels* is an inductive generalization. I'm saying something that's supposedly the cause of *all* historical phenomena. The method is to observe concretes—in this case, two countries—and then to observe many of the different concrete aspects of life in each country—economics, politics, art, literature, science, and so on. In each case, I try to bring out by analysis an underlying factor—"Philosophy in some form is shaping this, and this, and this." I don't have a great deal of quantity, only two countries, both from the modern era. And yet I come to a generalization at the end that applies to all of history. That is obviously a big inductive leap. What permits it? An implicit integration, going along with what we said before. I also bring in a certain view of the nature of man, which itself rests on earlier inductions: that man survives by the use of reason—that's a generalization acquired earlier, not argued for in my book; that reason requires a certain guidance—knowledge of the nature of the universe, of knowledge, of values—that is, a certain *philosophic* guidance, with the implication that philosophy has tremendous power by the very nature of man. This is a whole framework of principles that I bring to the historical observations. So I tie in, I integrate, the observations about America and Germany in all the concretes, with everything I know that's relevant about the nature of man. That's where the integration comes in.

I want to stress that, even so, this is a contextual issue. The rationalist would say, "Once you did all this, that's it. It's an absolute, philosophy is the cause of history, it's a dogma, you're omniscient." Of course, if and when any exception would occur, an empiricist would clap his hands in glee and say, "Ah, you see, another theory bites the dust." Now just for pedagogical purposes I want to suppose the worst, just to illustrate that it doesn't mean anything—let's suppose there is an exception to the theory of history put forth in my book. Suppose centuries from now we will discover that there is a precondition to this law of human history that we do not yet know. Obviously, since I don't know it, I can't tell you what it is. But let's make up a bizarre one. Let's suppose that philosophy is influential on human affairs only if men engage in sexual relations at least once a year. I never thought of that; everybody that I looked at had done that, so it just passed me by. I don't know why that would be, but let's just say it. And that if they are abstinent for very long periods, philosophy no longer has any power. Would that invalidate the thesis? Would it wipe out all the observations that led to it? Obviously not. They are all there, they are all true, they are all vital, but the point would be: We now learn that they hold only under a certain condition that we hadn't earlier identified; they hold only in a certain context, and now we've discovered a new condition. So the rationalist is wrong—you *have* to say that inductive knowledge can always be made more precise; you can always specify more fully what it depends on; it is not a dogma or a revelation. Does this mean then that we should always say, "How do you know? Maybe there's going to be a new condition next week or next century. Is it possible?" Every time I utter a generalization do I have to say, "I'm not a dogmatist; therefore, I have to add conscientiously, 'It's possible that this is going to be overthrown or specified or whichever at a later time'"? No. Only where there's a specific basis to say that it is possible. What you should say is, "So-and-so is certain within the framework of all the knowledge already obtained." You should not say, "It is *im*possible to discover anything new that's relevant," and you should not say, "It is *possible* to discover something new that's relevant." You do not have to say either, if you do not have any basis to say either. Go with the evidence. And if you do that, you will be entirely confident in the framework of what you *do* know, and if and when the so-called worst happens, it does not threaten what you already know. New knowledge does not invalidate old knowledge; it will not upset your inductions, if of course they were made by complete integration in the first place.

The rationalists are right that certainty is essential. But they are wrong in thinking that omniscience is the means to it. The empiricists are right that we're not omniscient, but they are wrong in thinking that therefore we have to dispense with induction. The solution is certainty within a specified context.

Point five—and going more quickly, because these next points are implicit in what we've already said—is the Objectivist attitude toward order or system. Yes, we are in favor of order or system, as against empiricism, but not an order or system allegedly dictated by reality without reference to our minds—an order or system based on the facts *and* the nature of our consciousness. There are options within the proper order or system. There are options in the order of learning originally and in the order of organizing or presenting what you've already learned. As to the order of learning, we've already covered the fact that there is no necessary order—you don't have to learn the concept "table" before "chair," or "the virtue of integrity" before "the virtue of independence"—whenever you have concretes under a given abstraction, they're all simultaneous in reality, and therefore, there are many options in acquiring the knowledge. There are, of course, *principles* of structure, of order, as we know from our hierarchy exercise, certain broad issues that have to precede others and make the learning possible. And this order you must follow. But that does not dictate every detail. So both rationalism and empiricism are wrong, rationalism in saying there are no options, and empiricism in saying that everything is an option. There are options within the framework of principles dictated by reality.

The same is true for organizing or presenting material already learned. There are many choices or options in a lecture, an article, or just in reviewing and thinking in your own mind. There's no one to say you must give concretes first and then the abstraction, or vice versa; there is no one to say you must first give the lesser principles and then the broader, or vice versa. You do have to make clear in *some* form what the key abstractions are and what their logical relationship is.

Point six, the Objectivist view of emotions in contrast to rationalism and empiricism. The rationalist is opposed to emotions, and in contrast to that, Objectivism is strongly in favor of emotions, feelings, because those are the expression of values. Objectivism is a philosophy of self-interest, and self-interest has to involve "I want X" as a crucial precondition or constituent. That means having a feeling and asserting it. However, as against empiricism, Objectivism is not emotionalist; it is not the whim-worshipping idea of Nietzsche that if you feel it, that makes it right.

Point seven, polemics. First, on the topic of the need of polemics—if you hold your philosophy in a chewed form, concretely related to reality, you will not feel vulnerable or threatened by disagreement. That doesn't mean, of course, that you can answer every objection; there are tremendously ingenious people coming up with tremendously warped arguments. And anybody can be thrown by something new, especially if they don't specialize in the field and they weren't expecting that particular nightmare. But I think what you *can* do is to get rid of an obsessive need to prove and prove and refute and refute. In a situation where you judge it appropriate, you may want to argue or refute; but you won't feel, "I have to force him and beat him down," which is a consequence and an expression of a failure in the way your own ideas are held in your mind.

With regard to the *method* of polemics, the proper method is to *reduce a dispute to basic premises.* Don't focus on internal inconsistencies of your opponent, like the rationalist does, and don't merely cite random facts at him, like the empiricist does. Recognize that his viewpoint rests on a certain foundation, and the only way to attack that foundation is through facts. If you recognize that it rests on a foundation, you will be attacking the empiricist approach, because you'll be going to the structure of his argument. If you recognize that you have to cite facts, you'll be attacking the rationalist method. A brief example (but just a schematic one): three right-wing people trying to refute socialism. A rationalist will typically argue like this—"You claim to be for freedom (which all socialists do), but actually your ideas lead to complete dictatorship, so you're contradicting yourself—allegedly you're for freedom, and yet we have no choice at all under your system." That's the attempt to show that he's internally inconsistent. And of course, the typical socialist, if he's studied Hegel, simply comes back and says, "It looks to you like you're not free, but really there's true freedom for the *real* self under socialism; it's just the ephemeral, superficial self that goes to jail." So it doesn't faze him. The empiricist tries to refute socialism by random brute facts. He says, "They're starving in Russia." He doesn't bother with why they are starving—"Who can explain anything?"—he just tosses out a fact, trying to obliterate a theory. And this, of course, cuts no weight, because the socialist says, "There are ten thousand reasons why they are poor in Russia—they've had bad leadership, they've had terrible weather for fifty-seven years," and so on. The Objectivist approach (again, just schematically) is, in principle: You cannot argue against socialism except by reference to its foundation. And by "foundation" here, you don't have to go all the way back to "A is A." You have to go back to altruism—that is the ethical root that the socialist is actually counting on and which his politics expresses. And then you have to explain, "*This* is the thing to argue about, not politics; this is what the issue is. Look at the facts—man has a certain nature, he has to live egoistically. If he doesn't, if he does what you do and sacrifices himself, then he has to give up his freedom, he has to give up his prosperity, and so on." You take the data, which the empiricist seizes on out of context, and you show that it follows from the foundation. That's very brief, but it gives you just an angle of the approach.

And now the last point: What is the philosophic foundation of this whole approach? It is not the intrinsicist view, and it is not the subjectivist view, but the *objective* view. That's the foundation. We are trying to know reality by a certain means, by using our consciousness, which has a certain nature and dictates a certain method. We have to adhere to the direct concretes out there, the percepts, but we have to grasp them by using concepts, abstractions; we have to unite the facts—reality—as grasped by our minds. If you remember the discussion of objectivity, that is exactly the opposite of either the intrinsicist view (where we wait for revelations), or the subjectivist view (where we're cut off from reality). In every one of these points, reality makes a contribution in our consciousness. For instance, reality gives us the absolutes, but our consciousness says they are contextual—we only learn them within a certain framework of knowledge; reality dictates the structure of our system, but our consciousness is volitional, so we have options and implementation; reality says you must go by reason and adhere to facts, and it's in the nature of our consciousness that we have to evaluate and emotionally respond to facts, so there has to be a place for emotion. If you went down the list, you would see throughout that it's always an expression of "Adherence to reality by a consciousness of a certain kind." The root of the Objectivist approach is what we've been calling the *objective*, as against the intrinsic or the subjective. And this is, perhaps, the deepest reason why the whole philosophy is called "Objectivism" to begin with—because it dictates the approach to cognition.

I now want to move on to one of the arguments that we discussed in the opening lecture: "What is the use of philosophy, or Objectivism, in daily life?" As I presented the argument, "I see that philosophy is important when you're a teenager, when you're starting out, because it gives you a basic direction. But after you're established and you have a political affiliation and a career and a lifestyle and so on, what then is the use or value of philosophy?"

The answer depends on how philosophy is held in a person's mind. If a person holds it either rationalistically or empiricistically—if he holds philosophy as floating abstractions, this argument is convincing. Floating abstractions, by definition, have no applications. If philosophy is just a generalized ritual, like what Miss Rand called "church on Sundays," that you just recite every once in a while, then of course it has no connection to daily life. So we could put the point this way: If ideas have no connection to concretes, they have no connection to life. But, on the other hand, if the principles are held in chewed, concretized, reality-oriented form, if they're simply your way of holding a mass of data, if they are your means of grasping, judging, evaluating concretes, then they are absolutely indispensable to living, and you can't get on without them. It all hinges on how you hold philosophic ideas.

Let's take some specific cases. Where does philosophy come up in daily life, and why does it come up? I'm going to leave out politics, because philosophy is not *primarily* for politics; it is not primarily to equip you to argue with people. Even if there were no politics, or if you were entirely apolitical and uninterested in the whole subject, philosophy would still be vital to your daily life. So I'm not going to say anything about the role of philosophy in helping you understand the state of the world, and fighting against today's trends; all of that should be obvious anyway. Politics should not be your primary tie to philosophy; if it is, you're missing the role of philosophy in life.

The argument that we're considering begins with the idea, "I had a lot of choices when I was growing up, when I was on the threshold of maturity; but now I've settled it, I've made my basic decisions." The answer is that however much you have settled, there is still a tremendous amount in any life that is not routine and not automatically settled. Everyone is continuously confronted by novelty, by the need to choose, the need to judge, the need to come to new conclusions, the need to evaluate. You simply cannot escape this if you are a human being. So you have to decide *somehow*—the only issue is how you do it. And *however* you do it, you're going to be acting on some philosophic viewpoint. It's only a question of "Do you know it, and do you approve of it?"

For instance, your evaluation of yourself. Nobody can escape the continuous need to evaluate himself—"Am I good or bad? Successful or a failure? Efficacious, impractical?" You cannot escape having a need for self-esteem, or, failing that, pseudo-self-esteem; something keeping you going with the idea, "I have some value." How are you going to satisfy this need in practice? You cannot say, "I already have my self-estimate. I reached it when I was eighteen. I decided that I was good, so who needs values and philosophy, and so on? I already answered that question." You cannot do it, even if you would like to, because ten thousand circumstances will arise—not only *can*, but *will* arise—to challenge or shake whatever estimate you came to, if you do not have principles to protect yourself, principles that you know and righteously, deliberately, consciously apply.

Take an example. You're at work, you think you're doing okay, the season for a raise comes around, and you don't get one, you were ignored. No explanation was offered—a typical state of affairs. Obviously, there are all kinds of questions here. However much of a routine you're in, you can't avoid wondering why—"Was my work good? Is the boss fair? Is this an injustice? Did I deserve to be passed over? Have my coworkers been agitating against me? Do they dislike me? What does this prove about me?" You can't avoid a dozen questions of this kind. Suppose you just say, "To hell with it. I made my fundamental conclusions long ago. I'm not going to think about this at all. I'm set on my course, I'm just going to go ahead." If so, your automatic functions are simply going to take over, and they can go entirely by chance. You have no way then of controlling them; they may go anywhere. For instance, you can decide, "I'm not thinking about this," and the dominant emotional sum is: You will resent the way you're treated; maybe rightly or wrongly, but you don't analyze, you're not for all this moralism. So you just feel resentful. And you get carried into becoming defensive. And whether you like it or not, the feeling occurs to you, "The boss is a swine, my coworkers are swine, nobody appreciates me, life is hell." So you end up with some version of the malevolent universe. Or, your subconscious may move you in a completely different direction: you may be shaken by this experience; you may begin to feel fear. You just let it go, and you begin to feel, "I'm no good, I deserve to fail, I'm worthless, they were right to do what they did," and you start to get depressed, miserable. Or, you have no particular emotion, neither anger nor fear, you just feel baffled. And you begin to feel life is puzzling, which to you it certainly *is*, because you have no answers. "Who can understand anything? Life is just brute chance." And after a little while of that, it's not surprising that your ambition begins to fade. Who can do or try anything if life is just a chaos where anything can happen? If you simply coast, whatever you do has disastrous consequences on your life and on your routine. It attacks your motivation, your relations with others, your hope, the degree of effort you put forth, and your very self-estimate, which was supposed to be impregnable and part of your settled routine.

Now contrast that with going to the same situation consciously by principles. You tell yourself, in effect, "I know the universe can be dealt with, so I'm not posing the question of 'Is life hell?' I know that self-esteem should be based on what you do, and can't be at the mercy of other people's opinions. I know that the world is intelligible, and I won't accept such a conclusion as 'Who knows? Everything is chaos.'" The sheer act of reiterating those obviously philosophic principles in that context already acts to abort all kinds of self-destructive, automatic reactions. And that's just the *beginning* of the role of philosophy—it's like a guardian. Every time you try to think about this question, even more specifically, you are counting on philosophic standards. If you're thinking, "Was my work good?" let's say, well, what do you mean by "good"? By what standard? How much can you properly expect of yourself? Suppose you catch yourself feeling, "Somehow, I should have done better; I shouldn't have made that mistake last week"—now that in itself could lead you to start having self-doubt. But suppose then you were philosophical and you say to yourself, "I know that human knowledge is limited, that we can't expect revelations (that's intrinsicism), and I have to come to conclusions on the basis of what I know, and I can make mistakes, and I can't blame myself for them." You're bringing epistemology into what you define as good work—have you got impossible, or rational, standards? Or, should you have been given an explanation? What does that mean? Maybe you'll say, "I'm no good; they don't even have to give me an explanation." But if you remember philosophy, you'll say, "In this context, whatever else is true, they should have been objective. It's not right for people to deal with one another without giving them an explanation of something crucial that one does that affects another in a joint enterprise." That's philosophy; that's the application of a broad principle in your particular situation. Do other people dislike you? You start to think about that, and it's very relevant to ask, "Are they right or wrong to dislike me? What standards do they use? What standards *should* they use?" That's philosophy.

There are dozens of issues involving your knowledge of what is justice, what is objectivity, what is the role of context, what is the nature of the universe, and so on, all of which are absolutely essential to coming out of this type of situation alive, healthy and functioning, rather than in a self-destructive way. If you just let it go by and say, "I'm already set," your philosophy will not automatically apply itself, even if you think it will. What will happen is that the automatic functions will take over, and they do not automatically apply philosophy, but merely the emotion of the moment. What they do is whittle away whatever principles you once *did* accept. If you suddenly find yourself thinking, "It's hopeless to deal with other people, it's all subjective, they'll never understand me," as soon as you say that, you should think, "No, I know this is wrong. Values are supposed to be objective. Therefore, communication of mutual apprecia-tion is *supposed* to be possible, so I *can't* draw that conclusion." What a proper philosophy, what Objectivism, does give you is the principles to judge and decide the actual concrete events of your life. It gives you the moral support when you're right, and the guidance of how to change when you're wrong. And that is literally indispensable if you're not to be mas-sacred by undirected automatic functions. There's no other way out of it.

On this issue of giving you moral support when right, I had asked people to hand in papers on the role of Objectivism in their daily lives. I wanted to read long excerpts, but I will read just a few brief ones:

I've always been opinionated and enjoyed the realm of ideas. Since Objectivism, both of these elements have been intensified.

Now that's a good example of the role of philosophy, because suppose somebody criticizes you for being opinionated, but you're militantly anti-philosophical; well, your subconscious may conclude, "I shouldn't talk so much." After all, everybody wants to be liked; there's nothing whatever wrong about that, as long as you're liked for the right things. But how do you know what are the right things that you should be liked for? Whether this is a valid charge against you or not, are you being criticized for your virtues or for a flaw? What *are* your virtues? What are *virtues*? You see, without philosophy, the complexities of life will whittle away whatever conviction you had, including whatever conviction you had in your own value. Who was it who said "Eternal vigilance is the price of liberty"? Eternal vigilance is the price of self-esteem, and the only method of vigi-lance is philosophic principles. There is literally no other way to do it.

296 ■ LEONARD PEIKOFF

That is just one example. There are loads of things that come up, besides your estimate of yourself, that you have to judge. However routine you might think your life is, you meet new people. However you restrict your social contacts, people periodically do unexpected things, sometimes much worse than you could have imagined, and sometimes much better. You constantly have to decide, judge, evaluate. "Other people are irrational." What is being irrational? How do you know that's irrational? Evaluations imply some method of evaluating. Without philosophic principles, you have no way to judge other people except blindly.

Another example: Suppose a friend lies to you, and you just react by your automatic function, "I don't need philosophy." You might be very upset that he lied to you; you feel it's bad—"He is no good." Or, you might like the person a lot, and feel, "I don't care if he lied to me, he's my friend." Or, you might feel, "I don't know which way to go, I'll just evade the whole question," and then you simply feel shaken and uncertain about the person. All three of these methods are hopeless. You may cut off a true friend who spoke an untruth absolutely innocently, or you may fall into the power of someone really evil just because you felt you liked him, or you may end up in perpetual self-doubt and be afraid to like or dislike anybody, because who knows? You cannot get out of it, unless you say, "How would you objectively judge the person who lied? What is the right conclusion? What is the status of lying? What does morality say?" And that is philosophy. And of course, philosophy would tell you there are different kinds of lies in different contexts, and so on. You either use philosophy, or you put yourself on automatic pilot. And if you put yourself on automatic pilot in cases where the pilot has not been programmed, it is a disaster.

This applies to millions of concretes—your estimate of movies, of books, of *anything* you go and see. Your friend disagrees with you when you go to see a movie—should you argue? What does it mean? Does it show that he's really completely opposite to you and he's a no-good person? Maybe everything is subjective, and it's hopeless to expect people to agree. Maybe there are options; maybe on some things you have to agree on the principles, but there is a lot of room for disagreement. Is this such a case? What *are* the principles? On even such a small thing as this, you either bring your philosophy consciously to bear or you just flounder helplessly. You can't escape *some* kind of philosophic conclusion. If you throw out philosophy, you're simply acting on it unconsciously, such as subjectivism, or the malevolent universe. You may for instance be an intrinsicist subjectively, unthinkingly, and you start to argue aggressively with this friend, "You were wrong, I *know* this is a great movie," when in fact it may be entirely optional, or there may be many aspects.

Another major area is that of *psychological problems*—how can you solve them, except basically through philosophy? I don't mean that that's the *only* thing you need; obviously a lecture in philosophy will not solve psychological problems. But what I would say is this: All attempts at self-improvement do involve philosophy as *an* essential ingredient, because involved in any attempt at self-improvement, you are using principles in the face of your automatized functions to the contrary—there's something about your reactions or whatever that you don't like, and the only way that you can change is, every time you're tempted or every time the problem reasserts itself, you have to cling to the knowledge, the principle that tells you, "Whatever you feel now, it is still true that so-and-so is the case," so that your philosophic standards become the beacons enabling you to improve yourself, to grow, to correct your errors. This course, in its own way, is an example of that. Suppose that you have a rationalist tendency—which you can certainly have without any evil—and you want to improve. How can you do it? Only by grasping a correct philosophy and then deliberately applying it. Again, that would not be enough. A rationalist probably would need psychotherapy, if he's a really deep rationalist, because there are psychological factors involved, and it's one thing to know the truth and another thing to be able to integrate it. But one essential element is that you have to know the truth that you're *aiming* to integrate; that has to be clear and conscious. Philosophy is what makes you a self-regulator, as opposed to just a passive, helpless reactor.

This nonphilosophy or anti-philosophy approach amounts to what philosophy? Pragmatism. Because what it means in practice is, "There are no principles, you don't have to integrate, you don't have to have any overview, you don't have to consider the long-range—just react to out-of-context concretes." And that means that you'll gradually atrophy, lose control of your life, yourself, your knowledge of your friends, and so on. It's the same issue that we discussed: Why do we need principles? Why do we even need ethics? Remember that we discussed, regarding the nature of man, why he needs conceptual guidance. And this is really the same issue. Philosophy is that set of fundamental principles required for guidance in *every* issue.

The moral is *not* saying that you have to become philosophers or spend your time thinking about it and writing papers. No. Nor am I saying it's important to argue with people about it. This is not a social issue. I'm saying you have to keep your philosophy alive in your own mind as your life guide. You have to know, in terms that you understand, the principles that are going to guide you in all of these daily choices. And you have to be able to apply them in the countless situations where you have to choose, where you can't rely on your automatic functions. I don't say you can *never* rely on your automatic functions. Obviously, if you could never rely on them, you'd be like a baby and would have to start everything from scratch; if you go to work, you don't have to sit down and analyze, "Why am I starting to type? What do I have to do? And the trader principle, for my salary"—that's all automatized, there's no problem. The point is that life is not *only* rote routine, and you cannot make it that, however you restrict your range (unless you just become catatonic and don't move at all).

My argument does not refer to today's world specifically. It is not true that this world today is so bad that we need to know a better view, but if you were brought up in an Objectivist heaven, you wouldn't need philosophy—that is not true. There would still be all the same questions, all the same choices to make; there would still be no way to judge or decide or keep on track except to go back to principles, which means philosophy.

I would now like to read from just one of the papers I received. This is from a student who happened to hear the first lecture, and I like it because this is what I regard as a proper scale of approach. This is philosophy for daily life, rather than for the ages, for the cause. And therefore, the homier, the smaller, the more folksy the example, the better. He gave three cases where he used philosophy in daily life:

> One, I use philosophy when I'm buying a new pipe. When I walk into a pipe store, I don't just buy the first pipe that strikes my fancy, because philosophy tells me that feelings are not tools of cognition—my liking a pipe doesn't make it a good one. It might get too hot when you smoke it. It might be improperly balanced, or too heavy to hold between your teeth. It might cost too much. I choose a pipe by means of reason. If I find several pipes that meet my requirements, I can then safely pick the one that I like best. Philosophy doesn't stifle my feelings; it simply prevents me from wasting time and money on faulty pipes, so I have more time to enjoy a good smoke.

That is really the idea of the objective—there are many options within the correct principle. So he's not taking a revelation that it has to be this one pipe, nor subjective, any pipe you feel like. And he goes on:

> Two, I use philosophy when I'm late for the bus—I'll run like hell to catch it, but if it's pulling away, I'll relax and light up my pipe. Philosophy tells me the difference between the metaphysical and the man-made. If the bus is gone, there's nothing I can do to change it, and no use getting steamed up over it. I think philosophy helps prevent stress. It also tells me that I should change what *is* in my power, for example, my alarm clock.

Now then, his last point is more social:

> The other day, philosophy sent a few hundred thousand people marching through the streets to protest the "arms race." A different kind of philosophy convinced me to stay at home. My philosophy armed me against a pacifist I met at a party that night, and it told me when it was useless to argue any longer.

That is the level—particularly points one and two, the pipe and the bus—that it's really very important to grasp, because that is where philosophy comes in in daily life. If you hold philosophy in a form where that's the level that you apply it, you are safe. If you can do that, it means your philosophy is concretized, it's tied to reality, it's functioning as it should. And then there's no worry, because you will never give up your philosophy, because that would be like giving up your eyesight. On the other hand, if you begin to feel, "It's all broad abstractions, and I already know what my goal is, and what party I belong to," it has to mean that ideas in your mind float, that you have no connection to the actual concretes of your life. So this whole argument comes back to the issue of how you hold ideas.

One student from this course gave what I thought was a very good summary of the role of Objectivism in his life, and I'll just quote one paragraph. He says:

> With Objectivism, two analogies can be made. One is that Objectivism is to me as my sense of life is to me—it's like a constant, ever-present awareness of my self and my goals. The other is that Objectivism serves the same purpose to me as a work of art—it provides me with emotional fuel to continue the struggle to achieve my values.

I would certainly endorse that. You may think I'm prejudiced because I'm a philosopher by profession, but I tried to indicate that this is not restricted to that profession. To me personally, the actual guidance of day-by-day life is entirely a function of philosophy. Any hope I have for the future depends on philosophy. It is like the invisible shield of self-protection protecting you from the slings and arrows of the world by constantly giving you the means to deal with them. I see philosophy wherever I look, whether it's methods of thinking or value judgments, or art, or politics, or people, or books, or newspapers. I would actually be helpless, I would feel I couldn't function at all without it.

I think that that's true of everybody on the face of the earth. But the difference is whether they admit it, and whether they do it in terms of a deliberate, conscious set of principles, or whatever hash they have automatized—that is the issue. That's my answer to "What is the role of philosophy in daily life?"

Lecture Nine Q & A

Q: Can you explain why it is only my philosophy teachers who insist that Einstein disproved Newton? Every science professor that I've spoken to about this agrees with you.
A: I'm glad to hear that about the science teachers—they obviously have not been corrupted. The philosophy teachers do so, of course, on a priori grounds. I venture to say no philosopher has ever had an opinion affected by a scientific discovery. They come to science with a certain philosophy. And this is unavoidable—philosophy dictates science, not the other way around, because philosophy dictates epistemology, so epistemology comes before science. And if you come to science, you can interpret it only from the framework of some philosophy. And therefore science, per se, apart from philosophy, doesn't prove anything. And it's understandable, therefore—if these people come to science from the perspective of extreme rationalism, they're prone to the idea that the choice is dogmatic revelation or skepticism. And then they see a revelation qualified, or undercut, or whichever, so it seems to them it's irresistible to apply their philosophy. So it's not really an aberration; it simply shows that philosophy is prior to science, and you cannot convince people who have a wrong philosophy by pointing to science; they'll just reinterpret science.

Q: Ayn Rand once said that the attribute that most distinguished her was not intelligence but honesty. Could she have been referring to a concept that subsumes the virtue of honesty, and the lack of any innocent dishonesty such as rationalism?
A: "Innocent dishonesty" strikes me as a self-contradiction. If a person is dishonest, then he's guilty; if he's innocent, he tried his best, then he was honest. So you probably mean the correct *method*—she was not only honest, but had the correct *method* of thinking. And was that simply the result

of honesty on her part? I have to respectfully disagree with Miss Rand's self-assessment. I never agreed with that, and I argued with her for decades on that point. I regarded myself as thoroughly honest, and I never came anywhere near coming up with her philosophy on my own. I think that to explain the origination of an actual new philosophy, honesty is a valuable and necessary condition, but does not go the whole way. You cannot get away from the fact that you have to be a genius on top of being honest. So that's what I would say about that. I think it's understandable that a genius would not think of himself or herself as a genius, because that is the issue of the range that they can integrate, and to them, that's obvious, that's how their mind functions, and therefore, it would be natural to think that other people who can't do that, they just simply aren't focusing on the reality out there. I think that's very common, that geniuses regard as obvious things that to lesser mortals are very difficult to grasp. So I can only speak from my own perspective.

Q: All of the items you mentioned concerning the identity of consciousness (conceptualization, choice, and so on) would have to be grasped by a process of introspection of one's own consciousness. By what method can one know that, upon introspection, one is not just observing something particular to one's own consciousness, but something in general to man's consciousness?
A: Integration, that's all. And in this case, you would have to do two kinds of integration—to what you know about the nature of your consciousness, its *essential* nature, and to what you know about the actions of others. Take two different cases. You observe that you have a limited capacity to focus; you can hold only so many units. Can you connect that to knowledge of the nature of your consciousness? Yes, obviously—your consciousness is limited, it's finite, it's capable of grasping only so much by the very nature of having an identity. *Every* consciousness would have to be limited or finite—you're tying it to the very principle of the law of identity. On the other side, do you observe evidence that this is applicable to other men? You can't observe their consciousness, but what can you observe? They can speak, they write, they talk, they function intellectually. And you can learn a tremendous amount about their consciousness from their external

behavior. Do we see signs of the crow epistemology being applicable to others, not that we can introspect their consciousness, but from observing their actions? Obviously. You just have to get up before a class and give them seventy-nine principles and sit down, and they just look at you, they can't take it in; it's hopeless; you can see their eyes glaze over, they just tune out. So you can integrate it in two different ways. This is true of any principle of consciousness, just like of matter. On the other hand, you are repelled by snakes—that's a datum of your consciousness—you loathe them. Can you say that snake antipathy is a principle of human consciousness? No. Why not? If you go to the nature of what you know about your consciousness, you know that your repulsion or attraction is a consequence of your evaluations, and therefore, if you connect what you know about how your consciousness operates, you'll say, "No, this is obviously a function of my values, and I wasn't born with those, so why would everybody have to hold that?" And then, if you look at people, you'll see there are people who pet snakes and raise them and have them for dinner, and whatever else. So you say no, this is not a principle of human consciousness. It's the same issue as any normal induction; there's nothing more tricky about it.

Q: Since knowledge always assumes a specific context, why not make the inductive leap with the thousand white swans? Why not say, "Swans are white within the context of the numerous swans that I've observed"? Discovering a black swan in the future would not contradict this, any more than your counterexamples about philosophy and history. A: What you're suggesting is why bother to integrate at all, why make such a big fuss about integrating your observations with the rest of your knowledge, why not just take any number of instances and at a certain point say, "This is it, this is my principle within my present context"? I would say that the reason you cannot do this is that you have no way to control what is an essential and what isn't, if you go only by quantity of instances. You have no way to control whether you have struck a coincidence or something real, if you go only by instances, only by number of instances. The role of integration is precisely why I said that when you validate an induction, you do it by integrating it with the sum of your other relevant knowledge. If it integrates, that shows that what you've reached here is not an accidental conjunction but an actual principle. If it doesn't, that casts doubt, such as that you know that color is irrelevant to a species's behavior, then a thousand white swans is still very suspect. Superstition and racial stereotypes both come from this type of approach. You see five black cats and they all cause bad luck; that's how these things get started. The person says, "Within my knowledge, black cats cause bad luck." If it is within his knowledge, he should avoid them then. He can have a number of instances, but that does not yet justify even a contextual induction, because he does not yet know that those instances are truly expressive of a principle and not just a coincidence. And the same thing with all these ethnic stereotypes—Scotsmen are tight, Frenchmen spend all their life in bed, and Chinese people do nothing but laundry. All of this comes from the attempt to induce only from instances, and it is simply invalid. A number of instances is just the introduction that justifies your raising the question, "Do I have something here or not?" But you have to integrate before you can even claim it as a contextual principle.

Q: Can you suggest the best steps to follow in concretizing?
A: There are three different elements. One is its definition. Another is a range of concretes that come under it, a broad range, so you get an idea of what this concept subsumes. And another is a series of *non*defining characteristics. Why do you need to know a definition? You want to bound it, you want to distinguish it from other concepts, because if you don't do that, you have no means of tying it to reality, you don't know what it stands for. So you have to give a definition. But a definition is just other concepts related to this concept. It still leaves open the possibility of floating abstractions. So what do you have to do to cover that? Point to concretes, concretize, give a range of examples. And why should you, if you have any doubt, throw in a series of nondefining attributes, which would be stated abstractly? What does that contribute? You then don't have a temptation to equate the concept with its definition. You don't have a temptation to think, "The way to acquire knowledge is just to deduce everything from this one attribute." And where I think emotion comes in is in

making it relatively automatic. If you have your emotions open, then as you utter the word and focus on the concretes, you'll think of the things that you love and the things that you hate. Let me illustrate this point with a very abstract concept: "logic." I can zip off "the art of noncontradictory identification." That is no use by itself; that distinguishes "logic" from various other concepts, but it's entirely floating so far. What would the concretes be, and where would emotions come in here? I'll tell you what my mind would do right away with something like "logic": It goes right away to an example of logical thinking that I like, a concrete example to which I have an emotional attachment. So for instance, I might think of "The noblest act you have ever committed is the act of your mind coming to the conclusion that two plus two equals four," which is a conclusion from premises, an example of reasoning, of being logical. Or, even faster, my mind would go to the obvious example bequeathed to us by Aristotle that all logicians feel a certain affection for, the syllogism "All men are mortal, Socrates is a man, therefore Socrates is mortal." So that would be a paradigm in my mind, an example of a syllogism, an example of actual reasoning, of actually thinking noncontradictorily, and that would be an example that my emotion would take to positively. But now, to get a whole range, I would want a *negative* instance. I'd want an example that I *don't* like, but that is also an example of reasoning, or at least an attempt at logic. I might think of Leibniz there and think, "If there's compounds then there must be simples, and if there's simples then there must be monads, and so on"—there's an attempt at noncontradictory identification; I don't like it, but it comes under a certain process. Since I've done a lot of work and taught this, I have a range of emotions for a whole bunch of concrete instances. But you just need three or four, and then, in the act of saying "art of noncontradictory identification," right away your mind is focused on certain concretes that are there implicitly, because this means something to you, and therefore, that's where your mind goes.

Q: Is the process you just went through an example of chewing?
A: Yes, this is an example of chewing, if you take "chewing" in the broadest sense as countering floating abstractions. But more specifically, this is

what I think of as the *reduction* of a concept, taking it back to reality. And you do that in three steps, in effect: by finding the definition, surrounding yourself with examples and then inducing their nondefining characteristics, and then seeing those characteristics as being united back in the definition. That whole process brings the concept to reality; that's what I call "reduction." And you see, the whole point is that it is the opposite of the rationalist idea, and it is the opposite of the empiricist idea—you don't just sit and give examples either. The whole thing is the union of the two; that's going to be my theme next week.

Q: Would the selection of examples precede the definition normally?
A: To learn a concept originally, you have to know concretes. So until I grasp that there were certain countries like Sweden and Britain and so on, "welfare state" would be just meaningless to me. It's only when I would recognize that there *are* such countries that I would try to grasp that concept, as opposed to "totalitarianism," and so on. So certainly the concretes have to precede the abstraction in learning. But we're talking about now once you have a concept and you're trying to clarify it in your own mind. I don't lay down as a law that first you must give a definition and then look for concretes at this stage. You might certainly do it in reverse. But the point is that you need the guidance of a definition very badly, very soon, because otherwise you won't know what examples to give and you're going to confuse yourself thoroughly—you now have so many concepts that if you don't quickly demarcate, you're going to give the example of Soviet Russia, or the United States in the nineteenth century, and so on, and then when you try to figure out the definition you'll be lost. So there must be an interplay between the concretes and the definitions, and practically, I find that the best thing is to blurt out a definition as your basic anchor in differentiation, then a range of concretes, then the nondefining characteristics, and then tie those back to the definition. That's the procedure I recommend for the systematic chewing of a concept.

Let's look at the concept of "welfare state" from the standpoint of nondefinitional characteristics. There's no way to identify these characteristics but to look at them. You can't do it by deduction from the

definition, because these are nondefinitional. So you have to do it inductively. Here are some: unemployment insurance, workman's compensation,
old age, Medicare or Medicaid or outright socialized medicine—there's a
whole constellation of those income-supplement programs that vary within
certain limits. You wouldn't say that "A welfare state is one that" and then
list twenty-five programs, because you couldn't hold it; and yet the presence
of those programs is significant and is essential to grasping the whole phenomenon. Other examples of characteristics true of all welfare states: the
proliferation of lobbying and pressure groups, progressive taxation, wage
and price controls. They are true of all of them, and you can show that
that comes from the nature of the system; they aren't part of the definition,
and you cannot deduce them from the definition, although when you observe it, you can relate it to the definition.

■

Emotions and Moral Judgment

Our topic in this lecture is the role of emotions in human life, including why repression is harmful and unnecessary, and why the alternative to it is not emotionalism. And I want to show that the very same errors that lead to distortions in people's attitudes toward emotions also lead to distortions in their idea of moral judgment, whether that moral judgment is passed on themselves or on other people. As is so often the case, there are three attitudes on these subjects: the rational/intrinsicist axis, the empiricist/subjectivist axis, and the objective or Objectivist axis. If you see these issues in terms of this trichotomy, it will be very illuminating, given the base we've already built up. Before turning to emotions, I want to look more broadly at the field of morality as such, the general issue of value judgments. I want to sketch, in broad strokes, the three basic approaches—the rationalist, the empiricist, the Objectivist. And then in terms of that framework, we'll turn to the specific topics for this evening.

The rationalist is an intrinsicist. He regards moral principles as commandments issued directly by reality, by some intrinsic entity out there, such as God or, in Kant's case, the noumenal self. The rationalist claims to know these principles by some direct, unmediated form of awareness—for example, intuition, conscience, sense of duty. He makes no bones about the fact that moral principles are *orders*—he calls them "commandments" or "imperatives." They're of the form "Thou shalt" and "Thou shalt not." There's no issue of the purpose they serve, because morality is not a means to an end. They are dogmatic absolutes. There's no issue of context or of the circumstances in which they apply. The rationalist is rigid, in the worst sense of that term: There are no choices, no options. Either you obey the commandment and are virtuous or you defy it and are wicked. So this gives us what's known conventionally as the rigid, moralistic type. In the most primitive version, it's put forth as a series of disconnected commandments, as in the Bible. In a more sophisticated version, à la Kant, there's only one commandment. (That's the monist element, you see—he has just one rule, and all the others are deducible from it in a neat, rationalist system.) But either way, it's the same essence.

I want you to observe that implicit in this approach is the equation of morality with selflessness. This is an issue of content now, not method, but it's a content inherent in the method. Morality apart from you and your interests, which is the rationalist approach, has to end up as morality *in opposition* to you and your interests. The whole rationalist approach implies that your welfare is irrelevant, your interests are beside the point, that is merely subjective; true morality is obedience to reality, and to hell with you personally, whether you like it or not.

We know that life requires a very specific course of action, which the rationalist approach thoroughly ignores. So the result is that morality, as he construes it, does not coincide with what is required to live. And consequently he ends up with a constant clash: Morality points in one direction, your life and needs in another. And hence the rationalist view: It is morality versus your welfare; virtue is self-sacrifice for the sake of morality; we reach the idea of morality as necessarily involving a struggle that is inherent in the intrinsicist approach: morality as self-overcoming, or self-conquest, or to put it another way, the self as the major obstacle that you must beat down in order to achieve morality. If you're an intrinsicist, then your desires, interests, choices, preferences are irrelevant. You should merely be mirroring and obeying reality.

What is the obstacle to virtue on this approach? Why doesn't everybody simply obey the commandments? The obstacle, the rationalist will typically say, is the fact that we have desires, wishes, hopes, preferences. That's what "distorts our actions." Instead of simply theoretically grasping our duty and then obeying, we are tempted by our "lower nature," as they call it. And our lower nature is our *personal* nature, our individuality, our desires—what you want, what you care for, what you prefer. On this view, you are led inexorably to the idea of emotions as the villain, the enemy of morality. Plato said this openly when he divided man into reason versus emotions; reason, in his interpretation, led us to the world of goodness and virtue, and emotions pulled us down into the muck of this world. And Kant had a variant of that view.

Therefore, for this approach, implicitly at least, the *moral* ideal is repression—keep down these emotions, because they are inherently immoral and irrational. Why? Because reason, on this rationalist view, means selfless adherence to your duties, and emotions are inherently self-oriented, they're not selfless.

So you see a perfect consistency in the rationalist viewpoint. In epistemology, he holds that emotions have no function—they're useless, they're corrupting, they make our thoughts subjective. And in ethics, he holds that emotions have no function—they're a low, distorting element of evil.

The reason that intrinsicists end up preaching selflessness is not *only* the Christian influence; it does not come only from the Bible. It comes from the essence of the approach of intrinsicists. And the best formula I have ever reached to connect their basic philosophy to their ethics is this: If you believe in effacing consciousness in epistemology, then you will efface the self in ethics. Consciousness in epistemology, we're told, is supposed to have no identity, and be a sheer passive mirror. The same is true in ethics—it is to contribute nothing; our interests, needs, desires are all irrelevant and to be swept aside. After all, what is the self? It's basically one's consciousness. And therefore, it is on this approach to be as much nothing in ethics as in epistemology. This was the central viewpoint of Plato, Christianity, Kant, and in fact all major philosophical trends except Aristotle; it's been the dominant line of Western ethics.

Now let's look at the empiricist approach to ethics. The empiricist is the subjectivist, the skeptic: There is no moral knowledge; there are no absolute truths, no principles; everything is uncertain or relative. Reality has nothing to say in ethics; we simply go by our feelings, our desires. "Good" means "I want it"; "bad" means "I don't want it." Period. There's no way to resolve conflicts, you each just feel what you feel. There are no answers to moral questions.

The empiricist regards this as empirical, because, he says, the only way to have an ethics is to observe what people desire, so he simply observes desires; "I take desires as such," he says, "as my data." One variation of this approach is to give people no guidance at all, to be openly skeptical like the Greek Sophists and say, "Deuces wild, do whatever you feel like, might makes right." Another is modern pragmatism, which is the same thing but pretends to be different. Pragmatism says abandon principles, but be practical; define your concrete goal of the moment, and then act to gain it; don't just plunge in arbitrarily, Dewey says, but study first what you want, how to get it, what is required, and then act. If you ask him, "But how are you to decide what you want? What if you decide differently tomorrow? Are there any absolutes?" the answer comes down to, "Whatever you feel today is good enough for today."

Observe that on all the key points that we've made about the rationalists, the empiricists seemingly take the exact opposite view. For instance, empiricists stress *purpose* in ethics, as against the rationalists. But what makes them empiricists? They say the purpose is subjective, anything goes—your purpose, your neighbor's purpose, Hitler's purpose, you have to start somewhere. Empiricists stress *context* in ethics, as against the rationalists. But, they go on to say, context varies according to the feeling of the individual (or the group, if they're social subjectivists). There are no universal objective rules; therefore, everything is inextricably subjective. The empiricist stresses options and choices in ethics, but he says that everything is optional, there are no principles, there are no absolutes.

What is the empiricist's view on the question of selfishness? Since he's the opposite of a rationalist, since he believes that everything comes from consciousness and that the whole nature of cognition is just to assert your consciousness, you might think that his ethics would be: "Just assert yourself—satisfy any desire you get no matter what. Run roughshod over others and cut their throats if you feel like it." There have been empiricists in history who have held this. The Sophists are an example, likewise Nietzsche, who is not exactly an empiricist but in some moods behaves like one. This type of approach gives us the idea of selfishness as equaling a brute running wild, selfishness as being the sacrifice of others to self.

But this model is not common among empiricists. The reason is that telling people to act on their feelings is not enough to give them any guidance or to get them acting. Feelings are not a primary. Where do they come from? What is their source? *Ideas*, value judgments. Empiricists don't advocate any value judgments on their own, being skeptics, but they can't get along without them. Consequently, they have to take over the value judgments of others in order to give some content to their own minds and thereby generate feelings. Where do they get this content? From rationalists. They go to church, to synagogue, to the schools, to the movies, they read the *New York Times*, and so on; they're written to and lectured at by rationalists, religionists, and all their derivatives, from morning to night, from birth until age fifteen, and their feelings therefore end up on the whole being just what the rationalist imperatives *say* they should be. And consequently you get people like Dewey and Bertrand Russell and so on, who are just as thorough altruists and advocates of selflessness as are Plato and Kant. Empiricism is not an original source of ethical ideas; it's a parasitic approach, as against rationalism, which *can* be innovative and original, even if incorrectly. In essence, both rationalism and empiricism end up being champions of selflessness—the rationalists because they claim that's the voice of God, or reality, and the empiricists because they claim that's the way they feel.

Now let's turn to Objectivism in this broad survey. On the objective approach, value judgments are objective. Value implies of value to whom and for what—it implies a valuer for a purpose. Morality is not an end in itself; it's a means to an end. And it is only for that reason that it can be based on reality. As against rationalism, as we've already pointed out, Objectivism stresses purpose, that sets our ultimate standard; context, which dictates and shows how our purpose applies in specific circumstances; and therefore, we reject dogmatic absolutes, and we certainly include ethical or evaluative options, about which we will have a lot more to say. I've been stressing the contrast to rationalism. What about the contrast to empiricism on these points? Are we then empiricists in stressing the role of purpose in ethics? No, because our purpose, according to Objectivism, has to be based on reality, not arbitrary. Morality *is* conditional. It's of the form, *"If* you choose to live, then you should follow such and such virtues," as against the intrinsicist dogma "Thou shalt do so-and-so." But our ultimate purpose is not arbitrary or optional. It's based on reality. Lecture two discussed in what way it's only the requirements of life that give rise to the possibility of, and need for, value judgments. So, in our fundamental approach to ethics, we combine a purpose-based ethics with the idea that the purpose itself is based on facts of reality; it is not arbitrary.

Again, with regard to context, Objectivism is a contextual ethics, but it says the context must be determined objectively, not by feelings or subjective personal variation. There are principles, and in the right circumstances those principles are absolute; where those circumstances don't apply, it's also an absolute that that is *not* a virtue (which is why it is okay to lie to a crook). Ethics is not subjective, emotional, or arbitrary. It's contextual, but "contextual" does not imply subjective. Again, on the question of options, as opposed to empiricism, there are options, but not *everything* is an option. There are absolute principles. Options, as we'll see, come in only in regard to concretes, not in regard to principles.

On the question of selfishness, if anything is known about the Objectivist view, it's that it's an ethics of self-interest. And all I want to do is show you in what way this follows from the basic approach. In ethics, we have to assert our self—that is, our consciousness. We can't accept any ethics that says, "Dismiss your consciousness, its needs, its requirements, overrule yourself," as the rationalists say. Because the first question we would ask is: Overrule yourself in favor of what? What should you give yourself up *for* or *to*? If you say intrinsic commands, of course the answer is that there are no such things. Suppose you say, "You should give up your self-interest for other people's selves." Why? Why should there be a double standard? Why should *they* get what *they* want, but *you* can't get what *you* want? Suppose you say, "There are more of them than there is of you, so therefore, they're more important." "Important" is a value term, and if you take the objective approach, the first thing you'll say is, "Important, *to whom and for what?*" And as soon as you say "to whom and for what," that should remind you that it's an issue to be resolved according to some objective standard of value—what is that, according to the facts of reality? And that should bring you back to the requirements of the life of each organism. If you take the objective approach to knowledge, you have to end up with the idea that each man is an end in himself. The identity of his consciousness is a crucial factor in cognition and a crucial datum in ethics. We have to start from "There's a reality, and we have a self that has desires, needs, requirements, and we have to take into account what it requires to achieve its ends." One is the reflection in ethics of the other. I stress that this is not a subjective issue, because consciousness is the faculty of perceiving existence. In epistemology, consciousness asserts its identity in conformity with reality, and the same is true in ethics—we have to assert the needs of our consciousness in conformity with reality. That's the objective approach, where each is involved. So reality dictates the standard, the ultimate purpose, and the principles to follow. Therefore, selfishness is not a subjective free-for-all, but selfishness in conformity to reality. And that's what Ayn Rand calls *rational self-interest*, and you see that both of those concepts are essential—the "self-interest" is what differentiates it from an intrinsicist ethics; the "rational" is what differentiates it from an empiricist or subjectivist ethics. And this, I think, is the deepest root of the Objectivist approach to ethics. It actually follows from the objective, as opposed to the intrinsic or subjective.

That is the general background: three different approaches to the whole realm of value judgments. Now let's turn to the issue of emotions.

The rationalist, as we've seen, is typically opposed to emotions. He regards them as a bad element of human nature, so he typically counsels repression. And usually this is tied in with a supernaturalist viewpoint: There are two worlds and two sides of human nature reflecting these two worlds, and your emotions are hooked up with the bad world—namely, this physical world. So repression for the rationalist is like a form of asceticism; it's a form of beating down the low, materialistic, worldly element within you. Since you have that element and can't get around it, ethics is a permanent struggle against temptation. Recall the famous quote (as I remember it) from Paul, "The good that I would I don't do, and the evil that I don't want to do I do do," and that's very poorly put—he put it much better*—but the idea is that he's in chronic temptation, where his mind tells him to do something but his passions pull him in the opposite direction, so if only he could obliterate them or tame them in some way, he'd be happy. And the Stoics went so far as to say that nonemotion was the standard of the good; apathy, nonfeeling was their term for virtue—kill this evil element.

In regard to emotions, the empiricists are the opposite. They are really emotion worshippers, in the sense that they cannot criticize or judge an emotion. An emotion to them has to have the status of a revelation, because by their viewpoint, their minds are helpless; they have no way of criticizing an emotion by reference to cognition, and therefore, feelings are their only guide to action. "Do whatever you feel," they say, "reality is irrelevant, unknowable."

So we have the repressor versus the emotionalist. That is the consequence philosophically of rationalism and empiricism. Each argues for its viewpoint typically by attacking the other one and saying that there's no alternative but the other.

I want to make a clarification here: I do not mean to imply that rationalism and empiricism are the only possible causes of these attitudes. There can be repressors or emotionalists for other reasons, quite apart from the issues of rationalism and empiricism. Many complex psychological factors could enter into the development of these kinds of psychologies, factors that I have not even hinted at, pertaining to early self-esteem, traumatic experiences, early events, for instance, in a child's development far before the time that he could reach such a sophisticated adult issue as

---

* "For what I do is not the good I want to do; no, the evil I do not want to do—this I keep on doing." Romans 7.

rationalism or empiricism. You could even argue, for instance, that repression comes first in time and is a precondition of the development of rationalism; it could be the case that through various traumatic experiences in childhood and wrong conclusions, a child becomes a repressor. Then he grows up and, let's say, he becomes an intellectual, which they don't all become. And then he decides to retreat to a safe, unemotional world of the intellect, and he finds rationalism and it's really congenial to him, and he falls for it entirely. And it turns out that it's congenial to him because he came to it as a committed repressor. You could even argue that if he *hadn't* been repressed, he would have been *repelled* by rationalism when he first heard it and never accepted it. On that model, repression could be a precondition of rationalism. I am neither challenging nor endorsing this. The point I am making is only this: However he gets to this development, once a person *is* a rationalist, he finds his earlier disdain of emotions (assuming he had it) philosophically supported, justified, and therefore immensely strengthened. His rejection of emotions is not just an implicit childhood error but a fully conscious viewpoint that he identifies with value, virtue, logic, reality. So you have a vicious circle, a reciprocity: repression leading to rationalism, leading to a more intense repression, and so on. And I think the same pattern is certainly conceivable on emotionalism leading to empiricism, and intensifying emotionalism. These are not topics that I want to get into this evening. They are topics of psychology on which I rush to say I am not very knowledgeable; there's a division of labor, but I want to delimit my remarks by saying that I'm speaking tonight philosophically. I'm leaving open many possible psychological patterns and factors. I'm simply saying this much: rationalism, *philosophically*, leads to and supports repression, and the same with empiricism, which leads to and supports emotionalism, regardless of the psychological factors that might be developed in the earlier phases to prepare people for this syndrome.

I want to disassociate Objectivism from each of these attitudes toward emotion. I want very quickly to get rid of the empiricist/emotionalist side. This has been stressed for a long time in Objectivist courses and literature, so it's either obvious to you at this stage or it never will be. Emotions, one more time for the record, are not tools of cognition; they are not a guarantee of correct conclusions or of the right course of action; whim worshipping is bad, you have to live by reason. You know there are three schools. Whenever you spend a tremendous amount of time fighting one school, there is always the tendency for some people in the audience to go to the other one. I do not want to qualify every attack on rationalism tonight by saying, "And by the way, this doesn't mean subjectivism or emotionalism." I want to say it once, flatly, at the outset, and then brush it aside. I have no weapon to prevent anybody from concluding that I am coming out for emotionalism simply because I do not reiterate my opposition at every paragraph. I feel that certain things have already been made clear, and therefore, I'm just letting that clarification go; I want to spend the time we have on the *other* side of this false alternative—namely, *repression*, because this one is *not* very much covered in the Objectivist literature, it's widely misunderstood, and it gives rise to the argument that we discussed opening night about subjectivism versus the self, or philosophy versus your inner life.

So I want to turn now to the phenomenon of so-called Objectivist repressors. I want to start with a few words as to the *causes* of this phenomenon (speaking from a purely philosophic point of view), a few remarks on what the appeal of repression might be to many Objectivists. As I see it, one crucial issue here is precisely that they attach great importance to morality. I'm not saying that's wrong, but they *do* something wrong within this attitude. The strong moral emphasis in the Objectivist literature and Ayn Rand's novels is obviously a key factor in attracting people to Objectivism. Her works broadcast the message, "There is right and wrong, it's crucial, it's possible, there's a strong moral code, there's good versus evil," and that's what it rests on, and if you're attracted to Objectivism, it's obviously very natural to feel, "It's important to live up to this code, to be moral," and consequently, if you ever depart from it, to feel guilt, self-reproach, condemnation. So far, that's completely understandable and no mistake.

The question now goes one step further—what do you take as a departure from morality? What do you take as a departure from the

Objectivist morality? I think one pattern that operates in many people is something like this: "Ayn Rand said that man is a being of self-made soul, so you're responsible for your nature, your subconscious, your character. Ideally you should be like Roark or Galt." And then the question that you start to ask—once you become familiar with what these characters are like—is, "Am I that way? Am I like them, and therefore I've got the right values and I live up to morality, or am I not like them, and therefore I'm somehow betraying or departing from them?" Many people haven't gone that far; they just go to the next step and say, "The way to tell your values is through your emotions." Your emotions, they think, are indicators of your basic values. After all, Objectivism includes the viewpoint that emotions are not primaries but come from your value judgments. Therefore, emotions must be indicators of your essential soul or character: If your emotions are good, you're good (they think); if your emotions are bad, you're immoral, evil.

If you hold this view, I think you must conclude that emotions are potentially disastrous, because they are indicators of your essence. It's possible on this view that they indicate something really bad about you, something opposed to morality, something opposed to Objectivism. And consequently they are a constant threat: "Who knows what's coming next from this underground where I hold value judgments that may throw my whole moral status off?" Thoughts and actions don't pose any comparable threat, because we can directly, volitionally control them—we can guide our thinking and the conclusions we come to, for example, "I choose capitalism and reject socialism." We can guide and control our *actions* by a direct act of will. Our emotions, however, are not in our volitional control. Of course, in the long run they are, but the long run can be very long, and that doesn't do you any good in the length of time intervening. So on a day-by-day experiential basis, emotions are experienced as the involuntary—you just react, you live, and you feel desire, anger, hatred, passion. But if at the same time you feel that your emotions are potentially significant or revealing, then you have a dreadful combination. Here is something, an element of your nature, which can reveal something profound about you, and at the same time it is out of your control, as against your heart, lungs and soul, which are *also* out of your control, but don't prove anything about you. You are the source of these, according to Objectivism, you're responsible, and at the same time you're helpless, and who knows what they show?

With this kind of approach, I think there is an understandable inclination to say, "Let's do away with the whole realm. If I don't experience emotions, I wipe out the whole threat. I just won't worry about what I feel. I'll just concentrate on what I know is right, I'll do what's right, and I'll just put a lid on this whole thing." Of course, I don't think you sit down one day on a Tuesday and say, "This is my solution." It happens automatically, gradually, as a pattern across time—the realm becomes threatening, you just don't look, you suppress it, and gradually it becomes a built-in mechanism. I think that's an operative pattern in many good Objectivists.

There are many errors in this whole approach that I've just given. For one thing, the idea that emotions reveal your basic values, subconscious self, or character is false (as I will be discussing in the next lecture). That viewpoint represents a complete misunderstanding of the nature of emotions and their significance. In fact, it is essential to the whole Objectivist approach that emotions cannot be judged morally, neither as good nor evil (another topic for next time).

For now I want to go to still another point that aggravates the situation. Anyone would have problems, just on the basis of these two errors, of judging his emotions and then taking them as indicative of his essence. Even if he understood Objectivism perfectly and acted on it consistently, he would still be prey to some random, out-of-context emotion, which in fact proves nothing, but which would nevertheless lead him to condemn himself. But add in yet another factor: imagine someone with an imperfect understanding of the actual content of the Objectivist morality. The type of misunderstanding I have in mind is this: Somebody reads *The Fountainhead* or *Atlas Shrugged*, they see a hero (Roark or Galt) projected, they admire the hero immensely—they want to be like him—but they then fail to differentiate a crucial thing: *In what respects is he normative, and in what respects is he not?* Roark, for instance, has a great number of characteristics. To give them to you in no order: He loves skyscrapers, he's an architect, he's very independent, he dislikes parties, he has orange hair, he refuses to compromise, he hates small talk, he's indifferent to people's reaction to him (which parenthetically was not true of Ayn Rand*). Clearly these are not traits on the same level. Some of them are essentials: they reveal abstract principles of his character, and they would be applicable to all virtuous men. Some of them are concretes: they are optional; they are his particular interpretation of those principles, or application; they are not mandated by any principle as such.

The problem is that the novel—*any* novel, particularly Ayn Rand's novels—presents forcefully and brilliantly a vivid, compelling image of an ideal, a thoroughly admirable man. But it cannot be a philosophical treatise; it does not have footnotes saying after each line of dialogue, "This is Roark's general principle," or saying, "This is just unique to him, don't take . . . ," and so on. She cannot analyze it as she goes. She presents the whole, with her genius for making a compelling, integrated whole out of it. She gives you the principles *and* the concretes that make him unique, and she leaves it to you as a kind of beacon. But some people are so overcome by the portrait as a whole that they do not know how to dissect the principles from the optional, personal elements. They take it as one undifferentiated portrait of the ideal. They take it as "This is perfection, in every detail. Any departure is guilt, low, evil." So, Roark or Galt become the role model, down to every concrete aspect, including hair color (I once met someone who died his hair orange).

The motive here is not necessarily bad. It can be hero worship,

---

* [Clarified in a later question period:] I didn't mean that she went around eager to find out what everybody thought of her. What I *did* mean is that she once told me in a discussion that she was different from Roark—that if I had said something to her, or someone she liked or respected said, "That's not how I see you," she would immediately want to know, "Well, how do you see me?" But in the novel, the theme was independence, and she was putting in those concretes that would show that. But that didn't mean that you're dependent if someone says, "That's not how I see you," and you like and respect them, to think, "Well, how do you see me?" I mentioned that deliberately because nothing would shock the intrinsicist more than to hear that there are respects in which Ayn Rand and Howard Roark are different.

idealism; it can be the real desire to live up to the good, as opposed to just saying, "It's a nice book, but you've got to be practical." But the method is very wrong. It's natural, but mistaken. It's natural to want to be like a character you admire. But if you have an imperfect understanding of the abstractions that make him, then all you have is the concretes of his life, and you are reduced to, "The only way to be like him is to copy him, to imitate him." This is typically a problem of young people. Young people don't yet know how to act, or even fully how to think in principles—that's not a flaw on their part—and therefore they copy out of helplessness, out of a desire for something they admire; they copy mannerisms of their parents or their older brothers or the Beatles or whatever it is that they happen to admire—all adolescents tend to imitate their favorite role models, because they haven't yet learned to abstract or think in principle. So I think this is, to a very significant extent, a problem of a young person seeking a moral ideal but not yet grasping principles, and therefore, becoming concrete-bound. What it amounts to is that he doesn't grasp the range of concretes that are possible under that abstraction. Thus, his abstractions float. To him, independence or integrity has no connection to reality except that one concrete, which is Roark. So the real problem here is floating abstractions, which makes you concrete-bound in actual practice—there's no way to know what to do except model yourself on the literal concrete. Again the root of the trouble is a wrong way of holding philosophic ideas. And if you do take this approach, it leads to a lot of trouble, because no human being can literally become another, or copy him successfully. If you try to do that, you're headed for disaster, because every assertion of your individuality thereby becomes a threat; everything that makes you *you*, as opposed to Roark, becomes weakness, imperfection, something low, nonideal.

If you feel in general "Emotions prove something about me, and they're out of my control; they're a potential threat to my status as a moral person," you're still a thousand times *worse* off, because your emotions will naturally reflect something about you as an individual. They will be a constant source of fear, self-doubt, self-condemnation. And then you will begin to automatize the idea, "To be moral, I must repress myself," and that becomes an issue of self-preservation. At a certain point, what happens is that you can't take it anymore, and finally you "assert yourself," and jump all the way to the emotionalist axis and say, "The only way to be myself is to say to hell with philosophy and principles," and run wild. And I've seen that pattern many, many times.

The error here is demanding conformity to concretes, as opposed to principles. It's judging yourself by relation to an archetype, rather than with reference to a chewed principle. To sum up so far: As I see it philosophically, there's a certain attraction to repression among Objectivists, partly out of fear that emotions will jeopardize their moral status—it will be some kind of revelation of their subconscious—and partly because they misinterpret what it means to be moral.

Now I would like to hit that approach on the head, so far as one lecture can. In the strongest and most unmitigated terms that I can use without turning you all into emotionalists, I want to come out for emotions. I want to try to formulate positively a proper view of emotions, their role in human nature, their proper use and functions.

Presumably you know the basic nature of emotions according to Objectivism: They're not primary; they're not physical or chemical; they're not unknowable; they're consequences of our ideas, above all, of our value judgments. Automatic consequences of premises, held knowingly or not. The reason-emotion relation is simply an illustration of the general issue of the mind-body relation—emotions are to value judgments or to thought as body is to mind. They're the expression, the obedient servant. The primary cause, the prime mover, is the mind, and emotions are one result of it. There's no inherent conflict any more than there is between mind and body. There can be a clash between reason and emotions only if there are contradictions in the underlying ideas. And then the solution would have to be in principle (however difficult in practice): clarify your thinking, make it consistent, and you will then reach the proper relation, which is harmony, integration.

To be against emotions, in any way, is no more sensible philosophically than to be against the body. It's the same philosophic issue. If you went around worrying, "My body might do X, it's some kind of demon

out of my control, it will sully my moral character," that would be ridiculous. Your body has a nature. I'm speaking now of your body *apart* from
your will, as a physical entity—you have to allow it to function according
to its nature—that is, its internal processes, its objective needs, and so on.
And if you do, there will be no clash between the mind and the body. The
body as a total instrument will then follow your mind, and work to achieve
your mind's ends. As against if you decide to fight your body, to starve it,
to torture it, to whip it into submission, then of course it will become
"rebellious" and make it impossible to function.

The exact same thing is true of emotions: They have a nature, they
have needs, they have processes that they must follow, and if they are allowed to function according to their nature, there will be no clash. You
have to be just as pro-emotion as you are pro-body, because it's the same
issue. Being pro-body, of course, does not mean being a materialist who
scorns thought. But it *does* mean you have to love the body, the physical,
and everything inherently connected with it, including sex and money
and physical pleasures. And the same is true with emotions: being pro-
emotion doesn't mean being a subjectivist; it doesn't mean trying to get
from emotions what they can't do. They're not substitutes for the mind.
But it *does* mean loving them philosophically and everything properly
inherently connected with them, giving them full play, enjoying them.
Repression is to emotions what asceticism is to the body. You know those
medieval ascetics who tried to undermine the body—they drank laundry
water when they were thirsty, they ate a mixture of sheep skull and ashes,
they slept on pillows that were rocks, they had themselves flagellated, and
so on—it was a war against the body. If you think that is absurd, irrational, anti-life, you're right. But my point is that repression is exactly that
same thing, only applied now to the war against emotions. You might say
to me, "But can't you have an inappropriate emotion?" Yes, but you can
have a diseased limb, too. The solution in both cases is restore the function
to health, not conduct a war against it.

Now I'd like to be a bit more specific. What role do emotions actually
play in life? Nothing in a living organism can be irrelevant to its survival;
every facet of its nature has some function, some role to play, and this is

also true of emotions. If you repress, this is not only philosophically wrong, it actually harms your ability to function, to deal with reality. And I would like to give you a brief, incomplete list of some of the functions of emotions, just to scratch the surface of their value.

Number one—and these are in no particular order—emotions are essential to action, which gives them a pretty high status. They are the automatized form in which we experience our value judgments, in which our value judgments actually enter moment by moment into our daily lives. They are the "lightning integrators" of the situation (quoting Galt). In other words, they are essential to the crow need. You don't have to figure out every value aspect of a situation intellectually. Your subconscious takes in the meaning of an event and sums it up for you in an instantaneous feeling that Galt called "a statement of profit or loss," like a running lightning total, without which you would be helpless, because the complexity in actual life is simply too great; you would be helpless to know what to do. Imagine, for instance, there was no such function as emotions, but somehow or other you could nevertheless have value judgments, and someone held a gun at you, and there was no fear, no automatic desire to escape, nothing like that. So you'd sit back and say to yourself, in effect, "He's holding a gun; now, let me see—this gun, I guess, must be aimed at property. Oh, yes, property is definitely a value. Why was property a value? We have to have rights, now I remember, because justice is a very crucial principle, and therefore, if he takes my property that violates justice. And why was justice important? It had something to do with rationality." By the time you figured out, and looked up in the various books all of the structure supporting value judgments, obviously the opportunity for action would be long gone, to say nothing of the fact that even if you finally did, by purely intellectual means, come to the conclusion, "This is an action I should oppose," you wouldn't *care*, because caring is also a feeling, an emotion. Without emotions, you could not decide what to do in the face of this kind of complexity (and that isn't very complex compared to some situations), nor would you have any motive to do anything; you would have no initiative, nothing would make a difference to you. You know that supposedly one of the major problems of people who are depressed is what is called "flat affect"—they just feel nothing—and they're incapable of anything but the very most primitive action, because they just don't care, nothing matters to them. There's no emotional life, to say nothing of the fact that the reason you're motivated is because you know you're going to, or you hope, have an emotional reward in the long run; you're going to enjoy the results, or at least not be miserable. And happiness, of course, is an emotion; the genus of "happiness" is "feeling."

Insofar as you cut down your emotional life, you cut down your whole life. You cut down your motivation, you cut down your ability to function except in a dutiful, bored way, and that will have repercussions on every virtue: on your initiative, your industry, your enthusiasm, your productiveness, and so on. You will be more and more reduced to dragging yourself through life, and you can do that only up to a point. Free will is not omnipotent—at a certain point, if you just don't care, nothing is going to get you functioning. And you have got to have an emotional life to care.

Two, emotions have a critical psycho-epistemological function. That's the issue we've already discussed of concretizing our abstractions. Here again, in the process of actually thinking, using abstractions, emotions keep our values alive and real to us in situations where it's impossible to make that a separate conscious assignment. If your emotions are functioning properly, they automatically keep you attuned to concretes, and thereby keep your concepts concretized, as opposed to the floating abstractions of the rationalist. What wrecks the rationalist is that nothing in his automatic functions keeps him tied to reality, because the only thing that could keep him automatically tied would be his *interests*—that is, his likes, his dislikes, his inner emotional experience. A quickening of interest leads you to contact reality; that kind of dead repression leads you to obliviousness and castles in the sky. Miss Rand used to be a strong advocate of what she called "the pleasure-purpose principle." She meant the idea that on any level, whether we're talking about thought or action, you cannot function without a purpose that brings you pleasure, something you want to achieve, that you enjoy achieving. You can see this in an everyday example in the contrast between getting up on a day when there's something that you like—I don't mean necessarily some grand passion to be captured by a novelist for the centuries, but just something: You're going shopping, or you're going to have a nice day at work, or you have a special date for lunch or something, and you have a little jolt of anticipatory pleasure—that is crucial to the whole quality of your functioning throughout the day, as against that kind of gray, dragging yourself through some dutiful routine, which can only go on for a limited period of time, after which you either end up giving up action and giving up generally, or else you say, "I can't stand philosophy," and you become an emotionalist. The point here is that pleasure—and we mean here *personal* pleasure, personal interests, your likes and dislikes—is essential to your functioning, in action and in thought.

Point three—this is a variant—is that emotions are crucial in creative work of all kinds. Not just in concretizing abstractions and understanding them, but in *any* kind of creative work. And here let me just tell you my own experience from writing, which I think would apply generally. As I understand creative work, it involves a *deliberate* mixture of reason and emotion; both are indispensable. Before I can engage in writing, I have to have an outline, so I have to figure out topics that I think are logically necessary, a structure that makes sense. And that, of course, is an intellectual assignment. Even there, though, I have to consider what I am interested in. Some topics on the outline arouse me, make me feel something, and others I jot down sort of dutifully with the idea, "It seems that this point is unavoidable, regretfully, but I'll see when I get there, maybe I can pare it down." So it's basically intellectual, but with a definite emotional input. Then I get to the stage of writing out the rough draft, and there I function on the idea that you have to be motivated by the unleashed subconscious, whatever pours out—desire, interest—you keep one eye vaguely on the outline, but the basic moving force is let it out, whatever you feel. What releases that material? Basically, it is your emotions taking charge. You get on a certain topic and it interests you, and you feel, "This is important, this is good, this is worth saying," and you ride that for all it's worth, and it starts to grow and develop, and at a certain place you say, "To hell with the outline; this is better than the outline," and you just keep going. You get to another point on the outline, you start to yawn, and I've found many times that that means your subconscious is giving you the message, "This is not really important to your theme; you thought it was necessary, but really it isn't, and that's why you're bored." Which is very often something you cannot decide on until you actually get there and see your emotional reaction in the moment. You have to be guided by this inner pleasure principle or you just dry out. Of course, if you're an emotionalist, you just stop there; you pour this stuff out and say, "That's it, that's the way I feel." But I don't say that. Now comes the last stage— editing. And here I'd say you have to be cold, objective, unemotional, but it's also very uncreative. You just clarify, you get rid of repetitions, you remove confusions, you say it more smoothly, and so on. You say, "This point is overdone, and this needs a little more elaboration." There is no clash with your emotions, because as soon as you see an error, your sub-conscious, having now released itself, is happy to correct it and make it even better. But I think you need this whole combination of oscillation. The rationalist tries to create by deduction, from some theoretical outline, without this personal motor, and I do not think that can be done. The valid procedure is reason *and* emotion in a certain combination. Your emotions tell you something about what is needed that you *could not know strictly intellectually in that context.* So they're crucial. But emotions are not infallible, because once they lead you to a certain point, then your objec-tive, intellectual mind has to take over. So I would summarize it this way: Emotions are aids, critical aids, to creative thought, without therefore being tools of cognition.

Point four is evaluations of things that you see around you—people and their products, including artworks. Without emotions, this is a hope-less task. Typically the data confronts you, in a concrete case, so thick and so fast, so much faster than you could identify intellectually and integrate, that if you did not have this chronic emotional reaction, you would just swim helplessly. For instance, once in a very early phase I tried to be a thorough intellectualist—that is, I was going to function exclusively cere-brally, without the aid of emotions (I was young at the time). And I remember very clearly that I went to a movie with the idea of having absolutely no emotions—that is, they would have nothing to do with my assessment of the movie and were just going to be pushed aside. I was going to try to judge purely intellectually as the movie went by. And I had a checklist in advance, certain criteria: I was going to judge the plot, the theme, the characters, the acting, the direction, the scenery, and so on. And my idea was to formulate to myself in words for each point where I thought something was relevant, how it stood on all the points on my checklist. And to my amazement, I was absolutely unable to follow the movie; I did not know what was going on. I needed to sit through it I can't remember how many times, and I discovered that what you have to do is simply react, let it happen, feel, immerse yourself in it. And what happens is that your emotions give you an automatic sum. You just simply attend to it with no checklist, no intellectualizing, no thought, just watch the movie, like a person. If there was a major point in the plot, you react to it; if there was beautiful acting, if there was some scene that was really depraved, your feeling is simply instantaneous, integrating, evaluating for you. It's your subconscious applying automatically all of your knowledge and value judgments. At the end, you have a lightning summation: you're exalted, or you feel like throwing up, or whatever it happens to be. Here again, without emotions to perform this function, it's hopeless, it's the crow epistemology—you have no way to take it in.

Does this mean emotionalism? No, because when you do get your emotional assessment, it's not necessarily the objective truth; it's possible to have emotions that came from mistaken conclusions. Maybe in the heat of the movie, you latched on to a nonessential; maybe one of your value judgments was purely associational and had nothing to do with the actual movie; maybe your attention wandered for a second and you missed a point and that's why the whole movie seemed unintelligible to you, which is not the fault of the movie. This is the point that is the parallel to editing in writing—after the movie and after the emotion, if you want to have an objective assessment, in a calm state, you try to review your feelings and identify: in response to what—what were the essentials about the movie, how would you objectively formulate the aspects to which those emotions gave you a clue? Using your emotional reactions as data, you then intellectually, rationally, reach an assessment. But both stages are crucial. A repressor cannot do the first part, so he is simply lost. And an emotional-ist can't do the second part, so he never gets to the movie, only an auto-biography of his reactions to it.

This applies to *all* complex judgments, emphatically including the judgments of other people, which we're going to discuss later. So let me summarize this way: Emotions are critical aids to cognition in many areas—in thinking, in creative work, in judgment, in action. They enable us to process a tremendous amount of data faster than we could intel-lectually take it in, even though we always remember that emotions are not the final word. If you can get that idea, you'll get the idea of the objec-tive versus the intrinsicist, who wipes out emotions, and the subjectivist, who wipes out reason. The truth has to be the union of mind-body inte-gration.

Here is the last function of emotions that I'm going to cover this eve-ning: Emotions are essential to choosing among optional cases. Let me begin with an example in regard to choice of a career. Ethics tells us that there is a certain principle involved in regard to choice of a career, and that is the virtue of productiveness—you have to earn your sustenance, as opposed to living a life of crime or a life on welfare as a moocher; you have to earn it by your thought and action in the achievement of pro-life values. And even further, you can make a moral principle out of the fact that you should survive not by a mindless job if you're capable of more, but by the active use of your mind and your intelligence—as against stagnating in some kind of rut. This much you can prove as a matter of moral principle. But now we come to the question: In what realm, what concrete application, should you make of this general injunction? And here, there is no moral principle to guide you. We have to remember that a principle is an abstract formulation in terms of essentials. It has to be derived from life as the standard, and mandated by reality. Remember the work we went into to establish the principle of honesty, and if you remember in our follow-up discussion I made a point of saying "Wearing raincoats in the rain" is not a principle; that is a concrete. Can you think of a principle that would dictate one specific career, or one specific career field? You could not do it, because by definition you would have to descend to concretes, rather than the whole broad area. Could you say, for example, as, believe it or not, I have heard people say, "Morally, everyone should be a philosopher"? If you ask them why, they say, "This is the most abstract field, and you're supposed to think; therefore the more abstract, the more thinking." Why shouldn't anybody apply the abstractions to actual life? What is the use of all those abstractions, if everybody just sat around thinking about them? Actually, you could make a perfect case in the reverse—that is, that philosophy is of no value except as a means to all the other fields that it leads to and makes possible. You could make the point that the abstraction inherent in philosophy is *bad*, that it is a deformation of a proper human function, and that a philosopher pays the price in personal frustration in the fact that he sees results only long after he's dead. But the actual point here is that the philosopher's only significance is in the culture he shapes; without that, he is just clacking his uppers. Every form of productive work is crucial, whether it's as a businessman, a philosopher, an artist, an engineer, a computer programmer; all of them properly approached take full intelligence.

If there are countless equally legitimate ways to apply the moral principle, how are you going to decide what to do with your life? There is no way but by consulting your feelings, your desires; there is no other way. There is no argument, for instance, against me being an architect, *except that I don't like it*. It is not me, and by that I mean it doesn't interest me; it's not what I like to do with my mind and time; it is not what I want. There is no way to choose among legitimate options, except by reference to feelings.

Are your feelings infallible? No, not even here. Emotions are never the whole story. It's always the same, whether you're talking about creative work, or judging movies, or the selection of a career—you have to consult your feelings, you have to know what you feel, and then try to judge objectively by your intellect. In this case, your feeling about the career you want *might* be influenced by errors. You may be, for instance, making a simple factual error—you decide to become a philosopher because you have the illusion that you're going to see the world change tomorrow, or that you're going to make a million dollars. And then you investigate the career and you discover that the effects will come a hundred years later, and that you will starve during your lifetime. Your feeling changes. Or your feeling may have psychological errors mixed into it. For example, you want to be a philosopher not because you really are interested in the work, but for the fame (assuming it had any fame). Here again, your feeling is not the last word; you have to know what it's based on; you have to introspect; you have to be able to say, in some terms, "What is it about philosophy, or architecture, or whatever, that I really like?" If it turns out to be something really inherent in the work, as opposed to something mistaken, then the point is that you have no other way to know what to do except "That is the work I *want* to do." You go by your emotion, as now objectively validated.

You may say, "But why do I have that particular emotion for philosophy rather than for medicine?" There is no infinite regress; you cannot go back forever. At some point, all you can say is, "The values involved in this field are the ones that were my point of contacting reality. They made the deepest impression on my soul in its formative years." Remember, a conceptual consciousness can plunge in at *many* different points, in regard to concept formation and in regard to value formation. The earlier you plunge in and start to focus on that, the more you begin to develop ramified values, complexities, more aspects, and it becomes a bigger and bigger part of your personality. There is nothing therefore ultimately to say except, "Confronted by the whole feast, this is the food that I chose." If you can say about a field, "X is my cardinal value, that's the thing that really matters to me, and it *really* is in this field, I see that it is," then that is the right career. And you can only find it by your desires. No other way. After all the analysis, there's nothing you can say except "I want this, and that's why I'm in it."

You might know the dilemma of Buridan's ass—Buridan was a medieval philosopher, and he hypothesized an ass between two bales of succulent straw. The ass was hungry, starving, but the two bales were absolutely interchangeable; there was nothing objectively to choose between the one on the left and the one on the right—the same configuration of straw, and the same wisps and the same odor, everything. And he (or his followers) said that in a situation like this that the ass would have to starve to death, because there is no reason to pick one rather than the other. The point is this—we're all in a way in a situation of Buridan's ass on all these optional concretes, except that it's ridiculous to starve because we *do* have a means of deciding. And that is, once you've done all the analysis, it comes down to, "This is what I want, I like that bale. And since I've got to eat something, what in the world should I go to the other bale for if I want this one?" It's just sheer perversity to demand some other means of choosing when, by the whole situation, they are exactly interchangeable philosophically. It's just as in epistemology, there are options within limits, chosen by our preferences. The same here—reality dictates the principles, we choose the concrete form of their application, and we can only do this by using emotion as the critical factor.

Let's take another example—motherhood. I've met several people who feel guilty about wanting to be mothers, because they got the idea that you're supposed to make "the fullest use of your mind," and in Objectivism, heroines are always engineers, and therefore, if you want to be a mother, you have to be unambitious, conventional, and so on. This is a perfect example of forgetting the *principle* involved, and turning it instead into an intrinsicist dogma, a kind of concrete-bound rule dictated by God—namely, in this case, "Thou shalt be a professional, not a mother." Now where is this stated? How would it be defended? How would you show that this is inherent in life as the standard, and in the facts of reality? I put it to you that you could not do that; you could not demonstrate that motherhood is incompatible with life. In fact, you could make a case for the reverse. The only thing that influences these people is that Ayn Rand had very strong feelings that she did not want to be a mother, which was her prerogative, but that is not a moral principle. That has no normative force for anyone else. Nor did she think it did.

The issue is: With regard to any desire (but taking the desire for motherhood as an example), what is the meaning of that desire in the context of any given individual? I can think of many different patterns, many different kinds of mothers. For instance, there could be someone who looks at it as a hardworking, complex, intellectually demanding job twenty-four hours a day. This absolutely would be morally on a par with being a philosopher, a truck driver, a computer engineer, or a railroad tycoon. Or I can think of someone going into motherhood completely as escapism, as a mindless breeding machine who never wants to lift a finger. Or I can think of a completely conventional person becoming a mother, neither heroic nor vicious, just the idea "Everybody does it, I'm going to do it too," sort of a moral middle-of-the-roader. Here we have three cases of the same overt choice, but with radically different meanings. In one case, it exemplifies the principle "Use your mind to the fullest"—perfectly Objectivist. In the second case, it would exemplify the principle "Abandon your mind." In the third case, it would exemplify the principle "Do whatever other people do, obey society." There are three different principles, all capable of being expressed in the same one concrete choice. The way they'll pursue the career or the activity varies enormously, but the actual decision to become a mother remains the same. And this simply illustrates that you cannot take one choice and say, "Aha, this is wrong according to Objectivism." It depends on the principle that the choice illustrates. You *can* show that certain careers—for example, crime— violate the proper principle. But once you're within the framework of productive careers, you cannot do it. Objectivism is an issue of principles, not concrete-bound dogmas. Within the proper principles, your emotions have to be *an* essential ingredient in your decision.

And once you do decide, you should respect your choice, because it was based on your desire. There's a general point here: If you have self-esteem, then you respect yourself, your thoughts and your feelings. You should be able to say proudly and righteously, "This is what I want in life. I know why it's based on reality, but the point here is *I want it.*" And if someone then says, "Ah, but that violates Objectivism—Ayn Rand never created a hero who did that," you have to say, "What principle does this violate?" Intrinsicism gives no principles, only concrete-bound dogmas. But Objectivism gives *only* abstract principles. And if you could see the principles chewed in relation to the whole range of concretes that they integrate, this type of problem would never arise.

I want now to give you another dogma from a different area, and then see what the proper principle would be and where emotion comes in. "Thou shalt love skyscrapers," and we've taken that as a symbol several times in this course. Now, that is obviously concrete-bound; the question couldn't have even come up until the twentieth century. This is not a principle, and it is not part of anybody's ethics. What would be the principle that you could formulate of which this would be a concrete? The most I could think of would be something like, "You should respect human achievement." That would be an aspect of the virtue of productiveness, the value of material creations. But once you've said that, it becomes obvious that a person can respect achievement without having any particular passion for skyscrapers. It simply does not follow deductively that one comes from the other. Suppose you happen to like wide-open spaces, you're from the country, you reach New York and it strikes you as congested, dirty, rude, undealable-with—so abstractly, yes, you admire skyscrapers, but that is absolutely not for you. Where is the immorality in this? How is this counter to Objectivism?

I'll give you a real-life example that I think is analogous to this: I have no particular emotion for the space program. There are a number of reasons for it—partly because I focus on how governmental it is, partly because I personally prefer the Lindbergh type, where it's just one man in a solitary plane rather than a huge group effort. But I do *not* put those reasons forth as applicable to anybody else. Far from it, exactly the opposite—I'm perfectly aware that that is a personal slant of mine, and that people whom I respect very profoundly have a completely different reaction—both Ayn Rand, when she was still alive, and my wife, Cynthia, now are passionate about the space program and its achievements. I recognize this. Am I in violation of Objectivism? I would defy you to prove it. You cannot deduce adulation for the space program from respect for human achievement.

What *would* be a violation of Objectivism? If a person's attitude were, "Tear down achievement, derogate it," or, "Loot the achievers for the benefit of the nonachievers." Then obviously the principle involved would be corrupt. But that is clearly not involved in this type of case, because people with ideas like that don't come near Objectivism to begin with. So to condemn yourself on the basis of your reaction to skyscrapers or the space program is fantastic. Whatever your feelings, you would—to be objective—have to acknowledge intellectually, "Yes, so-and-so is an expression of human achievement, and I respect it to that extent." But that does not mean you have to have the same degree of excitement about every achievement; that depends on your unique constellation of *concrete* values, which is an optional issue. So there is tremendous room for options in what we admire, without that being an issue of subjectivism.

Now let's take the issue of choosing friends or lovers. I've heard for instance this: "You should like all Objectivists and only Objectivists." I'd like to know how you get that. Isn't it possible that there could be Objectivists, sincere Objectivists, who share your philosophy but don't personally interest you? They don't have your personal interests, your likes, your dislikes, so you can respect them abstractly in general, if they're moral, according to your knowledge, but they mean very little to you personally. And by the same token, can't there be non-Objectivists with whom you share certain crucial values, which can be the basis for a close friendship, even if you end up disagreeing forever about many other important issues in politics or esthetics? Suppose you're convinced that another person has certain virtues and values, you personally admire these characteristics, and you *wish* the person were a hundred percent your way—you'd be even closer if he were—but still, he's not, and it's important to you that you found what you did up to the point you did. In a case like this, you could very well be absolutely true to your philosophy, and at the same time be more friendly to a non-Objectivist than to Objectivists, and it happens all the time.

I think you can demonstrate that for a complete soul mate, you would want harmony in every way—intellectually, emotionally, personally—and broad philosophic agreement is *an* essential, one out of many. But for friendship, which can be real, it's possible to feel very friendly and warm toward an "outsider" or "heretic." We do not have to have a checklist of philosophic principles, "Does this person agree with A, B, C, and D?" and if he does he's your friend, and if not, he's out.

What would be the principle here? (Because you need to approach these issues in terms of the principle, not dogma.) The most abstract principle would be justice, and justice as a virtue would tell you, "Judge men according to their nature; grant them what they have earned." That's fine; you can prove that. And within this framework, we can even formulate a narrower principle, but still a principle: "Choose friends according to values, rather than to flaws or needs." That's already a specification of justice. But from there, an awful lot depends on what your concrete values are, what you actually feel about various people, whether you want to see more of them. Does it mean that you just choose friends blindly according to your feelings? No, because you can like someone mistakenly through errors of knowledge. You could take a trait to mean something that it doesn't. You see somebody very hardworking and you just leap to the conclusion that he's an exponent of productiveness, when maybe he's really a Peter Keating, or maybe he's a workaholic escaping from life. Or you might like somebody for neurotic reasons, through improper dependence. Feelings per se are not infallible. You need the guidance of your feelings, your likes and your dislikes, whom you like and whom you don't, monitored by your objective judgment in order to choose friends. And there are plenty of options. Ten perfect Objectivists could choose ten very different people to like or to love, and none of them would violate any principle of Objectivism.

There's one more area I want to comment on besides career and friends, and that's the area of recreation, including art. In this area, intrinsicist dogmas abound: Horse racing is wrong, because Galt's speech has a crack against horse racing. Gambling in Las Vegas is mindless. To like Beethoven is wicked. Horror movies are depraved, and Ayn Rand hated them. At a proper party, all you do is engage in intellectual conversation. There is no principle in what I just stated—just narrow concretes. And in fact, every one of those that I just stated are false. Let me speak first for myself just on those concretes, because some of these give me great pleasure to blast after the years in which I've been subjected to them. I enjoy horse racing (I mean watching it), and I did as a youngster, and I still like to go occasionally. I like poker sometimes. I like 21 in Las Vegas. I loved horror movies as a child, and I still like them to some extent. I like some Beethoven very much, though he's not my favorite. And I *detest* the idea of a party where people discuss philosophy at great length.

How would you formulate a principle involved here? The only thing that I can think of as a principle would be this: Recreation or entertainment should not be mindless, it shouldn't be a violation of being pro-reason and pro-values, and that excludes, of course, a whole set of concretes, such as walking around roaring drunk and drug addiction. It should be a pleasure within the context of a functioning mind who is not betraying his values. That much you can establish. But when you start applying that to concretes, how do you do it? If we're talking about relaxation, that has to be something very different from problem solving. When you say it shouldn't be mindless, that doesn't mean it should involve thinking in the way you have to do it at work. It should be easy, among all other things. It should involve rest. It should involve cashing in on what you already know. It shouldn't take any effort. And it should have some reasonable value to offer. But what is a reasonable value? In my opinion, horse racing involves a perfectly reasonable value. It offers a spectacle, which includes skill on the part of the jockeys, something esthetically attractive and exciting, and it gives you a chance to make money within certain limits, if you know something about the principles of betting. I see absolutely nothing wrong or mindless about this. Of course, if your whole life is lived as a tout betting on hot tips and praying for luck, there are a dozen principles that you violate. Or if you pursue it as mindless escapism, even on one day, you could criticize it—suppose your wife is sick, she needs you, but you feel like going to the races, and you just run to the races, that's bad. But as an occasional entertainment, you could not make a case that that is mindless. And the same is true for gambling, and a whole range of perfectly legitimate entertainment.

Now take horror movies—it all depends on what you see in them. For instance, I was born in a relatively small town, and I liked horror movies because the characters were not like the people next door. Frankenstein was not like my aunts and uncles. So to me he was interesting and exciting, and I formed this clear association. I think that most horror movies are really stupid, but I still have a residual fondness for the genre. I don't know how many times I watch the first five minutes in disappointment, but nevertheless hope that they'll be as enjoyable as they were when I was growing up. But it did get me through a long stretch of time. Contrast this to Ayn Rand's approach: She regarded horror movies as a serious esthetic phenomenon; she took it as the presentation of man at his most depraved and deformed, as in effect an exaltation of evil. Of course, if that's what you see in horror movies, obviously they are depraved, and the principle involved is corrupt. But it depends on what the meaning is that you see in them. It is true that the element that I saw is there, although other elements are also. But if you had asked me if I wanted to grow up to be a Frankenstein, I would have said no, but if I had had to choose between that and my relatives, I probably would have said yes. So, it depends on the principle that your preference expresses.

As to parties, let me just say that there are a thousand different things you could do at a party—it depends on what you like. This is such an optional issue that the only thing I want to negate is the idea that proper conduct at a party means that you've got to sit in a somber discussion of philosophy and the futility of life, or the hopelessness of the future, which I have heard at some parties, and that makes me dread to go to those particular ones.

There can be no intrinsicist rules such as "You must" or "You can't" with regard to concretes. Only the principle "Don't abandon your mind or values." But that leaves enormous room for options within the context of recreation. Here again, your desire is relevant, along with your intellectual knowledge of the *meaning* of your desire. It does not mean that anything goes. It depends on the reason. You can make a case against many concretes, such as the modern wife-swapping orgies. You can say that things like this are not under *any* circumstances compatible with Objectivist principle.

Notice that you have options not only in the *general* type of thing you prefer in life, but also in what you want to do in any given day or mood. Even if you know you like a party where the main thing is food, the thing that really excites you is a seven-course sit-down dinner with all the trimmings—and even suppose you have a whole set of friends who are the type of people you like within the legitimate options, you still have many concrete choices to make: which courses you serve, which friends you invite, whom you are in the mood to see that day, whether you want something quieter, more lively, mixed, small, big, a celebration. And so on and so on. There is no way to decide these things except by "What do I *feel* like? What do I feel like eating? What would give me pleasure? Whom do I feel like seeing?" There are options not only in regard to your *general* preferences but in their implementation in the actual concretes of daily life. And on both levels, emotions have a key role to play.

I want to make a brief remark now on artistic choices. We could have a whole lecture, or two, on the rationalist/empiricist dichotomy in regard to art, but we can't because of time. But I do want to say this much: Art is objective; you *can* reach objective assessments. But that does not mean there's no room for options, legitimate options. Art is intensely personal. It involves your own sense of life, your own interests, your special values. And in that sense it's analogous to romance, where your uniqueness is involved. And so two people with the same philosophic esthetics and the same objective judgments of a given work could differ emotionally in their reaction to it on the basis of their different assessments of many optional elements within it. And here again, you have to know what *you* like, what you look for, what you respond to. Nor does that make it subjective, not if you're able to recognize the causes of your reaction and show that they really are in the work.

I'll give you an example. A writer whom I like very much is Fredric Brown. And I like him for specific reasons: He's very clear, very ingenious, has terrific plot twists and very unusual structures. He is also extremely macabre, very malevolent, and his endings are usually black in despair. I discussed him several times with Miss Rand, who saw the same elements I did, and even enjoyed him to an extent. But the macabre, the black, malevolent element put her off so much that it simply compromised her enjoyment past a certain point. I certainly recognized that there was this element, but there were so many values that were important, and *are* important to me personally, in my particular hierarchy, that I didn't bat an eye at the fact that he was malevolent. So here is a perfectly optional issue—I love certain of his books very much, and yet other people I know and like cannot even read him, for a reason that I also can understand. There is nothing subjective about that.

Take another case—I deliberately take cases where Ayn Rand and I disagreed, because I'm trying to combat this idea that every preference of hers is an Objectivist principle. She liked the old *Perry Mason* shows, and she had her reasons and she was very eloquent—good plots, well-condensed, skillful, justice, and so on (she's written about it).* I never could understand *Perry Mason* on TV. My crow, if you want to put it that way, could not take in that many characters as were introduced at the beginning. And every time I watched, I constantly had to ask somebody, "Is that the guy we just saw before?" So I always got lost. Also, I found Perry Mason simply too starchy; I much preferred James Bond and the much more flamboyant, flashy heroes. And Miss Rand could see this. And often we would be talking, and she'd say, "I'm going to go watch *Perry Mason*," and I'd say, "Fine, I'm going home." It was entirely optional. And yet if we wrote a philosophic treatise, we would not differ in our objective assessment of it.

You can multiply these homey concretes in every art. And I think the moral should be that you feel what you feel, you enjoy what you enjoy, you figure out why, and you *don't* conclude that it's all subjective. If you're objective, you can validate your response by saying, "Here are the things I like, and they're in the work; here are the things I don't, and this is why. But by *my* options, within *my* framework, this is why I like it," or "this is why I don't." Again, in regard to art as to every other thing, you can demonstrate that certain concretes are outside the legitimate principle. Modern nonobjective painting—if someone were to say, "You can do that with Fredric Brown, why can't I go up to one of these smears and say, 'This bright green really gets to me'? So that's my preference; in my hierarchy of values, bright green is number one." That I don't accept, but I would have to demonstrate to him then that it is violating the essence of the medium. And therefore, if you claim to like it *as art*, I can prove

---

* "Perry Mason Finally Loses," *The Ayn Rand Letter,* July 30, 1973.

objectively this is wrong. So it's not "Whatever you feel goes." That is not true. As a further reason, it is possible to grow in regard to your artistic tastes. There are things (many people have had this experience) that they didn't like when they first heard a piece of music. But when they expose themselves further and learn more, they find they *begin* to like it. The point is this—not that your emotions are infallible, but they are essential, and there is room for an optional element in response to art, as to everything else. There is no Objectivist mandate in the form of an intrinsicist dogma in this area, too.

Now a quick aside on music. As Miss Rand many times pointed out, there is no vocabulary worked out to judge music objectively, in terms of judging its *meaning*, as against just its technical structure. You can say that atonal music is invalid, because it violates the essence of the medium. But you cannot prove, the way you can in literature or painting, "This is the theme and this is the so-and-so." Consequently, moral judgments of *any* kind are simply inappropriate in regard to music. If you like a composer, within the framework of human music (and by that, I mean excluding the distinctively twentieth century), you just go ahead, you don't try to force it on anybody else if they disagree. At that stage, I think we literally have to say, "This is what I hear, this is what I like, you don't agree? Good luck."

The problem is that people do not distinguish principles from these intrinsicist rules. They hear Objectivist principles as floating abstractions, and then turn them into concrete-bound dogmas. In fact, when you hear a principle, you should do what we did with honesty: delimit it, define it, break it down, tie it to reality, and that is then the base for seeing what it does and does not mandate. If you do that, you will understand the role of emotions, and your right to have emotions, within the framework of reason and reality.

I want to cover one more topic briefly. We've been discussing errors that cause people to condemn themselves for perfectly legitimate optional preferences. This is the kind of error that turns you into someone distrustful of your own emotions, and therefore encourages repression. A person condemns himself for not living up to these dogmas. He's far too severe on himself; he's critical of the least element of spontaneity or innocent individuality. What I want you to see is that if you are too severe on yourself in this way, you are going to be too severe on others also. If a person is a dogmatic moralizer about his *own* status, if he condemns himself for any deviation from the intrinsicist commandments, he is going to be a dogmatic moralizer about other people too, denouncing them at the drop of a hat, just as he does himself. We *do* have to judge others, so I'm not implying emotionalism; but you have to do it properly. And here the point I want to make is that the rationalist in ethics tends to be overly condemnatory toward others. Since his basic set is to feel that their individuality and their desires are flaws or weaknesses, he is predisposed to look for flaws or weaknesses in them, and he is predisposed to attack them just as he attacks himself. Of course, the empiricist sees this, and he says, "The only alternative is don't judge others. Who are you to judge? Nobody has the answers; live and let live." And so we reach the false alternative of moralizing condemnation versus amoralism. Here again, amoralism is not worth discussing. I want to comment on what's wrong with the other side, the rationalist approach.

There are many possible reasons and factors involved in why someone would be overly condemnatory of others. For instance, statistically, you have more chance of being right. Or you may be generally uncertain about people, you don't know how to judge, you're afraid of making errors, so you want to remain aloof, keep yourself uninvolved, and therefore, if you're generally on the premise of "People are no good," you don't have to worry about getting involved with them, so it's protection. Or, there are people who come to Objectivism with an axe to grind—they regard themselves as rebels and outcasts in a hostile world. Such a person decides that Objectivism is the right philosophy because it tells him everybody's rotten, and he's a small minority of the virtuous, and he thinks he has found a home. There are people who are deeply misanthropic, who really hate mankind, and they interpret elements of Objectivism as supporting that, and so they gravitate toward it. There may be many factors involved in this over-condemnation. Rationalism feeds and reinforces this type of attitude, and it does so via the mechanism of arming the person with all sorts of concrete-bound rules. And then they just simply have to check off other people's depravity according to the concrete rules that they violate.

The rationalist's pattern of judging people is that first he represses his emotions, so he has no way to judge others; then the flood of data about the person goes by him—he doesn't know how to take it or deal with it, it's too much to take in, so he flounders altogether with regard to people; yet he knows it's very important to judge people—he gets that drummed into him from the Objectivist literature—"You shouldn't be amoral, you must pass moral judgments"; so he takes the typical rationalist method: Grab on to an axiom in the flux; find something in the chaos that seems to be clear-cut or unequivocal, and then deduce from there; find an axiom, like the base of a deductive system. And, of course, for the rationalist, it's perfect to find some concrete rule that the person violates, that stands out in the chaos and that becomes his axiom. He has no hierarchy, no context, no principles; everything whirls until something strikes him. For instance, he sees a person reacting to an unhappy movie or music, and he says to himself, "Aha, now I know what this guy's like. He responds to tragedy, so he has a tragic sense of life—inferior, philosophically corrupt, weak, no good." Can you respond to tragedy without having a tragic sense of life? Yes. Can you have a tragic sense of life without being in any way immoral, corrupt, or evil? Yes. Can you have a tragic sense of life and still be one hundred percent honest, rational, and moral? Yes, absolutely. But this rationalist has a dogma, "Thou shalt respond only to the benevolent." Or, he might come out with a statement like, "Ted Kennedy is just as corrupt as Andropov, they're both collectivists." Are there differences in degree? Are there differences in consistency? Does it make a difference that one came from Massachusetts and the other from the head of the KGB? For the rationalist, all of this is beside the point. "Anybody who doesn't subscribe to my politics is equally wicked." Is it possible for there to be different kinds of collectivists? Is it possible for there to be an honest welfare-statist (leaving aside a discussion of Ted Kennedy)? The point here is that there is no attempt to analyze, just a trigger-happy snap judgment.

Another example: "I just saw that guy say 'Good morning' to a priest.

Sanction of evil." Is politeness the same as a sanction of evil? Is every courtesy to someone else an endorsement of every sin of the recipient? Are all priests evil? Can some priests be better than others? Can it be proper to be friendly with a priest? None of this is asked, considered; it's just, "Religion is bad, thou shalt not touch it." Now that is dogma, not philosophy, not moral judgment. I've heard this one, "My parents are no good because they look forward to vacations and family gatherings"— because the idea is that you should be like Roark, who didn't have any use for his family; in fact, his family wasn't even brought into the novel. You can see how many ludicrous things are evaded in this idea: Is there no place for vacations in life? Is it possible for a man to have a job he doesn't like, without that reflecting on him, given factors outside of his control, so he really looks forward to vacations? Or, he needs a rest, and he really wants a vacation; or, he has awful coworkers, or an awful employer, and he has to get away, and so on; or, believe it or not, he actually likes his family, and he respects them and enjoys their company. It is no answer to this to say, "Ayn Rand was not big on family, so this guy is no good." None of this is proper moral judgment. It is just the flinging of concrete dogmas without relation to Objectivism.

To summarize: Yes, you should judge others, but *by principles in the proper context.* You can condemn someone as wrong if you can *show* that he violated a principle in the context where it's applicable. But that requires that you approach the whole matter in terms of principles, which have to be concretized, chewed, that you can therefore actually apply to real life.

I want to conclude with one brief word back on the topic of emotions. If you understand the framework from which I'm speaking, I would say self-expression is the good. That argument I presented on opening night about your self versus philosophy is absurd. You should not repress yourself; you should bring yourself into reality, recognizing that that does not mean subjectivism. If you don't take the false alternative of the intrinsic versus the subjective, you will see that real self-expression is the expression of what you think and feel, and that combination is precisely the objective, which is why I say that if self-expression is your concern, you have to be objective, and ultimately, an Objectivist.

Lecture Ten Q & A

Q: What were Ayn Rand's reasons for not wanting to be a mother?
A: Primarily I would say because she was committed from a very early age to a full-time career as a novelist and writer. She did not want to divert any of her attention to anything else. She wanted to pursue that full-time, and it was simply not worth it to her to divert any time from that goal, by her particular hierarchy of interests and values. Beyond that, she had no interest in teaching. She was very different, for instance, from me in that regard. She was not interested in taking someone and bringing them along step by step, which is essential to being a parent. She wanted a formed mind that she could talk to on the level as an equal. She had more of the scientific motivation, rather than the pedagogical motivation. So it was as simple as that.

Q: Aren't esthetic value judgments especially prone to the pitfalls of intrinsicism? How does one avoid being dogmatic, especially when one definitely distinguishes between good and bad works of art? All too often I come across the false alternative of esthetic relativism or an intrinsic esthetic absolutism.
A: The subjectivist error is obvious: It's not true that anything you respond to is either art or good art. But what would intrinsicism in esthetic judgment consist of? We'll restrict ourselves to one point: concrete-bound dogmas, as against abstract esthetic principles as your method of judging. The best example of intrinsicism was a school in the nineteenth century known as Classicism. They took the great buildings of Greece and Rome and the Renaissance, and they worked out certain rules that all buildings should follow according to the way the classical structures were erected. And they decreed in effect, "We have to imitate or copy those buildings in certain crucial ways." Roark's objection was, "When we come to the modern era, we have different materials, different purposes, and consequently we can't be bound by the concretes of a different context." Did it follow that Roark advocated subjectivism, whatever you feel like? No. Toohey advocated it; Toohey said, "There are no principles; it's whatever

is the consensus." But Roark had a very objective principle, which was an *abstract* principle, not "Thou shalt be a copy of the Parthenon." And his principle, which he got from real life, was "Form follows function." His principle was that there should be ornament, but the ornament should grow out of and stress the function of the building, as against, "It should be copied from some concrete masterpiece," or, "Do whatever you feel like." In every art form, there could be Classicists. In music, there were people who set up Bach and a few others as the authorities, and then dictated how many movements your pieces should have, and what tempos, and when you should recapitulate the theme, and so on, and they had a whole series of rules. The Romanticists came in and swept all this aside. Did this mean that there were no principles when the Romanticists entered the picture? Absolutely not. It was the moderns who said, "You can do anything, make a sonata out of sneezes if you want." They were the ones who stood for subjectivism and no principles. The Romanticists still had definite musical principles—development, resolution, tonality, intelligibility—but they did not have concrete strictures derived from traditional composers. You can do the same thing in regard to literature— there was a whole school attempting to take the classic drama of the Greeks and the French, and say how many acts a play should have, what the time span should be, and so on and so on. Again, this was thrown out by the Romantics, but that did not mean that they wrote *Waiting for Godot*. The typical Objectivist Classicist takes Ayn Rand's concrete works as the model to imitate, and then finds some departure and therefore denounces the work. To give you just one simple example, this idea that it has to have a happy ending; it's either "benevolent," or it's no good. But that is not a principle of esthetic judgment. I gave a whole lecture in my introductory course on Objectivism, which is presupposed for this course, and I tried to concretize what is meant by a *principle* of esthetic judgment—the artwork has to be intelligible, it has to be purposeful, the parts have to be integrated into a whole, it has to express implicitly or explicitly a view of life—and I showed what their application would be, and how they derive from the very nature of art. But this still leaves tremendous scope for options within the application of these principles. First of all, it leaves room for great philosophic disagreement among artists, because there's a big difference between judging esthetically and judging philosophically, so that someone like Shakespeare could present determinism and the doom of man, and have an unhappy ending, and still be great art, even if you disagree with him philosophically. Even Ayn Rand herself wrote a book with an unhappy ending, namely, *We the Living*, where her specific theme required a tragic ending. Kira dies. She does not get to America. So there is no way of making that into a benevolent ending. But her theme required it. And you cannot say, "This is bad because it has an unhappy ending." To take that is to take a concrete out of all context as a kind of dogma and say you have to mirror it.

Q: You implied that an Objectivist could find Ayn Rand's novels boring or unenjoyable. Have you had any experiences regarding this?
A: The implication that I see in this particular question is that all concretes are optional. The questioner seems to have concluded that philosophy defines principles and not concretes, and therefore seems to have gotten the idea, "So long as you subscribe to the Objectivist principles, it's completely optional what reactions you have to any concretes, because after all, concretes are the preserve of your private reactions." I can just say it one more time: Principles are integrations of concretes. That's all they are; they are not Platonic entities in another dimension. There are no separate worlds, the world of principles dictated by reason and the world of concretes, which are optional. If that's true, there is no such thing as philosophy. Who needs principles if they are not to be applied to concretes, and applied objectively? Now where does the issue of options on concretes come in? In only one type of case, *where the concrete in question is mixed*, where there's a good element and a bad element. Then, I think, you have the obligation to identify both elements. You can't still be blind and say, "Since I like the good element, I'm going to pretend the bad doesn't exist, and vice versa." You have an obligation to *identify* the two elements, and then, however within limits, I think it's optional which you prefer. But there are a lot of concretes that are not mixed, and I would say in those cases, if you can demonstrate it, there is no option. And if a person

likes the bad—the thoroughly, unmitigatedly bad—he simply is wrong, flatly wrong, regardless of his upbringing, his preferences, his choices, and so on. And vice versa for the good. If somebody said about Adolf Hitler, for instance, "He did a lot of wicked things, but on the other hand, he has a really cute mustache, and with my personal option I really love that kind of mustache, so I feel a kind of sympathy and warm feeling for him, that's my option," I say that is not legitimate. It is not legitimate because you are defying the essence of the concrete in that case; you are making a gross irrelevancy into a criterion even of your *optional* judgment, and that is completely defying reality.

With all due respect, I maintain that in the realm of esthetic judgment, Ayn Rand's works are to the good what Hitler is to the evil. She has a rational philosophy, in my judgment for the first time in history, brilliantly dramatized in matchless works of fiction, completely consistent from sense of life, characterizations, plot, and so on—I do not see any legitimate ground on which anyone could say, "I find this 'boring' or 'unenjoyable.'" The principles and their application to the concrete are so unmistakable that I do not regard that as a realm of option. It's a different question, "What would I think of a person if they didn't like her works?" Granted, I don't think the judgment is legitimate. Does it follow necessarily that this person is depraved? No, not necessarily. It altogether depends on why. I can imagine instances where I would not condemn such a person, where I would not hold it against them, even though I think it's mistaken. For instance, I've met people, and sometimes *nice* people, who say, "I like her works, but I can't read the speeches; they're just so long." I think this is a mistake. I think you can demonstrate that those speeches are necessary to the plot, that they simply can't be condensed. But to me it's graspable that someone on a certain level is just not that interested in ideas, and that does not prove depravity. I could think of an even more plausible case, where I would let the person off the hook altogether (I mean, I wouldn't care to relate to them very much, but I certainly wouldn't regard them as guilty): I've seen Objectivist parents drive their kids crazy with Objectivist dogmatism. They hammer it down the throats of these kids for fifteen years; every time the kid wants a Coke, he gets a lecture on "A is A." And after a while the kid just rebels in the name of human self-assertion, and the rest of his life he hates Ayn Rand and Objectivism as the thing that destroyed his childhood. This, to me, is a very understandable reaction. I know particular children who grew up this way, who will never endorse Objectivism, who don't have the objective capacity to realize it was a warped attitude on the part of their parents, but nevertheless, that's the situation as they see it. I want to cut this short by saying this: The moral of my talk on options was not that everything is an option. When you say that something is an option, you have to be able to show in the actual concrete, what are the good, what are the bad—they have to be balanced enough so that it's not like the Hitler mustache case; you have to be able to identify both, including the principles that you're using to make the comparison.

Q: What about Miss Rand's view of pain, guilt, and fear—didn't she see them as fundamentally unimportant, and doesn't that lead to de-emphasizing those emotions, and therefore, to repression?
A: Absolutely not. She regarded them as unimportant *metaphysically*: Pain and fear and guilt should not be the indication of the essential nature of life, or of the universe. But that is an intellectual-philosophic appraisal. Repression means that it's wrong to feel those emotions, at any time, in any context, and therefore you should never feel them. To say that something is not a reflection of the essential nature of reality is not to say, "Therefore, it's wrong ever to feel it," including to feel it very, very intensely, and for a long period of time (relatively speaking).

LECTURE ELEVEN

■

Intellectual Honesty

I want to continue our discussion about judging people, and this time with a specific focus: how to judge their intellectual honesty. When people advocate various ideas that are wrong, are they honestly mistaken or are they dishonest? And then, on the basis of *all* of our discussions of judging people, I want to take up the last argument from the opening lecture I have not yet covered fully. That's the issue of philosophy versus the world, or Objectivism versus people. Does life have to be a constant battle?

Let's turn to honesty. We previously defined "dishonesty" as "evading some fact or facts of reality, combined with some form of pretense, some form of manufacturing a new fact, that the person wants to be so, regardless of the actual fact." It is by no means obvious when a person is being honest and when he isn't. So we are on an advanced level of chewing now, not just the easy examples, but the complex real-life cases where it's not self-evident. And here I want to take one specific trait and observe the kind of complexities involved in deciding just that one issue. I chose honesty because, although it's not by any means the whole question in judging other people, it is a very important question. It's important in helping you get to the essence of another person, and therefore, in helping you to decide if you want to deal further with this person, so far as you have a choice. If you talk to a man, and you disagree about major issues, and you conclude that he is honest, that it's simply an honest difference in viewpoint from yours, then other things being equal, you don't write him off. You say he's merely mistaken, and you may very well decide, "He's a decent, good, honest person; I like other traits of his; I want to continue the relationship." As against if you decide, "This person is not merely mistaken, he is dishonest; he is an evader, he doesn't *want* to know. He wants to live in an unreal world, and he resents me for trying to blast him out of it"—well, if you conclude that about somebody, it makes all the difference in the world. And in that case, the appropriate conclusion would be: There's no use in arguing further with him; he's not open to evidence; it's a waste of time to try to convince him; you're merely courting frustration. Plus, you are then sanctioning evil—you are letting him get away with the pretense that he's open to an honest discussion. So practically speaking, this is an important question. It is unjust to judge an honest man as dishonest, and it makes you a perennial victim of his dishonesty. It sanctions and thus aids the spread of evil in the world.

This issue of honesty is very important in your general view of people. If you have a tendency to engage in snap judgments on this question—if whenever you hear disagreement you automatically conclude, "This guy is dishonest, he's a swine, he's vicious"—the fact is, since you're in a very small intellectual minority, if you're an Objectivist, you're going to quickly conclude that people in general are rotten and that life is miserable. And you will soon end up bitter, paralyzed, overcome with futility. Again, I'm trying to combat rationalist, improper condemnation, and the resulting malevolence. The empiricist tendency, of course, is the opposite—it's either not to judge other people at all or aggressively say, "Everybody is honest, there is no such thing as immorality, everybody is really wonderful, innocent, and so on." That is what you can call philosophic Pollyannaism. That's also wrong, and it's self-defeating. But it is not the typical error of Objectivists I have known, so don't take my emphasis as meaning that the proper alternative is to say nobody is dishonest.

When is a man being honest as against dishonest in intellectual issues? We know that in general, an honest man conforms to the facts of reality as he grasps them; a dishonest man *defies* the facts that he either does grasp or easily could if only he would look. The first thing to say then is that if you want to describe some belief as honest, you have to be able to point to *something* in reality, some data, some basis that would make that conclusion possible or understandable. Of course, I hasten to say, since the belief is wrong, the reality basis is being misconstrued by the person—he's misinterpreting the evidence, because his idea is false. But the point is that there has to be some glimmer of fact or reason that the person would accept it. If there was any idea such that there was absolutely nothing in reality, however generous your interpretation of the person, to suggest X or be a basis for X, then by definition that cannot be an honest belief.

Suppose a man says, "God must exist, because who created the universe?" In fact that is not a basis to believe in God; but he *thinks* there's a basis, and minds such as Thomas Aquinas have accepted variants of that type of argument—they thought, for instance, that the orderliness of the universe was evidence that there was a God. They were mistaken, but they could point to some seeming evidence. By that fact it was therefore not necessarily dishonest.

This is true of most errors—that in *some* context, you could imagine a plausible basis—but I want to say at the outset that it is not, in my opinion, true of *all* errors. There are some positions in which I would say by the very nature of the viewpoint, no matter what the context or ignorance of the person, to accept that viewpoint is necessarily dishonest. So I want to give you a nonexhaustive list that will define one extreme. In this axis, you can definitely say, "This person is dishonest no matter what," simply from what he says. And I'll divide up my list into three subdivisions.

Inherently dishonest positions: (A) any *explicit* repudiation of reason and reality—that is, the open statement, "To hell with reason, down with reality." You say to the person that his argument is senseless, and he says, "That's tough, I hold no brief with making sense." You tell him, "Your theory conflicts with reality," and he says, "There is no reality. It's a myth. Facts are whatever I want them to be, or whatever society wants them to be." Honesty is the attempt to conform to reality by the use of your mind, your reason. If you openly reject the mind and/or reality, you have to be dishonest, because that wipes out the whole base of honesty. Nobody, however ignorant, can think, "My way of conforming to reality is to reject it." That is simply too blatant. There could be no possible basis in reality for the idea that there isn't one. And this, by the way, is why I regard Kant as the major turning point—morally speaking—of the moral status of philosophers. I believe that in general, philosophers up to Kant were dominantly honest, albeit mistaken. Since Kant, and thanks to his influence, I think philosophers are dominantly dishonest. And the difference lies, and can be symbolized, by the difference between Plato and Kant on this point: Plato thought there was a reality; he was wrong about what it was, but he nevertheless said, "There is a reality and we must conform to it." And he thought that reason was essential to grasping it, up to a point, even if his view of reason was distorted, and even if past that point he thought you needed a mystic insight. That is an essentially different phenomenon from, "Reality, by its nature, is unknowable and beyond the capacity of our minds to grasp," which is Kant's view, "and reason, by its nature, is an agency of distortion, so that if your mind comes to a conclusion by that fact, it isn't so," which is the essence of Kant's view. Kant therefore really inaugurated the essence of dishonesty into the mainstream of Western philosophy.

A second subdivision of these intrinsically dishonest positions: (B) on the ethical or evaluative level: *any explicit attack on values as such*. Men have to live by pursuing values. Everybody does it in some form; everybody *knows* it in some form. To assault values as such, to tell people they have to get rid of values as such, has to be in defiance of every solitary thing the person could possibly get from even the most fragmentary glimmer of a glance at reality. Here I have in mind nihilism, as exemplified in, among other things, modern art—the idea of the destruction of the various art forms as an end in itself. Not the advocacy of a *new* school with *different* values—as, for instance, Naturalism versus Romanticism; both of those could be honest—but not the idea of art's essence being to strip away the essential values in every single field. I'm not saying every *advocate* of modern art is dishonest. I'm talking just about those who know its nihilist essence, and advocate it. We'll discriminate some other types of advocate later.

Another example of nihilism would be the Kantian view of sacrifice, as against the Christian. Christianity said, "Sacrifice yourself in the name of helping the weak, and for an alleged higher value, which is your happiness in the next life." Kant said, "Sacrifice everything *because* it's a value; destroy for its own sake." Egalitarianism is another example of this explicit attack on values as such. I'm thinking of John Rawls and the idea "Destroy the men who achieve values *because* they achieve values; cut down the virtuous *because* they're virtuous." That's what Ayn Rand calls hatred of the good. And all of those would be examples that I think are intrinsically dishonest.

And then finally, my third point: (C) politically, any advocacy of the totalitarian state, whether it be Nazism or communism. Not necessarily socialism. I mean the open declaration "Man should be a slave; he should have no right to think, to choose on any level; he should be a complete zombie, mindlessly obedient to a master," of which the extreme expression is a concentration camp. This is simply the same nihilism as point B: utter destruction, now in politics, and the same reasoning applies.

All of these points, A, B, and C, are absolutely devoid of any basis, even mistaken. They fly in the face of essentials that no one can escape if he gives the most *casual* attention to reality. They are inherently wicked, vicious, dishonest viewpoints. So I think there are some such things as dishonest viewpoints.

But I do want to say that the advocates of these types of views are definitely a minority in the world, and in the United States in particular. Mostly these views will emanate from the mouths of professional intellectuals, who have been steeped in years of corruption at colleges. Ordinary people do not utter such things as a rule. So the question then becomes, how do you judge the more typical cases where, from the nature of what the person says, he might be honest and he might not be? And here we have a much more difficult and complex question.

The general answer is that you have to consider the cognitive context of the individual. How much evidence was available to him? Did he have access to all the data *you* have and then evaded it, deliberately invented something to replace it, or was his context more limited, was his ability to grasp the truth, therefore, impaired, limited, and therefore his error does not prove dishonest? Well, how do you tell this? There are many factors relevant to deciding another person's intellectual context. One obvious factor is age. Inexperience, delimited knowledge of a young person, excuses a great deal; it mitigates a lot of intellectual senselessness that would be unforgivable in an adult. This is particularly true given the state of modern colleges. Teenagers are, by definition, ignorant, not in the sense that they are completely devoid of knowledge, but they're just in the process of acquiring knowledge; they are, by that very fact, capable of much greater errors than an adult would be. Plus the fact that the schools and colleges have assaulted their minds systematically for a decade or more, from the time they enter grade one, and make them incapable of thought for the most part, pump them full of falsehoods as the basic self-evident framework. It would take heroic independence on the part of one of these children even to conceive how rotten his whole educational system has been. Again, a dishonest teenager is a possibility. But, other things being equal, you should give the benefit of the doubt to someone who is young—up to a point. We don't have to haggle over how young is young, and at what age does he lose his dispensation; but I would say that once you're in your early twenties, you lose this excuse.

The context of the person also varies with the historical era that he lives in, because that determines *also* how much evidence is available to him. Andrei in *We the Living* thought Russia was a noble experiment, that the grief would last only a very short time, and thereafter it would be utopia. He was, of course, wrong, and Miss Rand herself thought that he was a fictional character who could not have a real-life counterpart. But at least in fictional terms, it was conceivable for such a character to exist at the time of the Russian Revolution. You could not, in Russia in 1983, have someone who thinks it's just temporary and all the concentration camps don't really mean anything, not with all the facts we now have available. Or, for instance, there is a very relevant difference between believing in God in the tenth century and in the twentieth, in the age of modern science. I don't here imply that all believers in God are dishonest, but merely that what you *could* say, I think, is that in the Middle Ages, virtually every believer was honest; they simply could not grasp the possibility of a nonreligious view of the universe at that time. Atheism was not a sin; it just simply was unconceived of; it was a prescientific culture, and that's a very different context than we have today.

Context also varies with a person's profession, with his area of specialization. In certain fields, there is specialized knowledge that you either have or are *supposed* to have, given your field. And you can be held responsible if you don't know it. There's a big difference here, for instance, between the man on the street who reads in some tabloid that the world is coming to an end because of the pollution and ecology, as against some left-wing scientist who comes out with doomsday scenarios in defiance of all known facts and of all scientific method, in order to foster his socialist conclusions. The scientists who do this are *prima facie* much more dishonest than the individual who reads the *Enquirer*. Or, as another example of this point, the man on the street who simply says, "There are no absolutes," and doesn't have the faintest idea of the philosophic implications, is in a very different position from the philosopher who *knows* what this means, and who knows that it's a complete assault, by implication, on reason and reality.

Another factor is plain ordinary intelligence. We don't expect as much from somebody who's mentally retarded or who's dull or who's average (going up the scale), as we expect from someone who is more brilliant. You'll have to work out, in your own experience, what other factors are relevant to inquire about if you have doubts. These factors will not yet lead you to a conclusion but merely give you a place to start. In judging honesty, you begin by asking, "Given everything I know about this person—his age, his era, his field, his intelligence, and so on—could he have known this point? Was there some basis in reality to lead him to what he went to, to throw him off, or was he defying evidence that he must have seen, given his cognitive context?"

Sometimes in trying to weigh this—and it's by no means easy to weigh; there are lots of cases in which I simply say, "I don't have the faintest idea if this person is honest or not"—but sometimes it's helpful to take yourself as a standard in judging this question, in the following way: If *you* could have once believed something honestly, then so could somebody else. So if you see someone who believes something wrong that you yourself once held, that doesn't prove he's honest, because he may have a much better context now than you had—he may be more knowledgeable—but at least it shows that it's possible for him to be honest if you have no evidence to the contrary. This is one ground on which I will swear until I die that it's possible for a rationalist to be honest, because I committed that error and I regard it as honest in my own case. But it does not always work in reverse—if a certain error was impossible to you, it doesn't follow that it's impossible to others, except for their dishonesty. It depends on whether their evidential context was as good as yours. Someone can be honestly confused or misguided about something that you are perfectly clear about. For instance, you read *Atlas Shrugged*, and you take some courses, and to you it's now perfectly clear what's the right politics. That does not prove that everybody who disagrees with you is dishonest. To you, now, disagreement on politics is impossible, but that would be dropping the cognitive context of others. And this is one of the tests of a good teacher or communicator—to be able not to take your own knowledge as the sole standard, to realize that honest confusion *can* exist, even though to the speaker himself perhaps the issue was always clear.

Let's assume you're trying to judge the person's context, and you make the comparison to yourself. Can I suggest any test of honesty to confirm or weaken your conclusion so far? Yes, I think there is a critical test, and that is the *method by which a person argues, or conducts himself in a discussion.* This exists, of course, on a whole spectrum, but to take the two extremes—if a person resorts to invective, *ad hominem*, aggressive changes of subject, evasion of your point of view, sarcasm, name-calling, name-dropping, and so on, that clearly suggests he's dishonest. It looks like he's actively working to ignore reality and sustain his fantasy. Contrast that with a person who listens, doesn't resort to personalities, tries to answer your points, or at least says, "I don't know, I can't answer, I'll have to think it over"—that gives you a completely different picture.

This test of method, although it's certainly helpful, is not always an absolute. I've seen a person resort to invective, evasion, and so on, where you would say, "This guy is a real louse," and then later, on his own, he apologizes. It turns out that in discussion he was threatened by what you said, he was thrown, he reacted emotionally, he was out of control, and later he calmed down, recognized what he had done, and admitted it to himself. This indicates obviously a better person who had a bad episode, but he wants to remain in contact with reality, and he owned up to it. That is not evidence of a dishonest person. So I think you have to go by the total picture. And it is pretty easy to judge this question. You just watch a pattern of his behavior across time. And after a few times, if he keeps throwing a fit, he loses the excuse of "This was just a temporary aberration"; that becomes his character.

You can have the reverse phenomenon. I have observed professors whom I know are dishonest intellectually. I know that from extensive private discussion, and from the nature of their views, which are beyond horrendous. But nevertheless, I have seen those very same professors (not all, but some), when talking to students, engage very calmly, with no invective discussion; they are the seeming model of rationality; they answer every point of the student quietly; from everything you would look at, you would swear they are honest, but the fact is that they are so trained in expounding their dishonest viewpoint that no student throws or threatens them at all; they just internally laugh at the idea of a student who thinks he can find a chink in their armor. So they enjoy the encounter, they remain absolutely in control. They come across as calm, reasoned, honest, when in fact they know perfectly well what they're doing, and they relish the process of crippling their students under the veneer of honest discussion. So you have to know the whole picture when you judge a person's method of arguing. And here, the content of his view is critical; that's why I opened with views that I think are intrinsically dishonest. That's overriding—if he is an avowed Kantian, or those other ones I mentioned, he is dishonest no matter how sweet his manner.

Let's develop this further. When we judge a person's context, we're trying to discover what he *could* have grasped if he tried. There's another factor relevant in that question besides the evidence available to him, and that is his psychology, especially what Ayn Rand called his *psycho-epistemology*, his automatized methods of thinking. Honesty involves two different kinds of factors: on the one hand, the objective evidence available to the person, and on the other hand, the ability of his consciousness to take it in, to process it correctly. And this last involves his psychology, above all his subconscious processing mechanism, the automatized thinking mechanisms with which he deals with the evidence. The evidence may be available to him, given his age and his profession and his field, and yet his psycho-epistemology may be so poor, so chaotic, that he is effectively deprived of the means to take in the evidence. So even though something would be obvious to the ordinary person, it would not necessarily be dishonest to this individual.

The arch-examples are rationalists and empiricists. Rationalism, as I said, can be a thoroughly honest error; not all rationalists are dishonest. But once they become rationalists, they are unable to keep ideas connected to reality, they become oblivious to factual data, they start deducing consequences from floating axioms. And up to a point, if you know that this kind of methodology is automatized in a person's mind, that is relevant in judging whether he's honest or dishonest. For example, take a man who advocates communism in regard to property—communism with a small "c," all property should be owned in common. And he projects in a rationalist void that if we had that kind of world, it would be a world of peaceful cooperation, some socialist utopia. In actuality, what he is preaching goes counter to the requirements of human life and would lead to disaster. But in his floating world, he shrugs off real-life examples as irrelevant, as distortions of his ideal, and he deduces in a void—"If everyone shared, then there would be no greed; if there was no greed, then everyone would love everyone; if everyone loved everyone, then there would be peace"—and it's all in some other dimension, like Leibniz drawing conclusions from premises. This is profoundly mistaken, not only in content but in method, but it is not necessarily dishonest.

Or take the example of an empiricist, the kind who is so distrustful of abstractions that he deliberately refuses to accept a theoretical conclusion, because he is suspicious of all theoretical conclusions. You argue with him about capitalism, and every example he brings up, every monopoly and every depression and every alleged instance of child labor, you answer. And you ask him, "Do you *now* agree with capitalism?" and he's still suspicious, because he has to be, by his method, suspicious of *any* system. As soon as you give it a "label," it's suspect. Again, up to a point, he has been destroyed intellectually by his in-built method. And it becomes like a self-made stupidity, in his case and in the rationalist's case. It's as though it's a self-made inaccessibility to facts. Remember that we said intelligence was relevant. Rationalism and empiricism amount to a self-reduced intelligence. It's like a person has a partial lobotomy. If you're young, this is theoretically curable. But if you're no longer young, you're not so flexible anymore, and bad methods of thought may become incurably entrenched. In such a case, I would say the person is not necessarily dishonest, but for practical purposes, it comes out to be the same as if he were, because it has the same result: You can no longer deal with the person.

The purpose of this discussion is to try to determine whom to pursue and whom to abandon. The extreme, entrenched rationalist or empiricist in practice—even if he is honest—you have to end up treating as though he were dishonest, because he is so (in the vernacular) "screwed up" that you can't reach him anymore, except possibly by many, many years of psychotherapy. It's as though he were psychotic; he may be very honest, but so what, what are you going to do with it? I hasten to add that he is *not* psychotic. And therefore I must stress that rationalism and empiricism, although they excuse a lot of errors (excuse in the sense that you cannot claim the person is dishonest), they do not excuse *everything*. At a certain point, the evidence becomes so blatant that even an honest rationalist has to admit that something is wrong with his viewpoint. For instance, however rationalistic a Soviet apologist, he cannot escape the facts of the Soviet system. Even his rationalism cannot literally blind him to the butchery of so many millions of people. So there you have to say if he is not psychotic, it doesn't make any difference if he's rationalist or what; he is dishonest. And the same principles apply to an empiricist. I received a good question from someone in this class when we gave that example in the empiricist lecture about the Korean airliner being shot down, and that empiricist professor had all these incredible concrete-bound questions, and the questioner said, "Okay, he's an empiricist, but how could he overlook the deaths of the passengers? Why didn't that have any effect on him?" And I think that is a very good point. I defer to the questioner: Even an empiricist doesn't become an actual moron. However concrete-bound he is, there are issues that even he cannot miss, so at a certain point, he is dishonest also.

There are other psychological mechanisms relevant to judging honesty besides rationalism and empiricism. I gave an example earlier about the person momentarily threatened by an argument you give, who becomes hostile, defensive, and so on. That's not necessarily the expression of a whole twisted psychology on his part. It's relevant to know, in such a case, if this person is being detoured by a subconscious mechanism, an unidentified emotion that is warping his performance, or is he just plain dishonest? And here, the test is his pattern of behavior across time. There *may* be subconscious mechanisms or unidentified defense mechanisms that temporarily warp an otherwise honest person, that detour him and throw him off the rails. That does not prove that he is essentially dishonest.

I am not counseling what Ayn Rand called *psychologizing*—that is, whenever anybody says anything, immediately hypothesizing what his deep subconscious psychology is, and then excusing him on the grounds that nobody can help what they do because of their Oedipus complex or whatever. In judging any moral or philosophical question, including honesty, you have to go by the facts, by the philosophic content, until and unless there is some specific evidence of a psychological malfunction that obtrudes itself blatantly upon you. At that point, then, you can investigate if you want to pursue the person. All I'm saying is this: You can't, on principle, say, "To hell with this man's psychology; I judge his honesty strictly on the basis of the evidence available." In some cases you do have to take his psychology into account, but you cannot use it arbitrarily to justify or explain away everything. You should give primacy to the conscious data, and consider the subconscious only when there's something really malfunctioning blatantly, like a real rationalist, where there's no other way to interpret his conscious statements except by the idea, "There's something wrong with the way his mind operates."

Another point with regard to judging honesty. When asking if, when someone believes X, is he honest, it's very important to know what he takes X to mean. Does it mean to him what it means to you? You cannot assume that everyone attaches identical meanings to every term or statement. A person may be guilty of a misuse of language, of a misnomer; he may be simply ignorant of the meaning of the term. For instance, a man on the street could advocate altruism, and to him that simply means giving a dime to a beggar, or helping someone in trouble, and it has no deeper meaning whatever. That's obviously not what's meant by altruism philosophically, and is entirely different from Auguste Comte, the coiner of the term, coming forth and advocating altruism, where it means the complete and utter self-sacrifice of man to the collective.

This is an important general issue in judging nonphilosophers who utter formulations casually, with little idea of their meaning. Most people are not formulators, and by "formulators" I mean people trained in, or even conscious of, methods of exact statement of their views. Most people have no such concept as "there is a way of expressing your philosophic or intellectual views exactly." They toss out terms or ideas casually, lightly, with no precise idea of the meaning or the implications. And one grave error on the part of a philosophical person judging a nonphilosophical one is to assume that every utterance of his has the standing in his mind that every utterance of yours has—that every utterance of his is weighed, considered, grasped in every implication. It may be un-thought-out—it may not even stand for a real belief on the person's part; he may just be groping something in words that the next day he wouldn't even remember saying. So when you're judging a person's honesty in believing X, you have to first find out what he really believes, if anything, on this question.

Even when a person does actually hold a bad belief—he believes something and it's wrong—it's still very important to distinguish the *implicit* from the *explicit*. A belief may imply a disaster without the person knowing it. I gave the example of the man on the street who denies absolutes, which implies wiping out all of reality. But that, obviously, is not known to him. Or to give you a more extreme example, I could prove that if you do not advocate private ownership of roads, that implies the principle of statism, which implies that man should be a pawn of the group, which implies an assault on the integrity of the mind. But if you were to say, "The ordinary person who believes in public roads is therefore hostile to man's mind," that would be ludicrous. Of course, as the implication of an idea becomes more obvious, then it's more reasonable to believe that the person saw it, or at least should have seen it. If somebody openly advocates the all-powerful state, including government controls of elections, the press, assembly, and so on—in other words, not just the welfare state, but totalitarianism—he ought to see, both from the theory and from the empirical data, that human slaughter is an implication. As opposed to the example I gave of the person who advocated public ownership of property, but projects a peaceful, free society otherwise. In such a case, the implication is more remote. The person doesn't necessarily see that if property is publicly owned, everything is destroyed; maybe he's so rationalistic that he can't see that. Of course, you do have an obligation to see *some* implications, but you don't necessarily see *every* implication.

There are many factors, therefore, to survey—the context of the person (the evidence available given his age, field, and so on); his psychology (his ability to process the data); his method of arguing; the actual content of the belief he holds; what he actually sees, as against what's merely implicit.

I have one last theoretical issue with regard to judging honesty. I think it's important to make a distinction between *dependence* and *dishonesty*. A person may be passive in regard to ideas; he may not have thought actively or independently but has merely gone along with the social consensus and accepted the prevalent view of the culture around him. I am not saying that this is admirable. What I *am* saying is that I do not think this is necessarily dishonest; it does not necessarily involve deliberate evasion to sustain a specific idea. Of course, a dependent may be dishonest, depending on the reasons for his conformity. I would say, as a general rule, that if a man sees the need to think about an issue and has some idea of how to go about it, and *then* defaults, then he's dishonest, because he's evading facts that he himself sees. And his motive in such a case might be laziness, parasitism, he wants a crutch, he's afraid of others, he wants to be popular, so he just shuts his mind down and goes along. A lot of this is immoral, in the sense that he's deliberately rejecting his own mind in the name of some emotion. Doing that requires sustained evasion, and therefore it is dishonest. But it's possible to have a dependent person, who goes along with others for a different kind of reason—through helplessness. And that's particularly true in regard to philosophic issues. Most people absorb philosophy from others, with no idea that what they're absorbing is controversial or that any alternative exists. They have a view that philosophy is a subject that can't be dealt with, it's all a matter of opinion, there are no answers, it's irrelevant to life—none of which you can blame them for having, given the way its advocates present the subject. Plus, even if these people accepted that the subject was important, they would have no clue as to how to go about thinking about it, which is itself a separate, complex skill. Yet people can't simply dismiss it the way they do nuclear astrophysics, because it is inescapable, so they end up conforming, accepting what they're taught, fitting in, not so much out of laziness or fear or parasitism as out of ignorance, helplessness, and not even knowing that there is an issue to think about or how to begin the process. They're caught in the position of officially believing that these issues are insignificant, and yet they can't escape, so they half believe. I think that in many cases, this represents inner chaos and confusion but not active deliberate dishonesty. So, I distinguish two types: the dependent by commitment, who *wants* to be dependent, and the dependent by default, who is essentially helpless.

Of course, there may be elements of *both* in a person. When you judge, you have to judge according to the salient, essential feature: Is this a basically helpless person, with an occasional evasion? That is still not the same as an essentially dishonest type. An occasional noncharacteristic evasion is not good, but it is not damning.

There is not much you can do with dishonest types, insofar as they are dishonest. But those who are conformists out of default are a different case. What I'm calling the "helpless dependent" may be a good man who is baffled. Even the neurotic evasive dependent is not as corrupt as the actively dishonest crusader or zealot for a given idea. The typical, garden-variety neurotic may be weak and lazy and therefore immoral to that extent. But he's not immoral in the sense that he's an essentially wicked Kantian, whom you should never deal with or sanction. I think the proper policy in regard to the weak dependents is to delimit your actions, deal with them in the realms where they're better. As I see it, even the weak dependent may have better areas; but the person I'm calling the dishonest advocate, the dishonest believer, who is not just going along with others but is actively evading and working to sustain his viewpoint, is essentially wicked, corrupt down to the roots. And that's why I think the distinction is important. I'll give it to you in a threefold way. What I'm calling the helpless dependent *can* be completely moral; the weak or neurotic dependent can be morally like a mixed economy; the real dishonest person (and this is the one we're trying to ferret out) is basically evil. And so I think there is a significant moral difference.

If you ask, "How do you tell which type you are dealing with?" one simple thing is to see what happens to a conformist when he grasps through *you* the enlightenment that he has been deprived of in school, when he grasps the nature of philosophy, its importance, the way to think about it, and so on. If, as does happen sometimes, this person who on the surface is just a Peter Keating who never had a thought and never disagreed with anybody, sometimes—and I know this from personal observation—such a person wakes up, he becomes excited, he starts to think, he's enamored of this whole world, and he couldn't care less about the views of the majority, although prior to that point, if you had followed him around, you would say this person is a real zero. That would be good evidence then that he was an honest person, but he just gave up. On the other hand, if, when you elaborate these points about philosophy, he becomes hostile and starts to rationalize and claim, "Nobody can know," then you can begin to hypothesize that he is the bad type of conformist.

Another test here, in trying to distinguish all these various subdivisions, is whether the helpless dependent is deeply involved in the issue. Perhaps he doesn't hold the wrong view as an integral, intense issue that's part of his mind, part of his soul. He mouths it, he utters it, but precisely because he's just going along, he doesn't think anybody can really prove anything, and it's not a big issue to him. He's simply not challenging others; he's routinely echoing them, but he doesn't really believe it. To some extent, of course, his actions will have to be involved with his wrong belief, but they will be minimal. That belief will be more or less peripheral to his life; he will tend to function more by common sense. And that already is a better sign of his honesty. As against someone who would mouth the same ideas, but who's an active, proselytizing debater, lecturer, arguer, activist. Take, for instance, the claimed nuclear freeze: The typical leaders, the instigators, the scientists who are out promoting that, I think are demonstrably dishonest. But the followers, on the whole, I don't think you can say that. And I think one of the reasons that there's a distinction is precisely that the followers go along with what they're told, and they hear ten trillion facts, and what do they know, and everybody's saying it, and that's all there is as far as they see it. They're wrong, they are not heroes of independent thought, but I don't think you can say they are dishonest, and that's the issue we're talking about. Some of them you can argue with—I actually had the experience once of arguing with a nuclear freeze type, and he said "Oh" when I gave him an argument; he hadn't thought of that point. And if that can happen once, it's possible. So when you say about a person, "Is his belief honest?" the question is, "Does he have a belief in the significant sense, or just a slogan that doesn't mean too much, even to him?"

Now let us briefly apply some of these distinctions to a few topics, and decide if this belief is honest and what the possibilities are.

Modern—that is, nonobjective—art. A person says to you, "I like modern art." How do you assess that in terms of honesty? I said that the *phenomenon* is intrinsically wicked, and that the nihilists who originated and passionately defended it are absolutely dishonest and not even subject to discussion. But does it follow that every advocate of modern art is therefore dishonest? No, I don't think it does. I think there is a whole spectrum of possibilities, and you would have to talk to the person if you were interested and see where they go, and how you would classify it. Here is just a touch of a pattern, by no means exhaustive.

The most innocent I could imagine would be an utterly ignorant person who likes certain things that he sees on the wall from the point of view of decoration. He doesn't see any issue at all; he knows zero about art or philosophy; he just likes certain smears; they've got a nice color and so on. I would say it doesn't prove anything about his dishonesty. It certainly shows that he has a lot to learn, and it might be discouraging to have to start the philosophic discussion if he's at that stage of the game, but it does not prove that he is dishonest. I think that this is uncommon, but it is a theoretical possibility that I'm projecting just to give you my most benevolent interpretation of the contexts that are possible. Most nonphilosophical people are not like that, because modern art is not popular with the average person. And I would say, therefore, that another pattern is much more common if it's a confused, helpless, but basically honest person. And that's when you hear a statement like this—"I don't know much about art. I don't like it, but of course who knows? It's just a matter of taste, and a lot of very knowledgeable people seem to like it. So who am I to know?" That's more the typical pattern. This person is simply ignorant in a more plausible way, because there are major issues involved, and he has no clue where to start.

On the other hand, take a person who actually endorses it in a more significant way. He really means that he likes it (or he tries to mean it). More likely he is motivated by fear, conformity, the desire not to offend his significant others, like his teachers and classmates and so on. This is obviously not a heroic independence; this would be a weak dependence. But so long as the person takes it as "It's not a big issue," it falls in that category of standard dependence.

Now take a con man, a conscious con man, who does not like it, but actively pretends to—he's an out-and-out hypocrite—in order to gain favor or prestige or a following or money. This is a real plain, ordinary fraud, like a bank robber. He is much more dishonest, because he is going directly counter to something that he knows.

Or take the type that we could describe as the pretentious New Yorker. This is not just the standard dependent whom you would find in Iowa, but the person who wants to be a part of the elite, with whom "pretentious" *means* he's pretending, but he's pretending to himself that he likes it; he's being tremendously phony. He's lying to himself. Whereas the con man just lies to others (and to that extent he preserves some tie to reality), this phony wants to be one of the elite, and therefore he masks his own actual attitude. It's much more dishonest than any of the preceding.

And yet even *that* is benign compared to the nihilists like Kandinsky and Schoenberg, who inaugurated it all. So you see that there's a whole spectrum. I personally draw the line at the con man. Further than that, I think there's no use in talking, or sanctioning them. But up to that point, I can see talking to even the conformist, if he's open to discussion. Sometimes it has an effect, sometimes not.

Now let's take a quick look at religion. Can religion, the belief in God, be honest? There are widely different answers that you would give, depending on where in the religious hierarchy you look. This is the issue of the context, what you expect people to know, how it stands in their minds. If I look at the leaders of some religion, such as the pope, or the priesthood or the nuns, or then all the way down to the laymen, one needs to decide how much they know about its meaning, about what it involves, how much they have to go against their knowledge. So much in judging honesty depends on what a person sees. It's dishonest to deny the knowledge available to you, *if* you realize that the position involves that. To judge this a relevant fact would be to ask how much of a factor religion is in a man's life. Almost nobody is religious today in the way it was once a rule to be. The whole Western world in the medieval period was extremely religious, and today, the most religious zealot in the United States would have been drummed out in the Middle Ages because he would have been hopelessly tainted with secularism. So religion is a dying phenomenon. It's not that big a factor in most people's lives. It's a casual utterance, which most people don't really act on. But, for some people, it *is* a real factor; they propagandize for it, they're zealous about it—that of course makes a big difference, and that would make it much more dishonest.

For most people even today, it can be honest. In my experience, religious people are intellectually dependent. They're not typically innovators, they do not have philosophic independence, but they think that there is some kind of reason you can give to believe in God. For instance, a perfectly standard claim is, "There has to be a God, because where else did the material world come from?" This implies the primacy of consciousness so deeply entrenched that they just take it as self-evident that if there's matter, there must be a consciousness that created it. They seemingly can't conceive of any alternative. And from their point of view—I have argued with some of these people long enough to be convinced—they truly can't get the point. So they are not being dishonest. Whether it's a bad psycho-epistemological method or they have an entrenched wrong metaphysics that would take years to correct, maybe it's worse to argue with them any further, but I do not think in many cases that that is dishonesty. In the same way that people can certainly believe that "some sacrifice is necessary," with no idea of what the whole issue is. If you took the typical American and sat him down for ten hours and you beamed at him the message, "It's America or religion, that's the choice," I do think he would give up religion in favor of America, and that is what makes me think that such people are basically honest. But if we were in Iran and you asked me what I think of believers of God, it would be entirely reversed. I'd say, "It's possible that you can find some honest ones, but I never have."

It's very important that we take into account what people take religion to mean. Many people equate religion with morality as such. They think that the only alternative to religion is rejecting all moral standards. This is certainly not evidence of dishonesty, but of confusion. And sometimes, if you meet such people and point out to them that there is such a thing as a rational ethics, they change. That's very different, in terms of psychology, from a person who equates religion deliberately with supernaturalism as such, who *wants* to escape from reality into another dimension, who says, "I hate this idea of science and this world."

One last example with regard to honesty: the believer in the welfare state, in effect. Here again, it really depends on what he believes in, how much, why, what he knows. For instance, if he believes in it the way that Karl Marx believed in it in the *Communist Manifesto*, as a deliberately calculated step on the road to complete totalitarianism, that's obviously outside the realm of honesty. That's not the same phenomenon as a dependent person for whom this is the way that politics has always been as far as he knows, he doesn't know anything about the subject, he's never had an idea in politics, and he just goes along. You cannot condemn a welfare statist as dishonest per se. It depends on how strong his conviction is, what kind of method of argument he uses, if he's open to argument, and if he's even clear what is involved. In the 1972 presidential election, I met many people who were for George McGovern on the grounds of ending the war in Vietnam, which was package-dealt with an expansion of the welfare state, and they just simply went along with it. It's also important to know how intent the person is on the welfare state. The typically apolitical person doesn't really care. That's very different from the kind who is zealously out to cut down the rich in the name of "social justice." The type who wants to just help out the weak a little is very different from the type who really wants to enslave, and for whom the welfare state is just a means of nihilism. You also have to take into account that the schools, for fifty years, have never even given people the idea that there *is* an alternative. And that context is very relevant. A welfare statist in the nineteenth century in America is an entirely different phenomenon than a welfare statist in the twentieth century, where he doesn't even remember that there ever was anything different.

In sum: Until a person has heard the argument against the welfare state, I tend to give him the benefit of the doubt, other things being equal. On the whole, knowing all the details and contextual factors that apply, I am a priori suspicious of someone who advocates modern art, and open on the question of religion and politics, until I see how it stands in their exact situation and mind. That will give you just a clue as to how you can apply some of these distinctions.

I now want to turn to the last of the three arguments against philosophy that I presented in the opening lecture of this course: philosophy versus the world—that is, the claim that philosophy brings you into perpetual conflict with the outside world or with other people, that it leads to an attitude of perpetual condemnation, malevolence, bitterness. This is the view that life is a kind of grim pilgrimage through an alien realm, where the rule should be tight-lipped solemnity in the presence of evil. This is a typically religious attitude toward life, the idea that this world is a realm of sinners, that it's wrong if you enjoy it, that you should be alienated and await heaven. There are some sincere and honest Objectivists who have a similar idea, but they substitute "Atlantis" for "Heaven." And they have the idea that someday, maybe centuries from now, we will have Atlantis and happiness, but here and now, people are rotten, there is no hope, enjoyment of the world is treason, suffering is one's destiny.

Although this would be a very understandable and even valid attitude if you were living in a concentration camp or a totalitarian dictatorship, it is not true of life in a free or even semi-free Western country. If you're talking about the United States today, the situation is mixed—there is evil and there is good, and your reaction should reflect the *mixture*, and not merely the negatives. There *is* enough good today in the world, in the United States particularly but also in Europe; there's enough achievement, enough freedom, enough justice, enough talent, enough virtue, so that any monolithic across-the-board condemnation of society, of the culture, of the people around you, is simply unjustified. Of course, there is also the bad. There is enough government regulation, injustice, dishonesty, stupidity, parasitism, unreason, and mediocrity so that a monolithic praising of everything around you would be utterly senseless and unjustified. Neither misanthropy (that is, hating everyone), nor Pollyannaism (loving everyone) is justified. The first condemns all men as rotten, and if that were true, even a semi-free country couldn't exist. The second, the Pollyanna viewpoint, holds that down deep, all of us are really good, honest, moral. If this were true of everyone including the leaders of the world, the state of the world would be inexplicable; no one could make that big of a mistake. Both of these warped characterizations are wrong. So the philosophic issue is how to get a balanced, rational appraisal of people, the culture, the world.

In answering the argument I gave you originally, I am *not* going to say that any conflict you might have with the world is entirely a result of philosophic error. In regard to the argument about philosophy versus the self, I did say that. Assuming that your self is not identified with irrational principles, there is no reason whatever to have a conflict between philosophy and your self. If you have such a conflict, it comes entirely from errors. But that is not true of the present case. I think we have a mixed issue in this case.

A sense of alienation from the world can have two sources. Given the state of today's world, part of it is valid and understandable; given the state of the culture, there are some battles you cannot avoid if you hold a philosophy. But there are some battles you can *and should* avoid. There are two different streams feeding this one conclusion of alienation. Partly it's a philosophic error that leads to this, and partly not. And first I want to look at the error side.

What kind of error could lead people to exaggerate the evil in the world, to focus only on the negative, the corrupt, the irrational? The philosophic error that has run through this whole course: the mind/body dichotomy, with all its ramifications. The mind/body dichotomy, as we've seen, leads straight to the moral versus the practical dichotomy. On this view, the moral comes out as the *inner*, the standards within your own mind, your own integrity, but that realm is regarded as necessarily in conflict with the *outer*, with the world, with people, with what succeeds. So if you choose the moral side of this dichotomy (as Objectivists typically do if they're going to commit the error), you have the resulting feeling, . "My idealism is just *my* standards; that's just my inner world. But in the world of other people, my standards have no power, no efficacy; they're going to be rejected. I will be impractical." This is simply another form of the same dichotomy that makes rationalists fear empirical facts and ignore them, or fear emotions and try to wipe them out. And here, the parallel is that the person fears other people as the element he can't control, the element that does not adhere to his inner standards, that will defeat him unless he brushes them aside, so he gives up relations with them and commits himself to a solitary existence.

I'd summarize it this way: The corollary of the rationalist in thought and the repressor in feeling is the misanthrope in relation to people. And it is three forms of the same basic mind/body dichotomy. It's all the same error in different versions and applications.

Once this basic mind/body dichotomy is implanted in a person's soul, it tends to become a self-fulfilling prophecy, because it makes a person act in ways that make him think that his basic viewpoint is ever more true. In pattern, first he decides on philosophic grounds—on the mind/body grounds—that you can't deal with other people; they're not like him, they'll never share his standards or admire him. Then, as a result of this view, he withdraws in action, keeps his distance, rarely if ever tries to make friends, and the result is that nobody *does* know or like him. In fact he *can't* deal with others, because he's never tried. And so after a while, it isn't just theoretical philosophy to him anymore; it seems to him that his actual experience bears out his viewpoint, his actual experience of people. And yet his experience was caused and warped by the underlying mind/body dichotomy.

Here's an alternative: First, either you advocate the mind/body dichotomy or you're brought up with it, and you take the rationalist path. And this leads you, by a route we've seen many times, to over-condemnation of others—you have no method of judging them, so you latch on to utterances out of context, you condemn them as vicious and dishonest, that's your characteristic method of judging. After a while, and not too long a while, on this policy, you come to feel, "Everybody I actually meet and deal with is irrational, they're all unjust, they're all dishonest." And then you think, "You see, I was *right* to distrust everybody." And yet, in fact, you were wrong, because the over-condemnation was a warped by-product of the mind/body dichotomy, which then worked to make it seem even more true.

I don't say this is the only issue involved, but I would say that if you have the right attitude on the mind/body question, including above all that you're not rationalistic, you will find any problems that you have with people are greatly reduced—not necessarily entirely gone, but certainly lightened in a major way, because there is definitely more good out there than the rationalists imagine. (Just to keep the record clear, I must add there is more evil than the amoralists imagine, but that is not my theme in this lecture.) But I come back to the point that most people and most cultural products today are mixed. Am I saying there is no black and white, only gray? Absolutely not. There is a tremendous amount of black—the museums of modern art, and Washington, D.C., are two outstanding examples—but there's also a tremendous amount of white, of good, honest people and achievements in a whole variety of realms. But my point now is that what we are confronted with is a mixture reflecting the mixture of basic premises in the world today. And if you judge in a nonwarped way, you should discriminate both elements. Am I saying that you should look for the good in everyone? No, because it's not always there. But *sometimes* it is, and then you should try to be objective, find it, notice it. When you see a mixture, it's always complicated, but you have to try to judge, as well as possible, what kind of a mixture? I'll give you three rough possibilities: (1) It (whatever you're judging) is dominantly bad with a few fragments of something better. In that case, I would say: Okay, condemn it, because that would be its essence. (2) It's dominantly good, with some traces of error. Again, say, "Okay, I think this is good, and I recognize these flaws." (3) It's very mixed, with big errors and evils and big virtues. Then you have to observe and recognize that, and be content with "It's mixed" as your final verdict. You can't conclude that because something is irreducibly mixed—it does not come out as really good or really bad, but really mixed—you cannot make that automatically let you decide, "Therefore, it's evil." It is not true that if it isn't essentially good, it has to be essentially evil, because an enormous number of things are just essentially mixtures, unquantifiable.

Now let's consider *E.T.*, the movie that I mentioned in the opening lecture. That was a movie that has real philosophic and esthetic flaws. It was certainly anti-adult (in fact, it was, incredibly, *banned* in the welfare state of Sweden because they thought it would foster a bad attitude toward adults). It was anti-science in a very senseless way—that standard science-fiction movie that is based on science and spends its time condemning science. There were scenes that, to me, were certainly not fully clear. So I think you could make a case that substantial criticism was certainly appropriate. But for all of that, I think there were some actually enchanting things in that movie. I found E.T. himself to be extremely likeable, and I took the whole thing as a love story between E.T. and the boy, sort of like Romeo and Juliet, star-crossed lovers who have to fight the world to preserve their love, and this time it had a happy ending. And I think there were many brilliant, if not always entirely clear, elements and touches in it. The film was ingenious, enjoyable—I certainly found it moving. I was in tears at the end of that movie. But I did not come out saying, "Spielberg is the new Objectivist director."

This is, within limits, a perfect case of an optional reaction. You could be put off by certain things and say, "I just can't take a movie like that," or you could pick the better side and say, "That was so enjoyable and so good that I'm going to just ignore the stupid message." What I *do* say is that it's wrong to come out of a movie like that and say, "Another sign of today's evil world." I'm not saying every movie and every person has got the hidden good qualities that you should ferret out. But I *am* saying in many cases of movies and books and people, where there may be a tendency to condemn them across the board, the person is not judging the total. He's seizing out of context some actual negatives in the rationalist manner, and this contributes profoundly to reinforcing a malevolent view of life.

The problem with adopting "life as a bitter struggle against an alien world" is that it's compounded by other factors beyond just the mind/body issue, and I want to mention one briefly. And that is a peculiar interpretation that Objectivists sometimes place on the principle "you must not sanction evil." I've met people who interpret this to mean that you are morally obliged, in order to be true to your values, to have a perpetual fight with everyone on everything, to get into a bitter argument at the drop of a hat with your boss, your professor, whoever. And if that's how you interpret it, it would certainly contribute to the sense, "My life is nothing but a fight, a constant war against the world." This particular interpretation of the principle that you should not sanction evil represents a major confusion. It takes the idea of not sanctioning evil as an intrinsicist dogma, out of context, and yet the context is critical, because that principle applies only in specific situations. You have to know what the exact situation is, what the alleged evil is, what your relationship to the perpetrator is, whether your silence means that you endorse what he is saying, and so on.

Much more could be said of the principle "You shouldn't sanction evil," what it consists of, how you validate it, and how you apply it. But I want to point out only this much: Ethics tells us only that we should not help out evil, whether actively or passively, because that will redound to your own long-range harm; the evil is the anti-life. But you have to know in each context what the evil is, and what a sanction would consist of. So let's take a couple of examples.

Earlier in the course, one questioner wrote me, "I have felt guilty for years because I didn't jump up and vehemently oppose my boss's irrationalism." I don't know this person's particular context, but I do want to say that typically you are not responsible for your boss's views; you were not hired to correct him or to tutor him philosophically. You're not obligated to tell your boss what you think of his opinions. There is no objective implication if you work for a man, that you agree with him about everything except what you explicitly denounce. An employee is not the same as a friend, and it's not a relationship of equals. It's very simple—you are there to do what he says in exchange for money. There's nothing in that context to imply that you condone his private views. Of course, I can imagine contexts where even an employee should speak up, so I'm not saying, "There is now a new Objectivist dogma, 'Thou shalt never speak up in the office.'" For example, suppose your boss explicitly asks you your opinion in a context where you think he really wants to know, and you have reason to believe (from his past conduct and so on) that he would be fair, he wouldn't penalize you for it, then I would say yes, you should tell him, not necessarily in the form of a tirade, but calmly and briefly. Or suppose your boss's irrationalism (as this questioner put it) necessitates you personally doing evil work, work that benefits some provable evil, for example, Soviet Russia, then you should certainly be concerned and refuse, and you should speak up and even quit, if necessary. But if it's the standard type of case, your silence does not objectively imply *anything* about your viewpoint, and there's no onus on you to volunteer your criticisms in that context. By the way, a decent boss—as anybody who has ever employed people knows—a decent boss realizes that there are a lot of controversial issues, that he is in a powerful position in relation to his employees, and he does not go around spouting off controversial views in front of helpless employees. That actually amounts to power lust on his part, and it disqualifies him from deserving to hear your views. You could simply be contemptuous of a boss like that and say to hell with him.

Let me take a different situation. In college, should you let the professor in the class know you disagree every time you do? Is your silence a sanction of evil? If it is, I certainly sanctioned a tremendous amount of evil in my fourteen years as a college student, so I have to come out as the world's greatest monster, next to Kant. This was my policy: Sometimes I spoke up, and sometimes I didn't, according to a whole constellation of factors. I realized that I couldn't speak up every time, because I disagreed with everything. And since it was philosophy, every disagreement was vital, so I would have had to have equal time with the professor and the rest of the class, which would be ludicrous. So I simply had to accept from the outset, "An awful lot is going to go by that is irrational, horrendous, depraved, and I will be completely silent about it. I have no choice about that." On the other hand, I did not simply say, "I'm going to just keep quiet and never speak up at all," because there were various specific purposes that I wanted to achieve by means of occasional raids or forays—for example, I wanted to know if there was anybody better in this class. And periodically I felt I had to let this professor know that there is some opposition out there, that he can't assume it's absolutely safe and uncontroversial to utter all that garbage. And partly, every once in a while, I was overcome with what you could call a sheer need of self-assertion—it was just simply the feeling at times, "Even if it doesn't accomplish anything, I'm going to go crazy if I don't say something about this particular insanity." How did I decide when to speak up? It was all a matter of context: How important was the issue? How difficult is it to say anything briefly, keeping in mind that there's no use saying anything if you can't begin to make a dent on a viewpoint? Another question I asked is how well do I know the issue? Since I have to let a tremendous amount go by anyway, why stumble and make an idiot of myself? Also, how big is the class? Because if you're in one of those huge lecture sections with two hundred, it wouldn't mean a thing whatever the professor says. If it's a seminar of three or six or ten people, there's much more implication in that context that your silence means agreement. Am I going to be graded down? Some professors—rarely, but *sometimes*, I found, professors graded you down, and therefore I kept quiet. Another factor was how strong did I feel on a particular day? Did I feel able to take another assault from the professor in the class, or was I just too tired or depressed or fed up? I picked my spots, not scientifically, but by a whole set of criteria such as this. Now and then I would speak up; much of the time I kept silent. And I do not regard that as a sanction of evil, and I could certainly not have survived fourteen years of university if every moment had to be total war against every utterance.

If you take a party among equals, as opposed to a professor/student or boss/worker situation, then it's more plausible that if somebody says something that you disagree with, you will want to speak up. But even here there are limits. You don't have to contest everything; you have to decide, "Is this person worth speaking to? Is there anybody who's going to listen to me? Is this an appropriate forum?" There's also an optional element—some people don't like arguing, and they have every right in the world not to, and there are other people who can't wait to start arguing, so they would rather argue. There is always the possibility of saying to someone in a perfectly amiable way, "I disagree with that, but this is hardly the place to go into it," and that's it; you don't have to say any more than that. There is certainly such a thing as improperly sanctioning evil, remaining silent when you should speak up, but it is a contextual issue. Often, you just have to shrug off statements you disagree with and go about your life, and that is perfectly moral; it's self-preservation to do so. Even in college, which is the worst situation I can imagine, life is not a constant battle.

I have been looking at some errors that make people feel that life is hell, people are rotten, existence is a constant battle. Now I want to look at the other side, where it is understandable if you feel somewhat isolated. It's true that there is a lot of corruption in the world, a lot of irrationality and injustice. And, if you're rational, you simply can't avoid seeing it, judging it, and reacting to it. Even if you're absolutely nonrationalistic, you're not a condemner on principle—you're benevolent, you're predisposed to look for positives, and so on—sometimes they are not there, and you get a full concentrated dose of evil or entrenched mediocrity, where it would be simply absurd to say, "Look on the bright side." This Pollyannaism—everyone is moral, everything is terrific—is a complete default of moral judgment and is self-defeating. You lose the ability of self-protection from evil; you become a pawn of everyone and anyone because you have no means to judge. And, in addition, this Pollyannaism is tremendously unjust; the symbol of it is Joel Sutton in *The Fountainhead*, who loves everybody equally.

Sometimes you have to expect to be momentarily overcome with the sheer force of the evil in a given situation. I want to speak for myself, from this point on, from my own experience, because I'm not prepared to make a universal law out of this, so I offer it to you for what it's worth. There are times and situations where, despite my knowledge of philosophy, I feel overwhelmed by the evil in the world—I feel isolated, alienated, lonely, bitter, malevolent—and this is, to me, inescapable at times in certain contexts. I'll give you an example. A few weeks ago, I went to a debate at a large university, on the subject of the nuclear freeze. One of the debaters, my friend, was eloquent, but it was a hopeless situation. The audience of college students was closed, irrational, hostile, dishonest by every criterion outlined tonight. They wouldn't listen for a moment, they were rude—they were real modern hooligans—and when they *did* speak up, it was utterly without redeeming features—a whole array of out-of-context questions, sarcasm, disintegrated concretes—it was a real modern spectacle in the worst sense of the term. After a couple of hours of this, I was angry, I was resentful, I was hostile. And I felt (and I underscore the word "felt"), "This is the way the world is. What is the point of fighting it? They don't want to know. I'm going to retire and stop lecturing and let the whole thing blow up, and to hell with it." I was depressed. And of course, once I was in that mood, I was more negative about everything, so when I saw the headlines in the *Times* the next day, I felt worse. Even the long lines at the bank were further evidence that the world is rotten.

The point here is that I don't think that I made a mistake. I think you have to react to concretes. You would be schizophrenic if, after such a blatant, protracted display of injustice and irrationality, you could blithely shrug it off and say, "What the hell—life is great, everything is wonderful, I'm happy." It has to affect you. That's the concrete reality that's been surrounding you. It has to make you miserable, depressed, malevolent— to an extent and for a time. You can't always get away from the rotten things. And that's what I think is the valid point in the belief in philosophy versus the world. There are going to be periodic attacks of despair. The point is, what to do about these attacks. First, recognize them as natural, unavoidable, legitimate (assuming that they really were provoked and it's not a rationalist construct that you manufacture). If you take ideas seriously in today's world, I think you have to allow yourself to feel that sometimes. Certainly Ayn Rand did. She has described the character of Dominique in *The Fountainhead* as herself in a bad mood, and she knew that mood intimately, and if you read the forthcoming book *The Early Ayn Rand*, she wrote *Ideal*, an entire play, based on the premise that the world is rotten and people are awful. And she did not change. She didn't come up with a benevolent statement in the end; it was malevolent in that way from beginning to end. She wrote this in the early 1930s at a time when *We the Living* (her first novel) had been rejected by I don't know how many publishers, *Night of January 16th* had been rejected, her money was running out, and she simply felt, "There is no way to break out, people are hopeless," and in that mood, she wrote exactly the kind of play that Dominique would have written if Dominique were a playwright—it's a beautiful, very bitter play. I do not think you can escape that kind of mood sometimes, if you do take ideas and values seriously.

Second, I would say, you should try to minimize the occasions for them. Sometimes there is nothing that you can do; you have to live in the world, and you just can't hide from what's going on. But sometimes you can. For instance, if you know that a party is going to be filled with particularly disgusting people, why go? If you know that a movie is going to turn your stomach, avoid it, unless there's some overriding reason. I don't say avoid every negative, but I also say you don't have to seek out situations where you know you're going to be revolted. Do it only if you think you're going to gain more than you'll lose. Every one of those cases is like an assault on your sense of life, on your benevolence, and so you have to be able to gain enough to make it worthwhile.

And that brings me to the third point—what to do with these attacks of despair. You have to estimate the situation appropriately in the full context of your knowledge. Let yourself feel the bitterness for a while. Not too short a time, either; otherwise, you will repress it. If you just feel bitter for three minutes, and then say, "I know it's a wonderful world," that is just a formula for repression. You have to feel it, you have to let the knife twist, you have to say, "It's a rotten world," let it out—but not to the point where it becomes self-indulgence. At an appropriate point, when you've felt it and when it's real to you, you have to start reminding yourself of what you know about life and the world and philosophy. That won't remove the evil, but it will reestablish the broader context and your overall perspective. For instance, on that debate, at a certain point I had to tell myself, "New York City is really worse than a lot of places in this country, and college kids are not typical of other groups. If they were, we couldn't survive. They're especially brainwashed and so on. And it's ideas that are really at the root that's causing them, so there's still a chance by combating those ideas. So if I give up, I'm letting the professors that I hate have the last word. After all, there were some better people at that debate who focused on a few things that weren't so bad." If you say this type of thing too soon, it's mechanical and it doesn't strike you. But at some point, you have to start. And if I can be personal, if you have a wife like mine (like Cynthia), you have an invaluable asset, because she knows just the right amount of moaning to permit me, and then she very gradually and unobtrusively comes in with a few questions that start to break the negative mold and restore perspective. So, after I was denouncing this debate for an hour and a half, she asked me straightforwardly, "Do you think these kids are typical of Americans?" I was sort of reluctant, but I had to say no, and I began to revive a better viewpoint. Ideally, this is one of the crucial helps that a partner in life can be to you—to help you restore your benevolence and perspective after a vicious assault. And I certainly know that Frank O'Connor was that to Ayn Rand, and vice versa.

A mixed culture, like a mixed person, is very hard to deal with. In regard to a person, you all know that there's a constant drive to simplify—you want to say that he's a saint or he's vicious. Either way, it's clear-cut, and you can deal with it. But when you have to say about somebody, "He's really good in part, and he's really bad in part, and I don't know what's coming tomorrow," it's very unsettling. So there is a constant tendency to swing from one assessment to the opposite. And the same is true with regard to today's culture. It's a mixture. One day you see the best side, you feel uplifted, you experience "People are great." And one day you see the vicious side and you feel "Life is hell and the world has gone to pot." Some oscillation, I think, is unavoidable, but both of the extremes are wrong. The trick is to try not to oscillate too much. And the method, as far as I know, is to use your conscious knowledge in conjunction with your feelings. So we come back to the reason and emotion union. When you're uplifted, you can say, "Fine, I love this moment," and you can even say, "This is life as it should be, this is the real essence of life." But somewhere—not to diminish your enjoyment—but somewhere within you, you have to know it's not going to be like this all the time. And vice versa—when you are blackly in despair, you say, "Okay, although I know the better side will exist also."

That brings me to my final point of the course. I think your greatest ally in keeping a balance of sanity in your viewpoint should be philosophy, and specifically Objectivism. And still more specifically, the mind-body integration with all of its corollaries, including chewed, concretized abstractions. Because if that's how you hold philosophy, it should be an enormous value in helping you judge people and events accurately. If your principles are chewed and concretized, you should be able to see them everywhere, and that will make the world seem better to you, more understandable. You will then really see that following your principles in the long run leads to success, happiness, and you will see that in the long run, evil really is impotent. Or, to put it another way, you will see that the moral is the practical, and reality will seem much better to you. It will seem to be basically on your side, which it *is* if you have a true philosophy. Philosophy, and particularly Objectivism, is supposed to be an aid in life; and if it's chewed and concretized, that's how it functions. And that's the main reason I wanted to give this course on understanding Objectivism. Objectivism should help you to enjoy life. It should help to make you glad that you're alive. And that is my sincere wish for you. Don't make Objectivism into a hair shirt, a constant source of guilt, repression, condemnation, and gloom. Make it a means of your rational self-interest in the full sense. Let it make you happier, not more miserable, because that is its purpose. And I wish you success in attaining it. I hope this course has been of some help in this regard.

ABOUT THE EDITOR

Michael S. Berliner is cochairman of the Board of Directors of the Ayn Rand Institute and senior advisor to the Ayn Rand Archives. He was the executive director of the Ayn Rand Institute from its founding in 1985 to January 2000. Dr. Berliner is the editor of *Letters of Ayn Rand* and *Russian Writings on Hollywood*. His editorials on such topics as Western civilization and multiculturalism have been published in the *Los Angeles Times*, *New York Post*, the *Australian*, and other major newspapers. He holds a Ph.D. in philosophy and taught philosophy and philosophy of education for many years at California State University, Northridge, where he served as chairman of the Department of Social and Philosophical Foundations of Education.

ABOUT THE AUTHOR

Leonard Peikoff is the preeminent Rand scholar writing today. He worked closely with Ayn Rand for thirty years and was designated by her as heir to her estate. He taught philosophy at several places, including Hunter College and New York University. He is the author of *The Ominous Parallels, Objectivism: The Philosophy of Ayn Rand*, and the forthcoming book *The DIM Hypothesis*.